LANGUAGE IN USE

INTERMEDIATE

TEACHER'S
BOOK

Adrian Doff
Christopher Jones

CAMBRIDGE
UNIVERSITY PRESS

Published by the Press Syndicate of the University of Cambridge
The Pitt Building, Trumpington Street, Cambridge CB2 1RP
40 West 20th Street, New York, NY 10011–4211, USA
10 Stamford Road, Oakleigh, Melbourne 3166, Australia

© Cambridge University Press 1994

First published 1994
Reprinted 1995

Printed in Great Britain at the University Press, Cambridge.

ISBN 0 521 43553 6   Teacher's Book
ISBN 0 521 43552 8   Classroom Book
ISBN 0 521 43555 2   Self-study Workbook
ISBN 0 521 43554 4   Self-study Workbook with Answer Key
ISBN 0 521 43560 9   Class Cassette Set
ISBN 0 521 43561 7   Self-study Cassette Set

Split editions:
ISBN 0 521 43558 7   Classroom Book A
ISBN 0 521 43559 5   Classroom Book B
ISBN 0 521 43556 0   Self-study Workbook A with Answer Key
ISBN 0 521 43557 9   Self-study Workbook B with Answer Key
ISBN 0 521 43562 5   Self-study Cassette A
ISBN 0 521 43563 3   Self-study Cassette B

Contents

Introduction

How the course is organised

Who the course is for

Language in Use Intermediate is a one year course at intermediate level. It can be used by students who have completed *Language in Use Pre-Intermediate*, or who have studied English using another course up to intermediate level. It is also suitable for students who are coming back to English after studying it at some time in the past.

The components of the course

The course contains 24 units, each designed to last for about three classroom hours. The students' materials are divided into two major components: a Classroom Book, for use in class by students working with a teacher; and a Self-study Workbook, for use by students working alone at home or in a self-access session. The Classroom Book and Self-study Workbook are each accompanied by two cassettes.

The syllabus

The course has a dual syllabus: a grammatical syllabus, which deals with the main structures of English that are important at intermediate level, and a topic syllabus, which deals with vocabulary. These two strands are reflected in Grammar units and Vocabulary units, which alternate through the course. For example:

Unit 1	Regular events	*Grammar unit*
Unit 2	Around the house	*Vocabulary unit*
Unit 3	Past events	*Grammar unit*
Unit 4	Money	*Vocabulary unit*
etc.		

This alternation of grammar and vocabulary units allows systematic coverage of the two major content areas of English. It also allows a natural recycling of language through the course: structures are recycled in Vocabulary units and vocabulary is recycled in Grammar units.

The Classroom Book

The Classroom Book contains the main presentation and practice material of the course, as well as activities in speaking, writing, reading and listening. (Examples of typical Grammar and Vocabulary units are shown on pages 3e and 3f).

After every six units, the Classroom Book contains:
– a *Review* section, which revises the main language dealt with so far
– exercises in *Conversational English*, which focus on key functions of spoken English.

There is also a *Reference section*, which includes a full summary of each unit.

The Self-study Workbook

The Self-study Workbook contains a variety of exercises which provide back-up for work done in class and give opportunities for further self-study:
– homework exercises focusing on grammar and vocabulary
– sentences for translation
– listening tasks
– reading tasks
– exercises developing writing skills
– exercises in pronunciation, stress, and intonation
– exercises focusing on phrasal verbs

(For more information about these exercise types, see *To the Student*, in the Self-study Workbook.)

After every six units there is a *Review* section, which contains informal tests and a short dictation.

What the course teaches

Grammar

The Grammar units cover the main grammatical areas that are essential at this level; these include verb tenses, the passive, conditional structures, modals, and structures involving adjectives and adverbs.

Our aim in *Language in Use* is to help students use grammar actively in communication, so the main activities in the unit are open-ended and give opportunities for communicative use of language.

Each Grammar unit also has a section called *Focus on Form*, which provides more controlled practice of the main structures of the unit. These exercises are optional, and can be used for extra accuracy and remedial work.

Vocabulary

The Vocabulary units cover a number of topic areas that are relevant to students at this level (e.g. money, the media, crime, the environment). Each unit introduces a range of key vocabulary, including not only individual words but also phrases, items of lexical grammar and common collocations.

As in the Grammar units, the aim is to help students activate vocabulary and use it in communication, so many of the activities are open-ended, and involve discussion and exchange of information.

Vocabulary work is also included in some exercises in the Grammar units. Examples are:
– jobs (Unit 1, Exercise 4)
– disasters (Unit 3, Exercise 4)
– climate (Unit 9, Exercise 3)

Functions

Important interactional functions of English are dealt with in the Conversational English sections (after every six units). Examples are: requests, offers, suggestions, making choices, asking for information.

Other functions are included in individual activities in both Grammar and Vocabulary units. Examples are:
– Asking/giving permission (Unit 5, Exercise 4)
– Giving advice (Unit 11, Exercise 4)
– Making 'small talk' (Unit 21, Exercise 3)

Other more general functions are linked to broader grammatical areas, and these form part of the grammar syllabus of the course. Examples are:
– Making predictions (Unit 11)
– Making comparisons (Unit 13)
– Expressing regret (Unit 23)

Speaking skills

Because *Language in Use* is concerned with active use of grammar and vocabulary, oral fluency is developed through many of the exercises in the Classroom Book, and especially through the freer activities in each unit.

Writing skills

Writing is developed through both the Classroom Book and the Self-study Workbook.

In the Classroom Book, writing is either a follow-up to oral work or an integrated part of a classroom activity; it takes the form of note-making, writing single sentences, and simple paragraph writing.

The Self-study Workbook includes guided paragraph writing, and also provides exercises which specifically develop writing skills (punctuation, cohesion, organising information); these exercises make up an independent Writing skills syllabus which runs through the course.

Listening and reading skills

There are two types of reading and listening activity: those which are designed for use in class with interaction between students and help from the teacher (which appear in the Classroom Book), and those which are designed for students working alone (which appear in the Self-study Workbook).

In the Classroom Book, listening and reading are used in each unit as a basis for presentation or as a stimulus for a speaking or writing activity. In addition, each Vocabulary unit contains an extended activity which integrates reading and listening.

In the Self-study Workbook, there are short tasks designed to develop particular listening and reading strategies.

Pronunciation

In the Classroom Book, there are pronunciation exercises at the end of every Grammar unit. These focus on particular features connected with the main structures of the unit.

In the Self-study Workbook, there are exercises which focus on particular features of pronunciation (reduced vowels, stress, links between words, intonation). This forms an independent Pronunciation syllabus that runs through the course.

Phrasal verbs

Phrasal verbs often pose a particular problem for intermediate students, and the Self-study Workbook contains exercises that deal systematically with the form and use of more than 50 common phrasal verbs. Like the Pronunciation and Writing skills exercises, these exercises form an independent syllabus running through the course.

Underlying principles

Flexibility

Language in Use takes account of the fact that no two language classes are alike: students vary in level, age and interests, and may have different cultural and learning backgrounds; classes vary in size, physical layout and formality; teachers have different teaching styles; and learners may have widely differing ideas about what and how they need to learn. The course caters for some of these variations by:

– providing open-ended activities, so that classes can find their own level, and so that both weaker and stronger students have something to contribute
– encouraging students to contribute their own ideas, and draw on their own knowledge and experience
– providing activities that can be adapted to a variety of different teaching styles and types of class.

Clarity

In any language course, it is important that students understand clearly what they are doing and why they are doing it, and have a clear idea of what they have learnt. In writing *Language in Use*, clarity (for both learners and teachers) has been a major consideration, particularly in the following areas:

– the organisation and design of the units
– instructions, explanations and examples
– the unit summaries at the end of the book
– the design of the teaching notes

Classwork and self-study

Activities in class are only one part of the language learning process; also important is individual work done by students in their own time, which gives them a chance to consolidate and build on what they have learnt. There are also certain kinds of activity that can sometimes be done more efficiently by students working alone than in class. These include, in particular:

– activities which students often prefer to do at their own pace (e.g. some listening and reading tasks)
– activities which some students may need more than others (e.g. pronunciation and writing skills).

For these reasons, the Self-study Workbook is not just a homework book accompanying the Classroom Book. Rather, there is a careful division of material between the two books so that each contains appropriate activities.

Learning and acquisition

We believe that both 'learning' and 'acquisition' are important elements in learning a language. In other words, it is useful to spend time consciously focusing on particular language items, and it is also important to provide opportunities for natural language acquisition through fluency activities.

Both these elements are therefore incorporated in *Language in Use*. Some activities involve careful use of language and focus mainly on accuracy; in others, students develop fluency through freer, more creative use of language. Similarly, some reading and listening tasks focus on specific language items, while others are concerned with fluency and skills development.

In addition, the dual syllabus gives opportunities for acquisition of both grammar and vocabulary. In Grammar units, the focus is on learning grammatical structures, and this allows vocabulary to be acquired naturally. In Vocabulary units, the focus is on learning vocabulary, and this allows the natural acquisition of grammatical structures.

Using the course

The teaching notes

The teaching notes are designed to help you to make the most appropriate use of the Classroom activities with your students. They are in two columns.

The main notes for each activity (in the left-hand column) give a simple and straightforward route through the material, and include explanations for students and ideas for blackboard presentations.

In the right-hand column are a variety of options and alternatives which include:

* suggestions for homework both before and after the lesson
* optional phases within the lesson such as sentence writing, comprehension checks, vocabulary work, role-play and extra practice
* alternative procedures suitable for
  – classes which are better/weaker than average
  – larger/smaller classes
  – monolingual/mixed-nationality classes
  – more formal / less formal teaching situations
* notes giving explanations and examples of further language points arising from the main presentation.

The teaching notes for each unit also contain a summary of the exercises in the Self-study Workbook, and suggestions for suitable homework exercises are included in the notes for individual activities.

Working in pairs and groups

Many of the classroom activities are designed to be done in pairs or small groups. Most of these activities naturally fall into three phases:

* *Preparation*. Introduce the activity and make sure everyone knows what to do. It is often helpful to give a model or a demonstration yourself first.

* *Pair-/Groupwork*. During the activity, move around the class, listening and giving help when necessary.
* *Round-up*. Ask a few students to report back to the rest of the class on what they've done.

If you have a large class, or students who are not used to working in pairs, it may be better to introduce pairwork gradually, using it at first only for clearly defined tasks such as filling tables and controlled grammar practice. Other activities can be done with the whole class together.

Correcting errors

In some kinds of classroom activity, it is important to monitor students' language and correct errors: otherwise the point of the activity is lost. These can be spoken or written, and include:

* the presentation phase of activities in Grammar and Vocabulary units
* *Focus on Form* exercises in Grammar units
* homework exercises, including those in the Self-study Workbook.

In freer, more communicative activities, especially those involving pair- and groupwork, students should be involved in using language fluently, and you should avoid interrupting the flow of the activity by correcting mistakes too often. If you notice particular errors that you consider important, it is usually better to wait till the end of the activity before dealing with them.

Many of the activities in the course include a short writing phase, often involving sentence-writing as a preparation for a speaking activity. This gives an opportunity for students to monitor their own language more carefully, and for you to move round the class giving help and correcting errors.

Listening

Some listening activities involve fairly short pieces of listening which form part of the presentation and are used to introduce new structures or vocabulary. With these, you should aim for students to understand almost everything they hear. If necessary, you can help them to do this by:

* giving extra preparation for the listening (e.g. pre-teaching vocabulary, talking about the topic)
* playing the tape several times, and perhaps repeating difficult phrases yourself more slowly
* at the end, letting students listen and follow the tapescript at the back of the book.

Other listening activities are concerned with more general skills development. These usually involve longer pieces of listening, with accompanying tasks. Here the aim is that students should understand enough to complete the tasks, but not that they should attempt to understand every word they hear. However, as students often want to know exactly what was said, it may sometimes be a good idea to play the tape through again at the end and let students follow in the tapescript.

Reading

As far as possible, get students to read texts silently (rather than reading aloud or following as the teacher reads). This allows them to read at their own speed, and in a more natural way.

As with listening, it is often unnecessary for students to understand every word they read. Very often, the task only involves grasping the main points, or reading for particular information. It is also possible in many cases for students to guess the meanings of unfamiliar words from their contexts.

Using the Focus on Form pages

Each grammar unit ends with a page of *Focus on Form* exercises. These exercises give simple intensive practice of the main structures that are covered in the unit. They are intended as optional back-up material, and you do not need to do them all or do them in any particular order.

The *Focus on Form* exercises can be used in a variety of ways. Here are some suggestions:

• *Pre-presentation check*

| Focus on Form exercise → Main exercise |

Begin with a *Focus on Form* exercise, to focus on the structure that you are teaching and to check that students can form it correctly. Then go on to the main exercise in the unit.

• *Basic structure practice*

| Main exercise → Focus on Form exercise |

Do one of the exercises in the unit. If there are no problems, go on to the next exercise. But if students are having difficulty, do a *Focus on Form* exercise to give quick extra practice of the structure.

• *Extra remedial practice*

| Whole unit → Focus on Form exercise |

Do exercises 1–4 in the unit, then do selected *Focus on Form* exercises at the end, choosing areas that students have had problems with or which you think need more practice. You could also do individual *Focus on Form* exercises for five or ten minutes at the end of a lesson, to give variety and a change of pace.

• *Revision*

| Series of units → Focus on Form exercise |

Leave out the *Focus on Form* exercises, then use them as a way of revising the main grammar points that you have covered over a number of weeks.

• *Self-access/homework*

Some of the *Focus on Form* exercises can be done in writing. Students could do these in a self-access session or as homework, as an addition to the Self-study Workbook.

Using the Self-study Workbook

There are three ways of using the exercises in the Self-study Workbook. You will probably want to adopt a mixture of these approaches.

Homework

In the teaching notes for each classroom activity, there are cross-references to Grammar, Vocabulary and Listening exercises which are suitable for homework. You can also set other exercises for homework, such as Reading and Writing skills. If you use the Workbook extensively for this purpose, you might prefer students to have the version without the Answer Key.

Independent self-study

Allow students to work independently, choosing exercises that suit their individual needs. This is a sensible approach to adopt for the Translation, Pronunciation, Phrasal verbs and Writing skills exercises, particularly with multi-national classes. Students can either use the Answer Key to check their answers, or give in their books periodically to be marked.

Classwork

Some Workbook exercises are also suitable for use in class. Some possibilities are:

– Listening exercises, which are usually closely linked to classroom activities
– Translation exercises, in monolingual classes
– Pronunciation exercises, in classes which have particular pronunciation problems.

Short cuts through the course

Language in Use is designed to provide plenty of material, and it is quite possible to cover the course without doing every single exercise. If you are short of time, or if you wish to move through the units quickly with a good class, there are various short cuts you can take through the book:

• with a good class, leave out the *Focus on Form* exercises.

• with a weaker class, leave out some of the freer, more demanding activities, and use the *Focus on Form* exercises instead.

• in the combined Reading and Listening activities, you could give the Reading for homework, and do the Listening only in class.

• limit the time you spend in class on material from the Self-study Workbook. If students have no time to work outside class, you could leave out the Workbook altogether and use only the Classroom Book.

Grammar units

Grammar units contain:
- three activities that introduce key structures.
- one freer communicative activity.
- a grammar checklist.
- optional exercises for controlled practice (*Focus on Form*).

Main presentation of Past perfect tense, involving reading and problem-solving. Shows how we use this tense for 'flashbacks' in a story.

Shows how we can express the same idea using Past or Past perfect tense. Simple sentence-making exercise, focusing on meaning.

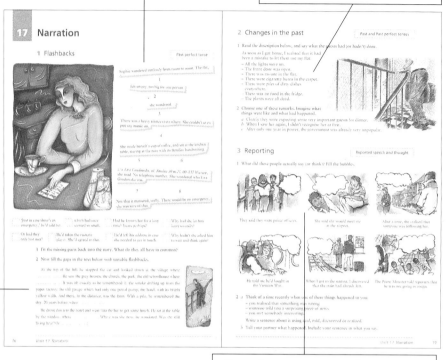

Part 2 – a chance for students to use their imagination.

Shows how we use tense changes in reported speech and thought. In Part 2, students talk about a real experience.

Vocabulary units

Vocabulary units contain:
- three activities linked by topic. Each activity focuses on a different area of vocabulary.
- an integrated reading and listening activity, for skills development.

A discussion activity. Introduces vocabulary of punishments.

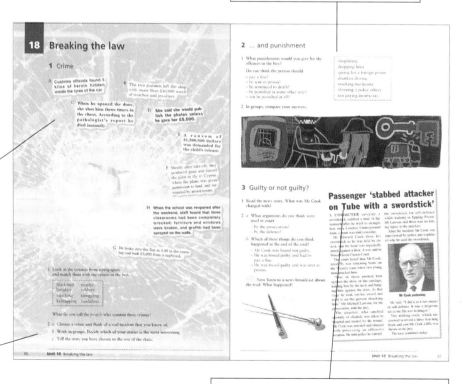

Introduces vocabulary of common crimes and criminals.

Part 2 – a chance for students to talk about their own experience.

An authentic newspaper story, for reading and discussion. Introduces vocabulary connected with courts and the law.

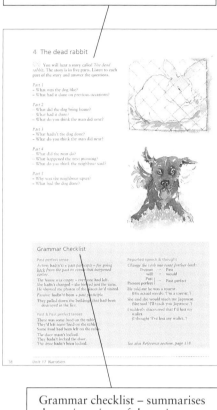

Students listen to a story, and predict what will happen next. Draws on all the language of the unit.

Focus on Form exercises. These are optional, and give extra controlled practice of key structures.

Every Focus on Form page ends with pronunciation practice.

Grammar checklist – summarises the main points of the unit.

Integrated reading and listening activity.

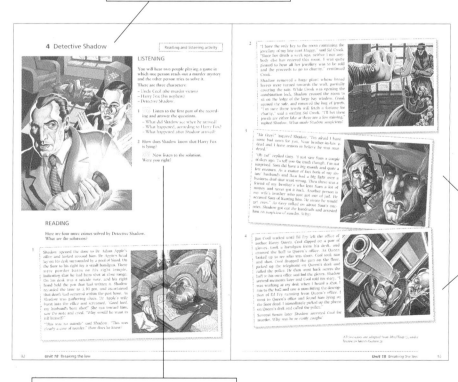

More murder mysteries for students to read and solve.

Students listen to a murder mystery and try to solve it. Then they hear the solution.

Guide to units

Classroom Book	Self-study Workbook

1 Regular events

Talking about regular events and actions; talking about current activities

Grammar: Present simple active & passive; frequency expressions; Present continuous

Grammar exercises
Listening: *Personality types*
Pronunciation: *The sound /ə/*
Reading: *How to saw someone in half*

2 Around the house

Vocabulary: behaviour in the home; household jobs & appliances; features of rooms

Reading and listening activity: *Snow house*

Vocabulary exercises
Listening: *A Spanish family*
Phrasal verbs: *Introduction*
Writing skills: *Punctuation: joining sentences*

3 Past events

Talking about past events and actions; saying when things happened

Grammar: Past simple and continuous; past time expressions; subject & object questions; Past simple passive

Grammar exercises
Listening: *Childhood memories*
Pronunciation: *Reduced and full forms*
Reading: *Two terrible tales*

4 Money

Vocabulary: cost and value; using money; expenses, bills & taxes

Reading and listening activity: *Can you make a million?*

Vocabulary exercises
Listening: *A waste of money*
Phrasal verbs: *Intransitive verbs (1)*
Writing skills: *Reference: pronouns*

5 Obligation

Obligation and permission in the present and past; freedom from obligation

Grammar: (don't) have to; (not) allowed to; can('t); make & let; freedom from obligation structures

Grammar exercises
Listening: *School rules*
Pronunciation: *Contracted forms*
Reading: *Three word games*

6 On holiday

Vocabulary: types of holiday; holiday activities; holiday equipment; festivals & celebrations

Reading and listening activity: *Culture shock*

Vocabulary exercises
Listening: *Going home*
Phrasal verbs: *Intransitive verbs (2)*
Writing skills: *Subject and object relative clauses*

Review Units 1–6

Conversational English

1 *Making requests*
2 *On the phone*

Classroom Book	Self-study Workbook

7 Past and present

Habitual actions in the past; describing changes; preparations

Grammar: used to; Past simple; Present perfect active and passive; not any more/longer

Grammar exercises
Listening: *Changed lives*
Pronunciation: *Syllables and stress*
Reading: *Two childhoods*

8 At your service

Vocabulary: having things done; using public services; evaluating services

Reading and listening activity: *Jobs we love to hate*

Vocabulary exercises
Listening: *On the phone*
Phrasal verbs: *Transitive verbs (1)*
Writing skills: *Punctuation: direct speech*

9 Imagining

Imagining things differently from the way they are; making wishes

Grammar: would; second conditionals; I wish + would / could / Past tense

Grammar exercises
Listening: *What would you do?*
Pronunciation: *Linking words: consonant + vowel*
Reading: *My perfect weekend*

10 Describing things

Vocabulary: describing objects by appearance and purpose; buying & selling

Reading and listening activity: *Great ideas?*

Vocabulary exercises
Listening: *Things for sale*
Phrasal verbs: *Transitive verbs (2)*
Writing skills: *Reference:* this *and* which

11 The future

Making predictions; hopes & expectations; giving reasons for predictions

Grammar: will/might; hope & expect; Future continuous; Future perfect; linking words

Grammar exercises
Listening: *When I'm 60 ...*
Pronunciation: *Stress in sentences*
Reading: *Crossing the Sahara*

12 Accidents

Vocabulary: describing accidents and injuries; dealing with emergencies; road accidents

Reading and listening activity: *You're on your own*

Vocabulary exercises
Listening: *Narrow escapes*
Phrasal verbs: *Transitive verbs (3)*
Writing skills: *Joining ideas: clauses and phrases*

Review Units 7–12

Conversational English

1 *Making suggestions*
2 *Finding things in common*

Classroom Book	Self-study Workbook

13 Comparing and evaluating

Comparing things; comparing the way people do things; criticising and complaining

Grammar: comparative adjectives and adverbs; (not) as ... as ...; too & enough

Grammar exercises

Listening: *Living in Britain*

Pronunciation: *Linking words: consonant + consonant*

Reading: *Left-handedness*

14 The media

Vocabulary: newspapers and magazines, and their contents; types of TV programme

Reading and listening activity: *Easy listening*

Vocabulary exercises

Listening: *Media habits*

Phrasal verbs: *Double meanings*

Writing skills: *Similarities*

15 Recent events

Announcing news; giving and asking about details; talking about recent activities

Grammar: Present perfect simple active & passive; Past simple; Present perfect continuous

Grammar exercises

Listening: *What has happened?*

Pronunciation: *Changing stress*

Reading: *Personal letters*

16 Teaching and learning

Vocabulary: learning things at school; skills and abilities; education systems

Reading and listening activity: *Improve your memory*

Vocabulary exercises

Listening: *Three school subjects*

Phrasal verbs: *Prepositional verbs (1)*

Writing skills: *Letter writing*

17 Narration

Flashbacks in narration; changes in the past; reported speech and thought

Grammar: Past perfect tense; reported speech structures

Grammar exercises

Listening: *Locked in!*

Pronunciation: *Linking words with /w/ or /j/*

Reading: *Strange – but true?*

18 Breaking the law

Vocabulary: types of crime; types of punishment; courts and trials

Reading and listening activity: *Detective Shadow*

Vocabulary exercises

Listening: *A case of fraud*

Phrasal verbs: *Prepositional verbs (2)*

Writing skills: *Defining and non-defining relative clauses*

Review Units 13–18

Conversational English

1 *Giving advice*
2 *Making choices*

Classroom Book	Self-study Workbook

19 Up to now

Saying when things started; saying how long things have (or haven't) been going on

Grammar: Present perfect simple/continuous + for/since; negative duration structures

Grammar exercises
Listening: *Favourite things*
Pronunciation: *Stress and suffixes*
Reading: *Four logic puzzles*

20 In your lifetime

Vocabulary: birth, marriage and death; age groups; age and the law

Reading and listening activity: *A Good Boy, Griffith*

Vocabulary exercises
Listening: *Birth and marriage*
Phrasal verbs: *Three-word verbs (1)*
Writing skills: *Joining ideas: showing what's coming next*

21 Finding out

Asking for information; reporting questions; checking

Grammar: information questions; indirect questions; reported questions; question tags

Grammar exercises
Listening: *Phone conversation*
Pronunciation: *Changing tones*
Reading: *A bit of luck*

22 Speaking personally

Vocabulary: ways of describing feelings; positive & negative reactions

Reading and listening activity: *What's in a smile*

Vocabulary exercises
Listening: *James Bond films*
Phrasal verbs: *Three-word verbs (2)*
Writing skills: *Sequence: unexpected events*

23 The unreal past

Imagining what would have happened in different circumstances; expressing regret

Grammar: would have done; 2nd and 3rd conditionals; I wish + Past perfect; should(n't) have done

Grammar exercises
Listening: *A better place*
Pronunciation: *Common suffixes*
Reading: *If things had been different ...*

24 Life on Earth

Vocabulary: environmental problems and solutions; endangered species

Reading and listening activity: *The Doomsday Asteroid*

Vocabulary exercises
Listening: *How green are you?*
Phrasal verbs: *Review*
Writing skills: *Organising ideas*

Review Units 19–24

Conversational English

1 *Making offers*
2 *In the street*

1 Personality types

Present simple tense

1 You want to find out what kind of person your partner is.
What other questions could you ask?

A culture-vulture

A sociable type

A home-lover

How often do you go to the theatre?
What kind of books do you read?
Do you ever go to art galleries?

Do you enjoy parties?

What do you do in the evenings?

An outdoor type

A workaholic

What sports do you do?

Do you work at weekends?

2 Interview your partner. What kind of person is he/she?

This unit deals with language for talking about regular events and actions, and contrasts this with language describing current activities. It focuses on:
– Present simple active and passive
– frequency expressions used with the Present simple
– Present continuous.

1 Personality types

In this exercise, students find out about their partner, by asking questions using the Present simple. This gives a chance to revise Yes/No and Wh- questions, as well as vocabulary connected with work, leisure activities, sport and entertainment. It also gives students an opportunity to get to know each other.

➤ Focus on Form: Exercises 1, 2
➤ Workbook: Exercise A

1 Presentation

- Look at each of the five 'types', and ask students to suggest some of the things they probably do, e.g.

  Culture-vulture: goes to the theatre, art galleries; reads the latest books.
  Sociable type: goes out a lot; enjoys parties; likes being with other people.
  Home-lover: buys furniture; does a lot of housework; doesn't go out much.
  Outdoor type: goes walking, running; plays sports; enjoys picnics.
  Workaholic: works a lot; takes work home; talks about work; doesn't relax.

- Check that students can form Present simple questions. If necessary, present these on the board:

Do you Does he/she	enjoy parties?

How often	do you does he/she	go to the theatre?

- Ask students to suggest questions to find out about each type, e.g.

  Sociable type: Do you go out much? How often do you go to parties?
  Home-lover: How much time do you spend at home? Do you watch TV a lot?
  Outdoor type: Do you go camping? How often do you go for a walk?
  Workaholic: How many hours do you work a day? Do you work in the evenings?

2 Speaking activity

- Pairwork. Students interview each other, asking further questions if necessary, and as they do so build up a 'profile' of their partner.

- After the interview, they report their conclusions to their partner – *You're quite sociable, and a home-lover, not a workaholic, and definitely not an outdoor type. You're quite cultured, but not a culture-vulture.* – and see if their partner agrees.

- As a round-up, ask a few students to tell you their partner's 'profile'.

Vocabulary note
A 'culture-vulture' is a common slang expression for someone who follows culture keenly.
A 'workaholic' is someone addicted to work (cf. alcoholic).

Presentation option
If necessary, remind students of positive and negative forms of the Present simple:

I	enjoy don't enjoy	parties.

He	enjoys doesn't enjoy	parties.

Practice option
Do quick transformation practice to check that students can form questions:
I work hard.
→ Do you work hard?
I go out. (How often?)
→ How often do you go out?

Alternative: class survey
Assign different 'types' to different groups or pairs of students. They move around the class asking everyone they meet their set of three or four questions.
As a round-up, each group reports on its findings, e.g. *There are two workaholics in the class, most of the rest work quite hard, and three don't work very hard at all.*

Homework option
Students write a profile of themselves, saying what they do and what they don't do.

2 How often?

This exercise focuses on expressions of precise frequency (twice a day, every 6 weeks), *and also practises questions with* How often? *and* How much/many?

➤ Focus on Form: Exercise 3
➤ Workbook: Exercise B

1 *Presentation*

- Write these three question structures on the board:

  > How often ...?
  > How much ...?
  > How many ...?

- Look at the remarks in the bubbles, establish what they might be about, and elicit possible questions, e.g.

  – How often do you go on holiday? – How often do you go to the dentist?
  – How many cigarettes do you smoke? – How often do you go to the cinema?
  – How often do you clean your teeth? – How much coffee do you drink?

- Write *once a week* and *every 6 months* on the board, and build up a range of frequency expressions that follow each pattern:

once	a day		hours
twice	a week		days
three times	a year	(once) every 6	months
...	...		years

2 *Speaking activity*

- Elicit possible continuations for Sentence a, e.g. *I write to them twice a month, I go to see them every three weeks, I phone them three times a week.*
- Pairwork. Students think of continuations for the other remarks.
- Go through the answers together. Possible answers:

  b She eats 15 a week. / She buys at least one a day.
  c He goes to church three times a week. / He prays five times a day.
  d We go there every two weeks. / We eat there twice a month.
  e He has three showers a day. / He changes his clothes twice a day.

Practice option
Students ask each other the same questions, and give real answers about themselves.

Alternative
Students sit in groups, adding one sentence each, e.g.
A I write to them once a month.
B I write to them once a week.
C I phone them every two days.
D ...

Optional extension
Students think of one or two frequency questions of their own, and ask their partner.

3 National statistics

In this exercise, students read statistics about the USA, and find appropriate verbs. This provides a natural context for using the Present simple passive.

➤ Focus on Form: Exercise 4
➤ Workbook: Exercise C

1 *Presentation*

- Ask students to identify active and passive forms in the first five statistics:
  Active: arrives, die.   *Passive:* are produced, is murdered, are born.

- Use the first example to show how passive sentences are formed:

  > **ACTIVE**: They produce 25,000 new cars.
  > **PASSIVE**: 25,000 new cars <u>are</u> produc<u>ed</u>.

  Point out that
  – the passive is formed with *is/are* + past participle.
  – the *object* of the active sentence becomes the *subject* of the passive sentence.
- Pairwork. Students fill the gaps in the sentences. Answers:

  are eaten (are killed); are stolen; are produced / thrown away; are published; dies / is killed; are sold (produced); are grown/produced; uses; delivers

Language note
The passive is used here because the focus is on the *cars*, not on who produces them.

Presentation options
1 Give your own examples, e.g. That shop sells books.
  → Books are sold in that shop.
2 Give equivalent sentences in the students' own language to make it clear how the passive is used, e.g. *On produit les voitures ...*; *Se producen coches ...*

2 *Speaking/writing activity*

- Pairwork. Students discuss what each statistic might be.
- Get a range of ideas from the class. Then read out the answers:

  2,500 bottles of Coca Cola are sold every second.
  200,000 couples get married every month. (The figure for divorces is just under half that number.)
  800,000 pairs of men's jeans are sold every day.
  The average person eats 51 kilos of red meat a year.
  During the summer season 100,000 people visit Disney World every day.

Optional extension
In their own time, students find out statistics for their own country (or the country where they are studying). In a later lesson, they ask if other students can guess them, e.g. *How many loaves of bread are bought every day?*

2 How often?

Twice a year if we can afford it.

About 20 a day.

Three times a day.

Every six months, but only for a check-up.

1 What are these people talking about?
   What questions do you think they're answering?

About once a week if there's anything good on.

About six cups a day.

2 Continue each of these remarks, using a frequency expression.

   a I like to keep in touch with my parents. I …
   b She loves hamburgers. She …
   c He's very religious. He …
   d That's one of our favourite restaurants. We …
   e He keeps himself incredibly clean. He …

3 National statistics

Present simple passive

In the USA...

25,000 new cars are produced every day.
Someone is murdered every 25 minutes.
Every second, one foreign visitor arrives in the USA.
500 babies are born every hour.
Every hour, about 100 people die from heart attacks.
Four million chickens _____ by Americans every day.
4,000 cars _____ every day.
10,000 tons of rubbish _____ every hour.
1,000 novels _____ every month.
Someone _____ in a road accident every five minutes.
Every day, 30 million newspapers _____ in the USA.
Every year, 3,000 million tons of wheat _____ .
Every day, the average American family _____ 600 litres of water.
Every day, the US Post Office _____ 300 million letters.

1 Look at the first five statistics. Which verbs are active, and which are passive?

   Fill the gaps with active or passive forms of the verbs in the box.

publish	die	produce
sell	kill	grow
eat	throw away	deliver
steal	use	

2 Here are parts of other statistics about the USA. Can you complete them?

   2,500 bottles of Coca-Cola

   200,000 couples

   800,000 pairs of men's jeans

   51 kilos of red meat

   100,000 people visit Disney World

4 At the moment ...

1 You will hear five people talking about their jobs.

  a Here are some of the things they say.
  Match the remarks on the left with those on the right.
  What do you think the five jobs are?

What do they do?	*What are they doing at the moment?*
I work for the *Daily Mirror*.	We're cutting down trees and mending fences.
I answer the phone.	I'm covering the American elections.
I spend a lot of time in libraries.	I'm doing some research on the First World War.
I drive a tractor.	We're building a dam in Ethiopia.
I work for the United Nations.	I'm typing out our annual report.

  b 🔲 Now listen to the recording. What else does each person say?

2 Think of a job, and write two or three sentences saying
  – what you do in general
  – what you're doing at the moment.

  Read out your sentences one at a time, and see if your partner can guess your job.

Grammar Checklist

Present simple tense

Third person singular: add **-s** or **-es**
Negatives: **don't/doesn't** + *infinitive*
I **like** old films.
She **works** in Madrid.
I **don't like** old films.
She **doesn't work** in Madrid.

Present simple questions

(*Question word* +) **do/does** + *subject* +
infinitive
Do you **like** old films? (*not* ~~You like~~ ...?)
Where does she **work**? (*not* ~~Where she works~~?)
How often do you **go** to London?

Frequency expressions

I see them **twice a week**. (*not* ~~in a week~~)
He has milk **four times a day**.
I go to London **every three months**.
  (*not* ~~every third month~~)

Present simple passive

is/are + *past participle*
They grow coffee in Kenya.
→ Coffee **is grown** in Kenya.
Too many people **are killed** on the roads.
The magazine **is published** twice a year.

Present simple & continuous

Present simple – *for regular actions and talking 'in general'*.
Present continuous – *for activities 'around now'.*

She **works** for a marketing company, and she often **visits** the USA. Just now, she's **attending** a conference in Boston.
I **study** German literature. At the moment, I'm **writing** a paper on Goethe.

See also Reference section, page 130.

---

4 At the moment ...

This exercise contrasts the Present simple (for talking about jobs and regular activities) with the Present continuous (for describing temporary activities). Students match sentences describing jobs, then listen to five short recordings in which people say what their jobs involve. The second part of the exercise is a guessing game.

➤ Focus on Form: Exercise 5
➤ Workbook: Exercise D

1 *Presentation & listening*

- Look at the two columns of remarks, and establish that
  - we use the Present simple to say what we do in general (what our job involves)
  - we use the Present continuous to talk about things we are doing 'at the moment' (= around now).
- Students match the remarks in the two columns and guess what the jobs might be. (At this stage, students may suggest various possible jobs, not necessarily those in the recordings.)
- 🔊 Play the recording, pausing to establish the answers:

  1 Journalist: works for the *Daily Mirror*; is covering the American elections.
  2 Secretary: answers the phone; is typing out the annual report.
  3 Research student: spends a lot of time in libraries; is doing research on the First World War.
  4 Farm worker: drives a tractor; is cutting down trees and mending fences.
  5 Engineer: works for the United Nations; is building a dam in Ethiopia.

- If necessary, play the recording again, checking for further details (e.g. the journalist reports on foreign news and spends a lot of time abroad).

> *Presentation option*
> Give other examples relating to your own job or the jobs of some of your students. (Ask: What do you do? What are you doing at the moment?)

> *Language note*
> The question *What are you doing at the moment?* can be answered in two ways:
> 1 *I'm doing this exercise.*
>   (= exactly now)
> 2 *I'm revising for exams.*
>   (= around now)

2 *Writing/speaking activity*

- To show how the activity works, think of a job yourself and make up some sentences about it. Read them out to the class, beginning with the least obvious, and pause after each sentence to see if students can guess the job, e.g.
  - I work for Swissair.
  - At the moment I'm working on the route to Singapore.
  - I serve meals and drinks to passengers.
- Students think of a job and write sentences about it.
- They read out their sentences one at a time, beginning with the least obvious. Other students try to guess the job. This stage can be conducted in groups or with the whole class.

> *Preparation option*
> Write names of jobs for the game on slips of paper, and give them out to students. Some possible jobs:
> pilot, waiter, receptionist, mechanic, police officer, student, gardener, writer, lorry driver.

> *Alternative*
> Students move freely round the class reading out their sentences to other students.

🔊 Tapescript for Exercise 4: *At the moment ...*

1 I'm a journalist. I work for the *Daily Mirror*. I report on foreign news, so I spend quite a lot of time abroad. At the moment I'm covering the American elections.

2 I work as a secretary for a firm of accountants, so I answer the phone, type letters, things like that. At the moment I'm typing out our annual report, which I have to finish by Friday.

3 I'm a research student. I spend a lot of time in libraries and on the phone to people, trying to get information. I study the history of medicine, and at the moment I'm doing some research on the First World War, finding out what kind of medicines they used in the army.

4 I work on a farm, a potato farm. I drive a tractor and I help with all the jobs around the farm. There's not much going on at the moment, being winter. We're cutting down some of the trees and mending fences, mostly.

5 I work for the United Nations as an engineer. I'm involved in development projects in Africa. Just at the moment there's a big project we're doing – we're building a dam in Ethiopia.

Focus on Form

1 *Present simple*

Present simple, positive & negative (1st & 3rd person)

- To introduce the exercise, go through the items, checking that students can make positive and negative sentences, e.g. *She speaks / doesn't speak Russian.*
- Working alone, students write guesses about their partner.
- Pairwork. Students tell each other what they really do/don't do.
- As a round-up, ask some students how many guesses they got right, and what they found out about their partner.

2 *Present simple: questions*

Present simple Wh- questions

- Pairwork. Students look only at their own texts, and find the missing information by asking questions.
- As a round-up, look at both texts with the whole class, and establish what the questions should be:

Text 1: Where do the Tuareg live? What do people call them? Why do they call them that? What do they wear? What do they breed? What do they take across the Sahara? Where do many Tuareg live now? What work do they do? (What do they work as?)

Text 2: Where do the Dinka live? What do the men look after / do? What does a boy's father give him? What does he do (to it)? What does he do when it dies? What do they get from their cattle? What do they hunt for meat? (How do they get meat?)

3 *Frequency*

Expressions of precise frequency

- Go through the items with the class, eliciting frequency expressions. Answers:
  - a twice a month; (once) every two weeks; once a fortnight
  - b three times a week; every two days; every other day
  - c four times a year; every three months
  - d every 20 minutes; three times an hour
  - e every two years; every other year
  - f three times a day; every eight hours
- Students write a few sentences using the expressions. These could be either true or imaginary.

4 *The passive: processes*

Present simple passive, singular & plural forms

- Either do the exercise orally round the class or in pairs, or ask students to write the sentences. Answers:

  Frozen peas: they're grown; they're picked; they're washed; they're cooked; they're frozen
  Car: it's assembled; it's painted; it's tested
  Fish: they're caught; they're cleaned; they're frozen
  Book: it's written; it's edited; it's printed; it's published

5 *Simple or continuous?*

Present simple vs. Present continuous

- Give time for students to fill the gaps, working alone or in pairs.
- Go through the answers together. Answers:
  - a is having; is enjoying; spends; doesn't have; is reading; (is) writing
  - b works; spends; travels; is building

6 *Pronunciation*

Ask students to try saying the sentences themselves, then play the recording as a model. Focus on these points:

a Reduced *do* in questions and elision with *you* /djə/. Reduced *does* /dəz/ in unstressed position in questions.

b Pronunciation of *often* /'ɒfən/ or /'ɒftən/.

c Past participle endings:
/d/ after voiced consonants (/n/, /l/, etc.)
/t/ after unvoiced consonants (/s/, /ʃ/, etc.)
/ən/ in irregular forms
/ɪd/ after /t/ or /d/

Self-study Workbook

Exercise A: Explanations
Positive and negative forms of the Present simple.
Completing sentences with correct forms from a box.

Exercise B: Frequency
Rewriting sentences with suitable frequency expressions.

Exercise C: Present simple passive
Students write 'advertising' sentences describing different products.

Exercise D: At the moment
The Present continuous.
Students write three short paragraphs from prompts.

Translation
Key sentences for translation.

Listening: Personality types
Someone talks about how he spends his time.
Students listen and decide what kind of person he is.

Pronunciation: The sound /ə/
The sound /ə/ in unstressed syllables in words, phrases and sentences.

Reading: How to saw someone in half
Students match a jumbled description of a conjuring trick with pictures, then try to work out how the trick is done.

Focus on Form

1 Present simple

Look at the list and make guesses about your partner. Write complete sentences.

Example: *speak Russian*

She doesn't speak Russian.

a speak Russian   e take sugar in coffee
b smoke   f enjoy cooking
c do crosswords   g like chewing gum
d like horror films   h bite his/her fingernails

Your partner will tell you what he/she really does and doesn't do. See how many guesses you got right.

2 Present simple: questions

Student A: Look at Text 1 on page 112. Ask B questions to find out the missing information.

Student B: Look at Text 1 on page 114, and answer A's questions.

Example: The Tuareg live in ....
A Where do the Tuareg live?
B (They live) in the Sahara region of North Africa.

Now do the same with Text 2.

3 Frequency

Express the following ideas using frequency expressions.

Example: *at 9 a.m. and 9 p.m.*

(once) every 12 hours
twice a day

a on the 1st and 15th of every month
b on Monday, Wednesday and Friday
c in January, March, July and September
d at 9.00, 9.20, 9.40, 10.00 ...
e in 1985, 1987, 1989, 1991 ...
f at 7 a.m., 3 p.m. and 11 p.m.

Now make sentences using the expressions.

Example: I listen to the news twice a day.

4 The passive: processes

Look at the products in the pictures. Say what happens to them before they are used. Use the passive form of verbs in the box.

Example: *a packet of frozen peas*

First the peas are grown. Then they're picked ...

5 Simple or continuous?

Fill the gaps with the correct form of these verbs.

build	have	spend	work
enjoy	read	travel	write

a Mary .... a good rest in hospital, and I think she .... the change from her usual routine. Usually she .... so much time working that she (not) .... a chance to relax. Now she .... a lot of magazines, and .... letters to friends, and she says it's wonderful.

b Richard .... as an engineer for a large construction company. He .... six months of every year in Africa, where he .... from country to country supervising irrigation projects. At the moment, he's in Mali, where his company .... a dam.

6 Pronunciation

How do you say the words and phrases below?

a Do you go out a lot?
What kind of films do you like?
What does he do at the weekend?

b How often do you clean your teeth?
How often does she see her parents?

c cleaned   sold   produced   published
   eaten   stolen   tasted   painted
The fish are cleaned.
The cars are painted.

▭ **Now listen and check your answers.**

assemble	freeze
catch	grow
clean	paint
cook	pick
edit	print
write	wash
test	publish

Around the house

1 Easy to live with?

1 🗔 You will hear five people talking about the people they live with.

Listen and match what they say with the pictures.
How did the speakers use the words in the box?

mess	leave	tidy up
noise	put away	use up
clean	switch off	wash up

2 Are you an easy person to live with? Write a list of the things you do and don't do.

Now change lists with your partner. Do you think you could live in the same house or flat?

This unit is concerned with things people do at home. It focuses on the following vocabulary areas:
– 'behaviour' in the home (e.g. keeping things tidy, making a noise)
– jobs in the home and labour-saving devices
– features of rooms (e.g. carpets, wallpaper, furniture).
The Reading and Listening activity is about igloos: how they are built and what they are like to live in.

1 Easy to live with?

This exercise introduces a range of action verbs associated with the home and how people are expected to behave: turning off lights, tidying things up, washing up, etc. These verbs are contained in short recordings that students match with the pictures on the page. They then write and talk about things they do at home themselves.

➤ Workbook: Exercise A

1 Listening & presentation

- To introduce the activity, write the words *tidy* and *untidy* on the board, and ask students what they mean (they can do this with reference to the pictures). Then ask a few students whether they are tidy or untidy people.

- 📼 Play the recordings, pausing after each one and asking students to match the remark with one of the pictures. Ask students to say *why* they think it goes with that picture, and in doing so focus on the words in the box. Answers:
  1 A She helps with *cleaning* the flat; *leaves* books and magazines lying around; never *puts* things *away*.
  2 D He never *makes a mess*; always *washes up*.
  3 C She *uses up* all the hot water.
  4 E His room's always *in a mess*; he never *tidies up*; never *puts* his clothes *away*; doesn't *make too much noise*.
  5 B She *leaves* the lights *on*; never *switches* the light *off*; *leaves* the doors *open*.

- Point out that several of the verbs in the box are phrasal (= two-word) verbs. The second word can come before or after a noun:

> **He never switches** **the light off.**
> **off the light.**

- Point out these structures with *leave*:
  + *adjective*   He left the door *open*.
  + *phrase*   He left the book *on the floor*.
  + *-ing*   He left the book *lying on the floor*.

2 Writing & speaking activity

- As a lead-in, tell the class some things you do (or don't do) at home (e.g. *I'm a fairly tidy person, and I don't leave lights on, but I like to get up very early and spend about an hour in the bath with the radio on.*) and ask them if they think you would be an easy person to live with.

- Working alone, students write a list of things they do and don't do at home.

- Students exchange lists with their partner. They read each other's lists, and discuss how well they think they could live together.

- As a round-up, ask a few pairs whether they could live together, and why or why not.

Presentation option
As you go through the answers, build up longer phrases on the board, showing how the words in the box are used, e.g.

> **makes a mess**
> **makes a noise**
> **leaves ... lying around**
> **she's not very tidy**

Language notes
tidy can be an adjective or a verb:
– He's a very *tidy* person.
– He always *tidies* his room.
– He *keeps* his room *tidy*.
In phrasal verbs, *up* often conveys a sense of completeness:
use up the water = it's all gone.
tidy up = there's no more mess.

Note
There are exercises on phrasal verbs in the Self-study Workbook (even numbered units). For word order with phrasal verbs, see Self-study Workbook, Unit 8.

Note
If you think your students would be embarrassed by the idea of sharing a flat with people of the opposite sex, do this activity with all-male or all-female pairs.

📼 Tapescript for Exercise 1: *Easy to live with?*

1 Well, she helps a lot with cleaning the flat, but she's not very tidy. She always leaves books and magazines lying around, and she never puts things away when she's finished using them.

2 He's only been in a couple of weeks, but he's a good cook, and he's very tidy. He never makes a mess when he's cooking, and he always washes up afterwards.

3 Oh no, I like Jane – she's really great. Oh, apart from one thing – she spends hours in the bathroom. I can never get

in to have a shower. And another thing – she uses up all the hot water.

4 Well, his room's always in rather a mess – he never tidies up, never puts his clothes away. Oh he's OK otherwise – he's quite quiet, doesn't make too much noise.

5 The worst thing about her is she leaves all the lights on. She never switches the light off when she goes out of the room, so I have to go round switching them off after her. And she leaves all the doors open.

2 Labour-saving devices

This activity introduces the vocabulary of household appliances and verbs associated with them. Students consider which labour-saving devices are the most useful, and then invent a device of their own.

➤ Workbook: Exercise B

1 Presentation

- Pairwork. Students complete the table, adding the uses for the other items, and then adding other labour-saving devices to the list.

- Go through the answers together, explaining or translating any items that students don't know. Possible answers:

  vacuum cleaner – cleaning carpets, vacuuming/hoovering
  food processor – preparing food, chopping vegetables, making soups, etc.
  fridge – keeping food cold/fresh
  iron – ironing clothes
  dishwasher – washing dishes / washing up
  electric drill – drilling, putting things up on walls, repairing things

- Ask students what other items they thought of, and build up a list on the board. This could form the basis for a general brainstorming activity. Some possible answers:

  sewing machine; microwave oven; freezer; hair drier; electric carving knife

- Ask students which items they think are the most and least useful, and why. Then take a class vote.

> **Presentation option**
> This is a good opportunity to present the structure *use for + -ing*:
>
> | **You use it**
It is used | **for washing clothes.** |
>
> The structure is formally presented in Exercise 10.1.

2 Speaking activity

- Look at the picture, and ask the class what they think it is used for and how it works. (It fills your bath automatically; you can decide what temperature you want and how deep you want the water.)

- In groups, students think of a labour-saving device, either one that is unusual or one that doesn't exist. They decide how it works and what it looks like, and make brief notes or a sketch.

- One student from each group tries to 'sell' their device to the rest of the class. The other students say whether they would buy it or not.

> **Help option**
> Write imaginary devices on slips of paper and give one to each group. Some possible ideas:
> – a burglar-catching device
> – a houseplant-watering machine
> – a breakfast-making machine
> – a window-cleaning device
> – a dust-attracting machine
> – voice-operated doors/windows
> – automatic lighting

> **Alternative**
> Students sit in new groups or move freely round the class, and try to persuade other students to buy their device.

3 A place to relax

Although intended as a freer fluency activity, this exercise naturally involves vocabulary for describing features of a room and its general atmosphere. Students hear a recording of someone imagining an ideal room to relax in; they then imagine their own ideal room in the same way.

➤ Workbook: Exercise C

1 Presentation & listening

- Ask a few questions to focus on the picture, e.g. *What sort of furniture has it got? What has it got on the floor? What about the walls? Does it have a view? Are there any ornaments? Does it look comfortable?*

- 🔲 Play the recording. Students listen and find similarities and differences between what they hear and the room in the picture. Differences:

  The room in the recording is small, has wooden walls, a view of the sea, a real dog. The woman's reading a book. (She doesn't mention a fireplace or pictures.)

2 Speaking activity

- Students work in pairs, and take it in turn to imagine a room. They should try to visualise the room as clearly as possible, and to imagine that they're actually in the room themselves – so it may help if they close their eyes! The other student in the pair should prompt by asking questions, e.g. *Are there any pictures? What's on the floor? What sounds can you hear? Is there a view? What are you doing in the room?*

- As a round-up, ask a few students to tell you briefly what kind of room they imagined, and if it was like any room they know in real life.

> **Vocabulary option**
> You could go beyond the picture, and develop this stage into a more extended elicitation of vocabulary:
> *Walls:* bare walls, painted walls, (plain or patterned) wallpaper
> *Floor:* floorboards, carpet, rugs, cushions
> *Furniture:* armchair, sofa, shelves, cupboards …
> *Objects:* ornaments, plants, vases, posters, paintings …
> *Atmosphere:* relaxing, elegant, cosy, lived-in, formal …

> 🔲 The tapescript is on page T15.

> **Homework option**
> With a good class, ask students to write a description of the room they imagined.

2 Labour-saving devices

1 Look at the labour-saving devices in the list.
What are they used for?
Add more items to the list.

Which do you think is the most useful?
Which is the least useful?

2 Think of an unusual labour-saving device
(either real or imaginary). Try to persuade
other students to buy it.

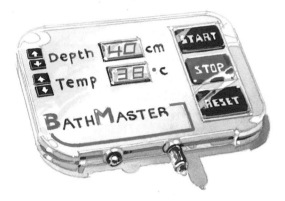

	Device	Use
washing machine	Washing clothes	
vacuum cleaner		
food processor		
fridge		
iron		
dishwasher		
electric drill		

3 A place to relax

1 🔲 You will hear someone imagining an
ideal room to relax in.

How similar is it to the room in the picture?

2 Imagine yourself relaxing in an ideal room.
– What are you doing?
– What's the room like? Think about the
things in the bubbles.

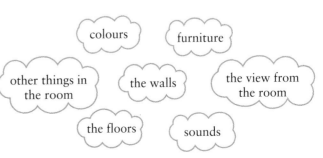

colours   furniture

other things in   the walls   the view from
the room   the room

the floors   sounds

4 Snow house

READING

1 Read the opening paragraph of the article *Inside the snow house*.

Look at the writer's questions. What do you think the answers might be?

2 Now read the rest of the article.

What were the answers to the writer's questions?

LISTENING

You will hear part of a TV programme in which someone builds an igloo.

1 🔲 The speaker demonstrates seven stages in building an igloo, but you will hear them in the wrong order. Listen and match what he says with the pictures.

2 🔲 Now listen to the whole description (in the right order) and write a sentence describing each of the stages 2–6.

Stage 1: Find an area of deep snow and mark out the shape of the igloo.

Stage 2:

Stage 3:

Stage 4:

Stage 5:

Stage 6:

Stage 7: The finished igloo.

4 Snow house

This combined reading and listening activity is about igloos. The reading text describes what it's like to live in an igloo, and the listening is a demonstration of how to build one.

READING

- Read the opening paragraph with the class, and ask students to imagine what the answers to the questions might be. Focus the discussion on what you would expect to find inside an igloo, how warm it would be, how it could be heated.

- Give time for students to read the text and find the answers to the questions in the opening paragraph. Then discuss the answers together. Possible answers:

  - *Too cold to sit down?* No, because there are skins and furs to sit on, and the igloo is quite warm inside.
  - *Able to stand up?* Yes, because the floor is below ground level.
  - *Light a fire?* An oil lamp, which doesn't make too much smoke (and the smoke goes out of the chimney).
  - *Melt the walls?* No, only a thin layer on the inside melts. Animal skins stop the water dripping down.

LISTENING

- ▭ Play the first recording, pausing after each section and asking the class which stage they've just heard. Ask students to say how they know, and focus on key expressions that indicate what stage is being described (e.g. Stage 2: he says 'cutting blocks' and 'entrance tunnel'). The stages in the first recording are:

  6 4 3 7 5 2 1

- ▭ Play the second recording (which is in the correct order), pausing so that students can write a sentence to describe each of the stages 2–6. Possible answers:

  Stage 2: Cut out blocks from the entrance tunnel.
  Stage 3: Cut out blocks from the floor to build the walls.
  Stage 4: Build the blocks around in a spiral.
  Stage 5: Push the last block into position.
  Stage 6: Cut a hole for a chimney, and pack snow over the outside.

> *Optional lead-in*
> Begin by asking general questions about igloos, to lead into the topic and establish some of the key vocabulary, e.g.
> *What are igloos made of?* (Blocks of snow.)
> *Where do you find them?* (In the Arctic.)
> *Who lives in them?* (Eskimos or Inuit.)
> *What kind of clothes do/did they wear?* (Animal skins, furs.)

> *Note*
> The demonstration is recorded twice, first in the wrong order and then in the correct order.

▭ Tapescript for Exercise 4: *Snow house*

(6) Now we'll cut a small hole for a chimney, and meanwhile John is packing snow over the outside just to make it all nice and strong and close up any gaps so the wind doesn't get through.

(4) Now we're building the blocks round and round in a spiral. They're very firm, very firm, and there's no chance of them falling in.

(3) Now we're cutting blocks from the floor of the igloo, so it will be below ground level, and we're building the walls from the inside.

(7) So that's it, and it's very strong, you see – well, take a chance here, here we go … Yes, I can climb on the top of it, no problem, no problem. And it's very strong. So, it took just over an hour to build, and that's not bad for a place to live.

(5) So now we've just got one block to put on the top. So I'm going to push it up through here and then let it fall into position – there, ah there, good. And now we're going to make the entrance tunnel.

(2) Now I've marked out a circle for the igloo, and I'm cutting blocks from the entrance tunnel first. So this, this will go down below ground level.

(1) Well, we've found some nice firm deep snow here, and it looks like a really good place to build an igloo. So we'll get started. So first of all we're going to mark out a shape for the tunnel and for the igloo itself.

(The second recording is in the order indicated by the italicised numbers *(1), (2)* …, above.)

A OK, I'd like you to imagine an ideal room, a place to relax.

B I see windows, big windows that look out on the sea. A small room with wooden walls, wooden furniture, wooden floors, a thick rug, a thick woollen rug on the floor, and a dog – I love dogs. On the floor also a table, a small table with papers, magazines, books on it. Music coming from a CD player.

A What about you? What are you doing?

B Reading. Listening to the music and reading at the same time. I'm reading a novel. And the room is warm – I'm alone.

Self-study Workbook

Exercise A: Good housekeeping
Students complete crossword diagrams with 'housekeeping' vocabulary.

Exercise B: Labour-saving devices
Students label pictures of labour-saving devices, then say which three they would choose, and why.

Exercise C: Features of rooms
Students answer questions about a picture of a room, using words in a box to help them.

New words
Space to record new words with notes and examples.

Translation
Key sentences for translation.

Listening: A Spanish family
A man compares the roles taken by different members of his family. Students listen and decide who does/did various household jobs.

Phrasal verbs: Introduction
Differences between phrasal verbs and 'normal' verbs. Students guess the meanings of phrasal verbs based on 'look'.

Writing skills: Punctuation: joining sentences
Use of punctuation and linking words to join sentences, focusing on comma, semi-colon, colon and dash. Students join sentences, then rewrite an advertisement using punctuation and linking words.

Inside the snow house

Spending the winter in an igloo isn't as uncomfortable as you might think

Every five-year-old knows what igloos look like from the outside, but what are they like *inside*? And what would it be like to live in one? Imagine yourself inside a hollow dome made of snow and ice, with more ice underneath you. Would it be too cold to sit down comfortably? Would you be able to stand up, or would you have to crawl around on your hands and knees? And how would you keep warm? Could you light a fire? Wouldn't the fire fill the igloo with smoke and start melting the walls? The more you think about life in an igloo, the more problems there seem to be.

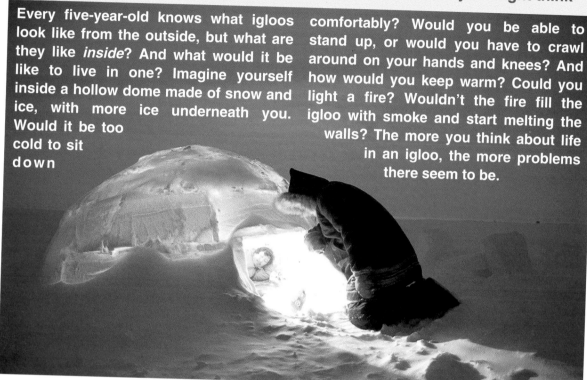

In fact, life in an igloo isn't nearly as uncomfortable as you might think. Let's imagine going into a traditional igloo out of a snowstorm in the middle of an Arctic winter …

Room to move

The first thing you notice after crawling down through the entrance tunnel is that the igloo is bigger than it looks from the outside. The floor in the centre of the igloo is quite a bit below ground level, and there's plenty of room to stand up without banging your head.

Heat

It's also quite warm inside. This is partly because the snow blocks that the igloo is made from provide very good insulation, and partly because of a stone lamp burning seal oil – the only form of heating in the igloo. So although it's −30°C outside, it's a fairly comfortable +10°C inside – warm enough to take your wet clothes off and hang them up to dry.

Naturally, the heat melts a thin layer of the snow wall, but to prevent drips (and to provide even more insulation) there are animal skins hanging across the ceiling and down the walls.

It isn't smoky inside, either – a small hole in the ceiling acts as a chimney, and allows the smoke from the lamp to escape.

Light

Above the entrance tunnel, there's a thin sheet of ice set into the wall, which acts as a kind of window. You can't see much through it, but during the few hours of daylight it lets quite a lot of light in. The rest of the time, you can see by the light of the lamp (which is also used for cooking).

A place to sit

Around the walls of the igloo is a wide platform (which is at the same level as the ground outside), where you can sit or lie down. You don't have to sit directly on the snow – the platform is covered with dry grass and animal bones, then with animal skins, and finally with animal furs, and there are more animal furs to use as blankets. So the platform is a comfortable place to stretch out – and warm, too, as it is near the top of the dome where the warmest air is trapped.

A temporary home

In many ways, an igloo is the ideal place to spend a really cold winter. When the weather gets warmer in spring, of course, you no longer need it – which is just as well because that's the time that igloos start to melt.

3 Past events

1 Scary stories

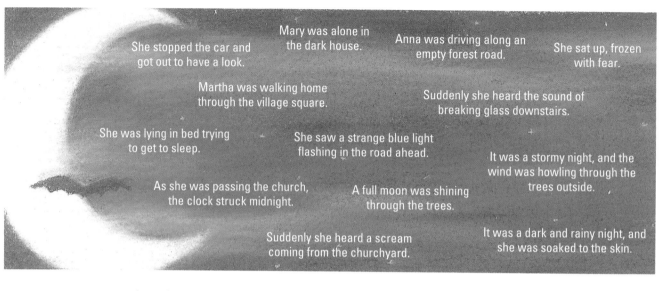

She stopped the car and got out to have a look.

Mary was alone in the dark house.

Anna was driving along an empty forest road.

She sat up, frozen with fear.

Martha was walking home through the village square.

Suddenly she heard the sound of breaking glass downstairs.

She was lying in bed trying to get to sleep.

She saw a strange blue light flashing in the road ahead.

It was a stormy night, and the wind was howling through the trees outside.

As she was passing the church, the clock struck midnight.

A full moon was shining through the trees.

Suddenly she heard a scream coming from the churchyard.

It was a dark and rainy night, and she was soaked to the skin.

1 *a* Look at these sentences. Can you put them together to make the beginnings of three different stories?

 b Which parts of each story give the *background*, and which give the main *events*?

 c Imagine what happened next.

2 Work in groups. Choose one of the pictures, and write the beginning of a scary story.
Think about these questions.

 – What time was it?
 – What was the weather like?
 – Where were the people?
 – What were they doing?
 – What did they see/hear/feel?
 – What happened?
 – How did they react?
 – What happened next?

This unit deals with language for talking about events in the past. It focuses on the following grammatical areas:
– Past simple and continuous tenses
– subject and object questions in the past
– past time expressions
– Past simple passive.

3

1 Scary stories

This exercise uses the opening sentences of horror stories to show how we use the Past simple and continuous tenses in narration. Students reorder the sentences to make three stories, and then develop a story of their own from the pictures.

➤ Focus on Form: Exercise 1
➤ Workbook: Exercise A

1 Reading & presentation

- Give time for students to read the sentences and fit them together to make three different stories. They could do this working alone or with a partner.

- Discuss the answers together. Expected answers:

  Martha was walking home through the village square. It was a dark and rainy night, and she was soaked to the skin. As she was passing the church, the clock struck midnight. Suddenly she heard a scream coming from the churchyard.

  Mary was alone in the dark house. She was lying in bed trying to get to sleep. It was a stormy night, and the wind was howling through the trees outside. Suddenly she heard the sound of breaking glass downstairs. She sat up, frozen with fear.

  Anna was driving along an empty forest road. A full moon was shining through the trees. She saw a strange blue light flashing in the road ahead. She stopped the car and got out to have a look.

- Use the stories to establish that
  – to give the *background* we use the Past continuous tense (*Martha was walking home, She was lying in bed, The wind was howling, Anna was driving, A full moon was shining*)
  – to give the *main events* of the story we use the Past simple tense (*The clock struck midnight, She heard a scream, She heard the sound of breaking glass, She saw a strange blue light, She stopped the car and got out*).

- If necessary, show how the two tenses are formed:

	PAST SIMPLE + -ed (or irregular)	PAST CONTINUOUS was/were + -ing
walk	walked	was walking
shine	shone	was shining

- Take each story in turn and ask students to imagine what happened next.

2 Speaking & writing activity

- Groupwork. Students choose one of the situations in the pictures and develop a story by thinking of answers to the questions. When the group has agreed on a possible storyline, they write it down with one person in the group acting as 'secretary'.

- In turn, each group reads out their story to the rest of the class.

Vocabulary option
Deal with any unfamiliar vocabulary, focusing especially on expressions that are typical of this style of writing, e.g. *frozen with fear* (= very frightened), *soaked to the skin* (= very wet), *the wind was howling* (= making a noise in the trees).

Language note
We can, of course, also use the verb *to be* for background description, e.g.
Mary *was* alone ...
It *was* a stormy night ...

Presentation option
If you like, give everyday examples of your own, e.g.
This morning I *was having* breakfast. I *was eating* toast. The sun *was shining* outside. Suddenly the doorbell *rang*, so I *got up* and *opened* the door.

Homework option
Students continue the story, adding a paragraph to what they have already written in class.

2 Information gaps

This exercise introduces questions using the Past simple and continuous, and deals with the difference between subject *and* object *questions. Students match questions with gaps in a text, then ask their own questions about other texts.*

➤ Focus on Form: Exercise 2
➤ Workbook: Exercise B

1 Presentation

- Look at the text and ask students to match the questions with the gaps. Then discuss what the answers might be. Questions (and possible answers):

  1 Who phoned you? (An old friend.)
  2 Where did you arrange to meet? (At the Metropole Bar.)
  3 What did he show you? (A letter.)
  4 Who was standing by the door? (A woman with dark glasses.)
  5 What was she holding? (A camera.)
  6 What happened next? (She took a photo of us.)

- Establish that
  – the questions on the left are *subject* questions. They ask about the subject of the sentence, and keep normal word order:
      Something *happened.* → What *happened*?
      Someone *was standing* by the door. → Who *was standing* by the door?
  – the questions on the right are *object* questions. They ask about other parts of the sentence, and have question word order:
      He *showed* me something. → What *did* he *show* you?
      She *was holding* something. → What *was* she *holding*?

Presentation option

If necessary, present basic Past simple and continuous question forms:

Past simple: *did* + infinitive
I went there →
    Where *did* you go?
Past continuous: change word order:
I was sitting →
    Where *were* you *sitting*?

2 Speaking activity

- Go through the texts and establish what the questions should be:

  Text 1: Who called round? What did he want? What did you tell him?
  Text 2: What attacked you? What did you throw at it? What did it do? What happened next?
  Text 3: Who was sitting by the window? What was she wearing? What was she reading? What did she say?

- Pairwork. Students ask the questions and make up suitable answers.

- As a round-up, ask a few pairs what answers they gave.

Practice option

Give prompts for students to make subject or object questions, e.g.

I saw someone →
    Who did you see?
Someone saw me →
    Who saw you?
Something happened →
    What happened?
I went somewhere →
    Where did you go?

3 The first time ...

In this activity, students talk about personal experiences, using the Past simple and past time expressions with when, while, before, after *and* during.

➤ Focus on Form: Exercise 3
➤ Workbook: Exercise C

1 Listening & presentation

- 🔲 Play the recording and establish when the people learnt to swim and how:

  1 When she was 11. / After she moved to the south of Germany. She jumped off the diving board.
  2 When he was five or six. / During the summer holidays. His father put a chocolate bar at the end of the pool.
  3 While he was at infants school. / When he was five or six. He went to swimming lessons. They used a long pole to help him.

Check that students understand how the words in the box are used. Point out that *while* is followed by a clause, but *during* is followed by a noun phrase:

> **He left** *while we were eating.*
> *during the meal.*

Optional lead-in

Use the pictures to elicit key vocabulary: *swimming pool, diving board, shallow end, deep end, pole, rubber ring, armbands.*

🔲 The tapescript is on page T18.

2 Speaking activity

- Groupwork. Students tell each other about 'first experiences'. Encourage them to use past time expressions, and also to give a few details (e.g. where they were, what happened, what it was like).

- As a round-up, ask a few students to tell you some of the things they said.

Alternative

Students go through the items quickly; then they each choose one to talk about in more detail.

Option

With some classes, you may want to be more adventurous, e.g. first alcoholic drink, first kiss. But first make sure no-one will be offended!

2 Information gaps

Subject & object questions

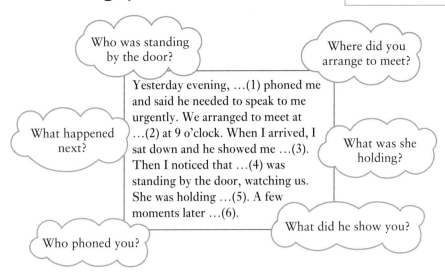

Who was standing by the door?

Where did you arrange to meet?

What happened next?

What was she holding?

Who phoned you?

What did he show you?

Yesterday evening, …(1) phoned me and said he needed to speak to me urgently. We arranged to meet at …(2) at 9 o'clock. When I arrived, I sat down and he showed me …(3). Then I noticed that …(4) was standing by the door, watching us. She was holding …(5). A few moments later …(6).

1 *a* Match the questions with the gaps. What do you think the answers might be?

  b What is the difference between the questions on the left and those on the right?

2 Ask (and answer) questions about these stories.

I was having dinner last night when …(1) called round. He wanted …(2), but I told him …(3).	We were walking across a field when a …(1) attacked us. I threw …(2) at it, and it …(3). Then …(4).	I got on the train and sat down. …(1) was sitting by the window. She was wearing …(2) and reading …(3). She looked up and said '…(4).'

3 The first time …

Past time expressions

1 ⬚ You will hear three people saying how they learned to swim.

  a When did they learn?
    Use words from the box.

when	before	during
while	after	

  b How did they learn?

2 Work in groups. Which of these things can you remember?

– learning to swim
– the first film you saw at a cinema
– smoking your first cigarette
– the first time you went on a long journey
– using English for the first time

SHALLOW END

DEEP END

4 Bad news

A The worst damage occurred in the city centre. Several of the older buildings collapsed and many others

B One village was completely cut off by the rising water, and many people were trapped in their houses for several hours. Eventually they

C The town came under heavy fire again last night as Government troops continued their advance. More than 100 civilians

D Passengers were thrown from their seats, and the driver, who was slightly injured,

E Police were attacked by crowds of youths throwing stones and home-made bombs. One police vehicle

1 *a* Which of the newspaper articles is about
  – a train crash? – a riot? – a war?
  – an earthquake? – a flood?

  b Which verbs in the articles are in the passive?

  Complete the sentences in each article. Choose verbs from the box.

destroy	trap	rescue
damage	kill	overturn
injure	take	

2 Choose one of the articles, and imagine what else happened. Write two or three sentences to continue the article.

Grammar Checklist

Past simple tense

verb + -ed (or irregular forms) – for talking about events in the past.

They **elected** a new President.
I **heard** the news last night.

Irregular verbs: see list on page 143.

Past continuous tense

– for talking about the background to past events (what was going on at the time).

We **were** living in France at the time.
I heard the news while I **was** having breakfast.

Subject & object questions

*If **Wh-** questions are about the **subject** of the sentence, they keep normal word order.*

Who **invited** her to the party?
What **happened** next?
Who **was sitting** next to you?

Otherwise, they have question word order.

Who **did you invite** to the party?
When **did they arrive**?
What **were you doing**?
  (*Not* ~~What you were doing?~~)
Why **was he sitting** outside?

Past time expressions

We became friends **during** the war.

I met him | **when** / **while** | I was in Spain.

She worked there | **before** she went abroad. / **after** she left university.

Past simple passive

was/were + *past participle*

They **took** him to hospital.
→ He **was taken** to hospital.
The Chinese invented gunpowder.
→ Gunpowder **was** invented by the Chinese.

See also Reference section, page 131.

4 Bad news

This activity uses the context of natural disasters to introduce the Past simple passive. Students read short extracts from newspapers, and then add sentences to them.

➤ Focus on Form: Exercise 4
➤ Workbook: Exercise D

1 Reading & presentation

- Look at the five topics in Question 1a and check that students understand what they mean. Then give time for students to read the extracts and decide what each one is about. Answers:

  A earthquake B flood C war D train crash E riot

- Build up two lists on the board, one of active and one of passive verbs:

ACTIVE	PASSIVE
occurred	were thrown
collapsed	was injured
came	was cut off
continued	were trapped
	were attacked

- Show how the Past simple passive is formed:

  WAS/WERE + Past participle

  | The driver <u>was</u> | |
  | Several people <u>were</u> | slightly inj<u>ured</u>. |

- Students complete the sentences using verbs from the box. Possible answers:

  A … were badly damaged.
  B … were rescued by helicopter.
  C … were injured but no-one was killed.
  D … was taken to hospital.
  E … was overturned and several policemen were injured.

2 Writing & speaking activity

- Groupwork. Students choose one of the news items, and write two or three more sentences, drawing on the verbs from the box. Some possible answers:

  A Many people were injured, and were taken to hospital.
  B Large areas of farmland were flooded and at least 500 sheep and cows were killed.
  C Buildings in the city centre were destroyed. Several foreign tourists were trapped in the Hilton Hotel, but they were later rescued.
  D None of the passengers were injured. Several people were trapped in one of the carriages.
  E Twenty people were arrested. Several shops were damaged.

- As a round-up, ask some groups to read out what they have written.

Vocabulary option
Discuss briefly what happens in each, and use this to introduce key vocabulary, e.g.
Earthquake: *collapse*, *damage*, *trap*

Language note
In these news items it is natural to use the passive to talk about people because we are mainly interested in what *happened to* them, rather than in what they *did*.

Practice option
Give a few active sentences and ask students to give passive equivalents, e.g.
Something damaged the building.
→ The building was damaged.

Alternative round-up
Students read out their sentences, and the others guess which news item they have chosen.

Optional extension
Bring in a picture of an accident or natural disaster (e.g. a capsized ship, a burnt-out building), and ask students to write an imaginary news item based on it.

🔊 Tapescript for Exercise 3: *The first time …*

1 How did I learn to swim? It was when I was 11. It was just after we had moved from Berlin to the south of Germany to a small village and I was the last one in the class of 28 who could not swim, but as I was very good in sports otherwise I decided that I will be able to swim in no time. So I didn't want to be taught, I just stepped on the diving board and jumped in and somehow struggled with the water and managed to move back to the side of the river bank and got out, and that was it.

2 I learnt to swim when I was about five or six during the summer holidays, and I remember my father putting me in the swimming pool in the shallow end and at the other end of the pool he put I think it was a chocolate bar on a plate, and he said 'If you can swim to the other end all on your own you can have the chocolate bar,' and I did.

3 It was while I was at infants school, which would make me five or six, I suppose. My brother and I used to be taken for lessons on a Tuesday evening. My brother learnt to swim a lot sooner than I did, and so I used to watch him jumping into the deep end, while I was sort of guided up and down the shallow end on the end of a pole. I used to look forward to the hot chocolate that we used to buy in the foyer afterwards.

Focus on Form

1 *Events and circumstances*

> Past simple and continuous

- Read the example, and demonstrate the exercise by giving a background sentence yourself and asking the class to find the event from the list (e.g. I was crossing the road ... → ... when a car nearly ran me over).
- Students do the exercise in pairs.
- To introduce the second part of the exercise, give an example situation and ask what happened next, e.g. 'I was crossing the road when a car nearly ran me over. I shouted at the driver but he only laughed.'
- Students write down one of the situations they thought of, and add a continuation.
- Ask a few students to read out what they have written.

2 *Asking questions*

> Subject & object questions about the past

- Explain that the point of the exercise is for students to make their own questions from the facts in the back of the book.
- Working alone, students look at their own facts and write quiz questions.
- Pairwork. Students ask each other their questions.
- Ask different pairs what their questions were and what answers they gave. The questions should be:

Student A
1 Who became Prime Minister of Great Britain in 1979?
2 When did the Second World War begin?
3 What was Archimedes doing when he shouted 'Eureka'?
4 Who wrote the song 'Yesterday'?
5 Who played James Bond in 'From Russia with Love'?

Student B
1 Who beat George Bush in the 1992 American Presidential Election?
2 What was Isaac Newton doing when he discovered gravity?
3 Who invaded Russia in 1812?
4 In Shakespeare's play, who did Othello kill?
5 How many times did Björn Borg win the men's tennis championship at Wimbledon?

3 *Saying when things happened*

> when, while, during, before, after

- Either go through the exercise with the class, eliciting a variety of continuations, or let students work through it in pairs and then go through the answers together. Possible answers:

  a while he was skiing / when he slipped over.
  b during the lesson / while I was driving.
  c after she had a baby / before she got more qualifications.
  d during the journey / after I retired.
  e before I went abroad / when it expired.

4 *Past simple passive*

> Past simple passive, singular and plural forms

- Read the example, so that students can see how the exercise works. Then read out *b: I didn't lose my credit cards*, and ask students to find a continuation and change it into the passive: *They were stolen.*
- Students do the rest of the exercise in pairs.
- Go through the answers together. Answers:

  c She was sacked last week.
  d He was pushed.
  e It was found on a bus.
  f He was brought up by his grandmother.
  g We weren't invited.
  h It was painted by my daughter.

5 *Pronunciation*

Ask students to try saying the sentences themselves, then play the tape as a model. Focus on these points:

a Reduced *was* and *were* in *he was* /hi wəz/, *they were* /ðeɪ wə/, *what were* /wɒt wə/.
b Full *did* in Yes/no questions: /dɪd/.
   Slightly reduced *did* in Wh- questions: /waɪ dɪd/, /wɒt dɪd/.
c Pronunciation of past tense forms: *destroyed* /dɪˈstrɔɪd/, *damaged* /ˈdæmɪdʒd/, *injured* /ˈɪndʒəd/, *rescued* /ˈreskjuːd/, *murdered* /ˈmɜːdəd/.

Self-study Workbook

Exercise A: Short stories
Past simple and Past continuous.
Students complete some single-sentence stories.

Exercise B: Subject and object questions
Students write questions for answers given in brackets.

Exercise C: When did it happen?
Students write about real experiences, saying what happened and when.

Exercise D: Active or passive?
Students fill gaps in a text about Bonnie and Clyde with active or passive forms of verbs in a box.

Translation
Key sentences for translation.

Listening: Childhood memories
Students listen to two people describing childhood memories, and complete a gapped summary.

Pronunciation: Reduced and full forms
Full and reduced forms of *for*, *from*, *to*, *some*, *was* and *do*, depending on their position in a sentence.

Reading: Two terrible tales
Students reorder two mixed up stories, and try to guess the endings.

Focus on Form

1 Events and circumstances

Choose one of the events below and decide what was happening at the time. See if your partner can guess which event you are thinking of.

Examples:

A I was eating some lamb chops last night …
B … when I broke a tooth.
A While I was cycling through the park a few days ago …
B … a dog started chasing me.

My parents came home.
I tripped over.
All the lights went out.
A car nearly ran me over.
A dog started chasing me.
I broke a tooth.
Someone stole my wallet.
I fell asleep.
Someone shouted my name.

Now choose one of the situations you thought of and write one or two sentences saying what happened next.

2 Asking questions

Examples:

Alexander Fleming discovered penicillin in 1928.
Q Who discovered penicillin?
Columbus discovered America *in 1492.*
Q When did Columbus discover America?

Read your facts in the back of the book and ask your partner questions.

Student A: Your facts are on page 112.
Student B: Your facts are on page 114.

3 Saying when things happened

Imagine when these things happened. Complete the sentences, using *when*, *while*, *before*, *after* or *during*.

Example: *They decided to get divorced …*

… during their honeymoon.
… after they had their fourth child.
… when they both fell in love with other people.

a He broke his arm …
b It was so embarrassing! I fell asleep …
c She found it difficult to get a job …
d I had plenty of time to read …
e I forgot to renew my passport …

4 Past simple passive

Example:

A He didn't die of a heart attack.
B He was murdered.

Student A: Read out the sentences below.

Student B: Choose suitable continuations from the box, and change them into the passive.

a He didn't die of a heart attack.
b I didn't lose my credit cards.
c She doesn't work there any more.
d He didn't fall out of the window.
e I've got my brief-case back.
f His parents died when he was three.
g We didn't go to the party.
h Actually, it's not a Picasso.

His grandmother brought him up.
Someone pushed him.
Someone stole them.
My daughter painted it.
Someone found it on a bus.
They didn't invite us.
Someone murdered him.
They sacked her last week.

5 Pronunciation

How do you say the words and phrases below?

a He was sitting next to me.
They were watching television.
What were they watching?

b Did you know?
Why did she phone you?
What did she say to you?

c destroyed damaged injured
rescued murdered
He was murdered.
Several buildings were damaged.

Now listen and check your answers.

4 Money

1 You and your money

1 Do you spend more than you earn?

2 What do you most enjoy spending money on?
3 What do you least enjoy spending money on?

4 What do you think is good value for money?
5 What do you think is a waste of money?

6 What can you afford that you most appreciate?
7 What can't you afford that you would most like to have?

a Life insurance – I'm not planning to die just yet. And expensive haircuts.

a Potatoes, rice, pasta, things like that. They're cheap, and they fill you up!

b I like being able to buy good quality food and clothes, and not having to look around to find the cheapest of everything.

b A plane ticket, when I can afford it. That gives me a really great feeling.

c A really nice, old, classic car. My first choice would be a Jaguar XK150.

c Oh, lots of things — fur coats, caviare, designer shoes and unnecessary make-up, for example. And tobacco.

d No, but I don't save anything either.

d This stupid Government tax. I don't think students should pay taxes.

e Take-away restaurants which take your order over the phone and deliver the food right to your door — free.

e A round-the-world plane ticket, with lots of stopovers in nice places.
A car plus enough money to keep it running.

f Boring things like suits and white shirts and ties to wear to work. And buying train tickets every day to get to work and back.

f Yes. I have to borrow from my parents, and also from a student loan company.

g A really good night out at the weekend. Or preferably two.

g I'm pretty lucky to have enough money to study, and to do a bit of travelling.

1 Here are the answers two people gave to the questions at the top of the page.

Can you match their answers to the questions?
What can you tell about each of the people?

2 Spend some time thinking of your own answers to the questions.

Now work with a partner. Interview each other.

This unit deals with three vocabulary areas related to money:
– talking about cost and value
– language used in buying, selling and spending money
– talking about the cost of living (bills, taxes, etc.).

The Reading and Listening activity is a reading game in which students read cards and make career choices until they make £1 million or reach the age of 36.

4

1 You and your money

This exercise uses the context of a magazine questionnaire to introduce a range of expressions connected with cost and value. Students match two people's answers with the questions, then answer the questions themselves.

➤ Workbook: Exercise C

1 Reading & presentation

- Write these words and expressions on the board: Ask students to use them in sentences, and establish what they mean and how they are used. Focus on these points:

  > **earn**
  > **spend**
  > **good value**
  > **a waste of money**
  > **afford**

  – *earn* = to make money from working
    (She earns £200 a week.)
  – *spend* = to use money to buy things
    (He spends £50 a week *on* food.)
  – It's *good value* (*for money*) = it's not expensive
    (The meals here are good value – you get large portions, and they're cheap.)
  – It's *a waste of money* = it's a useless way to spend your money
    (The exhibition was a waste of money – it cost a lot and it wasn't at all interesting.)
  – I can't *afford it* / *afford to* … = It's too expensive for me
    (I can't afford to go by taxi.)

- Pairwork. Students look at the questionnaire and match the two people's answers to the questions. Answers:

  Left-hand column: 1d 2g 3f 4e 5a 6b 7c
  Right-hand column: 1f 2b 3d 4a 5c 6g 7e

- Discuss what the two people seem to be like. Possible answers:

  Person on left: Male, in his 20s or 30s, works in an office, travels to work, is quite well off and expects to get richer, not very fashion-conscious, goes out a lot.
  Person on right: Student (actually female, though this is not clear from what she says), around 20, lives cheaply, hasn't got much money, is in debt, has a practical attitude to life, likes travelling.

2 Speaking activity

- Working alone, students think about their own answers to the questionnaire, and make brief notes.
- In pairs, students interview each other in turn.
- As a round-up, go through some of the questions, asking different students what answers they gave. You could also get students to interview you.

> *Presentation option*
> Ask a few questions round the class using the key items, e.g.
> Do you think the food at … is good value for money?
> Did you go out last night? How much money did you spend?

> *Vocabulary option*
> As you go through the answers, check that students understand any unfamiliar vocabulary (e.g. *life insurance*, *take-away restaurants*, *fur coats*, *stopovers*, *loan company*).

> *Alternative: class survey*
> Give each student (or pair of students) one of the questions. They move freely round the class, asking other students their question. As a round-up, ask students to tell you what different answers they got to their question.

2 Exchanges

This exercise introduces a range of expressions used in money transactions (e.g. changing money, paying bills). Students match pairs of remarks together, then listen to five short scenes; then they improvise similar conversations themselves.

1 Presentation & listening

- Ask students to find pairs of remarks they think fit together. Establish briefly what situations they might be used in, e.g. *I'd like to pay my bill please, Do you take credit cards?* – paying a restaurant or hotel bill.
- 🔲 Play the recording. After each scene, pause and establish what is happening. Answers:

  1 She's *borrowing* £20 from a friend (wants the friend to *lend* her £20).
  2 She's paying her hotel *bill*, wants to *pay by credit card*.
  3 He's bringing a shirt back to a shop, wants a *refund*; hasn't got a *receipt*.
  4 She needs *small change* / wants to *change* a £10 note. She asks at a kiosk, the assistant will only give her change if she buys something.
  5 She's *cashing traveller's cheques* (at a *bank* or *exchange office*).

2 Writing/speaking activity

- As a lead-in, choose one of the remarks from the bubbles and write it on the board. Ask students to suggest other remarks that might come before or after it, and together build up a dialogue, e.g. *A: Could you lend me £20? B: What do you need it for? A: I want to buy my sister a birthday present …*
- Working in pairs, students choose one of the remarks and develop it into a dialogue of their own. They could either do this in writing, as in your example on the board, or orally.
- Ask students to act out their conversations in turn. Ask other students whether it is clear who the people are, what they want, and what happens.

3 The cost of living

This exercise introduces vocabulary for talking about living costs and the economic systems of a country. In the second part, students use this language to write a manifesto for an imaginary political party.

1 Presentation

- Use the general words shown in the picture to elicit particular expenses that apply to the students' own country. Build these up on the board, e.g.

BILLS	TAXES	INSURANCE
rent	income tax	property insurance
medical bills	sales tax	health insurance
heating bills		life insurance
repair bills		car insurance

2 Writing/speaking activity

- Read the manifesto and ask students to think of a suitable name for the party (e.g. The Motorists' Party, The Private Car Party, The Car Owners' Party).
- Focus on these verbs, which are useful for talking about government policies:
  - *increase/reduce*
  - *halve/double*
  - *introduce/abolish* (a tax)
  - *ban*
- In groups, students think of another political party that might represent a particular group of people. They decide what name to give it and what the party's aims should be. Then they write a 'manifesto' similar to that in the example.
- As a round-up, each group in turn talks about the aim of their party and reads out their manifesto.

> ➤ Workbook: Exercises A, C

Presentation option
As you discuss the answers, build up a list of key words and expressions on the board.

🔲 The tapescript is on page T23.

> ➤ Workbook: Exercises B, C

Language note
We say *the cost of living*, not ~~the cost of life~~.
We also talk about our *standard of living*.

Help option
Suggest suitable parties, or get ideas from the class and write them on the board. Some possible ideas:

The Anti-Car Party
The Teenagers' Party
The Working Mothers' Party
The Business Party
The Health Party
The Old People's Party
The Music Lovers' Party
The Vegetarian Party

Optional extension
Students vote for any of the parties except their own, and you find out which party wins the 'election'.

2 Exchanges

Can you give me change for a £10 note?

I can pay you back on Friday.

Can I just buy some chewing gum, please?

Did you bring your receipt with you?

Do you think you could lend me £20?

I'd like to pay my bill, please.

You'll need to sign them just here, please.

Do you take credit cards?

I'd like to cash some traveller's cheques.

I'd like a refund, please.

1 📼 You will hear five short conversations about money. Look at the remarks in bubbles. Which two remarks do you think you will hear in each conversation?

Now listen to the recording, and see if you were right.

2 Work in pairs. Choose one of the remarks and develop it into a conversation of your own.

3 The cost of living

1 Think of an average family in your country. What are the main expenses they have to pay?

2 Read this election manifesto. What do you think the name of the party is?

The ▮▮▮▮▮▮▮ Party

ELECTION MANIFESTO

1 We will spend more money on roads and motorways.

2 We will spend less money on public transport.

3 We will reduce the price of petrol.

4 We will abolish car tax.

5 We will halve the price of car insurance and driving lessons.

6 We will provide free parking in all city centres.

In groups, form your own political party.

– What is your party called? What is its aim?
– Write your election manifesto.

4 Can you make a million?

READING

This is a reading game in which your aim is to make £1,000,000.

Start at Card 1, and decide what you want to do. Then turn to the card indicated by your choice. For example, if you decide to go to university, go on to Card 12, which is on page 114.

Each card represents at least two years of your life.

As you play, make notes in the table below. The game ends either when you reach 36 years of age or when you have £1,000,000.

> **1** You're 18, and it's time to leave school and decide what to do with your life. Your best subjects were maths and economics, but you are also interested in art and graphic design.
>
> Your parents would like you to study economics at university for four years, and then follow a career in the Civil Service. Or you could go to design college for two years, and then go into advertising. A third possibility would be to get a job in a bank, where you can use your maths and start earning money straight away.
>
> Your savings at the moment total £5,000.
>
> | | | |
> |---|---|---|
> | Go to university | ➤ **12** | (p.114) |
> | Go to design college | ➤ **10** | (p.113) |
> | Join a bank | ➤ **18** | (p.115) |

Age	Card no.	Place	Occupation	Money
18	1	Home	Leaving school	£5,000
18–20				
20–22				
22–24				
24–26				
26–28				
28–30				
30–32				
32–34				
34–36				

LISTENING

🔲 You will hear parts of an interview with someone who made £1,000,000.
Listen to each part and follow his career, starting with Card 1.

Part 1
– Which card is he on now?
– What do you think he'll do next?

Part 2
– Which card is he on now?
– What do you think he'll do next?

Part 3
– Which card is he on now?
– What finally made him a millionaire?

---

4 Can you make a million?

This combined reading and listening activity is a game in which students try to make £1 million by the time they are 36 years old. The reading part of the activity consists of a series of cards which students read and make choices about their careers. The listening part is an interview with someone who successfully made £1 million, and so provides the 'answer' to the reading activity.

Note: Short cuts

This reading and listening activity is longer than most in the book, and may take more than a lesson to complete. If you are short of time, you could make the activity shorter in one of the following ways:
– letting students read the cards at home before the lesson, working out the best way to become a millionaire. In the lesson you could discuss which is the best route, and then play the interview as a check.
– doing the reading activity in class, but stopping when the first group has finished, so that the activity becomes a race.
– letting students read the tapescript as they listen to the interview instead of following the man's career from card to card.

READING

- Divide the class into groups of three or four. Begin by establishing how the game works:
  - Students should imagine they are 18 years old, about to leave school, and have £5,000 in the bank.
  - Their aim is to make £1 million by the age of 36.
  - They start at Card 1, and then decide which card to go to next. Nearly every card represents two years of their life.
  - One person in the group should keep a record in the table of what they decide to do and how much money they have.

- Students play the game, moving from one card to another and deciding together what to do. They carry on until they have made a million or until they are 36 years old.

- If you are short of time, stop the game when the first few groups have finished – otherwise let all the groups finish the game. Find out how much money each group made.

Vocabulary option

The reading cards contain a number of useful words and expressions connected with money. You could focus on these by writing them on the board at the beginning of the lesson, and establishing what they mean: *economics*, *make a loss*, *bank balance*, *salary*, *invest money*, *accountant*, *shares*, *go bankrupt*, *savings*, *inflation*.

Alternatively, give each group a dictionary and let them look up any words they need to know.

LISTENING

- Explain that the career of the man in the recording follows the best route in the game to become a millionaire.

- 📼 Play the recording, pausing from time to time to give students a chance to follow his career on the cards. Stop after each part, and get answers to the questions. Answers:

Part 1: He's on Card 20.
Part 2: He's on Card 25.
Part 3: He's on Card 21. He designed the Galactosaurs.

📼 The tapescript is on page T23.

Note

The millionaire's route follows these cards:
1–10–14–20–7–25–3–15–21
See the diagram on page T144, where his route is shown by a thicker line.

Homework option

Students write an account of the course that they followed themselves, using the same style as the person in the interview.

📼 Tapescript for Exercise 2: *Exchanges*

1 A Do you think you could lend me £20?
　B Um, well I'm not sure.
　A I can pay you back on Friday.
　B Well OK, here you are. (Thanks)
2 A I'd like to pay my bill, please.
　B Right yes, it's all made out. There you are.
　A Thanks. Do you take credit cards?
　B No, I'm afraid we don't. You can pay by cheque or by cash if you've got it.
3 A I bought a shirt here the other day and it's got a little tear here (Oh yes, yes) on the back of the collar, so I'd like a refund please.
　B Right. Did you bring your receipt with you?

　A No, I haven't got one.
　B Well I'm afraid without the receipt we can't really give you a refund.
4 A Excuse me, I'm sorry to bother you. Can you give me change for a £10 note? I need to make a phone call and I haven't got any change.
　B Sorry, I can only give you change if you buy something.
　A Oh really? OK well, can I just buy some chewing gum, please?
5 A I'd like to cash some traveller's cheques, please.
　B Certainly. Can I see your passport? (Yes) Right. Thank you. OK, you'll need to sign them just here, please.

📼 Tapescript for Exercise 4: *Can you make a million?*

A So Gareth, you're going to tell us how to make a million.
B Well, to go back to the beginning, um I went to study graphic design after leaving school. And I was there for two years, and when I left college I decided to go off and see a bit of the world.
A Where did you go?
B Well a friend of mine got a job in Brazil, so I decided to go and have a look at Brazil. And I had a wonderful time. The social life was terrific, and I made a lot of wonderful friends. Some of these friends then decided to drive up to the USA. It seemed like a very good opportunity to see some more of the world, so I joined them. But we had a bit of a mishap in Central America. We were kidnapped by bandits, believe it or not, (Good Lord) and it was two years before I got away from them.
A What an extraordinary experience …

B … And eventually that was the way that we escaped from them, by paying our way out.
A So what happened then?

B Well, having got away from there I went to the States, as I planned to do two years before, to Los Angeles, without any money of course, and for four years I drove a cab in LA.
A Did you meet any of the stars? …

B … But when she died only a year later, she left me half a million pounds in her will.
A That is extraordinary. What a stroke of luck. So what did you do?
B Well, fortunately a friend wrote to me to say that she was starting up her own toy-making business. So I came home and I worked helping her design, and of course business was very slow to start with. But then I had a great stroke of luck. I found a design that was very popular – I designed the Galactosaurs (Of course) which are a family of toy dinosaurs, and they proved to be a great hit all over the world. And that was the beginning of my great good fortune, and I've just become a millionaire.
A And congratulations.

Self-study Workbook

Exercise A: Using money
Vocabulary concerned with using money.
Students add missing sentences to dialogues.

Exercise B: The (6) of living
Vocabulary relating to expenses, bills, taxes.
Students fill gaps in a text to complete an acrostic.

Exercise C: Similar meanings
Verbs relating to money.
Students rewrite sentences using particular verbs.

New words
Space to record new words with notes and examples.

Translation
Key sentences for translation.

Listening: A waste of money
Two people discuss what they think is a waste of money. Students decide what the speakers' main point is, and write brief notes on what they say.

Phrasal verbs: Intransitive verbs (1)
Basic intransitive phrasal verbs, mostly with a 'literal' meaning (e.g. *get up*, *come in*). Students find pairs of opposites, then put them appropriately in sentences.

Writing skills: Reference: pronouns
Use of pronouns (*one, ones, some, any, mine, yours, his,* etc.) to avoid repetition in a paragraph. Students correct sentences, then rewrite a text, replacing nouns with appropriate pronouns.

2 Congratulations! You got your degree in economics. You can now get a well-paid job in the Civil Service, with good chances of promotion – this is what your parents would like you to do.

Or you could drop everything and go to Brazil – a friend of yours is working there and says she could probably find you a job.

You didn't spend much in the last two years at university – you have £1,000 less than you did two years ago.

Join the Civil Service   ➤ **11** (p.113)
Go to Brazil   ➤ **14** (p.114)

3 You're enjoying life – you and your friend work well together, you're living in a nice part of the country, and you've made a lot of new friends.

Designing toys is hard work – there seem to be so many already on the market – and it's taking you time to build up contacts. In your first two years you made a slight *loss* – nothing to worry about, but you now have £15,000 less money than two years ago.

You *could* get a nice safe job with a firm of accountants, but on the other hand, perhaps the toy business will take off ...

Stay in the toy business   ➤ **15** (p.114)
Join a firm of accountants   ➤ **24** (p.116)

J&B DESIGN STUDIO

4 After two years in the Caribbean as a crew member of the yacht *Passing Clouds*, you've begun to suspect that something illegal is going on. You've often seen your passengers talking in whispers and exchanging mysterious packages – and isn't £30,000 a year a bit *too* much for the job you're doing?

You could leave the ship now and go back home (your father says there's a job in the Civil Service still open for you) – or take a risk and carry on working on *Passing Clouds*. You've added £50,000 to your savings over the last two years.

Stay in the Caribbean   ➤ **23** (p.116)
Join the Civil Service   ➤ **16** (p.115)

5 You've had a good two years. You were promoted twice and you're now earning a good salary – with plenty left over to invest. You invested money at the right time, too – share prices doubled over the last year, and altogether you now have 50% more than you had two years ago.

But you're bored – you could carry on in the Civil Service, or you could just drop everything and go off on a trip round the world ... you never know what might happen to you.

Stay in the Civil Service   ➤ **13** (p.114)
Go round the world   ➤ **17** (p.115)

5 Obligation

1 Overseas experience

Obligation structures

1 *a* Look at this advertisement. What other questions might you ask?

Do I have to pay tax?

Do I have to pay my own fare?

Do I need a work permit?

Can we go away at weekends?

Are we allowed to use the hotel's facilities?

Do I have to ...?

Can I ...?

...?

Work abroad this summer
in an Interplex international hotel

✔ **No formal qualifications needed**

✔ **Varied and interesting work**

✔ **Free accommodation**

✔ **Earn money and see a foreign country**

b Now read the information sheet on page 112. What are the answers?
Talk about things you

– can / are allowed to do
– can't / aren't allowed to do
– have to / need to do
– don't have to / don't need to do.

2 Choose one of these advertisements.

Student A: You're interested in finding out more. Think of some
questions. Then find out the answers from B.

Student B: You represent the company that placed the advertisement.
Think of the information you will give. Then answer A's questions.

Au pairs needed for European families

Learn a foreign language in the country of your choice. Full board and pocket money given in return for child care and light housework.

Learn English in Britain this summer

● 4-week residential courses in beautiful countryside
● Fully qualified teachers
● Friendly accommodation with local families.

Why not work on a farm this summer?

Fresh air, good food, lots of exercise: what better way of spending the summer? And you'll be earning money instead of spending it!

This unit is concerned with obligation in the present and past. It focuses especially on:
– basic obligation and permission structures (e.g. *have to*, *be allowed to*)
– *make* and *let*
– structures expressing freedom from obligation (e.g. *wherever you like*, *as long as you like*).

5

1 Overseas experience

This exercise introduces basic structures for talking and asking about obligation: have to, need to, can, be allowed to. *Students look at an advertisement for hotel work, and use these structures to ask about their rights and obligations; they then read an information sheet to find out the answers. The second part is a role-play, in which students find out about other imaginary jobs.*

➤ Focus on Form: Exercise 1
➤ Workbook: Exercise A

1 Presentation & reading

● Look at the advertisement and the questions, and ask students to suggest other questions they might ask. Build up a list of these on the board. The questions should mainly be with *Can I/we ...?* or *Do I/we have to ...?*, but could include others as well. Some possible questions:

Do we have to work in the evening?
Do we have to share a room?
Do we have a room in the hotel?
Can we leave if we don't like it?
Can we choose what kind of work we do?

● Write this table of structures on the board:

have to need to	don't have to don't need to
can are allowed to	can't aren't allowed to

Point out that *don't have to* and *don't need to* both mean *it isn't necessary*: *You don't have to go = You can stay (if you like)*.

● Give time for students to read the information sheet on page 112. Then go through each of the questions, and get students to make a sentence (if we know the answer) using one of the structures on the board. Possible answers:

You have to pay local tax.
You have to pay half the fare.
You need (to have) a work permit, but you don't need to arrange it yourself.
You aren't allowed to go away at weekends, but you can go away for one other day a week.
You're allowed to use the hotel facilities outside working hours, but you have to pay for them (at 40% of the normal rate).

● Briefly discuss whether students think the job sounds worth doing or not, and why.

2 Writing/speaking activity

● To start off the activity, look quickly at the three advertisements and elicit a few of the questions students might ask, e.g.

Au pair: How much pocket money do you give? Can I go out in the evenings?
English courses: Do we have to do homework? What do we do at weekends?
Farm: What work do I have to do? / How many hours do I have to work?

● Divide the class into pairs. Each pair chooses one of the advertisements. Then, working alone, they prepare questions or answers, making brief notes.

● When they are ready, they get together and ask and answer questions.

● As a round-up, ask a few students if the job or course seemed worth doing or not, and why.

Language note
You could add to the table:

must   (= have to)
needn't (= don't need to)
mustn't (= can't)

These are all modals, and are usually used in *giving* orders or instructions, e.g.

Parent to child: 'You *mustn't* make so much noise. You *must* do your homework. You *needn't* get up early tomorrow.'

Alternative 1
Choose one of the advertisements, and elicit a series of questions from the whole class, writing them on the board. During the preparation stage, students either think how to answer the questions or prepare one or two further questions of their own.

Alternative 2
Choose one of the advertisements, e.g. the English courses. Divide the class into three groups of 'course directors' and three groups of 'students'. In turn each group of students questions each group of course directors.

As a round-up, ask each group of students which school they would choose and why.

2 Strict or easy-going?

This exercise introduces the verbs make *and* let, *and shows how they are related to the structures in 5.1. In the second part, students write sentences with* make *or* let, *and other students guess what situation they are referring to.*

➤ Focus on Form: Exercise 2
➤ Workbook: Exercise B

1 Presentation

- Look at the captions, and establish the difference between the two teachers: one is *easy-going*, the other is *strict*.
- Ask students to give you equivalents of the sentences in bubbles, using *make* and *let*, and write these up as examples on the board:

> She <u>lets</u> us wear what we like.   She <u>doesn't let</u> us talk in class.
> She <u>doesn't make</u> us do much work.   She <u>makes</u> us do lots of homework.

- Establish that
  - after *make* and *let* we use the infinitive <u>without</u> *to*: so we say *lets us wear*, not ~~lets us to wear~~.
  - otherwise, *make* and *let* are like normal verbs (not modals): so we say *She lets*, not ~~She let~~ in the Present tense.
- Elicit other possible sentences about the two teachers, e.g.

  She lets us eat sandwiches in class.   She makes us speak English all the time.
  She doesn't make us do homework.   She doesn't let us use dictionaries.
  She lets us talk to each other.   She makes us do a test every week.

2 Writing/speaking activity

- To show how the game works, give two or three sentences yourself, and ask the class to guess which people you chose each time, e.g.
  - They let me wear jeans and a T-shirt. (easy-going employers)
  - They let me sleep on the bed. (easy-going dog owners)
  - They make me practise the piano every day. (strict parents)
- Give time for students to write one or two sentences.
- Students read out their sentences in turn, and the others guess who they are.

Presentation option
With a single-nationality class, it might be useful to give the equivalents of *make* and *let* in the students' own language.

Practice option
To practise the equivalence between *make/let* and the obligation structures from 5.1, give sentences using *have to*, *can*, etc., and ask students to say them using *make* or *let*, e.g.
I'm not allowed to go out.
→ They don't let me go out.

Note
So that the answers aren't too obvious, sentences should begin with *They*, and refer to *me* or *us*.

Alternative
With a large class, this stage could be done as pair- or groupwork.

3 Punishments

This exercise introduces obligation in the past. Students listen to people describing punishments they received, then talk about punishments they remember themselves.

➤ Focus on Form: Exercise 3
➤ Workbook: Exercise C

1 Listening & presentation

- 🔲 Play the recording. Pause after each item and establish what the person did wrong and what the punishment was. Answers:
  1. She stayed in the school building at lunch time. She had to go to the class below for a week.
  2. She held her prayer book too low at morning prayers. She had to recite a prayer in front of the class.
  3. He was rude to the teacher. He had to write out 'I must not be cheeky' 500 times in Latin.

- As a preparation for the next stage of the activity, check that students know the past forms of the obligation structures from 5.1 and 5.2. You could do this by giving the present forms and asking for the past equivalents (*I have to* → *I had to*, *He lets me* → *He let me*).

2 Speaking activity

- Students sit in groups of four or five, and think of interesting or unusual punishments they remember – these could be at home or at school.
- Each group chooses the most interesting punishment they talked about. In turn, one person from each group tells the rest of the class about it.

Optional lead-in
Look at the (Latin) handwriting, and ask students to suggest what kind of punishment it shows.

🔲 The tapescript is on page T26.

Blackboard option
Build up a list of past obligation structures on the board:

> **I had to / didn't have to**
> **I could/couldn't**
> **I was/wasn't allowed to**
> **He made / didn't make me**
> **She let / didn't let me**

Homework option
Students write two or three short paragraphs describing the punishments they heard about.

2 Strict or easy-going?

1 What's the difference between the teachers of these two students? Talk about each one using *make* and *let*.

Imagine other things that the two teachers do and don't do.

We're allowed to wear what we like in class.

We don't have to do much work.

We're not allowed to talk in class.

We have to do loads of homework.

2 Choose one of the pictures and write a sentence about them using *make* or *let*. See if other students can guess who you chose.

Strict parents

A strict dog-owner

A strict boss

A strict government

Easy-going parents

An easy-going dog-owner

An easy-going boss

An easy-going government

3 Punishments

Past obligation structures

1 🔲 You will hear three people talking about punishments they received when they were at school. For each one, say

– what they did wrong
– what the punishment was.

Do you think the punishments were fair?

2 Work in groups. Tell the others about something you had to do (or weren't allowed to do) as a punishment.

Choose the most interesting punishment and tell the rest of the class about it.

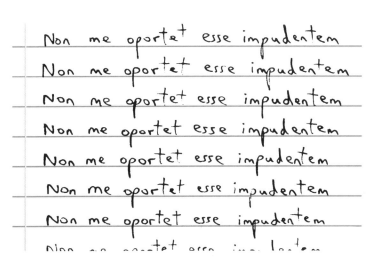

Non me oportet esse impudentem
Non me oportet esse impudentem
Non me oportet esse impudentem
Non me oportet esse impudentem
Non me oportet esse impudentem
Non me oportet esse impudentem
Non me oportet esse impudentem
Non me oportet esse impudentem

4 Feel free

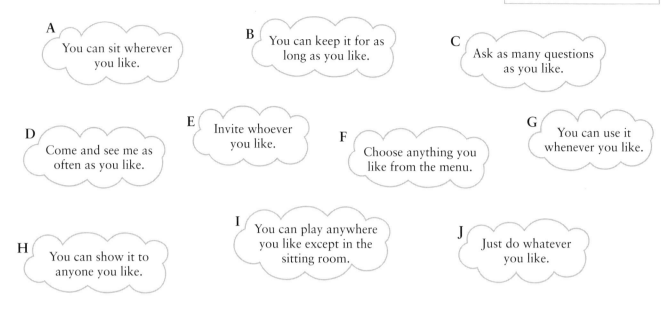

A You can sit wherever you like.

B You can keep it for as long as you like.

C Ask as many questions as you like.

D Come and see me as often as you like.

E Invite whoever you like.

F Choose anything you like from the menu.

G You can use it whenever you like.

H You can show it to anyone you like.

I You can play anywhere you like except in the sitting room.

J Just do whatever you like.

1 Look at the remarks in bubbles. Make a list of
   – words like *wherever*
   – words like *anywhere*
   – expressions with *as … as*.

2 Imagine you're staying with a friend who's very easy-going.
   How might he/she answer these questions?
   – Where shall I put my coat?
   – Can I watch the news on TV?
   – Can I have one of these apples?
   – What time shall I get up?
   – Can I phone my sister?

   Now continue with questions of your own.

Grammar Checklist

Obligation

(don't) have to; (don't) need to

You **have to** show your passport at the border.
You **don't have to** wear a tie.
We **don't need to** be there till 7 o'clock.

Do I have to show my passport?
Do we **need to** buy tickets?

Permission

can('t); are(n't) allowed to

Sorry – you **can't** smoke in here.
She's **allowed to** have visitors.

Can I smoke in here?
Is she **allowed to** have visitors?

make & let

make & let *are followed by infinitive <u>without</u>* **to**.

Her parents **make** her **tidy** her own room.
 (= she has to tidy it)
They **don't make** her **cook** her own meals.
 (= she doesn't have to cook her own meals)
They **let** her **stay** up late at weekends.
 (= she's allowed to stay up late)
They **didn't let** me **use** the phone.
 (= I couldn't use it)

Freedom from obligation

| You can ask | whoever anyone | you like. |

| You can sit | wherever anywhere | you like. |

You can eat **as** much **as you like.**
They can stay **as** long **as they like.**

See also Reference section, page 132.

4 Feel free

This exercise introduces a range of structures for expressing complete freedom from obligation. These follow three patterns: structures with -ever, structures with any-, and structures with as ... as. The first part of the exercise simply focuses on language; in the second part, students make up sentences for an imaginary situation.

➤ Focus on Form: Exercise 4
➤ Workbook: Exercise D

1 Presentation

• Look at the remarks, and ask students what they might be about. Possible answers:

A To a guest in your house, an audience at a meeting, etc.
B You've lent someone a book, a video.
C To people at a meeting, someone being interviewed.
D To a friend who's lonely, to a new acquaintance.
E Parent to teenager who's giving a party.
F Someone who's invited a friend to a meal in a restaurant.
G Letting someone use a car, a computer, etc.
H About a photo, a letter.
I Parents to children, at home; or perhaps to a musician.
J A wide variety of situations, e.g. a dancing instructor to a class.

• Give students time to note down the key structures, then build them up as a table on the board:

anywhere any time anyone anything	OR	wherever whenever whoever whatever	you like

as	long many questions often	as you like

Point out that
– the structures *any-* and *-ever* are used to answer questions with *Who? Where? When? What?*
– the structures with *as ... as* are used with adjectives or adverbs (to answer *How far ...? How much ...?*, etc.).

2 Speaking activity

• Go through the questions, and establish what the answers might be:

– You can put it wherever/anywhere you like.
– You can watch anything you like. / You can watch it whenever you like.
– You can have as many as you like. / You can eat anything you like.
– You can get up whenever you like. / You can get up as early as you like.
– You can phone anyone you like. / You can use the phone whenever you like.

• Pairwork role-play. One student is the guest, and the other is the easy-going host. The guest asks the questions on the page, and then continues with other questions of his/her own.

• As a round-up, find out what other things the hosts allowed their guests to do.

> *Practice option*
> Ask simple questions, and get students to answer using the target structures, e.g.
> How much sugar can I use?
> How fast can I drive?
> Who can I talk to?
> Where can I go?
> What can I say?
> When can I leave?

🔲 Tapescript for Exercise 3: *Punishments*

1 The worst punishment I can remember was when I was at primary school, and I'd stayed in the school building at lunch time, because I felt it was too cold to go out. And for that they made me go down to the class below, and do all their lessons for a whole week. And I wasn't even allowed to see my own friends during the break times.

2 I remember I was about seven and I got punished because I held my prayer book too low in morning prayers. They made me stand up in front of the class and recite a prayer in front of everybody, and I was terribly embarrassed.

3 When I was about eight years old and I was at school, I remember we were having a Latin lesson, and the teacher asked me something, and I was extremely rude back to him. And to punish me, he made me write out 'I must not be cheeky' something like 500 times in Latin one Saturday afternoon.

Focus on Form

1 *The law: obligation structures*

> Obligation structures (present tense):
> *(don't) have to; can('t); are(n't) allowed to*

- Either go through the exercise together, discussing what is true of the students' own country, or let students discuss the items in pairs, and then go through the answers together.

2 *Make & let*

> Structures with *make* and *let* in the present and past

- Check that students can form positive and negative sentences with *make* and *let*, in the present and past. Focus especially on:

  PRESENT: He *lets / doesn't let* me stay up late.
  PAST: He *let / didn't let* me stay up late.

- To show how the exercise works, give one or two 'let' sentences yourself, and ask students to find an equivalent 'make' sentence.

- Students do the exercise in pairs.

- Go through the answers together. Possible answers:

  - The teacher doesn't let us use our own language in class.
    She makes us speak English all the time.
  - My boss let me have the day off.
    She didn't make me come into work.
  - My parents didn't let me wear jeans to go to the concert.
    They made me wear a suit.
  - I never let my cat sleep on the bed.
    I always make it sleep in a basket in the kitchen.
  - They let us go straight into the cinema.
    They didn't make us wait in the queue.
  - The manager didn't let me pay by credit card.
    She made me pay in cash.
  - Her parents didn't let her boyfriend stay the night.
    They made him go home.

3 *Past obligation*

> Obligation structures (past tense):
> *had to, didn't have to; could(n't); made, let*

- To show how the exercise works, think of a situation yourself, and let students find the correct continuation, e.g. *Last weekend I was out with my family, and on the way home we bought a take-away pizza, so …*
  … we didn't have to cook.

- Students do the exercise in pairs, taking it in turn to think of a background situation.

4 *Do whatever you like*

> 'Freedom from obligation' structures with *any-*, *-ever* and *as … as*

- Either do the exercise with the whole class, or let them do it in pairs and go through the answers together. Answers:

  a They let him watch anything/whatever he likes.
  b We can have lunch whenever / any time you like.
  c She can borrow as many books as she likes.
  d I'll take you wherever/anywhere you like.
  e You can drive as fast as you like. (at any speed you like)
  f You can phone anyone/whoever you like.
  g They can have as much (money) as they like.

5 *Pronunciation*

Ask students to try saying the sentences themselves, then play the tape as a model. Focus on these points:

a Reduced *to* in *have to* /ˈhæf tə/, *need to* /ˈniːd tə/, *allowed to* /əˈlaʊd tə/. Tendency for /v/ to become /f/ in *have to*. Linking /r/ sound in *we're allowed to* /wɪər əˈlaʊd tə/.
b Weak forms in *them* /ðəm/.
c Pronunciation of *wherever* /weəˈrevə/, *whoever* /huːˈevə/, *however* /haʊˈevə/.
   Reduced *as* in *as long as* /əz ˈlɒŋ əz/.

Self-study Workbook

Exercise A: Obligation structures
Students fill gaps in sentences with obligation structures.

Exercise B: Make and let
Students rewrite sentences about army life using *make* and *let*, then write sentences of their own.

Exercise C: Past and present obligations
Students contrast what their life was like as a child with what it is like now.

Exercise D: Utopia
'Freedom from obligation' structures.
Students choose from a list of 'ideal' objects, places, institutions, etc., and imagine what they are like.

Translation
Key sentences for translation.

Listening: School rules
Three people talk about school rules. Students match questions and statements with what each speaker says.

Pronunciation: Contracted forms
Students hear examples of common contracted forms. Then they look at sentences and predict which words will be contracted when they are spoken.

Reading: Three word games
Descriptions of three word games that students can play themselves in English. Each game is followed by 'Test yourself' questions.

Focus on Form

1 The law: obligation structures

Change these sentences (if necessary) so that they are true of your country.

a Passengers in cars don't have to to wear seat-belts.
b You're not allowed to drive faster than 100 kph.
c You don't have to pay for local phone calls.
d Everyone has to carry an identity card.
e Foreigners can't own land and property.
f Men and women have to retire at 65.
g You're allowed to smoke on buses and trains.
h Men and women have to do two years' military service.

2 Make & let

Student A: Choose an item from Box A, and make a positive or negative sentence with *let*.

Student B: Choose an item from Box B, and make a sentence with *make*. Your sentence should mean the same as A's.

Examples:

A His parents don't let him stay up late.
B They make him go to bed early.

A My dad let me stay up late last night.
B He didn't make me go to bed early.

Box A:
let

stay up late
use our own language in class
have the day off
wear jeans
sleep on the bed
go straight in
pay by credit card
stay the night

Box B:
make

pay in cash
wait in the queue
go home
come into work
wear a suit
sleep in a basket in the kitchen
go to bed early
speak English all the time

3 Past obligation

Student A: Choose a sentence from the box, and imagine what happened beforehand.

Student B: Can you guess what happened next? Choose one of the sentences in the box.

Example:
A Last night we went to the cinema, and it finished so late that we missed the last bus …
B … so we had to walk home.

… we had to walk home.
… we didn't have to buy one.
… they made us wait till the interval.
… they finally let us go home.
… we couldn't get out.
… we let them stay with us.
… we didn't have to cook.
… we had to leave a note.

4 Do whatever you like

Change these sentences so that they end in
… *you like*, … *she likes*, etc.

Examples:

She's allowed to eat crisps, sweets, ice-cream …
She's allowed to eat whatever she likes.

You can sleep for 8 hours, 9 hours, 10 hours …
You can sleep as long as you like.

a His parents let him watch cartoons, westerns, soap operas …
b We can have lunch at 12.00, 1.00, 2.00 …
c She can borrow one book, two books, three books …
d I'll take you to the museum, to the zoo, to the park …
e You can drive at 90 kph, 120 kph, 150 kph …
f You can phone Ken, Laura, Stephen …
g They can have £100, £200, £300 …

5 Pronunciation

How do you say the words and phrases below?

a I have to stay here.
   Do you have to do homework?
   Do we need to pay?
   We're allowed to go out.
   You aren't allowed to look at it.

b She made them work.
   He let them stay up.

c wherever   whoever   however
   You can sit wherever you like.
   They can stay as long as they like.

🖭 **Now listen and check your answers.**

6 On holiday

1 Away from it all

St. George's

Gren On Tuesday morning we arrived at the port of St. George's, Grenada's capital city. Most people decided to join the ▮▮▮▮ round the island, which included a ▮▮▮▮ to a spice plantation and Carib's Leap, the cliffs where, in the 17th century, the last of the Carib Indians are said to have jumped to their death rather than become slaves. Some of the group, including myself, preferred to look around St. George's itself. We spent a fascinating morning in the ▮▮▮▮, where you could buy all kinds of ▮▮▮▮ produce: fruit, spices, straw hats and rugs (popular as ▮▮▮▮) and a bewildering variety of fish. For lunch, we ate crab soup and turtle steaks (both local ▮▮▮▮), and drank rum punch, which was a bit strong for my taste. Later on, we went ▮▮▮▮: we saw the cathedral, the 18th century Fort Rupert (now the headquarters of the Grenada police force) and, surprisingly, a zoo, before rejoining the rest of the party for an early evening barbecue on a sandy ▮▮▮▮ a few kilometres along the ▮▮▮▮. Then a last stroll along the harbour, and back to the ship.

1 Here is part of a travel article. Fill the gaps with words from the box.

souvenirs	market	coast
specialities	visit	local
sightseeing	excursion	beach

Now look at these pictures. Make a list of activities for each type of holiday.

2 You are either a *travel agent* or a *tourist*.

Travel agents: Think of a holiday destination and decide what you will say about it. Then visit each group of tourists in turn.

Tourists: Decide what you want to know about each place. Then listen to each travel agent and ask any questions you have.

Which holiday destination will you choose?

This unit is concerned with three areas of language for talking about holidays:
– types of holiday and holiday activities
– clothes and equipment associated with holidays
– ways of describing festivals and celebrations.

The Reading and Listening activity is about culture shock: the misunderstandings that can arise when people go to a different country from their own.

6

1 Away from it all

This exercise is about types of holiday and typical holiday activities. The first part introduces basic vocabulary for talking about holidays. The second part is a role-play, in which students take the parts of tourists and travel agents and find out about various holiday destinations.

➤ Workbook: Exercises A, B

1 Presentation

- Look at the postcard from Grenada, and ask students to imagine some of the things they might do on holiday there.

- Working alone or in pairs, students read the text, which describes part of a Caribbean cruise. They fill the gaps with words from the box.

- Go through the answers together. Answers:

  excursion; visit; market; local; souvenirs; specialities; sightseeing; beach; coast

- Look at the other pictures, and ask students to identify the types of holiday shown. Answers:

  skiing holiday; coach tour; seaside holiday; camping holiday

- Give time for students to note down holiday activities they think might go with each picture. Then go through the answers together, building up key vocabulary on the board, e.g.

walking	*sunbathing*	*going to restaurants*
camping	*windsurfing*	*taking photos*
climbing	*dancing*	*buying souvenirs*
sightseeing	*waterskiing*	*going on excursions*
skiing	*sailing*	

> *Vocabulary option*
> Pre-teach some of the more difficult words in the text, e.g. *spice, plantation, slaves, straw hats, crab, turtle, stroll.*

> *Grammar option*
> Point out that we often use the structure *go + -ing* to talk about many of these activities:
> You can *go* sightsee*ing*.
> We *went* sail*ing* every day.

2 Writing/speaking activity

- Choose three or four students to be 'travel agents'. Divide the rest of the class into three or four groups – they will be groups of 'tourists'. The travel agents will each talk about one holiday destination: write these on the board at the beginning.

- To prepare for the role-play, the travel agents think of what to say about their holiday destination, and the groups of tourists think of questions to ask.

- The travel agents take it in turn to visit each group of tourists. They tell them about their holiday destination and answer their questions.

- As a round-up, ask the groups of tourists to decide which of the holiday destinations they would choose, and why.

> *Note*
> For the travel agents, choose students who have been to or come from somewhere interesting, and who would be able to talk about it. Or let students volunteer.

> *Alternative*
> The travel agents stand up in turn and talk about their holiday to the whole class, answering questions that any of the tourists may have.

2 Packing list

This exercise introduces a range of vocabulary for things you might take on a holiday: clothes, equipment, accessories and medicines. Students choose a holiday and write a packing list for it – this encourages them to explore vocabulary areas they are interested in.

1 Presentation

- Look at the packing list, and establish that the person is going on a walking/camping holiday, probably somewhere fairly remote or cold. Then clear up any unknown vocabulary items in the list (She's taking an anorak in case it's cold and wet. So what's an anorak?).

2 Writing/speaking activity

- Groupwork. Each group chooses a type of holiday and a place. Together, they decide what they would take with them, and write a 'packing list' of about ten items. They should include things which are relevant to the type of holiday rather than general items (such as socks, toothbrush).

- In turns, groups read out their packing list, pausing every few items. The others guess where they are going and what they're going to do.

> ➤ Workbook: Exercise B

Language note
This is a good opportunity to introduce *in case* and *so that*, both used for giving reasons, e.g.
I'm taking an anorak …
… *in case* it's cold.
… *so that* I don't get wet.
These structures are presented systematically in Unit 11.

Suggestion
Have bilingual dictionaries available, so that students can look up words they need.

Option
To ensure a range of holidays, you could assign a holiday type to each group. Some possibilities: sightseeing holiday in a big city; seaside holiday; hitch-hiking across Europe; skiing holiday; safari in Africa; boat trip up the Amazon.

3 Festival

This activity is about national festivals and celebrations, and their origins. In the first part, students listen to someone describing the Chinese Dragon Boat Festival. In the second part, they discuss what they know and don't know about festivals in their own country.

1 Listening

- Look at the picture (which shows a Dragon Boat race in Hong Kong), and ask students to tell you anything they already know about the Dragon Boat Festival, or that they can guess from the picture. Focus on the questions, and check that students understand what all the items mean.

- 🔲 Play the first part of the recording, which is about the origin of the Dragon Boat Festival. Then discuss the questions. Answers:
  - He threw himself in the river to protest against the government.
  - They raced boats to scare away the creatures in the river.
  - They beat drums to scare away the creatures in the river.
  - They threw dumplings in the river to feed the fish (so that they wouldn't eat Chow Yen's body).

- 🔲 Play the second part of the recording, which describes what people do today, and discuss the questions. Answers:

  They eat the dumplings. They hold boat races. There is a large drum in each boat, and the racers have to row to the rhythm of the drums.

2 Presentation & discussion

- Divide the class into groups. Each group chooses a festival they know something about. Together, they discuss what they know about it, and also what they don't know or are not sure about. They write two lists, e.g.
  Christmas
  Sure: It's on 25 December. St Nicholas brings children presents.
  Not sure: Is it the same day in all countries? Why is it on 25 December? Who was St Nicholas?

- In turn, each group tells the rest of the class what they do and don't know about their festival, and see if other students can answer their questions.

> ➤ Workbook: Exercise C

Alternative
Tell students they will hear these words: *national hero, drowned, boats, race, drums, dumplings, fish.*
Ask them to guess how they might fit together in the story of the origin of the festival.

🔲 The tapescript is on page T31.

Alternative: single culture classes
Choose one festival and ask all the groups to make notes on it.

Alternative: mixed culture classes
Divide students into groups according to their culture. Each group gives the name of one of their festivals, and these are written on the board. Other groups think of questions they want to ask about the other festivals. Then groups take it in turns to answer the questions.

2 Packing list

1 Look at the packing list. Where do you think the person is going?

two jumpers
map
water bottle
anorak
matches
tent
binoculars
insect repellent
sleeping bag

2 Choose a holiday destination and imagine what kind of holiday it might be.

Make a list of 10 things you would take with you. Use a dictionary to help you.

Other students will guess where you're going.

3 Festival

1 ▭ You will hear someone talking about the origin of the Chinese Dragon Boat Festival. What does the speaker say about

– Chow Yen?   – drums?
– boats?   – dumplings?

▭ Now listen to her describing what happens in the Festival. What do people do with boats, drums and dumplings now?

2 Work in groups. Choose a festival in your own country.

What do you know about it?
What aren't you sure of?

Write questions to ask other students.

4 Culture shock

1

- ◆ Don't be surprised if people you don't know well ask you how much you earn or how much your car cost. This is quite normal.
- ◆ If you are invited for a meal, people will always offer you a second helping. You should always say 'No', so as not to appear greedy. This will be understood, and your host will give you more anyway. If you really don't want any more, cover your plate with your hand.
- ◆ It is polite to leave some food on your plate at the end of a meal – if you eat everything, it's a sign that you want more.
- ◆ Don't drop litter – even cigarette ends. It will be noticed, and you'll be fined. You can also be fined if you fail to flush the toilet in a restaurant or other public place.
- ◆ In general, it is considered insulting to give tips, and many places have signs saying 'No tipping'.

2

- ◆ Greetings can go on for some time – 'How are you? How is the day? How's business? How's the family?' … Your answer should always be 'Fine', even if you're not. If there's a gap in the conversation, this is usually filled with more greetings.
- ◆ Holding hands is common, even between strangers. Don't be surprised if someone showing you the way down the street leads you by the hand.
- ◆ In general, the left hand is used for 'unclean' activities, so use the right hand for giving things to people, handling food, etc.
- ◆ People younger than you will avoid looking you straight in the eye. This is not rude – on the contrary, it is a sign of respect.
- ◆ Hissing is a common way of attracting a person's attention, and is not rude. It's quite normal to hiss to call a waiter to your table.

READING

1 Here are some texts containing tips for visitors to five different parts of the world. Which text do you think is about
   - Britain?   – Thailand?
   - Spain?   – West Africa?
   - Singapore?

   Which tips are illustrated in the pictures?

2 According to the texts, where is it either *polite* or *impolite* to

   a leave food on your plate?
   b visit someone without an invitation?
   c touch food with your left hand?
   d ask someone how much they earn?
   e look your boss straight in the eye?
   f open a present immediately?
   g arrive on time?

3 Imagine yourself in one of the five places. Which customs would you find it

   – easy to get used to?
   – difficult to get used to?

4 Imagine that someone from one of the five places is coming to visit you.

   What tips would you give them about your own country?

A

LISTENING

▭ You will hear someone talking about something that happened to him in the Sudan. The story is in three parts.

Part 1
- What was he doing?
- How many people were there?
- What did they start doing?
- What do you think the speaker did next?

Part 2
- What did everyone eat?
- Why do you think they didn't eat the tomatoes?

Part 3
- Why didn't they eat the tomatoes?

4 Culture shock

This combined reading and listening activity is about culture shock: the experience of going to a different country and finding customs and behaviour different and difficult to understand. The reading is a series of tips taken from travel guides for visitors to five different parts of the world where customs may be different from their own. In the listening, students hear a story about a misunderstanding that happened to someone while travelling in the Sudan.

READING

- To introduce the activity, write 'Culture shock' on the board, and ask students to tell you what it means. If necessary, give examples yourself of misunderstandings that can arise between people with different customs.

- Divide students into pairs or groups. Give time for them to read the texts and decide which countries they refer to. Then discuss this together. Answers:

  1 Singapore   3 Spain   5 Thailand
  2 West Africa   4 Britain

- Discuss what tips the pictures go with. Answers:
  A Spain. It's common to see young children in restaurants.
  B Britain. You have to go to the back of the queue and wait.
  C Thailand. If you're calling a waiter, do it with your palm down.
  D West Africa. It's normal for strangers to hold hands in public.
  E Singapore. Don't tip in restaurants in Singapore.

- Look at Question 2 with the class. Ask students to find places in the text which answer the questions. Answers:

  a Singapore: polite.
  b Thailand: polite. Spain: impolite.
  c Thailand: impolite.
  d Britain: impolite. Singapore: polite.
  e West Africa: impolite.
  f Thailand: impolite.
  g Britain: polite.

- In pairs or groups, students choose one of the countries and discuss Question 3. Then talk about this with the whole class.

- Students write a few tips for visitors to their own country. Then ask them to read them out, and build up a list of tips on the board.

> *Optional lead-in: mixed nationality classes*
> Ask students to tell you things that they have found odd or surprising in the country they are visiting.

> *Alternative: mixed nationality classes*
> Students sit in pairs or groups according to their nationality. Together, they write a list of tips for foreigners coming to their country. Then each group reads out their list to the rest of the class.

LISTENING

- Check that students know where the Sudan is. Explain that they will hear a story in three sections and you will ask them to guess how it continues.

- ▱ Play the recording, pausing after each section so that students can answer the questions and predict what will happen next. Get a range of predictions each time before going on to the next section. Answers:

  Part 1
  - He was travelling by train, sitting in the compartment.
  - There were seven others apart from him.
  - They started bringing out food to eat.

  Part 2
  - Bread, beans, lamb, etc. – all the food except his tomatoes.

  Part 3
  - Because he'd used both hands to break them up. (In the Sudan you are supposed to touch food only with your right hand.)

> *Optional lead-in*
> To set the scene for the listening, ask students what they know about the Sudan (e.g. It's in North-East Africa, it's a poor country, it's hot, a lot of it is desert).

> ▱ The tapescript is on page T31.

The Dragon Boat Festival commemorates the death of a national hero, Chow Yen, who threw himself into the river and drowned himself in protest against a corrupt Government, and that happened about oh over 2,000 years ago in China. But the people saw the incident and they felt very sorry for him, and they collected a fleet of boats and beat the drums, made a lot of noise and raced the boat in the river trying to scare away the creatures in the river which were about to eat Chow Yen's body. And other people made up dumplings of rice, meat, beans, and they threw these dumplings into the river to feed the fish and other creatures in the river. That's how it started originally.

And nowadays people still make dumplings but they do not throw the dumplings into the river any more. They eat the dumplings, which is really very delicious. And they still hold boat races, anywhere in China, in Hong Kong and any parts of the world where there is a sizeable Chinese community, they still hold dragon boat races. The dragon boats are quite narrow and long and they have the head of a dragon in the front and the tail of a dragon at the back and they have about 22 people on each boat. They have a drum, a big drum at the end of the boat as well, so while the people are racing one person will be beating the drum and the people have to row together to the rhythm of the drum.

I was travelling in the Sudan by train and the journey I had to make was going to last about 48 hours and about an hour into the journey someone in my compartment, I think there were another seven people in the compartment, someone spread a large cloth on the floor and people began to bring out food. No-one had a knife, so people were breaking up the food and placing it on the cloth …

… I realised this was the thing to do so all I had was three or four tomatoes. So I broke up my tomatoes and put them on the cloth and then we all started to eat the food. And there was bread and beans and lamb and many different things and people were eating and I noticed that no-one was eating my tomatoes. So I encouraged them to eat and everyone smiled very politely but wouldn't actually take any. And slowly the food disappeared and disappeared and my tomatoes were left. So at the end of the meal there was nothing left except my tomatoes. And I felt slightly uneasy about this, I didn't know why …

… I thought probably it was because I was a foreigner and perhaps the Sudanese people didn't want to take a foreigner's food from them. So in fact I ate the tomatoes myself. It was only some time later that I realised that in fact the reason that people hadn't eaten my tomatoes was because I had broken up the tomatoes with both hands.

Self-study Workbook

Exercise A: Holiday activities
Students write paragraphs about different kinds of holiday, using vocabulary in a box to help them.

Exercise B: Holiday puzzle
Students find vocabulary relating to holidays hidden in a wordsquare.

Exercise C: Festival
Students answer questions to build up a paragraph about a festival in their own country.

New words
Space to record new words with notes and examples.

Translation
Key sentences for translation.

Listening: Going home
A travel courier describes an incident that happened at the end of a holiday. The listening is in two parts.
In Part 1, students predict the order in which events took place. They then listen to Part 2, and write an outline.

Phrasal verbs: Intransitive verbs (2)
More intransitive phrasal verbs, mostly with 'idiomatic' meanings (e.g. *carry on*, *turn up*). Students guess their meanings, then use them to replace phrases in a text.

Writing skills: Subject and object relative clauses
Use of relative clauses for identifying people, objects and places; difference between subject and object relative clauses. Students add relative clauses to a text, then rewrite sentences using relative clauses.

B

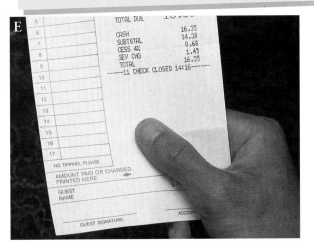

C

3

◆ People regard their homes as very private places, so if you're asked out to a meal it'll probably be to a restaurant rather than to the person's house or flat.

◆ It's common to see young children eating in restaurants with their parents, even quite late at night.

◆ Evening activity starts late. Restaurants start to fill up around 10 o'clock, and nightlife can carry on till four or five in the morning – or even later.

◆ Kissing (on both cheeks) is a common form of greeting between women, and between women and men. It is unusual between men, except when greeting a member of the family or a close friend.

◆ If it's your birthday, you're expected to invite friends or colleagues for a drink or a meal. You're the host, so you're expected to pay.

D

4

◆ Kissing is not common as a form of greeting unless you know someone well. It is especially unusual between men, who usually shake hands or just say 'Hello' without touching. People usually kiss on one cheek only.

◆ Unless you know someone well, it's impolite to ask them how much they earn, or how much they paid for something.

◆ In shops and at bus stops, go to the back of the queue and wait. If you 'jump the queue', other people will angrily tell you to wait your turn.

◆ Punctuality is important. If you arrange to meet someone, try not to be more than a few minutes late.

◆ On trains, especially underground trains, people tend to sit in silence and read. If you try to start a conversation with the person next to you, don't be surprised if you don't get much of a response.

E

5

◆ The head is considered the most spiritual part of the body, and the feet the dirtiest part, and it is very impolite to point your foot at someone, especially at their head. So don't sit with one leg crossed over the other, and never put your feet up on a chair or a desk.

◆ It is also rude to point at people with your finger. If you must point at someone, do it by nodding your head. If you want to call a waiter, do it with your palm down, moving your fingers towards you.

◆ It's quite normal to visit people at home without being invited. If you do, take a small gift with you.

◆ If you give someone a gift, they will usually thank you for it and put it aside without opening it. Don't be offended – it's bad manners to open a present in front of the person who has given it.

Adapted from *Britain, Singapore, Spain, Thailand* in the *Culture Shock* series; *The Rough Guide to West Africa*.

Review: Units 1–6

Find out

1 Find out how often other students do these things.
   – drink coffee   – go on holiday
   – wash up   – go to the bank

2 A Think of someone interesting that you know. What's his/her name?
   Other students: Find out what the person does, and what they're doing at the moment.

3 A Ask questions to find out as much as you can about what B did last weekend.
   B Answer A's questions, but don't give any information that he/she doesn't ask for.

Role-play

1 A You've seen an advertisement for a room to let. Ring up and find out what it's like.
   B A is interested in renting a room from you. Tell him/her what it's like.

2 A You're at an exchange office. You want to change some US dollars, and change some traveller's cheques. Make sure you get a receipt.
   B Serve the customer. Don't forget to ask for his/her passport.

3 A You're visiting a friend in prison. Find out what some of the rules are.
   B Tell your friend what you have to do and what you are(n't) allowed to do.

Conversational English

1 Making requests

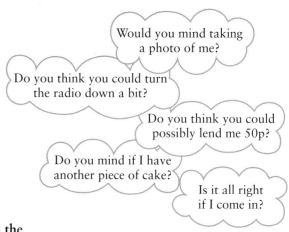

Will you take a photo of me?

Would you turn the radio down a bit?

Could you lend me 50p?

Could I have another piece of cake?

Can I come in?

Would you mind taking a photo of me?

Do you think you could turn the radio down a bit?

Do you think you could possibly lend me 50p?

Do you mind if I have another piece of cake?

Is it all right if I come in?

1 Compare the requests on the left and those on the right. Why do you think the second speaker is asking more carefully?

2 Make suitable requests for one of these situations.
   – You're in hospital. Think of some things to ask the nurse.
   – You're staying at a hotel. Think of some things to ask the receptionist.
   – You're on a bus. Think of some things to ask the person next to you.

   Now think of some real requests to ask your partner.

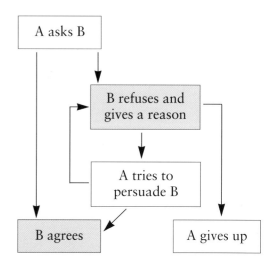

A asks B

B refuses and gives a reason

A tries to persuade B

B agrees

A gives up

Find out

1 Revision of language from Unit 1

- Establish what the questions should be, and a range of possible answers (e.g. How often do you drink coffee? Three times a day).
- Students ask each other questions in pairs. Then ask students to tell you what they found out from their partner (e.g. She drinks coffee three times a day).

2 Revision of language from Unit 1

- Think of someone yourself, and get students to ask you questions. Use this to focus on the difference between 'What does he/she do?' and 'What is he/she doing (at the moment)?'
- Groupwork. In turn, students think of people they know, and the others find out about them.
- Round-up. Ask each group to tell you about the most interesting person they talked about.

3 Revision of language from Unit 3

- Get students to find out what you did last weekend. Don't tell them anything unless they ask, so that they are forced to ask lots of questions. Check that students are forming Past tense questions correctly.
- Pairwork. Students find out from each other what they did at the weekend.
- Round-up. Ask a few students what they found out.

Role-play

1 Revision of language from Unit 2

- Preparation. Establish some of the questions students could ask, e.g. Is it furnished? What furniture has it got? Is there a desk? Can I cook meals? Is it quiet? How much does it cost? Has it got a nice view?
- Pairwork. Students improvise the conversation.
- As a round-up, ask a few students whether they decided to take the room, and why / why not.

2 Revision of language from Unit 4

- Preparation. Establish some of the things each person might say, e.g. I'd like to change some dollars into francs. Can I change traveller's cheques? Could I have a receipt, please? Could I see your passport, please? Sign your name here.
- Pairwork. Students improvise the conversation.

3 Revision of language from Unit 5

- Preparation. Establish some of the questions the friend might ask, e.g. When are you allowed to have visitors? Do you have to share a cell? Can you get up when you like? Are you allowed to go out at all?
- Pairwork. Students improvise the conversation.
- Round-up. Find out from a few pairs whether conditions in their prison were strict or not.

1 Making requests

This exercise practises ways of making requests, and focuses on the difference between casual and more careful requests.

1 Presentation

- Look at the two columns, and establish that
  - those on the left are casual requests: the speaker is asking for something that is quite unimportant, and which is easy for the other person to do
  - those on the right are more careful requests, using more polite language: we might ask like this if we felt we were asking something difficult (e.g. the other person is in a hurry, listening to his/her favourite music, has very little money, has only one piece of cake left, is changing his/her clothes).
- From the examples, build up a table of request structures on the board:

CASUAL	CAREFUL
Will you ...?	Would you mind -ing ...?
Would/Could you ...?	Do you think you could (possibly) ...?
Can I ...?	Do you mind if I ...?
Could I ...?	Is it all right if I ...?

2 Practice

- Using the first situation (in hospital), go through the flow-diagram, getting students to suggest what the people might say following different routes, e.g.
  - Could I use the telephone?
  - No, you've got to go to sleep now.
  - Oh please. I'll be very quick.
  - All right, but hurry up.
- Pairwork. Students have short conversations based on the three situations, then continue with requests of their own.

Talking points

This activity revises language from all six units:

– *Rice: from the field to the table*	Unit 1
– *Labour-saving devices*	Unit 2
– *Last week's news*	Unit 3
– *Bargains*	Unit 4
– *Things that are a waste of money*	Unit 4
– *The cost of living*	Unit 4
– *Strict parents*	Unit 5
– *What people do on holiday*	Unit 6
– *Festivals*	Unit 6

The activity can be played as a game round the class. One student chooses a topic and says a sentence or two about it. Another student then continues, adding another sentence, and so on.

As a preparation, you could let students choose two or three of the topics and look back at the appropriate unit to recall things they might say. If they like, they could also make brief notes.

Words

1 *Revision of language from Unit 2*

- Give time for students to make their lists of jobs.
- Ask students to read out their lists, and focus on any vocabulary that they seem to find difficult.

  Note: This could lead into a general discussion of male and female roles in the home.

2 *Revision of language from Unit 4*

- Students write down as many expressions as they can think of.
- Build up a list of expressions on the board, e.g. by cheque, by credit card, in cash, by opening an account.

3 *Revision of language from Unit 6*

- Give time for students to write down lists of items.
- Ask students what they wrote, and build up two lists on the board.

4 *Revision of language from Units 2, 3, 4 & 6*

- Ask the questions to the whole class, and use them to focus on key vocabulary from the units, e.g.
  Untidy person: *leaves* things *lying* around, doesn't *put* things *away*, never *tidies up*, *makes a mess*.
  Earthquake: buildings *collapse / are damaged / are destroyed*, people *are killed / injured / trapped*.
  Receipt: given when you *buy something*, or when you *pay a bill*.
  Sightseeing: visit *museums, art galleries*; look at famous *buildings (cathedrals, mosques, palaces)*; *take photographs*.

2 On the phone

This exercise practises basic telephone language, focusing on common opening remarks and replies.

1 *Presentation & listening*

- Look at the remarks and establish which would be made by the person making the call, and which by the person receiving it. Answers:

  Making the call:
  Hello. Is that Carol?
  Hello. Could I speak to Mr Taylor, please?
  Hi. This is Bill.
  My name's Linda Holden.
  Oh, OK. Can I leave a message?

  Check that students understand the meaning of *put you through* (= connect you), *leave a message*, and *Speaking* (= That's me).
  Point out that when phoning in English we say *This is (Bill), Is that (Bill)?*, not ~~I am (Bill), Are you (Bill)?~~

- Choose two or three pairs of students to have short conversations using the remarks (there are of course many possible variations).

- ▭ Play the recordings. Establish if any were the same as the ones the students made up.

2 *Practice*

- Divide the class into pairs, and give students in each pair a letter, A or B. Give a short time for students to read their own instructions and think of what to say.

- Students improvise the conversations.

▭ Tapescript for *On the phone*

1 A Hello. 305 8442.
  B Hello. Is that Carol?
  A Speaking.
  B Hi. This is Bill.
2 A Hello. Fletcher's Bookshop.
  B Hello. Could I speak to Mr Taylor, please?
  A Certainly. Can I have your name, please?
  B My name's Linda Holden.
  A Hold on. I'll put you through.
3 A Hello. Fletcher's Bookshop.
  B Hello. Could I speak to Mr Taylor, please?
  A I'm afraid he's not in at the moment.
  B Oh, OK. Can I leave a message?

Self-study Workbook

There is a review test of Units 1–6 on pages 34–5. The test is in six parts:
Sentence rewriting, Asking questions, Vocabulary, Fill the gaps, Writing paragraphs and Dictation.

Talking points

Choose one of these topics. Take it in turns to say a sentence or two about it.

Rice: from the field to the table

Labour-saving devices

Last week's news

Bargains

Things that are a waste of money

The cost of living

Strict parents

What people do on holiday

Festivals

Words

1 What jobs do you do around the house?
What jobs do other people do?
Make two lists.

2 How many ways of paying for things can you think of?

3 Think of some things to take
– to the beach
– on a visit to London.

4 Answer these questions.
What does an *untidy* person do?
What happens in an *earthquake*?
When do you get a *receipt*?
What might you do if you go *sightseeing*?

2 On the phone

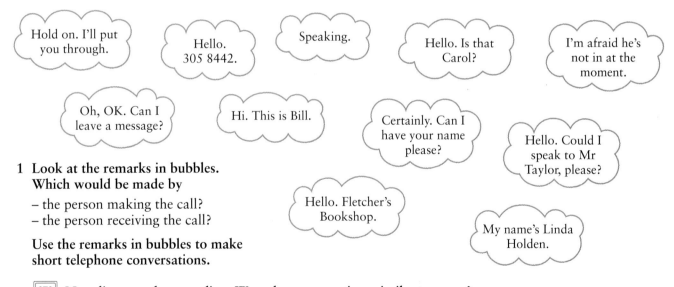

Hold on. I'll put you through.

Hello. 305 8442.

Speaking.

Hello. Is that Carol?

I'm afraid he's not in at the moment.

Oh, OK. Can I leave a message?

Hi. This is Bill.

Certainly. Can I have your name please?

Hello. Could I speak to Mr Taylor, please?

Hello. Fletcher's Bookshop.

My name's Linda Holden.

1 Look at the remarks in bubbles. Which would be made by
– the person making the call?
– the person receiving the call?

Use the remarks in bubbles to make short telephone conversations.

Now listen to the recording. Were the conversations similar to yours?

2 Work in pairs. Read your instructions and have two short telephone conversations.

Student A	Student B
1 Phone Harvey's Department Store and ask to speak to Mrs Davies.	1 You work at Harvey's Department Store. Mrs Davies is out having lunch. Ask if the caller wants to leave a message.
2 You're Sophie's mother/father. She's busy doing her homework. She can't come out tonight because she's got too much to do.	2 Phone your friend Sophie and ask her if she wants to go and see a film tonight.

Past and present

1 Ancient civilisations

used to • Past simple tense

1 *a* Look at the picture and read the three descriptions.
     Only one of them is true. Which one?

  b When do we use *used to*?

Detail from a scroll by the T'ang painter Chang Hsüan, 9th century AD

In ancient China, it was common for girls to get engaged at the age of 9 or 10. At the engagement ceremony, the women of the family used to hold up a length of cloth which the girl had to pass under. A bowl of flower petals, symbolising fertility, was placed on the cloth and the mother used to take petals from the bowl and scatter them over the girl's head.

In ancient China, ironing silk was a skilled job that was done by several people working together. The silk was so long that instead of using an ironing board, the women of the house used to iron it in mid-air. Two women pulled on the ends of the silk to stretch it out, while a third ironed it using a small pan filled with hot coals.

In ancient China, dining tables in wealthy households used to have handles, rather than legs. At mealtimes, the table was brought from the kitchen and two servants used to hold it for the entire length of the meal, while another served the different courses one at a time. Educated people used to eat standing up, as this was believed to help digestion.

2 Choose one of the pictures on page 116,
  and imagine what the people used to do.
  Write a few sentences to accompany the picture.

This unit focuses on the relationship between the past and the present, and deals with two main language areas:
– *used to* and the Past simple, for saying what things were like in the past
– Present perfect (active and passive) for saying how things have changed.

1 Ancient civilisations

This exercise introduces used to *and the Past simple for describing habitual events in the past and past states. Students read the three interpretations of the picture and decide which of them is true. Then they write similar paragraphs based on pictures in the back of the book.*

➤ Focus on Form: Exercise 1
➤ Workbook: Exercises A, C

1 Reading & presentation

● Give time for students to read the three descriptions. If necessary, give help with difficult vocabulary, e.g. *ceremony, petals, fertility, scatter; silk, ironing board, coals; handles, courses, digestion.*

● Establish what the three interpretations are: an engagement ceremony; ironing silk; serving a meal. To check more detailed comprehension, ask what different parts of the pictures are according to each text (e.g. the thing the woman is holding = an iron; the long white thing = a roll of silk, a cloth or a table; a bowl of petals or a dish of food).

● Ask students to vote on the interpretation they think is true. Answer:
Ironing silk.

● Focus on the examples of *used to*, and establish that
– we use *used to* to talk about things in the past that are no longer true (They used to iron silk in mid-air – now they don't).
– we use *used to* for repeated events (e.g. people used to eat standing up) or for past states (e.g. tables used to have handles).
– instead of *used to*, we can use the Past tense:

The family ~~used to hold~~ up a length of cloth.
                 held

● Show how *used to* has negative and positive forms like other verbs:

I ~~used to~~ walk to work.
  ~~didn't use to~~

Did you use to walk to work?

● Point out that *used to* is only used in the past (we cannot say 'Now they use to …').

2 Writing & speaking activity

● In groups, students look at the pictures on page 116, which show scenes from the Aztec civilisation. Together they imagine what people used to do and what life used to be like, and make notes. They can either give a serious explanation or make up something improbable, as in the presentation texts.

● Students develop their notes into a coherent paragraph, using the presentation texts as a model.

● In turn, each group reads out their paragraph. Other students look at the picture and decide if they agree with the interpretation.

● As a round-up, tell the class what the pictures actually show:
– A steam-house (rather like a modern-day sauna).
– People playing a board game, with stones and dice.
– A man having his nose pierced in order to wear a piece of jewellery.

Presentation option
Give other examples of your own, e.g.
I used to get up at 6 (now I get up later).
People used to wash clothes by hand (now they use washing machines).

Language note
We can also say 'They *used not to* …', but this is more formal in style.

Presentation option
Point out the difference between these two structures:

used to + infinitive
I used to wear a uniform
(= earlier, not now).

be used to + *-ing*
I'm used to wearing a uniform (= I often wear one, I'm accustomed to it).

---

2 Changes

This exercise shows the relationship between used to, *the Present perfect tense, and the structure* not any more/longer. *The second part is an information gap activity, in which students find differences between two pictures.*

➤ Focus on Form: Exercise 2
➤ Workbook: Exercises B, C

1 Presentation

- Establish the difference both in *form* and *meaning* between the three remarks:
  - the first remark uses *used to*, to say *how things were before*.
  - the second remark used the Present perfect tense, to say *what has changed*.
  - the third remark uses the Present tense, to say *what things are like now*.
- Present the structure
  not … any more/longer:

  She doesn't live here <u>any</u> <u>more.</u> longer.

- Ask students to make two sentences for each of the remarks A–E, using the two other structures. Possible answers:

  A He used to live here. He's moved (away).
  B I used to smoke. I don't smoke any more.
  C She plays the guitar now. She's learnt to play the guitar.
  D He used to be quite thin. He isn't thin any longer.
  E She's cut her hair. She doesn't have long hair any more.

> **Language note**
> *Any more* and *any longer* come at the end of the sentence. We cannot say 'She doesn't any more live here'.
> (It *is* possible to say 'She no longer lives here', but this is rather formal in style.)

2 Speaking activity

- Divide students into pairs, one A and one B, and ask them to look only at their own picture. They each describe their picture, and together they decide what has changed. They could note these changes down on a piece of paper.
- Go through the answers together. Possible answers:

  They've got older / had children / bought a colour TV, new furniture and a carpet/ painted the walls blue / put up some pictures / sold the piano. He's put on weight / grown a beard / lost most of his hair. She's started wearing glasses.

> **Blackboard option**
> As you go through the answers, build up a list of common 'verbs of change' that use the Present perfect, e.g.
>
> **has got**
> **has bought**
> **has grown**
> **has started**

3 Preparations

The Present perfect tense is often used to talk about preparations for a future activity, and it is shown in this context in this exercise. The exercise shows how passive forms are used when the agent is either unknown or unimportant.

➤ Focus on Form: Exercise 3
➤ Workbook: Exercise D

1 Presentation

- Students look at the sentences and decide which ones belong together.
- Go through the answers together. Answers:

  Wedding: food, flowers, photographer
  Journey: sandwiches, car, cases
  Hotel: chef, pool, rooms

- Show how the Present perfect passive is formed:

  The room <u>has</u> been cleaned. The rooms <u>have</u>

  Point out that the passive is used when the action is done by someone else, not by the people themselves. Compare:
  – They've serviced the car. (= themselves)
  – The car's been serviced. (by someone at the garage – it isn't important who)

- Ask students to suggest a few more sentences for each situation, e.g. *They've sent out the invitations. They've locked all the doors and windows. The windows have been cleaned.*

> **Optional lead-in**
> Establish the idea of the Present perfect for preparations by giving a simple situation (e.g. we're going on a school trip) and asking students to suggest possible preparations.

> **Practice option**
> Cue passive forms by giving active sentences, e.g.
> They've painted the fence.
> → The fence has been painted.

2 Writing/speaking activity

- Groupwork. Give one of these situations to each group:
  – *You're giving a class party.*   – *You're going abroad for a year.*
  – *You're going camping.*   – *You're going on a business trip.*
  – *You're going out on a date.*   – *You're taking an English exam.*

  Working together, students write a list of preparations they have made.

- In turn, each group reads out their sentences, starting with those that give the least obvious clues. Other students try to guess what they are planning to do.

> **Alternative**
> Students in each group write only one sentence for their situation. They then pass their paper to another group, who add a sentence, and pass the paper on again. Continue until the class has built up five or six sentences for each situation. Then ask students to read out the lists of preparations.

2 Changes

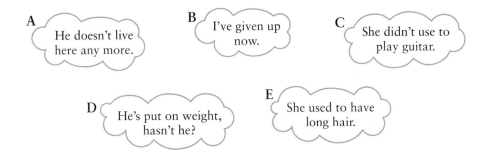

She used to ride a motorbike.

She's sold her motorbike now.

She doesn't ride a motorbike any longer.

1 *a* What is the difference between the three remarks above?

b Look at the remarks below, and make two more sentences about each situation.

A He doesn't live here any more.

B I've given up now.

C She didn't use to play guitar.

D He's put on weight, hasn't he?

E She used to have long hair.

2 Work in pairs. You will see a picture of a couple sitting in their living room.

Student A: Look only at the picture on page 113, which shows how things used to be.

Student B: Look only at the picture on page 115, which shows how things are now.

How many changes can you find?

3 Preparations

Everything's ready for the wedding ...

They're ready to set off on their journey ...

The hotel's ready for the new holiday season ...

The food has been delivered.

They've hired a new chef.

The pool has been filled.

The rooms have been redecorated.

They've ordered the flowers.

They've made some sandwiches.

The car's been serviced.

They've hired a photographer.

They've packed their cases.

1 Look at the sentences in the boxes. Which preparations do you think go with each? Add a few ideas of your own.

2 The teacher will give you a situation. Write a list of preparations you have made.

4 For and against

1  You will hear people talking about these inventions, and saying whether they think they have had a good or bad effect on people's lifestyles.

  a Which invention is each speaker talking about? Does he/she think the effect has been good or bad?

  b Think of an argument that gives a *different* point of view about each invention.

2 Work in groups. Decide together where to mark each invention in the table.

	very good	*good*	*–*	*bad*	*very bad*
television					
calculators					
computers					
convenience food					
video recorders					

Grammar Checklist

used to

used to + *infinitive – for regular past events and past states.*

My grandfather **used to** walk to school.
  (*not ...* ~~was used to~~ ...)
I **used to** live in France (when I was a child).
I **didn't use to** smoke (but I do now).
Where **did** you **use to** spend your holidays?

Present perfect tense

have/has + *past participle – for talking about changes and recent events. (See also Unit 15.)*

He's (= he has) **given** up smoking.
They **haven't** painted the room yet.
Have you packed the suitcases?

Irregular verbs: see list on page 143.

not ... any more/longer

They **don't** live here **any longer**.
  (= They've moved away.)
He **doesn't** have a beard **any more**.
  (= He's shaved it off.)

Present perfect passive

have/has + **been** + *past participle*

They've painted the room.
→ The room **has been** painted.

Someone has ordered the books.
→ The books **have been** ordered.

See also Reference section, page 133.

4 For and against

This is a listening and discussion activity, which is about the good and bad effects that recent inventions in technology have had on people's lives. Students listen to a series of opinions and then assess the impact of each invention themselves. Although there is no specific language focus in this exercise it naturally draws on all the structures introduced in the unit.

1 Listening

- Look at the photos, and establish what inventions they show.

- 📼 Play the recording, pausing after each section to establish which invention the speaker is talking about and how he/she regards it. Answers:

  1 Video recorders. Good.
  2 Convenience food. Bad.
  3 Television. Good.
  4 Computers. Good.
  5 Calculators. Bad.

- As you play each section, ask students to think of opposing arguments about each invention, e.g.

  1 They encourage you to watch more TV instead of doing more useful things.
  2 Before, people used to spend hours preparing food.
  3 TV turns people into vegetables – they stop reading / talking to each other.
  4 Once, you only needed a pen. Now you need a computer, disks, a screen, a printer, and a course of lessons ... just to write a letter.
  5 They save you time – you can make complex calculations easily.

2 Discussion

- Divide the class into groups. They discuss each invention and try to agree where to mark it in the table.
- As a round-up, draw a table on the board, and find out where each group put their marks.

> *Optional lead-in*
> Find out how many students in the class have or use these inventions, how often they use them, and what for.

> *Optional extension*
> Choose inventions where groups put marks in different places, and ask each group to justify their opinion.

> 📼 Tapescript for Exercise 4: *For and against*
>
> 1 Well I have to get up very early in the mornings, so I have to go to bed very early the night before. So it's great for me because I can, when there's good programmes on, I can record them late at night and watch them later on.
> 2 The problem is they just taste so awful. In the old days food used to really taste of something, but this stuff just tastes of nothing.
> 3 In the old days, say 50 years ago, nobody knew what was going on in the world. But nowadays you can actually see what's happening anywhere in the world, almost as it's happening.
> 4 I type with two fingers, and when I used to type letters I'd always make a mistake and then have to type the whole letter all over again – drove me crazy. But now I can just correct it on the screen as I go along, and when I'm happy with it I'm finished. It's perfect, brilliant.
> 5 At school I learnt how to add up in my head, and children just can't do that any more. My son can't add up at all.

Focus on Form

1 *Forms of used to*

> Positive, negative and question forms of *used to*

- Ask the first question round the class, getting a variety of answers.
- Students ask and answer questions in pairs.
- As a round-up, ask a few students what they found out about their partner.

2 *Present perfect tense*

> Present perfect questions. Long and short answers

- If you like, prepare for the activity by building up a list of key verbs on the board:

clean	sweep	wash	throw away
tidy	mend	wash up	clear away

- Give students letters, A or B, alternately round the class. Working alone, they look at the picture and write a list of jobs to do. You could set a time limit for this (e.g. five minutes).
- Students form pairs, one A and one B. A finds out how many of the jobs on his/her list B has done, e.g.

  A Have you tidied the bedroom?
  B Yes I have.
     No I haven't (but I've made the bed).

- As a round-up, find out which student managed to do the most jobs.

3 *Present perfect passive*

> Present perfect passive and 'change' verbs

- As a preparation, go through the items in Box B, eliciting the passive forms, e.g. They've redecorated it – It's been redecorated. As you do this, check that students know what the verbs mean.
- Students do the exercise in pairs.
- Go through the answers. Answers:
  ... it's been pulled down.
  ... he's been sacked.
  ... it's been redecorated.
  ... it's been cut down.
  ... it's been fenced off.
  ... it's been banned.
  ... he's been promoted.

Alternative: Go through the exercise using only the active (e.g. ... but now they've turned it into a cinema), and then ask students to do it a second time, changing the sentences into the passive.

4 *Pronunciation*

[cassette] Ask students to try saying the sentences themselves, then play the tape as a model. Focus on these points:

a Reduced *to* in *used to* /juːst‿tə/.
b Pronunciation of short forms used with the Present perfect: *I've* /aɪv/, *She's* /ʃiːz/, *He's* /hiːz/, *They've* /ðeɪv/. *John has* /dʒɒn (h)əz/, *My parents have* /maɪ ˈpeərənts (h)əv/.
c Pronunciation of Present perfect passive: *'s been* /z bɪn/, *have been* /həv bɪn/.

Self-study Workbook

Exercise A: Used to
Positive, negative and question forms of *used to*.
Students rewrite sentences with *used to*.

Exercise B: □□□□□□ □□□□ □□□□□□□
The Present perfect tense; past participle forms.
Students choose verbs to complete a text, and enter them in a grid. This spells out the name of the exercise.

Exercise C: How have they changed?
Students look at three pairs of pictures, and write sentences about the ways in which people have changed.

Exercise D: Present perfect passive
Students write sentences about pictures, choosing verbs from a box.

Translation
Key sentences for translation.

Listening: Changed lives
Three people talk about how their lives have changed. Students complete gap-filling and true/false questions.

Pronunciation: Syllables and stress
The number of syllables in individual words, plus primary and secondary stress. Students look at examples and identify stressed syllables.

Reading: Two childhoods
Extracts from an interview in which a man contrasts his own childhood with that of his seven-year-old son. Students look at remarks, and decide which 'child' they would expect to say them.

Focus on Form

1 Forms of used to

Student A: **Ask B about when he/she was seven years old.**

Student B: **Answer A's questions.**

Examples:

A What TV programmes *did you use to* watch?

B | I *used to* watch a lot of cartoons.
    | I *didn't use to* watch much TV.

or

A *Did you use to* watch much TV?

B | No, not really.
    | Yes. I *used to* watch it every day after school.

a watching TV	*e* eating sweets
b going to bed	*f* holidays
c playing with toys	*g* school
d reading	*h* homework

2 Present perfect tense

The picture shows A's flat as it was this morning.

Student A: **It's B's job to clean your flat. Write a list of all the jobs you wanted him/her to do in your flat. Then find out how many of them he/she's done.**

Student B: **You've just finished cleaning A's flat. Write a list of the jobs you've done. Then answer A's questions.**

Example:

A Have you changed the sheets?

B Yes I have.
    No I'm afraid I haven't.
    No I haven't, but I've made the bed.

Now compare your flat with someone else's. Which is cleaner?

3 Present perfect passive

Student A: **Read out the sentences in Box A.**

Student B: **Complete each sentence using an item from Box B in the Present perfect passive.**

Example:

A That building used to be a theatre …

B … but now it's been turned into a cinema.

A	B
That building used to be a theatre … There used to be a castle on that hill … He used to have a good job … This room used to have red wallpaper … There used to be a big tree in the square … We used to go for walks in that field … They used to let you smoke in the cinema … He didn't use to earn much money …	redecorate it pull it down cut it down promote him sack him turn it into a cinema ban it fence it off

4 Pronunciation

How do you say the words and phrases below?

a I used to drink coffee.

b I've She's He's They've
    He's packed the suitcase.
    John has left home.
    My parents have come to stay.

c The room's been cleaned.
    Ten people have been arrested.

🖭 **Now listen and check your answers.**

1 Yellow Pages

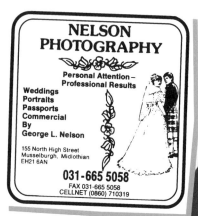

NELSON
PHOTOGRAPHY

Personal Attention –
Professional Results

Weddings
Portraits
Passports
Commercial
By
George L. Nelson

155 North High Street
Musselburgh, Midlothian
EH21 6AN

031-665 5058

FAX 031-665 5058
CELLNET (0860) 710319

FOR HAIR REFLECTING STYLE
63 SHANDWICK PLACE, EDINBURGH
TEL: 031–229 1582
CAMERON TOLL TEL: 664 6849

BONNYRIGG

Scott Christie B.D.S.
Dental Surgeon

64 HIGH STREET
BONNYRIGG

031-663 9271

*FAMILY DENTAL CARE
ALL EMERGENCIES SEEN*

**THE ELECTRICAL
REPAIR MAN** EST 1974

**OFFICES
SHOPS
HOUSES**
Electrical
Repairs
& Installations.

031-229 8370

Estimates Free on New Work & Rewiring
A.A.E.S.   Mobile: 0850 423451
244 Morrison St. Edinburgh EH3 8DT

It pays to
SPECIALEYES

Qualified Opticians · Free Frames
One Hour Service · Contact Lenses
Designer Frames

EDINBURGH 031-558 3306
31 St James Centre,
Edinburgh.

MUNRO CLEANERS

Bathgate	42 George Street	0506 630825
Broxburn	Unit 4, Argyll Court	0506 858630
Bruntsfield	141 Bruntsfield Pl	031-228 6365
City Centre	123 Hanover Street	031-226 2931
	3 Elm Row	031-556 0603
	90 Nicolson Street	031-667 4420
Corstorphine	12 Ormiston Terrace	031-334 6439
Cupar	8 Bonnygate	0334 55944
Dalkeith	9 High Street	031-654 1277
Davidson Mains	68 Main Street	031-336 2657
Dunfermline	14 East Port	0383 620457
Easter Road	7 Easter Road	031-661 5899
Glenrothes	6 Unicorn Way	0592 611468
Gorgie	156 Gorgie Road	031-313 2190
Haddington	31 Market Street	062082 4893
Haymarket	18/20 Dalry Road	031-337 0542
Kirkcaldy	77 High Street	0592 262227
	254a High Street	0592 269182
Leith	75 Gt. Junction St	031-554 3733
Linlithgow	73 High Street	0506 670660
Livingston	10 Almondvale South	0506 441351
Morningside	350 Morningside Rd	031-447 2140
Newington	95 Newington Rd	031-668 4767
Penicuik	24a John Street	0968 679834
Portobello	100 High Street	031-657 4958
St. Andrews	27 Church Street	0334 78831
Stockbridge	45 Deanhaugh St	031-332 3298
Tollcross	21 Home Street	031-229 0927

Contract Drycleaning Collection & Delivery Service
Curtain Cleaning, Pleating & Flame Proofing
Duvet & Pillow Renovation
17 Swanfield, Bonnington Rd, Leith. 031-554 3825

EDINBURGH

G. W. MARTIN LTD OF MORNINGSIDE

AA SPECIALIST
• SERVICING & REPAIRS OF MOST MAKES OF CARS
• FULL COMPREHENSIVE FACILITIES AVAILABLE
• STEERING, BRAKES, SUSPENSION, CLUTCHES ETC

031-447 6185

FAX: 031-452 8740 11 JORDAN LANE (OFF MORNINGSIDE ROAD) EDINBURGH

**M.O.T TESTING
WHILE-U-WAIT** (INCLUDING DIESEL TESTING)

1. Look at these advertisements from Yellow Pages. What services do they offer? What can you have done at each place?

   Example: At the photographer's you can have your photo taken.

2. Choose one of the advertisers and think of a reason for ringing them up. What questions would you ask? What would you expect them to ask you?

   Now have a telephone conversation with your partner.

This unit is concerned with three language areas:
– having things done (e.g. having a car serviced, clothes mended)
– language associated with using public services (e.g. post office, library)
– evaluating major public services: police, health and education.
The Reading and Listening activity is about jobs that people 'love to hate'.

8

1 Yellow Pages

In this exercise students talk about places that offer services and the things you can have done at them. It focuses on the structure have something done *as well as on vocabulary. The last part of the exercise is a role-play in which students make enquiries by telephone based on advertisements.*

1 Presentation

- Check that students understand what *Yellow Pages* are: the commercial telephone directory which contains advertisements for shops and services.
- Read quickly through the advertisements and establish what they are for:

  photographer, hairdresser, dentist, electrician, optician, garage, laundry / dry cleaner

- Use the first advertisement to introduce the structure *have something done*:

  A photographer takes your photograph.
  You can <u>have</u> your photograph <u>taken</u>.

- Go through the other advertisements, and establish what you can have done at each place. Possible answers:

  Hairdresser: you can have your hair cut/washed; have your beard trimmed.
  Dentist: you can have your teeth filled/cleaned; have a tooth (taken) out.
  Electrician: you can have your fridge/washing machine repaired/mended.
  Optician: you can have your eyes tested; have your glasses repaired.
  Garage: you can have your car repaired/serviced/tested.
  Laundry / dry cleaner: you can have your clothes/sheets washed; have your suit/dress/coat cleaned.

2 Speaking activity

- Ask students to suggest questions they might ask if they telephoned one of the companies in the advertisements. Build a list up on the board, e.g.

  How much **does it cost?**
  do you charge?
  Can I make an appointment?
  When are you free?
  Can you give me an estimate?

- Students choose one of the advertisements. Working alone, they prepare questions to ask.
- Pairwork. Students take it in turns to be the customer and the company. They act out a telephone conversation, using the questions they have prepared and improvising suitable answers.
- As a round-up, ask a few students whether they decided to have anything done by the company they spoke to.

➤ Workbook: Exercise A

Language note
The structure *have something done* is a form of the passive, sometimes called the 'have' passive. Compare:

He *took* my photo.   (active)
My photo *was taken*. (passive)
I *had* my photo *taken*.   ('have' passive)

Get is often used as an alternative to *have*:
I must *get/have* my car *serviced*.

Vocabulary option
Ask students to think of other places where you can have things done, e.g. *shoe mender* (have your shoes mended); *dressmaker* (have a dress made); *jeweller* (have a ring/necklace made/repaired).

Alternatives
1 Small classes
Choose one of the services. Half the class are customers, the other half are rival companies offering the same service. Customers move freely round the class, 'phoning' two or three different companies in turn. They then decide which company to use.

2 Role cards
To give more structure to the activity, you could give out role cards, e.g.

A Your filling has fallen out. Make an appointment to see the dentist as soon as possible.
B You're the dentist. You're very busy, but you can see emergency cases on Wednesday afternoon.

Optional extension
Ask students where they really go to have the things done that are in the advertisements, or if they know places locally where you can have these things done.

2 What's the system?

This exercise is concerned with public services which involve a system that people have to learn how to use. Students focus on key vocabulary and then listen to people explaining how the system works.

➤ Workbook: Exercise B

1 Presentation & listening

- Check that students understand the meaning of *library* (= a place where you borrow books – not a bookshop) and *parcel*.
- Students look at the words and decide which might be used to talk about each service. Then discuss this together, getting students to make sentences, e.g.

  You can take out books from a library.
  There's a reference section in the library where you can find dictionaries.
  As you do this, build up lists of words on the board under each category.

- 🔲 Play the recording. Pause after each section, and establish which words the speakers actually used, and how they used them. Answers:

  Phone: receiver, dial
  Library: join, take out, pay a fine, reference section
  Post office: weigh, stamps, customs form, registered

Option: vocabulary expansion
This discussion provides an opportunity to elicit or provide other words that students might find useful, e.g.
Phone: phone box, local call, long distance call, directory enquiries, operator.
Library: borrow, bring back, renew, overdue, (non-)fiction.
Post office: air mail, surface mail, express, recorded delivery.

🔲 The tapescript is on page T41.

2 Speaking & writing activity

- As a lead-in to the activity, discuss what differences there are in the way the systems work in the students' own country.
- Students work in groups. Together, they choose one of the services and design a leaflet explaining to foreigners what to do. They should think carefully about the *appearance* and *design* of the leaflet – adding illustrations or diagrams if necessary, using eye-catching headings, and listing points clearly.
- At the end, leaflets can be passed around the class for other groups to look at.

Optional 'editing' phase
Students show their leaflet to another group. The other group comments, and suggests changes and/or additions. Then the group makes a final version of their leaflet.

3 Public services

This is a freer activity, in which students evaluate the police, health and education systems in their own country. Short newspaper extracts about Britain are used to help focus on what the issues might be; then students give each service a score, which they discuss with their partners.

1 Reading & discussion

- Look at the newspaper extracts and check that students understand what they mean. After each one, ask students if the article could apply to their own country (e.g. Is the crime rate going up in your country? Do most people think the police are doing a good job? Are the police prejudiced against any group of people?).

Vocabulary option
Use the newspaper articles to build up a list of new words on the board, explaining the meaning or giving examples, e.g.
the *crime rate* = the number of crimes; a *burglar* steals things from people's homes – this is a *burglary*.

2 Speaking activity

- Working alone, students give a score out of 10 for each service in their own country. As they do so, they think of reasons for their score and make brief notes (e.g. *Classes are too big; not enough teachers; too many examinations*).
- Pairwork. Students compare their scores, and explain why they gave the score they did. If the students are from the same country, they compare their opinions; if they're from different countries, they compare the services in the two countries.
- As a round-up, ask how many students gave 10, 9, 8 etc. for each service. Ask a few students to explain the reasons for their score.

Alternative
Groupwork. Each group chooses one of the services and tries to agree on a score. Together they write a list of plus and minus points for the service they are discussing.

As a round-up, one student from each group reports their conclusions to the rest of the class.

Homework extension
Students write sentences giving plus and minus points about one or more of the services they discussed.

2 What's the system?

1 You will hear people explaining how to do these things
   in Britain.
   – use a public phone
   – use a public library
   – send a parcel abroad

   How do you think they will use the words in the box?

receiver	take out	join
registered	dial	customs form
stamps	weigh	reference section
pay a fine		

   [cassette icon] Now listen to the recording.

2 Think of one of these services in your own country.
   How would you explain to a foreigner how to use it?
   Design a leaflet.

How to send a parcel abroad

● **Write the address clearly in block capitals.**

3 Public services

Yet again the crime rate is up:
Burglaries are UP by 4%.
Violent crime is UP by 6%.
And car crime is UP by a staggering 14%.

Most people in Britain still think our police are doing a good job, a survey reveals today.

Police are still prejudiced against members of ethnic minorities, and do not understand their special needs, a spokesman for the Asian

Most junior hospital doctors work 70 hours a week and some work as many as 90.

63-year-old Janet Gould has been waiting for more than TWO YEARS for a simple operation – and she's typical of thousands of others around

When asked about the rise in prescription charges, Mr Baker replied that children, old age pensioners, pregnant women and unemployed people do not pay for medicines at all.

1 Look at these newspaper reports about Britain.
   Which of them could be true of your country?

2 Think about the police, health and education services
   in your country. Give a mark out of 10 for each.

   Compare your marks with your partner's.

Why is it that after 5 years at school, some 10% of British children cannot read or write?

Many primary school classes still contain more than 30 pupils, in spite of a Government promise to

More secondary school students are going on to university and other forms of further education than ever before.

	Mark out of 10	Notes
Police		
Health		
Education		

4 Jobs we love to hate

It's a lonely life. Clive Brown at work.

HELP
NOBODY
LOVES US!

They've got the jobs we love to hate ... from traffic warden to nightclub bouncer, we found out what it's like when nobody, but nobody, loves you.

READING

1 Read the opening descriptions of the three people's jobs.
   What do you think these expressions mean?

   private eye   taking her life in her hands   a strapping 6ft 9in
   insurance claims   like gold dust
                     tempers can flare

2 All three people answer the same six questions. What do you think the questions were?

3 Which of the people do you think

   a has the most dangerous job?   *c* is most interested in the money?
   b spends most time talking to people?   *d* is most interested in job security?

4 Which of these adjectives do you think describes each person best?

calm	friendly	cynical
cheerful	helpful	self-confident

LISTENING

1 🔲 You will hear four people talking about jobs they 'love to hate'.
   What are the four jobs?

2 Which jobs do these statements apply to?

   a They try to sell you things you don't want.   *e* They keep you waiting.
   b They don't tell you what's going on.   *f* They ask stupid questions.
   c They disturb you when you're busy.   *g* You can't trust them.
   d They don't keep their promises.   *h* They waste your time and money.

4 Jobs we love to hate

This combined reading and listening activity is about unpopular jobs. The reading is taken from a magazine article in which a private investigator, a traffic warden and a nightclub bouncer are interviewed about their work and people's attitudes to it. In the listening, a number of people talk briefly about the jobs they dislike most.

READING

- To check that students know what the three jobs are, ask them to say briefly what each of them involves:

  Private investigator: follows people and watches them, e.g. to see if they're doing something illegal.
  Traffic warden: checks that drivers have parked legally, and have paid to park.
  Nightclub bouncer: stops people causing trouble in a nightclub.

- Give time for students to read the opening descriptions. Then discuss what the expressions mean:

  private eye = private investigator
  insurance claims = when people ask for money from their insurance company
  taking her life in her hands = risking her life (this is of course an exaggeration)
  like gold dust = very hard to find, very valuable
  tempers can flare = people often lose their temper, get angry
  a strapping 6ft 9in = he's big and strong (2.05 metres tall)

- Working alone or in pairs, students read through the rest of the text, and answer Questions 2, 3 and 4. Then go through the answers to Question 2 together. The actual questions were:

  1 Why did you decide to do the job?
  2 Do you tell people what job you do?
  3 Have you ever been attacked?
  4 Have you ever made anyone cry?
  5 Has anyone ever made you cry?
  6 What do you like most about your job?

> *Vocabulary option*
> At this point deal with some of the difficult vocabulary in the texts, e.g.
> Private investigator: *disguise, security consultant, batter, a cheque bounces*
> Traffic warden: *redundancies, promotion, civil service, sob, chatterbox*
> Bouncer: *wrestler, violence, tactful, social*

- Discuss Questions 3 and 4 with the whole class. Ask students to say why they chose the answers they did. Possible answers:

  3 *a* private investigator (people often attack him)
  b traffic warden (she's a chatterbox) or bouncer (it's part of his job)
  c the private investigator (it's his reason for doing the job)
  d the traffic warden (it's her reason for doing the job)
  4 *Private investigator:* cynical, calm
  Traffic warden: cheerful, friendly, helpful
  Bouncer: calm, friendly, self-confident

- Ask students which of the people they would most like to spend an evening with, and why.

LISTENING

- [cassette icon] Play the recording, pausing after each section to establish what job the person is talking about (the names of the jobs are 'bleeped out' in the recording). Answers:

  1 receptionists; 2 politicians; 3 telephone salespeople; 4 shop assistants

> *Optional lead-in*
> Elicit unpopular jobs from the class, and write them on the board. As you play the recording, match what the people say against this list (and add to it if necessary).

- [cassette icon] Students look at the statements and mark the names of the jobs against them (*R, P, T* or *S*). Then play the recording again and discuss the answers together. Answers:

  Receptionists: b, e, h
  Politicians: d, g
  Telephone salespeople: a, c, f, (h)
  Shop assistants: a

  After each section, ask the class whether they agree with the speaker, and what they think about people who do the job.

> [cassette icon] The tapescript is on page T41.

> *Optional extension*
> Ask students to think of a job they 'love to hate', and write a sentence saying why they hate it. They read out their sentence, and other students guess what job they are describing.

📼 Tapescript for Exercise 4: *Jobs we love to hate*

1 I hate it when you ring up a big company, for example, and you're trying to get through to someone, and all you get is the ▨▨▨▨▨ who tells you to hold the line. And then they just leave you there – they don't tell you what they're doing, sometimes they play a horrible little tune that repeats itself over and over again, and you just – you don't know what's happening at all. And it's particularly annoying if it's a long-distance call, because it's costing a lot of money.

2 I don't like ▨▨▨▨▨ because I think that a lot of the time they take advantage of your vote. And they tell you that they're going to do one thing, but they're not, they don't have any intention of doing it. They're liars, basically. And I think that you put your trust in them by giving them your vote, and nine out of ten times they let you down.

3 I hate ▨▨▨▨▨, you know the people who ring you up and try and sell you something over the phone. And they always start off with a really stupid question like 'Would you like to make more money?' or 'Do you care about the environment?' And they always seem to ring up at the worst possible moment, like when you've just sat down to have tea or something. And they sound so cheerful, they really annoy me.

4 Oh, ▨▨▨▨▨ that try and sell you things that you don't want. You go into a shop, you want to buy a dress, you try it on, it doesn't look good, you come back out of the changing room and say 'No, thank you'. The ▨▨▨▨▨ says 'Oh well why don't you try another size?' You say 'No, I'm fine about it, I don't want it.' 'Oh well why don't you try another colour?' 'No, I don't want another colour.' They won't let you get out of the shop – it drives me mad.

📼 Tapescript for Exercise 2: *What's the system?*

1 To use a public telephone, first you lift the receiver and then you put in the coins. You can use as many coins as you like, because at the end of the call the coins which haven't been used are returned. And then after putting in the coins, you dial the number. Alternatively you can use a phone card, with which you can talk until the number of units on the telephone card has been used up.

2 To use libraries in England, you join the library. They'll give you a ticket, that means that you can keep books that you take out for up to two weeks. If you bring the books back late you have to pay a fine. There's also a reference section which you can use, but you can't take those books out, you can just use the books in the library.

3 To send a parcel abroad, you take the parcel to the post office, and have it weighed. And they give you stamps, which you stick on the parcel, and they also give you a customs form which you have to fill in, and then you stick that on the parcel as well. Now if you want to send something valuable, then it's normal to send that by registered post, which is rather more expensive than normal post.

Self-study Workbook

Exercise A: Having things done
Names of services, plus *have something done*.
Students label pictures of places that provide services, and imagine what they had done at each.

Exercise B: How do you do it?
The vocabulary of libraries, phones and postal services.
Students fill gaps in dialogues with words from a box.

New words
Space to record new words with notes and examples.

Translation
Key sentences for translation.

Listening: On the phone
Students listen to three phone conversations about services (dentist, photographer, garage), and complete a short task for each.

Phrasal verbs: Transitive verbs (1)
Phrasal verbs used with object noun or pronoun (e.g. *turn on the radio, turn it on*). Students match verbs to their context.

Writing skills: Punctuation: direct speech
Use of quotation marks, full stops, commas and capital letters in direct speech. Students correct punctuation in sentences, then rewrite a text, adding punctuation.

JOB: PRIVATE INVESTIGATOR	JOB: TRAFFIC WARDEN	JOB: NIGHTCLUB BOUNCER (official title 'Persuader')
Name: Clive Brown, 44 **Qualifications:** police training plus common sense **Home life:** married with two children **Salary:** over £35,000 a year **Being a private eye in real life isn't nearly as exciting as it is in detective stories. Clive Brown is on call day and night, investigating large insurance claims, dishonest employees, and unfaithful husbands and wives.**	**Name:** Linda Jackson, 35 **Qualifications:** on-the-job training **Home life:** single **Salary:** £16,000 a year **For the past 13 years, traffic warden Linda Jackson has been taking her life in her hands. In the few square miles of city streets where 5ft 4in Linda has her beat, parking spaces are like gold dust and tempers can flare.**	**Name:** Jim Allen, 42 **Qualifications:** none, but all the right physical attributes **Home life:** married, no kids **Salary:** £65 a night **Bouncer Jim, a strapping 6ft 9in, has been standing on the door of the Black Cat nightclub in Leeds for the last 20 years making sure that trouble stays out and only the right kind of people get in.**
I became a private eye because I was unemployed and had a family to support. I used to be a policeman so this was an obvious business.	Basically for security. The company I worked for was making redundancies. Traffic wardens' money was good and so were the promotion prospects.	I wanted work where I could meet people as I do enjoy it very much. Obviously, I'm also pretty strong physically, being an ex-professional boxer and wrestler.
I might not admit I'm a private investigator, but there are plenty of ways to 'disguise' what I do, such as calling myself a 'security consultant'.	If I'm meeting someone for the first time I might say I work for the Civil Service. Then if they ask further I tell them because I'm quite proud of my job.	Well, I don't like to be too obvious at the club, but I'd never lie about my job. I'm not out to give people any trouble.
Oh, you bet! You come across a lot of rather unpleasant characters. Someone who's been battering his wife, for example, isn't going to think twice before he starts battering me!	I was very nearly attacked once, when I had to call the police to help me deal with a man who got extremely nasty. He was arrested – and he got a ticket from me as well!	Some people get a bit upset at the door and won't be told to go quietly. But I never use violence myself. If anyone starts a fight, I always call the police.
Not that I can think of, but, in fact, if I'm doing my job properly I shouldn't have much contact with the people I'm investigating. They shouldn't even be aware I'm interested in them!	Quite often I come up against people with a problem – someone ill at home, for example, and they have to get to the chemist. But I'd never stand there and argue or reduce them to tears. I just help as best I can.	No! To be a bouncer, you need to understand people and to know about life. I think I'm very tactful. If I made the customers cry I might as well be working on a building site.
Just every now and then, when a client's cheque bounces. That really brings the tears to my eyes! But, seriously, I try not to get emotionally involved in my job; otherwise I wouldn't be able to do it.	Some of the horrible things people say have upset me, but I wouldn't give them the satisfaction of crying. Anyway I'd look pretty stupid in a uniform sobbing on the street.	Do what?
I'd like to say the satisfaction of helping my fellow men and women, but to be honest the thing I really like best about it is the money it brings me.	Meeting people – I'm a real chatterbox and love talking. I used to be shy, but the job soon changed that!	The people, without a doubt! I can mix with the crowd for most of the time so it's a nice social job.

Imagining

1 What would you do?

would

Situation 1

Your 14-year-old daughter thinks that the only reason you have a phone is so that she can talk to her friends all evening. You've told her that she can't phone them any more – so now her friends phone her instead.

4.00pm What would you do?
This week the panel looks at some of the problems that parents have with children – and children have with parents.

1 Look at the first situation. You will hear part of a radio programme in which three people discuss what they would do. Who do you agree with most?

2 Choose one of the other situations. Say what you would and wouldn't do.

Situation 2

Some older pupils at school are bullying you. You would like to ask your parents' advice, but you're afraid that they might rush round to the school and make a big fuss, and that this might only make things worse.

Situation 3

Your 3-year-old daughter won't eat her meals. Apart from cheese, she will only eat 'junk food' like chips, crisps, cake, sweets and ice-cream. You've told her that she can't leave the table until she eats her meal, but that doesn't work: she just sits and looks at it without eating.

Situation 4

You belong to a very close family who have always done things together. You're 15 now, and you would like to spend more time with your friends, especially at weekends. But your parents always organise family activities that fill up the whole weekend, and say you're too young to go off on your own.

This unit covers a range of language which is used for imagining – that is, talking about things which we see as 'unreal'. This includes the use of *would* and *could*, second conditionals, and structures with *I wish*.

1 What would you do?

This exercise shows how we use would/wouldn't *when imagining ourselves in an 'unreal' situation (one we are not actually in). The exercise focuses on problems between parents and children; students listen to people discussing a problem, then they discuss other problems themselves.*

➤ Focus on Form: Exercise 1
➤ Workbook: Exercise A

1 Listening & presentation

● Read through Situation 1, and briefly discuss with the class how much they or their children use the phone to chat to friends (the form this discussion will take will depend on the age of the class).

● 🔲 Play the recording, and establish the main point of view that each speaker expresses:

1 Try to reason with her; ask her to keep the conversations short.
2 Only let her receive one call every evening.
3 Encourage her to see her friends instead.

Ask students which point of view they agree with most.

● Point out that the speakers use *would/wouldn't* because they are not really in the situation described – they are just imagining it. If necessary, present these forms of *would*:

| **I'd** / **I wouldn't** | let her use the phone. |

2 Speaking activity

● Groupwork. Students look at one of the other situations and decide what they'd do. Either give each group a different situation to look at, or let them choose the one that interests them most.

● As a round-up, each group reports back to the rest of the class, saying what solutions they thought of. Some possible solutions:

Situation 2: Ask a brother or sister what to do; ask your parents, but make it clear you don't want them to make a fuss; tell your teacher; keep out of the way of the boys who are bullying you; go to judo classes.

Situation 3: Stop having junk food in the house; let her have small amounts of junk food, e.g. sweets every Sunday; make different meals with cheese on the top; say she can have some sweets or cake after she finishes her meal.

Situation 4: Try to explain to your parents that you're not a child any more; get your parents to invite your friends to join in your family activities; get a friend's parents to invite you to stay for a weekend.

Alternative for small classes
Choose three good students to be the 'panel' and organise the activity as a radio programme in front of the class.

Optional extension
Students write down real problems that they've had with their own parents or children (or which they know about from other people) and 'send' them to the radio programme.

Homework option
Students choose one of the situations they have discussed, and write a paragraph saying what they would do.

🔲 Tapescript for Exercise 1: *What would you do?*

A Your teenage daughter has started using the telephone to chat to her friends in the evening and quite often she talks for more than an hour, and it means that you can't use the phone yourself. Now you've told her to stop phoning her friends but now her friends phone her instead. Now what would you do about that? Rebecca?

B Er, oh it's a difficult one. I think I'd try to reason with her and say – I mean I wouldn't say 'You must not ring your friends and your friends must not ring you' because I think that's unfair. What I would say is 'If your friends ring you, can you just keep the conversation a bit short so that other people can use the phone?', which seems quite reasonable to me.

A Nick, what do you think?

C I think what I'd do is stop my daughter from answering the phone and monitor the calls as they came in. And she would only be allowed to take one call in the evening from a friend, and any other calls that came in from her friends, we'd say 'No I'm sorry, she's already talked to Angela, or Julia or whatever and so she can't talk to anyone else' and take control of it that way.

A Aisha, do you agree with that?

D Not really. I think you should always try and remember what it felt like at that age and actually how important it felt to try and talk to your friends. What I'd do I think is really encourage her to visit her friends and to have her friends round more so they could actually talk in person rather than on the telephone.

2 If ...

This exercise builds on the language introduced in Exercise 1. It presents complete 2nd conditional structures (If + Past, ... would ...) for imagining unreal situations. Students think of continuations for incomplete If sentences, then make up If sentences of their own.

➤ Focus on Form: Exercises 2, 3
➤ Workbook: Exercise B

1 Presentation

● Choose one of the sentences and ask students to suggest ways to continue it. Write one or two continuations on the board, e.g.

If I saw a tarantula,	I'd kill it. I'd scream.

Establish the structure of the 2nd Conditional:
If + Past ... would ...
Point out that we use this structure to imagine things we don't expect to happen (we're not expecting to see a tarantula – we're just imagining the situation).

● Students write continuations for the other sentences.
● Students read out their sentences.

2 Writing/speaking activity

● Students think of the beginning of a 2nd Conditional sentence themselves, and write it down.
● They pass their sentence to another student, who completes it.
● Students read out their completed sentences.

Presentation option
Contrast this with 1st Conditional structures, e.g. *If I see her, I'll ask her to phone you* (I *am* expecting to see her – it's a real possibility).
Note: For more on the difference between 1st and 2nd Conditionals, see *Focus on Form* Exercise 2 and the *Reference section* on page 134.

Game option
Students only read out the second half of their sentences. Other students guess what the first part of the sentence was.

Note
With a less imaginative class, you could write sentence beginnings on pieces of paper to give to students. Some possible beginnings:

If I were a man/woman ...
If everyone spoke one language ...
If I found $100 in the street ...
If we didn't need to sleep ...
If men had babies ...
If I didn't have to work ...
If I were the only human being left in the world ...

---

3 Cool thinking

In this activity, students imagine the consequences of a drop in the world's temperature, and then read a text about it. This is a freer activity, but it naturally involves the structures introduced in Exercises 1 and 2.

1 Discussion & reading

● Read the opening paragraph of the article and ask students to imagine what might happen if the temperature of the world fell by 5°C. If you like, build up ideas on the board under the headings Climate, Food and People, e.g.

CLIMATE	FOOD	PEOPLE
colder, more snow more wind? some countries uninhabitable	more expensive different crops	they'd starve they'd move to warmer countries

● Give time for students to read the article. then ask them to tell you any information that was different from ideas you already discussed.

2 Discussion

● Groupwork. Students discuss consequences of a drop in temperature for their own area. Ask them to make notes summarising the main ideas they had: they could include both general problems (e.g. the sea would freeze in winter, it would be impossible to grow oranges) and things that would affect them personally (e.g. I'd take up skiing, we'd need central heating).
● As a round-up, ask each group to report back their most interesting ideas.

Vocabulary option
Students make a note of three words in the text they don't understand. Ask them to read them out, and discuss with the class what they mean.

Homework option
Students write a short version of the article, describing only what would happen in their own area.

2 If ...

2nd conditional

If human beings lived for 150 years...

If cigarettes were banned...

If people could communicate by telepathy...

If I saw a tarantula...

If I had six months to live...

1 Here are the beginnings of six *If* ... sentences.
   Why are the verbs in the Past tense?
   How do you think the sentences might continue?

2 On a piece of paper, write the first part of an *If* ... sentence, and give it to another student to complete.

If I met the President of the United States face to face...

3 Cool thinking

A NEW ICE AGE?

MOST OF THE TALK these days is about global warming. But in fact the opposite could happen: it would only take the tiniest change in the Earth's orbit round the Sun to bring another Ice Age. A change of as little as 5°C would have a dramatic effect on life on Earth.

1 Here's the first paragraph of a magazine article.

   What do you think would happen if the temperature of the world fell by 5°C? Think about
   – climate
   – food
   – people.
   Now read the complete article on page 117.

2 How would a new Ice Age affect the place where you live?
   How would it affect your own life?

4 Wishes

I wish I had a
better car.

I wish I didn't live in
such a cold climate.

I wish I could play
the guitar.

I wish I lived in a
smaller house.

I wish my children
would leave home.

I wish I had time to
do more exercise.

I wish I could take more
time off work.

1 **Look at these wishes. Which ones do you think
   would be made by**

   a a 20-year-old student?
   b her father, a 50-year-old businessman?

   [cassette] Now listen to the recording.
   What can you tell about the daughter and the father?

2 **What do you wish?**
   Write three sentences using *I wish* ... and show them
   to your partner.

Grammar Checklist

would

What **would** you do?
I**'d** speak to his teacher.
I **wouldn't** let her use the phone.
   (*not* ~~wouldn't to let~~)

2nd conditional

If + *past*, ... **would(n't)** ... – *for imagining
unreal or unlikely situations*.

If I **won** the national lottery, I**'d** retire.
   (*not* ~~If I would win~~ ...)
If I **had** a car, I**'d** take you to the station.
If you **didn't drink** so much coffee, you**'d**
   sleep better.
The roads **wouldn't** be so crowded if they
   built a by-pass.

I wish

I wish + *past* – *for talking about the present*.
I wish I **had** more friends.
I wish the roads **weren't** so crowded.

I wish + *could/would* – *for things you want to
do and things you want to happen*.
I wish I **could** go abroad.
I wish they**'d** build a by-pass.

See also Reference section, page 134.

---

4 Wishes

This exercise introduces structures with I wish *for expressing wishes about things you consider 'unreal' (i.e. unlikely to happen or impossible). The contexts in which these structures are used is similar to that of 2nd conditionals. Students listen to two people (a father and daughter) making wishes, then write wishes themselves.*

➤ Focus on Form: Exercise 4
➤ Workbook: Exercise C

1 Listening & presentation

- Working alone or in pairs, students decide which wishes would be made by each speaker.

- 🔲 Play the recording, and check the answers. Establish what we know about the daughter and the father:

Daughter: she studies in the North of England, sharing a large house with other students. She lives at home during the vacation (the father says 'I wish my children would leave home').

Father: he works at home, he has grown-up children, he's probably not very rich (he can't afford a new car).

- Use the examples to present *I wish* structures:

> | I wish | + would/could |
> |--------|---------------|
> | | + past tense |

Point out that
- we use *I wish + would/could* to talk about things we want to do and want to happen (e.g. he wants to take more time off work, he wants his children to leave home)
- we use *I wish + Past tense* to talk about the present situation (She doesn't have enough time to do exercise, she lives in a cold climate).

2 Writing/speaking activity

- Students write three sentences about themselves beginning *I wish*.

- They show their sentences to their partner and talk about them (e.g. say why they wish these things, whether it's likely to happen).

- As a round-up, ask a few pairs to tell you the most interesting wish they talked about.

> **Language note**
> *I wish* can also be followed by the Past perfect tense. This structure is used for expressing regret, and is dealt with in Unit 23.

> **Language note**
> *I wish* is used about things we regard as *improbable* or *impossible*. Compare:
> - I hope I win some money. (I think it's quite possible.)
> - I wish I could win some money. (I don't think it's likely.)

> **Optional lead-in**
> Tell the class a few things you wish, and explain why.

> 🔲 Tapescript for Exercise 4: *Wishes*
>
> *Father:* I wish I could take more time off work. I work at home, and I find it very difficult to stop at the end of the day.
>
> *Daughter:* I wish I had time to do more exercise. I used to do a lot of aerobics, but now that I'm studying I find that I have very little time to attend the classes.
>
> *Father:* I wish I could play the guitar. I used to try to teach myself, but I wasn't very good, so I gave up.
>
> *Daughter:* I really wish it was warmer in the North of England, that's where I study, and I pay a lot of money for the rent and electricity to heat up the house. It would make me a lot happier to study in a warmer country.
>
> *Father:* I wish I didn't have such an old car. I'd like to have one with central door locking and power steering and an open sun roof.
>
> *Daughter:* I wish I lived in a smaller house. The house that I live in at the moment is very big. There are six of us living there, and it gets very noisy sometimes. In a smaller house I'd feel more comfortable and I'd have the quiet that I need to study.
>
> *Father:* I wish my children would leave home. They're over 20, but they're still living with us, and they use the telephone all the time, and they invite all their friends around, and they're very nice kids but I just wish they'd go.

Focus on Form

1 *Questions with would*

> Questions beginning *Would you ...?*; answers with *I would* and *I wouldn't*

- Go through the exercise and establish what the questions should be, e.g.

  a Would you give a lift to a hitch-hiker at night?

- Pairwork. Students ask each other the questions.
- Go through the answers together, finding out what most students would do in each situation.

2 *1st & 2nd conditional*

> !st and 2nd conditional structures

- Look at the two sentences. Establish that
  - in sentence 1 (1st conditional), the speaker has probably been to a job interview. There is a real possibility that he/she may be offered the job.
  - in sentence 2 (2nd conditional), the speaker doesn't expect anyone to offer him/her a job – he/she's just imagining it.
- If necessary, show the structure of 1st and 2nd conditionals:

  1st conditional: *If + present ... will/won't ...*
  2nd conditional: *If + past ... would(n't) ...*

- Working alone or in pairs, students complete the sentences. Possible answers:

  a If you miss your bus ...
  b If I found some money in the street ...
  c ... you'll have a heart attack.
  d If everyone spoke Esperanto ...
  e ... they'd get more customers.
  f ... I'll never speak to you again.
  g If I have time ...
  h If you had a holiday ...

3 *Advice: 2nd conditional*

> 2nd conditional structures, used for giving advice

- In pairs, students make *If* sentences as in the example.
- Go through the answers. Answers:

  took your jacket off ... you'd feel more comfortable.
  didn't hit your children ... wouldn't be frightened of you.
  took your dog for a walk ... wouldn't bark so much.
  got a diary ... wouldn't forget so many appointments.
  didn't drink so much coffee ... you'd sleep better.
  left a key ... parents would be able to get in.
  didn't leave food lying around ... wouldn't have mice ...
  didn't play music ... you'd be more popular ...

4 *Wishes*

> *I wish* + Past tense; *I wish* + *could/would*

- Either elicit sentences from the whole class, or let students work through the exercise in pairs and then go through the answers together. Possible answers:

  a I wish I wasn't so shy; I wish I could meet more people; I wish someone would invite me out.
  b I wish I didn't live with my parents; I wish I could leave home; I wish I had more money.
  c I wish everything didn't cost so much; I wish I didn't pay so much tax; I wish I could afford a holiday.
  d I wish I wasn't on this island; I wish it wasn't so hot; I wish I had some books with me; I wish I could escape.

5 *Pronunciation*

▭ Ask students to try saying the sentences themselves, then play the recording as a model. Focus on these points:

a Full *would* in Yes/no questions: /wʊd/.
  Reduced *would* in statements and Wh- questions:
  It would /ɪt (w)əd/, *What would* /wɒt (w)əd/ *Where would* /weə (w)əd/.
b Pronunciation of *wouldn't* /wʊdn̩t/.
c Reduced *could* in statements: /kəd/.

Self-study Workbook

Exercise A: Would and wouldn't
Students look at pictures and imagine what would happen if ...

Exercise B: Second conditionals
Students complete conditional sentences, by adding either the first or second half.

Exercise C: Wishes
Students look at pictures and imagine what the people in them might be wishing.

Translation
Key sentences for translation.

Listening: What would you do?
Two people answer some of the questions from *Focus on Form* Exercise 1 (above).
Students listen and complete a table.

Pronunciation: Linking words: consonant + vowel
'Links' between words ending in consonants and words starting with vowels. Students hear examples, then read sentences and predict where the links will be.

Reading: My perfect weekend
A magazine-style interview.
Students match the questions with the answers, then answer other comprehension questions.

Focus on Form

1 Questions with would

Find out whether your partner would do these things.

a give a lift to a hitch-hiker at night
b give money to a beggar in the street
c swim in the sea in winter
d cheat in an examination
e drive a car after drinking alcohol
f give up a seat on a bus for an elderly person
g kill someone in self-defence

Which of them would you do yourself?

2 1st & 2nd conditional

Look at these two conditional sentences. What is the difference?

1 If they *offer* me the job, I*'ll* probably take it.
2 Of course, if someone *offered* me a better job, I*'d* probably take it.

Now complete these *If ...* sentences.

a ... I'll give you a lift to the station.
b ... I'd hand it in to the police.
c If you carry on working like this ...
d ... no-one would need to learn English.
e If they weren't so rude to everyone ...
f If you don't apologise ...
g ... I'll come round and see you.
h ... you'd feel much better.

3 Advice: 2nd conditional

In pairs, make *If ...* sentences giving advice.

Student A: Choose items from the *Advice* box. Begin the sentence using *If* + past.

Student B: Complete the sentence with a suitable item from the *Reason* box.

Example:

A If you turned the sofa on its side ...
B ... it would go through the door.

Advice
Turn the sofa on its side.
Take your jacket off.
Don't hit your children.
Take your dog for a walk.
Get a diary.
Don't drink so much coffee.
Leave a key with a neighbour.
Don't leave food lying around.
Don't play music after midnight.

Reason
Your parents would be able to get in.
It would go through the door.
You wouldn't forget so many appointments.
You wouldn't have mice in your flat.
They wouldn't be frightened of you.
You'd be more popular with your neighbours.
You'd sleep better.
You'd feel more comfortable.
It wouldn't bark so much.

4 Wishes

Make sentences with *I wish ...* for each situation.

Example: *It's cloudy; the water's cold; you can't go swimming.*

I wish it wasn't so cloudy.
I wish the sun would come out.
I wish the water was warmer.
I wish we could go swimming.

a You're shy; you want to meet more people; no-one invites you out.
b You live with your parents; you want to leave home; you haven't got much money.
c Everything costs too much; you pay a lot of tax; you can't afford a holiday.
d You're on a desert island; it's very hot; you haven't got any books with you; you want to escape.

5 Pronunciation

How do you say the words and phrases below?

a Would you help them?
   It would look better if you washed it.
   What would you do?
   Where would you go?

b I wouldn't go home.
   It wouldn't help.

c I wish I could sing.
   I wish we could visit them.

📼 Now listen and check your answers.

Describing things

1 I don't know what it's called but …

1 *a* ▭ You will hear students describing five objects they don't know the names of in English.
Which objects do they describe?

b Describe the other things in the pictures.

2 Think of three common objects whose names you don't know in English, and write a sentence describing each one.

Find out if other students know what your objects are called.

This unit deals with two vocabulary areas that are important in describing objects:
– describing things according to their physical appearance (shape, size, materials, features)
– describing and naming things according to what they are used for.
The unit also introduces functional language involved in buying and selling second-hand goods.
The Reading and Listening activity is about Victorian inventions.

1 I don't know what it's called but …

This exercise introduces language for describing everyday objects, in terms of what they look like, what they are made of and what they are used for. This language is especially useful for describing objects that students may not know the names of in English. In the first part, students hear foreign learners describing objects, and then they write descriptions of objects themselves.

➤ Workbook: Exercise A

1 Listening & presentation

● ▢ Play the tape, pausing after each description and asking students to match the description with the pictures. As you go through, tell students the names of the objects in English. Answers:

1 Picture I: (a pair of) pliers
2 Picture H: a spatula
3 Picture J: correcting fluid (Tipp-Ex, or white-out)
4 Picture G: chopsticks
5 Picture D: (bathroom) scales

▢ The tapescript is on page T49.

● Use the examples on the tape as a basis for presenting the following language:
– general nouns for describing things:

| It's a | thing
tool
liquid | … |
| | | |

| It's | white
sticky | stuff … |

Presentation option
You could do this by referring back to some of the descriptions, e.g. What did she say about the spatula? That it's made of metal.

– adjectives for describing *shape* and *size*:

| long – short
wide – narrow | round – square
thick – thin |

– saying what things are made of:

| It's made of | wood.
metal.
plastic. |

| A | wooden
metal
plastic | bowl. |

Language note
Most nouns of this type are also used as adjectives, e.g. a *metal* knife, a *plastic* bag. The adjective from *wood* is *wooden*.

– the structure *use + for + -ing*:

| You *use* chopsticks
Chopsticks *are used* | *for* eating Chinese food. |

Language note
These are active and passive forms of the same structure. It is also possible to say: Chopsticks are used *to eat* Chinese food.

● Students use the language you've presented to describe the other objects shown in the pictures. Possible answers:

A *Plaster:* It's a kind of bandage that you put over a cut, and it sticks.
B *Clothes peg:* It's made of wood or plastic; it's used to keep clothes on a line.
C *Plug:* It's a small round thing, made of rubber or plastic. You use it to stop the water running out of a sink or bath.
E *Corkscrew:* It's a metal thing you use to take the cork out of a bottle.
F *Car jack:* It's a tool you use to raise your car off the ground so you can change a wheel.

2 Writing & speaking activity

● Working alone or in pairs, students think of a few common objects, and write descriptions of them.
● They read out their descriptions to the rest of the class, to see if other students can identify the object and say what it is called in English.

Alternatives
1 Single nationality classes
Write the names of objects on pieces of paper in the students' own language.
2 Flashcards
Give out flashcards showing common objects. Students describe the picture without showing it, and other students guess what it is.

2 Things with a purpose

This exercise introduces common noun phrases which refer to particular types of object (e.g. types of paper, types of knife*). Many of these words define what the object is used for (e.g.* writing paper*) or where it is used (e.g.* kitchen table*).*

1 Presentation

- To show students what to do, write one of the words from Box A on the board (e.g. *typing*); ask them to find a matching word from Box B (*paper*) and say where they would find it (*in an office*).
- Give time for students to find pairs of words. Then go through the answers. Expected answers:

    Office: filing cabinet, typing paper, word processor, address book, phone book
    Handbag: hairbrush, address book, car keys, reading glasses
    Kitchen: food processor, frying pan, tin opener, carving knife

- Show how the phrases follow three patterns:

-ing + noun	noun + noun	noun + -er/or
typing paper	phone book	word processor
reading glasses	car keys	tin opener

    Then say something about what the object is used for, e.g. typing paper = paper that is used for typing, car keys = keys you use to unlock/start your car.

2 Writing/speaking activity

- Give time for students to think of other kinds of paper, knife and book, and write them down.
- Ask students what ideas they had, and build up lists on the board. As you do so, elicit other items yourself (e.g. *What about a knife you keep in your pocket?*). Possible answers:

    – writing paper, newspaper, notepaper, wrapping paper, toilet paper
    – bread knife, penknife, pocket knife, fruit knife, hunting knife
    – notebook, exercise book, cookery book, coursebook

3 Things for sale

This activity is about buying and selling second-hand goods. It draws on the language of Exercises 1 and 2, and also involves other language functions: offering, enquiring about price, accepting and refusing. Students interpret the advertisements, and then use them as a basis for a role-play.

1 Presentation

- Establish that these are advertisements for second-hand goods that people want to sell; they might be found in a newspaper, or a shop window.
- Read through the advertisements, focusing on anything students don't understand (e.g. *mileage* = how many miles it has done; *o.n.o.* = or near(est) offer, so *£120 o.n.o.* = £120 or less).
- Go through the advertisements together, asking students to suggest possible questions, e.g. *How long have you had it? Is it in good condition? Was it new when you bought it? Would you accept £20 for it? Can I try it out?* If you like, build up a list of questions on the board.

2 Speaking activity

- As a lead-in, choose one of the items and demonstrate the role-play with a good student. You can act as buyer or seller.
- Pairwork. Students choose one of the items and improvise a conversation. They then choose another item and have a second conversation, changing roles.
- As a round-up, ask a few students whether they managed to sell their items.

➤ Workbook: Exercise B

Language note
Noun + noun patterns are usually written as two words, but a few commonly used forms are written as one word, e.g. *hairbrush, penknife, newspaper, notebook, saucepan.*

Optional extension ideas
1 Pass the paper
Students write a 'category' noun (e.g. *machine, boat, table, boots, bag, basket, jacket*) on a piece of paper. They pass the paper to other students, who write down particular kinds (e.g. *sewing machine, washing machine*).

2 Categories
Write a list of category nouns on the board. For each one, students write one type. They score 1 point for each correct answer, and 2 points if they have something no-one else has.

Discussion option for mixed nationality classes
Ask students where people put advertisements like this in the students' own country, and what kind of things people most often buy second-hand.

Optional extension
In class or for homework, students write similar advertisements for something of their own they would like to sell.

Post the advertisements around the class. Students move freely around the class looking at the advertisements, and then find out more information about any they are interested in.

2 Things with a purpose

1 Use one word from each box to make objects that you might find

   – in an office
   – in a handbag
   – in a kitchen.

A
filing   typing   word
food   hair
address   frying
phone   car   tin
reading   carving

B
keys   opener
pan   paper   glasses
knife   brush
processor
cabinet   book

2 Can you think of two other kinds of

   – paper?
   – knife?
   – book?

3 Things for sale

1 Look at these advertisements. What questions might you ask the owners?

PUPPIES FOR SALE

Contact: Jean Wright
Phone: 987304

SPANISH GUITAR

Good condition. With case.

£50

Phone Steve at 325444

SECOND-HAND

TYPEWRITER

Good working condition.
Recently cleaned and repaired.
Ideal for typing practice.

£25   Tel: 331256

FOR SALE

1976 VOLKSWAGEN

Dark green. Low mileage.

£120 o.n.o.

Phone: 331865 (after 5 pm)

BRASS BED
FOR SALE
150 years old. Genuine antique.
With mattress.
£150
phone: 322113

2 In pairs, choose one of the advertisements.

Student A: You're interested in buying the item. Find out more about it.

Student B: You want to sell the item. Answer A's questions.

4 Great ideas?

READING

Here are three ideas from inventors who lived in Victorian times.
Do you think they would work? What problems do you think
there might be?

A SPHERICAL, TRANSPARENT VELOCIPEDE

Imagine a hollow sphere made of some transparent but strong material, with a built-in door, and a seat attached to the sides, as shown.

Once inside, the rider simply 'walks' down the side of the sphere and the sphere starts to move forwards. If he wants to go right or left, he just leans his body slightly in the desired direction and the sphere will follow. To stop, he simply presses his feet against the place where the sphere touches the ground. If he wants to go backwards, he simply reverses his steps and the sphere will respond immediately.

But that is not all. He arrives at a river—let us suppose that it is not too wide—and the rider, going as fast as he can, rolls down the bank with enough speed to bring him to the other side of the river. The sphere floats on the water and continues to revolve until it has reached the opposite bank.

For this to work, the sphere must, of course, be airtight. But this is not a serious problem, as it contains more than 140 cubic feet of air—enough for the rider to keep breathing for up to two hours. [1884]

LISTENING

🖭 You will hear three people commenting on the three inventions.

1 What problems do they identify for each one?
  Write three lists.

2 Did you think of any problems that the speakers didn't?

4 Great ideas?

This combined reading and listening activity is about Victorian inventions. Students read the descriptions of the inventions and discuss whether they think they would work. They then listen to people commenting on the inventions and compare what they hear with their own ideas.

READING

- As a lead-in, look at the pictures and discuss briefly what the three inventions are, e.g.

  1 It's a form of transport. It's a glass ball; you sit in it and make it move with your feet, a bit like a bicycle.
  2 It's a kind of suit to wear if your ship sinks. It floats and keeps you warm.
  3 It's a flying machine. You sit in a cage and birds pull you through the air.

- Students work in groups. If you like, let them read quickly through all three texts, then ask them to concentrate on the one they find most interesting. They read the text and discuss whether they think the invention would work and what the problems might be. They should make a list of problems in note form, e.g.
  – *How does the man breathe?*
  – *He would fall over.*
  – *Is the ball made of plastic? If so, it would get scratched.*

> *Help option*
> Give each group a dictionary, so that they can look up any difficult words.

LISTENING

- ▱ Play the recording once to establish which invention the speaker is talking about. Then play the recording again, pausing from time to time. Students listen and make brief notes, listing the problems the speakers mention.

- Build up three lists on the board:

  Velocipede
  It would go too fast – you couldn't stop it.
  You'd be washed away in a river.

  Flying machine
  How do you get in?
  Where do you find ten eagles?
  How do you put their jackets on?
  They couldn't fly far.

  Life preserver
  Claustrophobic.
  The food would smell.
  Going to the toilet?
  You'd get seasick.

- Ask students what other ideas they had themselves, and add them to the lists on the board.

▱ Tapescript for Exercise 4: *Great ideas?*

1 It looks rather dangerous because if you were at the top of a hill, could you hold yourself so that you just didn't go down the hill really, really fast? I don't know. And then it says here that it floats on the water. Well that's fine, but if you were in a fast moving river and you were trying to get across, surely the water would take you with it and you'd just go on and on and never be seen again.

2 This is called a natural flying machine, but it doesn't seem very natural to me. How do you get the man inside, in the middle bit of this machine? And where do you find ten eagles? How do you actually put them inside their jackets? And just because we know that eagles can carry heavy weights, I mean we don't know how long they can

carry heavy weights for. So they may be able to lift a man for ten seconds or something, but they may not be able to keep going. But it's a nice idea.

3 My main fear is that it looks really claustrophobic once you're in there, especially with the lid down. It says you can have enough supply of food, a month's supply of food and drinking water in there – I'm a bit worried about the smell, for instance, of the food going off. Also, there's no mention of how you go to the toilet in it. Also, I should imagine you'd get quite seasick in it, especially with the lid on.

1 I need a pair of those things you use for pulling nails out. They look like scissors but they're not sharp.
2 Have you got one of those spoons that I can use because I'm frying eggs in the frying pan and I need something to turn them over. You know those big spoons made of metal I can use.
3 Please, I'm writing my composition and I've made a mistake. Do you have this white stuff that you use for correcting mistakes? You know, it's got a little brush and you paint it over the wrong word.
4 Have you got one of those things to eat Chinese food? You know those long sticks, and they're usually made of wood or plastic.
5 I'd just like to find out how much fatter I've become. Have you got this thing I can stand on and find out how much I weigh?

Self-study Workbook

Exercise A: Identifying objects
Students match pictures of objects with their names and their definitions. They then write three definitions of their own.

Exercise B: Compound nouns
Students find the names of compound nouns from clues and enter them in a grid. Letters from the grid spell out a sentence.

New words
Space to record new words with notes and examples.

Translation
Key sentences for translation.

Listening: Things for sale
Two phone conversations about things for sale. Students construct a 'small ad' for one, and answer true/false questions about the other.

Phrasal verbs: Transitive verbs (2)
Transitive phrasal verbs with an idiomatic meaning (e.g. *give something up*, *put something off*). Students match verbs with their objects, then use them to replace phrases in sentences.

Writing skills: Reference: *this* and *which*
Use of *this* and *which* to refer back to ideas in a sentence or paragraph. Students fill gaps in sentences, then match sentences together and join them using *this* or *which*.

A LIFE-PRESERVER

Mr Traugott Beek of Newark, New Jersey, has invented a floating life-preserver, which gives complete protection to people who have been shipwrecked. The upper section is large enough for the wearer to be able to move his head and arms about, and a month's supply of food and drinking-water can also be stored in it. The cover can be closed in rough weather, and the wearer can see through the window in the front, and breathe through a curved pipe. The life-preserver is made of waterproof cloth attached to circular metal tubes, which protect the wearer against sharp rocks and hungry fish. [1877]

Adapted from *Victorian Inventions* by Leonard de Vries, 1991.

A NATURAL FLYING MACHINE

Baltimore, 30th August, 1865

Dear Editor—

I would like to suggest an idea for a natural flying machine.

There are many birds, such as the brown eagle, which are both strong and can fly long distances. If these birds can carry up to 20 pounds each (we know that they are strong enough to carry off babies and lambs) one would need ten such eagles to carry an adult person through the air.

The eagles would have jackets fitted round their bodies, attached to circular metal tubes. These tubes would carry a metal basket large enough to hold a man. Strings passing through the hollow tubes would allow the passenger to control the direction of flight by pulling the head of the bird to one side or the other.

Would not this invention lead to an extremely simple and inexpensive means of air transport?

11 The future

1 Were they right?

will do • will be done

The 1990s: Decade of Depression

▼ The depressed '90s
The 1990s will be a period of depression, affecting the whole world. Many large corporations will be wiped out and millions of jobs will be lost. Prices will fall and taxes will rise sharply.

▼ City violence
Large cities will become so violent that they will be very unpleasant places to live in. As a result, people who can afford it will move out of the city altogether and settle in smaller towns.

▼ Legalised drugs
During the depression of the 1930s, the ban on alcohol was lifted in the USA. In the same way, the ban on illegal drugs will be lifted during the depression of the 1990s, in an attempt to control violent crime and raise money.

▼ The changing world map
The 1990s will be a profitable time for map-makers. We will see the break-up not just of the Soviet Union, but of India, Canada, China, Yugoslavia, Ethiopia and other countries.

▼ Nuclear terrorism
Governments will find it more and more difficult to fight terrorism. Terrorist groups will become more powerful and more dangerous. They will manage to obtain nuclear and chemical weapons, and won't be afraid to use them.

▼ The rise of religion
During the 1990s, people in many countries will turn more and more to religion. Religion – particularly Islam, but other religions as well – will become increasingly important in world politics.

Adapted from *The Great Reckoning* by James Dale Davidson & William Rees-Mogg, 1991.

1 The predictions in the text come from a book which was written in 1990.

Which of the predictions do you think

– have already come true?
– might still come true?
– probably won't come true?

2 What is the difference between the verbs in these two sentences?
Prices *will fall*. Millions of jobs *will be lost*.

Find two other examples of each structure in the text.

Now make some predictions of your own.

This unit deals with a range of structures used in making predictions about the future:
– *will* + active and passive infinitive
– *expect* and *hope*
– future continuous and future perfect tenses
– giving reasons for predictions using *in case, so that, because* and *otherwise*.

1 Were they right?

In this exercise, students discuss predictions that were made about the 1990s in a book published in 1991. The text is used to present will *followed by active and passive infinitives.*

➤ Focus on Form: Exercise 1
➤ Workbook: Exercise A

1 Reading & discussion

● Explain that the text is from a book published in 1991 which made predictions about what would happen during the 1990s.

● Give time for students to read through the text, and deal with any unknown vocabulary.

● Ask students to summarise the main message of each section:
  – There will be economic depression throughout the world.
  – Cities will become too violent to live in.
  – Drugs will become legal.
  – Large countries will break up.
  – Terrorists will get nuclear weapons.
  – Religion will become more important.

● Divide the class into groups. Ask each group to focus on one or two of the predictions. They should discuss whether the events have already started to happen, and whether they think they will happen.

● Ask one student from each group to report their conclusions to the rest of the class.

> *Vocabulary option*
> Focus on key vocabulary by writing words on the board as students read the texts, e.g. *depression, violent, settle, profitable, terrorism.* Then discuss with the class what the words mean in context.

2 Presentation & writing activity

● Look at the examples, and use them to present active and passive infinitives after *will*. You could do this by relating them to the present tense:

| ACTIVE: | **Prices fall** |
| | **Prices _will_ fall** |

| PASSIVE: | **Jobs are lost** |
| | **Jobs _will be lost_** |

Ask students to find other examples in the text. Answers:
will be/rise/become/move/settle/see/find/manage/turn
will be wiped out / be lost / be lifted

● Expand the presentation to show how we use *will (probably)* and *(probably) won't* in making predictions:

| Prices | will (probably) | fall. |
| | (probably) won't | |

| Jobs | will (probably) | be lost. |
| | (probably) won't | |

> *Language note*
> *probably* and similar adverbs (e.g. *definitely, certainly, possibly*) come after *will* but before *won't*.

● Working alone or in groups, students write a few predictions of their own, using the structures you have presented.

● Students read out their predictions. Ask the class to say whether they think the predictions will come true.

> *Homework option*
> Using these predictions as a starting point, students write paragraphs like those in the text, but about the decade to come.

2 Hopes and expectations

This exercise introduces expressions with I hope *and* I expect. *The first part focuses on the form and meaning of the two structures; then students use them in sentences to fit imaginary situations.*

1 Presentation

- Pairwork. Students look at the situation and decide what thoughts they would have. Then discuss this with the whole class.
- Look at the sentences again, and establish these differences between *hope* and *expect*:
  - *I expect* means 'I think this will happen'.
  - *I hope* means 'I want this to happen'.
  - *I hope* is usually followed by the Present tense.
  - *I hope* has no negative form (we say 'I hope he doesn't go', *not* 'I don't hope he goes').
- Build up two tables on the board to show how the two structures are formed:

I expect	I'll see him.	I hope	I see him.
I *don't* expect			I *don't* see him.

2 Writing & speaking activity

- Students write one or two 'thoughts' for each situation, using *hope* or *expect*. They then show their partner what they have written.
- As a round-up, ask a few students what they wrote.

3 In five years' time

This exercise focuses on the Future continuous and Future perfect tenses for talking about a particular point of time in the future. Students listen to someone being interviewed and imagine what her life will be like. Then they make predictions about their own future lives.

1 Listening & presentation

- [cassette] Play the recording, and establish what the woman says about each of the topics. Answers:

  She's got a job in a hospital; she's getting married before she leaves; they're not planning to have children yet; they want to travel as much as possible; she gets a free apartment; she'll be paid twice as much as now.

- To present the Future continuous and perfect, ask students to imagine the woman in five years' time. This is what she might say:
  'I'*m* in Australia now.' 'I'*m living* in Australia.' 'I'*ve moved* to Australia.'
  To talk about these things in the future, we add *will* to these sentences:
  In five years' time …
  … she'*ll be* in Australia.
  … she'*ll be living* in Australia.
  … she'*ll have moved* to Australia.
- Show the structure of the Future continuous and Future perfect tenses:

will + be + -ing	will + have + Past participle

- Ask what else the woman will be doing and will have done. Possible answers:

  She'll be working as a nurse; she'll be earning a lot of money; she'll have got married; she'll have left England; she'll have seen a lot of the Far East.

2 Writing & speaking activity

- Students complete the table for themselves. They then add one or two more predictions, using either of the two tenses.
- Students turn to the person next to them and compare what they have written. This should lead naturally into a discussion of the reasons for their predictions, and of what they hope will and won't happen.

➤ Focus on Form: Exercise 2
➤ Workbook: Exercise B

Presentation option
Show how we use *so* and *not* with *expect* and *hope* in answer to a question:
Do you think he'll come?

I expect I <u>don't</u> expect	<u>so.</u>

I hope	<u>so.</u> <u>not.</u>

Alternative: guessing game
Groupwork. Each group chooses one of the situations, and together they write a few 'thoughts'. Then they read out their sentences, and other students guess the situation they chose.

You could give more situations for students to choose from, e.g.

You're going abroad for a holiday.
Your aunt is coming for dinner.
A friend has asked you to look after her dog.
You're getting married next week.

➤ Focus on Form: Exercises 3, 4
➤ Workbook: Exercise C

[cassette] The tapescript is on page T52.

Practice option
Give other situations to elicit sentences using these structures, e.g.
After this lesson I'm going to go for a swim. Think of me in an hour from now. What can you say?
  - You'll be swimming.
  - You'll be at the swimming pool.
  - You will have changed.
  - You'll have taken your watch off.

Optional lead-in
Make a few predictions about yourself, including some based on the table. Ask the class whether they believe you.

2 Hopes and expectations

expect & hope

1 You've been invited to a party by some people you don't know very well. Which of these thoughts do you think would go through your mind?

> I expect I'll meet lots of interesting people.

> I don't expect I'll enjoy it much.

> I hope there's someone there that I know.

> I hope the food's good.

> I hope I don't have to dance.

> I hope there won't be too many people there.

2 What would you hope or expect in these situations? Write down your thoughts.

– You're about to go for a job interview.
– It's your birthday next week.
– A friend's children are coming to stay for the weekend.
– You're you, now.

3 In five years' time

will be doing • will have done

1 🔲 You will hear someone being interviewed about her present life and future plans. What does she say about

– work?   – travel?
– marriage?   – a place to live?
– children?   – money?

Think of her in five years' time. What will her life be like? What will she be doing? What will she have done?

2 Now think of yourself in five years' time. Which of these things do you think will be true?

	I'll be married.
	I'll still be living in the same place.
	I will have travelled round the world.
	I'll have three children.
	I'll be working in an office.
	I will have written a novel.

What else will you be doing?
What else will you have done?

Compare your answers with your partner's.

4 Survival

1 There are four ways of completing the piece of advice in the table. What are they?

You should wear a life jacket …	
… because	you might drown.
… Otherwise	you don't drown.
… in case	the boat might capsize.
… so that	the boat capsizes.

Now give reasons for these pieces of advice.

a You should have a radio with you …
b You should make sure the boat's got an engine …
c You should carry a compass …
d You should take some warm clothes with you …

2 What advice might you give to one of these people?

– someone who wants to cross the Sahara Desert
– someone planning to go across Europe on a motorbike
– someone who wants to spend the summer in Britain

Grammar Checklist

will, might & won't

+ *active infinitive*

They'll probably **give** him the job.
There **will be** more cars on the road.
You **might feel** thirsty.
I **won't see** them till next year.

+ *passive infinitive*

The book **will be** published next year.
You **might be** attacked.
Bus fares **won't be** increased.

expect & hope

| I expect
I don't expect | he'll come to the party. |

| I hope | he comes
he doesn't come | to the party. |
| | (*not* ~~I don't hope~~ …) |

Future continuous tense

will + be + -ing – *for things that **will be going on** at a point in the future*.

They'll still **be living** here next summer.
I'll **be waiting** at the station at 4 o'clock.

Future perfect tense

will + have + *past participle* – *for things that **will be completed** at a point in the future*.

He'll **have left** school by then.
I **won't have** finished it by lunchtime.

Linking expressions

You should wear a coat **because** it **might** rain.
You should wear a coat **in case** it **rains**.
(*not* … ~~it will rain~~.)

Take a map. **Otherwise** you **might** get lost.
Take a map **so that** you **don't** get lost.

See also Reference section, page 135.

4 Survival

This exercise is concerned with the precautions you need to take to ensure survival. It focuses on linking expressions used when giving reasons for advice: because, otherwise, so that and in case.

➤ Focus on Form: Exercise 5
➤ Workbook: Exercise D

1 Presentation & speaking activity

- Ask students to complete the advice in the table. Answers:

  ... because the boat might capsize.
  ... Otherwise you might drown.
  ... in case the boat capsizes.
  ... so that you don't drown.

  Point out that:
  – *in case* it happens = *because* it might happen.
  – *in case* and *so that* are followed by the Present tense, although they refer to the future.

- Discuss the reasons for the other pieces of advice. Try to get students to use a variety of linking expressions in their answers. Possible answers:

  a In case you want to call for help.
  b So that you can still move if there's no wind.
  c Otherwise you might lose your way.
  d Because it might get very cold on the open sea.

2 Writing & speaking activity

- Divide the class into groups, and ask each group to focus on one of the three topics. Together, they think of advice they would give and reasons, and make brief notes, e.g. (Sahara):

  Take plenty of water (thirsty)
  Take a gun (in case you're attacked)
  Take an Arabic phrase book (ask the way)

- One person from each group moves to the next group. Using the notes, they give the group advice and answer any questions.

- As a round-up, ask groups whether they thought the advice they were given was good or not.

Presentation option

To establish clearly how *in case* is used, give other examples, e.g.

Take an umbrella because it might rain. →
Take an umbrella *in case* it rains.

Alternative

Find out what outdoor activities students know something about, and build up a list on the board, e.g.

fishing	parachuting
diving	mountaineering
skiing	catching snakes
walking	canoeing

Students who know about the activity think what advice they would give. Other students choose an activity they want to know about, and prepare questions.

They then sit with the 'expert' and find out about the activity.

Note

Advice about crossing the Sahara is given in the Self-study Workbook reading for this unit.

🔲 Tapescript for Exercise 3: *In five years' time*

A So when are you planning to leave for Australia?
B I'll be going in a few months' time. I'm supposed to be staying there at least five years, but I don't know, I'll have to wait and see if I like it.
A And do you have a job to go to?
B Oh yes, I'm a nurse. I'm going mainly for the job that I've found there. I've found quite a good job in a university hospital, and I get a free apartment and I'll be earning twice as much as I do now, so it's not bad.
A That's good. And are you going by yourself?
B No, no I'm going with my boyfriend, who will by then be my husband. We're getting married before we go.
A And is he going to be working out there?
B Well hopefully he'll find a teaching job out there.
A And will you stay in one place in Australia?
B Oh I hope not. We really want to travel as much as possible. There's so much to see, I mean the whole of the Far East and the Pacific Islands, yeah.
A So you won't be starting a family straight away?
B Er, not just yet.

Focus on Form

1 *Will do & will be done*

> *will* + active and passive infinitive

- Read the example, then ask students to complete the sentences. Answers:
  - a ... they'll send him / he'll be sent to prison.
  - b ... they'll sack her / she'll be sacked.
  - c ... we'll sell them / they'll be sold.
  - d ... they'll cancel the show / the show will be cancelled.
  - e ... they'll take her / she'll be taken to hospital.
  - f ... someone will steal it / it will be stolen.

2 *I expect & I hope*

> Positive and negative sentences with *I expect* and *I hope*

- Use one of the items to establish the possible forms, e.g.
  I (don't) expect there'll be a world war.
  I hope there is/isn't a world war.
- Pairwork. One student writes sentences with *I expect*, the other with *I hope*. Then they compare answers, to see if their hopes match their expectations.
- As a round-up, use a show of hands to find out the hopes and expectations of the class as a whole.

3 *Will/might be doing*

> Future continuous tense with *will*, *will probably* and *might*

- To introduce the exercise, ask a few students what they'll be doing five minutes after the lesson ends.
- Pairwork. Students compare their answers with their partner. Alternatively, they could write sentences about themselves, and then read them out to their partner.

4 *Will have done*

> Future perfect tense

- Either go through the situation with the class, or get students to write sentences for each situation and then go through the answers afterwards. Possible answers:

> *Julia:* She will have gone to school. She will have learnt to walk/talk. She will have grown taller.
> *Ian:* He will have left school. He will have started college. He will have left home.
> *Mary & Tom:* She will have got her degree. He will have found a job. They will have got married.

5 *In case & so that*

> Giving reasons for advice, using *in case* and *so that*

- Look at the example and point out that *in case* and *so that* are followed by the Present simple.
- Either do the exercise round the class, or let students work through it in pairs and then go through the answers together. Possible answers:
  - a You'd better leave the door unlocked in case they don't have a key / so that they can get in.
  - b You'd better leave early in case the traffic's heavy / so that we don't get stuck in the traffic.
  - c You'd better wear boots in case it's muddy / so that your feet don't get wet.
  - d You'd better take sandwiches in case they don't provide a meal / so that you aren't hungry.
  - e You'd better take a coat in case the weather changes / so that you don't get cold.
  - f You'd better give them a map in case they don't know the way / so that they don't get lost.

6 *Pronunciation*

Ask students to try saying the sentences themselves, then play the tape as a model. Focus on these points:
- a Reduced vowels in *I expect* /aɪ ɪkˈspekt/ and *I don't expect* /aɪ dəʊnt ɪkˈspekt/.
- b Short *'ll* (dark l) /[ɫ]/ and reduced *will* /wə[ɫ]/ in Future tense: *I'll* /aɪ[ɫ]/, *he'll* /hiː[ɫ]/, *she'll* /ʃiː[ɫ]/, *they'll* /ðeɪ[ɫ]/, *Mary will* /ˈmeəri (w)ə[ɫ]/.
- c Reduced vowels and modified *h* in *I will have* /aɪ wəl (h)əv/.
- d Pronunciation of *should* /ʃəd/, *in case* /ɪŋ keɪs/, *so that* /səʊ ðət/.

Self-study Workbook

Exercise A: Optimism and pessimism
Active and passive forms of the future tense; *probably*.
Students write optimistic and pessimistic predictions.

Exercise B: Expect and hope
Students rewrite their optimistic and pessimistic predictions from Exercise A using *hope* and *expect*.

Exercise C: Will be doing and will have done
Students read imaginary newspaper clippings from near the end of the 21st century, and write a paragraph.

Exercise D: Giving reasons
Otherwise, *in case*, *because* and *so that*.
Students write sentences giving reasons for advice.

Translation
Key sentences for translation.

Listening: When I'm 60 ...
Someone imagines his life at the age of 60. Students answer true/false questions and complete a summary.

Pronunciation: Stress in sentences
Stress patterns in questions and answers. Students look at two-line conversations and predict where the stress will come.

Reading: Crossing the Sahara
Students read advice about crossing the Sahara Desert, and answer comprehension questions.

Focus on Form

1 Will do & will be done

Complete these sentences, using verbs from the box (1) in the active (2) in the passive.

cancel	sell	send to prison
sack	steal	take to hospital

Example: *When they realise we're missing …*
… they'll rescue us.
… we'll be rescued.

a If they catch him …
b If she turns up late again …
c When the puppies are six weeks old …
d If they don't sell more tickets …
e As soon as the ambulance arrives …
f If you leave your car unlocked overnight …

2 I expect & I hope

Student A: Do you expect these things will happen during your lifetime? Write sentences with *I expect*.

Student B: Do you hope these things will happen during your lifetime? Write sentences with *I hope*.

There'll be a world war.

They'll find a cure for cancer.

Smoking will be made illegal.

Elephants will become extinct.

We'll make contact with beings from another planet.

Now compare your hopes and expectations.

3 Will/might be doing

Picture yourself at the times below. What do you think you'll be doing? Compare your answers with your partner's.

Example: *five minutes after this lesson ends*
I'll probably be waiting for the bus.
I might be having a cup of coffee.
I'll still be sitting here.

a five minutes after this lesson ends
b at 10.00 tonight
c tomorrow morning at 7.45
d next Saturday at 11.00 a.m.
e next Sunday at 3.30 p.m.
f at this time next week
g at midnight on December 31st

4 Will have done

Think of three things that these people *will* (*probably*) *have done* in five years' time.
Example:
Julia will have stopped wearing nappies.

Julia, 1, baby

Ian, 14, schoolboy

Mary, 19, student   Tom, 21, unemployed

5 In case & so that

Give advice based on these situations, using *in case* or *so that*.

Example: *They might keep you waiting.*
You should take a book …
… in case they keep you waiting.
… so that you don't get bored.

a They might not have a key.
b The traffic might be heavy.
c It might be muddy.
d They might not provide a meal.
e The weather might change.
f They might not know the way.

6 Pronunciation

How do you say the words and phrases below?

a I expect he'll write to you.
  I don't expect they'll win.
b I'll   he'll   she'll   they'll
  I'll be waiting.
  Mary will be working.
c I will have finished by then.
d You should take some water with you …
  … in case you feel thirsty.
  … so that you don't get thirsty.

 Now listen and check your answers.

12 Accidents

1 Narrow escapes

1 You will hear three people talking about narrow escapes they have had.

  a Look at the pictures. What do you think happened?
  Use words from the box to help you.

ambulance	drown	smoke
catch fire	choke	slip
fire brigade	swallow	

  b 🔲 Now listen to the stories.

2 Think of a narrow escape that you (or someone you know) has had,
  and make some notes about it.

  Tell other students what happened.

This unit is about accidents and emergencies, and focuses on the following vocabulary areas:
– verbs that describe accidents and injuries (e.g. *burn, choke, drown*)
– ways of dealing with emergencies (e.g. *call an ambulance, put a bandage on*)
– words connected with driving and road accidents (e.g. *overtake, skid, crash*).

The Reading and Listening activity is a true story of how a passenger had to take over the controls of a plane and land it.

1 Narrow escapes

In this exercise, students listen to three 'narrow escape' stories, which include key vocabulary for talking about accidents and injuries. They then tell their own 'narrow escape' story.

➤ Workbook: Exercise A

1 Presentation & listening

● Look at the pictures and ask students to guess what happened, using words from the box. As you do this, check that students know how the words are used in context. If necessary, give simple explanations and examples to make their meaning clear. Focus especially on these phrases:
– call *an* ambulance, call *the* fire brigade
– catch fire = start burning (the house is *on fire*; they *put out* the fire)
– choke (on something) = you can't breathe, because of smoke or because something is stuck in your throat.

● 🔲 Play the recording. Pause after each story and establish which picture it refers to. Then ask students to say what actually happened. Again get students to use the words in the box to talk about each story. Possible answers:

1 The lid of the record player *caught fire*; the room was full of *smoke*; she threw a wet towel over the record player; she called the *fire brigade* and they put the fire out.
2 He *slipped* and fell in the pond; he nearly *drowned*; his mother pulled him out.
3 The baby *swallowed* a coin; it got stuck in his throat and he was *choking*; she called an *ambulance*; the next-door neighbour turned the baby upside down and the coin came out.

2 Writing/speaking activity

● Give time for students to think of a narrow escape story and make brief notes. (The notes are just to help them organise their ideas, not to be given in or corrected.)
● Students sit in groups and take it in turns to tell their story.
● As a round-up, ask each group to tell their best story to the class.

Vocabulary option

Present other words describing accidental death, e.g. *suffocate, starve, die of hunger/thirst/cold, be electrocuted.*

You could elicit these words by giving examples (e.g. Imagine you're in the desert and you've got nothing to drink …).

Optional lead-in

Tell the class a narrow escape story of your own. If you like, show them how you would prepare for it by writing notes on the board.

🔲 Tapescript for Exercise 1: *Narrow escapes*

1 Well I had these friends round to dinner and, I don't know, for some reason I had this candle and I put it on the plastic lid of the record player, and forgot all about it. We went into another room to have some coffee, and I went into the kitchen to get some more coffee for a top-up, and as I went out I noticed this dreadful smell of burning. And I realised that the lid of the record player was on fire, and I looked in, there was this thick black smoke everywhere. So, well I didn't really know what to do – so I thought 'Don't throw water, get a wet towel', and I threw that over the record player lid, and went to call the fire brigade. And luckily everything was OK.

2 Well my mother tells me that when I was small, just around about a year, I very nearly drowned. I was playing by the pond in the garden, and apparently I slipped and fell in, and somehow I stood up just enough so my mouth was sticking out above the water. And I didn't cry out – I was apparently just too busy trying to breathe. And eventually my mother, who was wondering where I'd got to, came out, found me standing in the pond with my head just above the water, and she pulled me out before anything bad happened.

3 Oh, it was awful. I'd left some money on the table, and I turned round just for a second to do the dinner, and the baby put it in his mouth. It got stuck in his throat, and he couldn't breathe properly – he was choking. Well I had no idea what to do, so I called an ambulance … But what happened was Jacky, my next-door neighbour was there, and she just turned the baby upside down, slapped him on the back, and the coin came out.

2 Emergency

In this activity, students discuss what they would do in five different emergencies, and then read advice from the back of the book. This is a free exercise, but it involves the language of 'dealing with emergencies'.

Reading, writing & discussion

- Quickly read through the situations, and deal with any new vocabulary (e.g. *poisonous*, *heart attack*).
- Working alone, students write a few sentences for each situation, saying what they would and wouldn't do (e.g. I'd tie something round my leg; I'd shout 'Help!'; I wouldn't try to walk).
- Students exchange papers with someone else. Then they turn to the advice given on page 117, and use this to 'mark' their partner's paper (e.g. they could give one point for each correct answer up to a total of five).
- As a round-up, find out who got the highest score for each situation.

➤ Workbook: Exercise B

> *Alternatives*
> *1 Pairwork*
> Students work together in pairs, helping each other write one set of answers. Then they swap papers with another pair.
> *2 Whole class*
> With a weaker class, do this stage with the whole class, building up ideas on the board and helping with new words. Then look at the back of the book to see how many of your ideas were correct.

3 Bad driving

This exercise introduces a range of verbs for talking about driving and road accidents. Students use the verbs to complete gapped sentences, and then discuss what caused the accidents in the pictures. The last part of the exercise is a short role-play.

➤ Workbook: Exercise C

1 Presentation

- Look at the verbs in the box, and check that students understand what they mean.
- Students complete the sentences using correct forms of verbs in the box. Then go through the answers together. Answers:

  I had to *swerve* …
  He *braked* hard … only *missed* me by a few inches.
  Every time I tried to *overtake* her, she *accelerated*.
  She suddenly *turned* left … and almost *ran over* …
  He *skidded* on the ice and *crashed* …

> *Language note*
> *Run over* is a phrasal verb: we can say 'He nearly *ran over* a rabbit' or 'He nearly *ran* a rabbit *over*'. For other phrasal verbs of this type, see Self-study Workbook Units 8, 10 and 12.
> *Overtake* is a one-word verb: 'He *overtook* a bus.'

2 Speaking activity

- Look at the pictures and discuss briefly how the accidents might have happened (but without going into too much detail at this point). Possible answers:

  1 A was trying to overtake B, then swerved to avoid a car coming the other way (and skidded off the road).
  2 A braked because a child on a bike was in the road, and B crashed into him.
  3 A came out of a side road and crashed into B.

- Pairwork. Students choose one of the situations and take the part of A or B. They improvise an argument.
- As a round-up, ask a few pairs what conclusions they came to.

> *Optional lead-in*
> To prepare for this stage, look at the situations together and discuss what the people might say (e.g. 'It's your fault – you weren't looking.').

> *Alternative*
> Choose one of the situations. Divide the class into pairs and give each pair a letter, A or B. Together, students in each pair prepare what to say. Then students form new pairs, so that each pair has one A and one B, and act out the conversation.

2 Emergency

How good would you be in an emergency? Write down what you would do
(and what you wouldn't do) in these situations.

1 You're out walking and you get bitten in the leg by a poisonous snake.

3 You're in a hotel room on the 5th floor and the fire alarm goes. You see smoke coming under your door.

4 Someone in your family knocks a pan of boiling water off the cooker. The water goes over his/her arm.

2 You're preparing food in the kitchen when you accidentally cut yourself deeply on the hand.

5 You find an elderly relative lying on the floor. She tells you that she thinks she's had a heart attack.

Now change papers with someone else, and check their answers at the back of the book.
Give up to five points for each.

3 Bad driving

1 Fill the gaps using verbs from the box.

turn	overtake	run over
crash	miss	accelerate
skid	brake	swerve

2 *a* Look at these accidents. How do you think they happened?

b In pairs, choose one of the accidents. Imagine you are the two people involved. Try to decide whose fault it was.

He suddenly pulled out of a side road and I had to .... to avoid him.

He .... hard and managed to stop in time. But it was close – he only .... me by a few inches.

She just wouldn't let me get past. Every time I tried to .... her, she ....

She suddenly .... left without indicating, and almost .... two pedestrians.

He was going much too fast. He .... on the ice and .... straight into the back of me.

4 You're on your own

READING

1 Look at the headlines and the pictures. What is the story about?

2 Now read the opening paragraph.
When Les Rhoades had a heart attack

– what were he and Alan Anderson doing?
– what did Anderson do?
– what did Robert Legge do?

3 Now read the rest of the article.
Which of these sentences are true of

– Anderson?   – Legge?   – neither of them?

a He had never been in a plane before.	*e* He gave very clear instructions.
b He didn't know how to use the radio.	*f* He was terrified.
c He was a flying instructor.	*g* He made a perfect landing.
d He took off as soon as he heard the emergency call.	*h* He wants to learn how to fly.
	i He was shocked by his experience.

4 What was particularly impressive about the behaviour of

– Anderson?   – Legge?

LISTENING

🔲 You will hear a reconstruction of part of the radio conversation between Legge and Anderson.

Before you listen, read the notes in the box.

Now listen to the recording. What does Legge tell Anderson to do at each of the stages 1–4 in the picture?

When you're flying a plane ...

- ... you hold the *control column*. Move it forward to drop the nose of the plane; pull it back to raise it.
- ... you *bank* (or turn) by moving the control column left or right.
- ... you open the *throttle* to speed up, and close it to slow down.
- ... you control the *rudder* with *rudder pedals*; when you're on the ground, these act as brakes.

4 You're on your own

This combined reading and listening activity describes a real event in which someone who had never flown before had to land a light aircraft single-handed. The reading is an adaptation of a newspaper article describing what happened, and the listening is a reconstruction of parts of the actual conversation between the pilot and a flying instructor who helped him to land.

READING

- Look at the headlines and the pictures, and get students to guess what the article is about and what happened. As you do this, write key vocabulary on the board (e.g. *pilot*, *land*, *heart attack*, *instructor*, *emergency*).

- Give time for students to read the opening paragraph, then check answers to Question 2. Answers:
  - He was flying the plane. Anderson was sitting in the plane as a passenger (on his first flight).
  - Anderson took over the controls, and called for help on the radio.
  - Robert Legge flew along behind him and told him how to land the plane.

  If necessary, focus on some of the difficult vocabulary in the paragraph (e.g. *nightmare*, *collapse*, *fatal*).

- Students read the rest of the article and answer Questions 3 and 4. Answers:

  3 *a* Anderson
     b Neither (Les Rhoades had shown Anderson how to use it.)
     c Legge
     d Neither (Legge was already in the air.)
     e Legge
     f Anderson
     g Anderson (and Legge!)
     h Neither
     i Anderson

  4 *Possible answers:*
     Anderson didn't panic although he was terrified, and managed to land the plane safely.
     Legge kept calm, and was able to show him how to land the plane.

LISTENING

- Read through the notes with the class. If necessary, explain some of the items, e.g.
  - the *control column* is a lever – looks like the gear lever in a car.
  - the *throttle* is like the accelerator in a car.
  - the *rudder* is at the back – like the rudder on a boat.

- Play the recording, stopping after each section to establish what Legge tells Anderson to do. Answers:

  The tapescript is on page T57.

  1 Forward on the controls. Let the plane fly itself. Read the air speed. Relax.
  2 Turn/Roll to the left. Keep at the same height. A little more power.
  3 Bank (turn) to the right. Pull the control column back. Close the throttle. Relax.
  4 Press both rudder pedals (which act as brakes). Turn the ignition keys off and take them out. Unstrap yourself.

■□ Tapescript for Exercise 4: *You're on your own*

A Forward on the controls. That's fine. Let the aeroplane fly itself.
B I wish it would.
A Read the air speed.
B The air speed is about 105.
A I am on your right-hand side. Just relax ...

A ... We are going to do a left-hand circuit. Try to keep that height. Keep the turn going all the way round again.
B I understand but how do you stop it?
A Maintain the height, little more power. That's good ... keep turning to the left. Roll the aircraft in a gentle bank to the left. That's fine ... gently bank to the left, if necessary a little bit of power ...

A ... I'm going to attempt to get you down.
B Going down, are we?
A We are shortly, yes. Bank gently to the right. We are aiming for the wide tarmac strip to the right of the white and red lights. Can you see it?
B Affirmative.
A Pull back very gently on the control column. Close the throttle, just hold it there. Hold it. Hold it. Hold it. Hold the control column back ... relax. OK ...

A ... Press the top of the rudder pedals. You will find the brakes. Press both rudder pedals together ... you will find the brakes.
B The engine still hasn't stopped.
A Can you see some keys in the ignition?
B Affirmative.
A Turn the keys to 'off' and take them out. The engine should then stop.
B The key's out.
A Has the engine stopped?
B Just stopping now.
A Unstrap yourself and the emergency services will see to you.
B Thank God.
A You're welcome. All in a day's work.

Self-study Workbook

Exercise A: Bad luck
Students write short descriptions of accidents, based on pictures and given vocabulary.

Exercise B: Dos and don'ts
Students say what you should and shouldn't do in three kinds of emergency.

Exercise C: On the road
Car and driving vocabulary.
Students solve an acrostic puzzle.

New words
Space to record new words with notes and examples.

Translation
Key sentences for translation.

Listening: Narrow escapes
Students hear the start of two 'narrow escape' stories, and try to predict how they will continue, with the help of questions. Then they listen and check their answers.

Phrasal verbs: Transitive verbs (3)
Transitive phrasal verbs with a person as object (e.g. *make someone out, let someone down*). Students put them appropriately in sentences.

Writing skills: Joining ideas: clauses and phrases
Joining ideas using *because, although* or *except that* followed by a clause, or using *because of, in spite of* or *except for / apart from* followed by a phrase. Students complete sentences, then use key items to join together groups of ideas.

PASSENGER LANDS PLANE AFTER PILOT DIES

It's the air passenger's nightmare ... the pilot collapses and you are forced to seize the controls to save your own life. For Alan Anderson, 24, it became reality when his girlfriend's father Les Rhoades suffered a fatal heart attack at 2,200 ft over the Welsh coast on Sunday. The pilot of a second light aircraft, Robert Legge, responded to his radio call for help and, trailing behind, calmly gave instructions on how to land.

Alan Anderson: "I'll never fly again"

ALAN ANDERSON had never flown before. So he was looking forward to an exciting time when his future father-in-law, Les Rhoades, aged 63, invited him up for a ride in his light plane. What he hadn't expected was that Mr Rhoades would suffer a heart attack while they were in the air. Fortunately for Mr Anderson, Mr Rhoades had shown him how to operate the radio, so he was able to radio for help.

MAYDAY MAYDAY

Robert Legge, an instructor with the Cardiff Flying School who was in a plane a few miles away, was asked to help by air traffic controllers after they received an emergency call from Mr Anderson, saying: "Mayday, Mayday, my father-in-law has had a heart attack and I don't know how to fly."

Mr Legge pulled alongside Mr Anderson's plane and told him by radio how to fly the aircraft. He took him through a practice landing and then helped him bring the plane down safely at Cardiff Airport just after 7 p.m.

INCREDIBLE FEAT

Mr Legge said last night: "It was an incredible feat for anyone, let alone someone for the first time ever in a light aircraft. He was fantastically calm. When I kept telling him what controls to use, the repeated reply was 'OK, but I've never done this before', but he never sounded frightened."

He added: "We had one chance to get it right and, thank God, we succeeded. The worst bit was coming over the runway for the landing when I felt as though I was no longer in control, but he made a perfect landing. He did marvellously well."

DEEP SHOCK

After his ordeal, Mr Anderson was put under sedation for deep shock, and is now resting at his fiancée's home near Cardiff. He said yesterday: "After what I have been through, nothing will get me on a plane again. I've never been so terrified in my whole life, but I knew I had to keep calm." And he thanked Mr Legge, saying: "I didn't have a clue what to do, but Robert put me at ease and I just gritted my teeth and concentrated on the job in hand."

Robert Legge: he flew alongside

The plane's cockpit: a nightmare line-up of knobs, dials and lights

31 March 1992

Review: Units 7–12

Find out

1 A What can you remember about your early childhood?
  B Help A to remember by asking questions.

2 Find out what other students would do
  – if they were stuck in a lift
  – if they won £1 million
  – if someone pulled out a knife in the street and said 'Hand over your money.'

3 A Imagine yourself at the age of 65. What will you be like? What will you be doing? What will you have done? Answer B's questions.
  B Ask as many different questions as you can.

Role-play

1 A You're having a party tonight. What have you done to prepare for it? Make some notes, then answer B's questions.
  B Write a list of things for A to do. Then check whether he/she's done them.

2 A You've got a bad toothache. Ring up the dentist and make an appointment.
  B You're the dentist. You're very busy. Do your best to give A an appointment.

3 A You're going camping for the first time. Ask B for advice about what to do, what to take, what to expect.
  B You're an experienced camper. Answer A's questions, and give reasons for your advice.

Conversational English

1 Making suggestions

1 🔲 You will hear some suggestions. Which suggestions do you think go with each situation?

Make a list of the structures you heard.

2 Work in groups. How many suggestions can you make for each of these situations? Use a range of structures for each one.

– It's your teacher's birthday next week.
– One of you is thinking of taking a holiday job.
– You want to give a party with a difference.

Find out

1 Revision of language from Unit 7, and also Unit 3

- Establish a range of possible questions (e.g. Who did you play with? What did you do at the weekend? Did you have many toys?), and get one or two students to answer each of the questions. Focus on opportunities to use *used to* in answering the questions.
- Pairwork. Students take it in turns to ask each other questions.
- Round-up. Ask a few students what they found out.

2 Revision of language from Unit 9

- Groupwork. Students think of different things they would do in each situation.
- Look at each situation in turn, and ask each group what they would do.

3 Revision of language from Unit 11

- Tell students how you imagine yourself at the age of 65, and get them to ask you questions. If necessary, use this to focus on *will be doing* and *will have done*.
- Pairwork. Students take it in turns to imagine being 65.
- Round-up. Ask a few students what they found out.

Role-play

1 Revision of language from Unit 7

- Preparation. Establish a few examples of questions B might ask and the answers A might give (e.g. B: Have you bought paper plates? A: Yes, I've bought 200 *or* No, I haven't. I've already got plenty of plates at home).
- Working alone, students write lists of preparations.
- Pairwork. B finds out what A has and hasn't done.
- Round-up. Ask a few students whether their partner was well prepared for his/her party.

2 Revision of language from Unit 8

- Preparation. Establish some of the things that A and B might say (e.g. *A* Can I make an appointment for today? It's very urgent. *B* I'm afraid I'm very busy. I can't see you today. Could you come tomorrow morning?).
- Students improvise the conversation.
- Round-up. Ask a few students how soon they managed to get an appointment.

3 Revision of language from Unit 11

- Preparation. Establish some of the topics that A might ask about (e.g. where to go, clothes, equipment, food, insects). Build up a few useful expressions on the board (e.g. *Should I ...?, in case, so that, You'll probably need ..., It's a good idea to ...*).
- Pairwork. Students improvise the conversation.
- Round-up. Ask a few 'campers' what advice they were given.

1 Making suggestions

This exercise practises a range of expressions for making informal suggestions which include yourself (e.g. Shall we ...?, Why don't we ...?, Let's ...*) and others (e.g.* Why don't you ...?, You could ...*).*

1 Listening & presentation

- Play the recording, pausing after each remark, and asking students which situation it goes with. Answers:

  I don't feel like cooking tonight:
  – We could always just have some bread and cheese.
  – Why don't we try that new restaurant?
  – How about getting a take-away pizza?
  It's a lovely day. What shall we do?
  – Shall we drive down to the coast?
  – What about going for a picnic?
  Oh no! The TV's not working!
  – Let's have an early night.
  – I suppose we could just talk to each other.
  – We could always play cards.
  It's getting a bit hot, isn't it?
  – Let's go and get a Coke.
  – Why don't you go and sit in the shade?

- Build up a table of suggestion structures on the board:

Let's ...	What/How about ...?
Why don't we/you ...?	We/You could (always) ...
Shall we ...?	I suppose we/you could ...

2 Practice

- Groupwork. Students look at each situation in turn, and go round the group making as many different suggestions as they can.
- As a round-up, go through the situations together.

> Tapescript for *Making suggestions*
>
> – Shall we drive down to the coast?
> – We could always just have some bread and cheese.
> – Let's have an early night.
> – I suppose we could just talk to each other.
> – What about going for a picnic?
> – Let's go and get a Coke.
> – We could always play cards.
> – Why don't we try that new restaurant?
> – Why don't you go and sit in the shade?
> – How about getting a take-away pizza?

Talking points

This activity revises language from all six units:

– *The past five years: good and bad changes*	*Unit 7*
– *Making an international phone call*	*Unit 8*
– *A job you wouldn't like to have*	*Units 8, 9*
– *'I wish ...'*	*Unit 9*
– *Buying things second-hand*	*Unit 10*
– *Next year's news*	*Unit 11*
– *'I hope ...'*	*Unit 11*
– *Dos and Don'ts on the road*	*Unit 12*

The activity can be played as a game round the class. One student chooses a topic and says a sentence or two about it. Another student then continues, adding another sentence, and so on.

As a preparation, you could let students choose two or three of the topics and look back at the appropriate unit to recall things they might say. If they like, they could also make brief notes.

Words

1 Revision of language from Unit 8

- Students write sentences. Then go through the answers, focusing on the structure *have something done*.

2 Revision of language from Units 8, 10 & 12

- Students write down as many words as they can think of.
- Build up lists of expressions on the board, e.g. book, ticket, member, librarian, fine, bring back; plastic, leather, stone, paper, rubber, cotton; smoke, flame, ash, fire brigade, fireman, water.

3 Revision of language from Unit 10

- Students write definitions for each of the items. Then go through the answers together. Possible answers:

  It's a small thing made of metal that you use to make pencils sharp. It's a machine for washing the dishes after you've finished eating. It's a big knife that you use for cutting (carving) meat. It's a square piece of wood; you play chess on it.

4 Revision of language from Units 11 & 12

- Use the questions to focus on key vocabulary from the units. Possible answers:

  You might get an electric shock / be electrocuted.
  You might (fall in the water and) drown.
  It might get stuck in his/her throat; he/she might choke.
  You might crash into another car / have an accident.

2 Finding things in common

This exercise practises short answers used for finding similarities and differences between yourself and other people (e.g. So do I, Nor have I, I don't).

1 Presentation & practice

- Ask students to match the replies to the remarks. Answers:

  I love computer games.
  – So do I. I spend hours playing them.
  – I don't. I think they're a complete waste of time.
  I've never been to Los Angeles.
  – Nor have I, but I'd love to go.
  – I have. I went when I was a baby.
  My dad was really strict when I was little.
  – So was mine. He was always telling me what to do.
  – Mine wasn't. He let me do whatever I liked.

- Use the examples to focus on the key structures, and present them on the board:

So	do did can have will	I.	I	do(n't). did(n't). can('t). have(n't). will (won't).
Nor				

- Point out that to avoid repeating 'my father', 'my friends', 'my car', etc., we simply say *mine*.
- Pairwork. Students have two-line conversations, either finding things in common or not.
- As a round-up, go through each item, asking different pairs what they said. Possible replies:

  – So have I. Nor have I. I have. I haven't.
  – So was I. Nor was I. I was. I wasn't.
  – So does mine. Nor does mine. Mine does. Mine doesn't.
  – So would I. Nor would I. I would. I wouldn't.
  – So do I. Nor do I. I do. I don't.
  – So am I. Nor am I. I am. I'm not.

2 Speaking activity

- Students write one or two sentences about themselves.
- Groupwork. Students read out their sentences, and find out if others in the group are similar.
- As a round-up, ask each group to tell you what they have in common.

Self-study Workbook

There is a review test of Units 7–12 on pages 60–1. The test is in six parts:
Sentence rewriting, Verb forms, Vocabulary, Fill the gaps, Writing paragraphs and Dictation.

Talking points

Choose one of these topics. Take it in turns to say a sentence or two about it.

The past five years: good and bad changes

Making an international phone call

A job you wouldn't like to have

'I wish ...'

Buying things second-hand

Next year's news

'I hope ...'

***Dos* and *Don'ts* on the road**

Words

1 **Why might you go to these places?**
   – a dry cleaner's   – a hairdresser's
   – a photographer's   – an optician's

2 **Add words to these lists.**
   – library, borrow ...
   – wood, metal ...
   – fire, burn ...

3 **What are the following?**
   – a pencil sharpener   – a carving knife
   – a dishwasher   – a chessboard

4 **Say what might happen if**
   – you mend a light without switching it off
   – you go sailing without a life jacket
   – you give a small child peanuts to eat
   – you overtake someone on a bend.

2 Finding things in common

1 *a* Look at the three remarks on the left, and find two replies for each.

   What replies would *you* give?

I love computer games.

I've never been to Los Angeles.

My dad was really strict when I was little.

Mine wasn't. He let me do whatever I liked.

I have. I went when I was a baby.

I don't. I think they're a complete waste of time.

So was mine. He was always telling me what to do.

So do I. I spend hours playing them.

Nor have I, but I'd love to go.

b Work in pairs. Have similar conversations starting with these remarks.
   – I've *seen / never seen* a UFO.
   – I *was/wasn't* a very quiet child.
   – My mother *goes out / doesn't go out* to work.
   – I'd *like / wouldn't like* to live in Hawaii.
   – I *believe / don't believe* in ghosts.
   – I'm */ I'm not* interested in politics.

2 Work in groups. Think of one or two sentences of your own – facts about yourself, opinions, things you like or don't like. Find out how much you have in common with the others.

13 Comparing and evaluating

1 National differences

Comparison structures

1 You will hear people from France, Japan and the USA talking about differences between Britain and their own country.
What do you think their opinions will be? Complete the sentences.

> .... is much more crowded than Britain.

> Britain's a safer place to live than ....

> In Britain, people have much more respect for the law than in ....

> In .... , people are more interested in each other than they are in Britain.

> The British don't spend as much time over their meals as the ....

> People aren't as honest in Britain as they are in ....

Now listen to the recording and see if you were right. Do they mention any other differences?

2 Write down three differences between your own country and another country.

This unit deals with language used for making comparisons and evaluating good and bad features. It focuses on three main areas of grammar:
– comparative forms of adjectives and adverbs
– comparative structures with *(much) -er than*, *(much) more … than* and *not (nearly) as … as*
– expressions of degree, using *too* and *not enough.*

1 National differences

In this activity, students hear people making comparisons between Britain and their own country. This is used to focus on key comparison structures, and then acts as a model for them to make similar comparisons.

➤ Focus on Form: Exercises 1, 2
➤ Workbook: Exercises A, D

1 *Listening & presentation*

- Look at the opinions, and ask students to decide which person is most likely to express each one. Students fill each gap with one of the three choices, e.g. *Japan is much more crowded than Britain.*

- 🔲 Play the recording, and check the answers:

  The Frenchman: The British don't spend as much time over their meals; they have more respect for the law.

  The American: American people are more interested in each other; Britain's safer.

  The Japanese woman: Japan is more crowded; the British aren't as honest.

- Point out that all the examples on the page use comparative structures. Use these as a basis for building up two tables on the board:

| X is | (much) (far) | more dangerous | than Y. |
| | (a bit) (slightly) | safer | |

| Y isn't | (nearly) | as | dangerous | as Y. |
| | (quite) | | safe | |

> **Language note**
> *Y isn't nearly as beautiful* means *X is much more beautiful* (a big difference)
> *Y isn't quite as beautiful* means *X is slightly more beautiful* (a small difference)
>
> **Practice option**
> Make sentences from one of the tables and ask for equivalent sentences from the other, e.g.
> Horses are much bigger than dogs.
> → Dogs aren't nearly as big as horses.
> London isn't quite as warm as Paris.
> → Paris is slightly warmer than London.

2 *Writing & speaking activity*

- To show how the activity works, choose a country yourself and write a few sentences on the board comparing it with your own country (but without naming the country you've chosen). See if the class can guess the country.

- In pairs or groups, students choose a country and write sentences.

- Students read out their sentences and the rest of the class try to guess the country.

> **Alternative for mixed nationality classes**
> Students write sentences comparing the country they are visiting with their own country. They show their sentences to other students from the same country and see if they agree. This could lead into a general class discussion.

🔲 Tapescript for Exercise 1: *National differences*

1 In France most of the people want to have a very long time for lunch. In Britain it doesn't seem to be important because people take a cup of tea and a very quick sandwich and it's OK.

2 Another very surprising thing for the foreigner is the way the people obey the law – you seem to have much more discipline than in France, and you respect the police much more than we do. For instance, people park their car everywhere, and they know it is forbidden but they do it – in Britain people don't do that.

3 In England it's easier to feel alone, people don't bother you, don't look after you or worry about you so much, so it's easy to get sort of, to get lost or to hide away here. When you're in the United States people want to know who you are, they tend to speak to you, to find out who you are, what you're doing.

4 Yes, one thing I should mention is that the United States is I think a much more exciting place to be than England, but there is a drawback and that is, you do have this sense of danger in the United States, especially in big cities, that you don't get so much in England or Britain as a whole. You feel safe in England.

5 Japanese houses are really small and people live close to each other, and there aren't so many parks, there aren't so many places where you can play when you are little, and it's very difficult for people to relax.

6 Japan is quite safe, and you can leave your handbag behind when you leave the room without being really careful about it. But in Britain you really have to keep eye on your handbag when you leave the room, and you have to take it with you when you leave.

2 Who does it best?

This exercise takes the form of a logic puzzle. It contrasts adjectives and adverbs, and introduces comparative structures using adverbs.

1 Reading & presentation

- Working alone or in pairs, students work out who is the best at each activity, and complete the table with numbers 1, 2 or 3. Then go through the answers together, completing a table on the board:

	swim	sing	English	write
Amanda	1	2	2	2
Brian	2	1	3	3
Claire	3	3	1	1

- Ask students to identify adjectives and adverbs from the texts:
  Adjectives: (a) *better* (swimmer), (he's) *better, fluent, bad*.
  Adverbs: *neatly, well, fast, fluently, beautifully,* (speaks English) *better*.

- Show how we form comparative structures with adverbs:

He writes	faster more neatly	than I do.

  Point out that
  – adverbs that add *-ly* form the comparative with more (e.g. *more quickly*).
  – adverbs that are *the same as adjectives* add *-er* (e.g. *faster, earlier*).
  – *well → better* is irregular.

- Practise these forms by asking students to make sentences from the table, e.g.
  Amanda swims faster than Claire. Claire writes more neatly than Brian.

2 Speaking activity

- Divide students into groups of three. They discuss the activities and find out who does each one best.

- As a round-up, ask each group what they found out.

3 Not good enough

This activity introduces the language functions of criticising and complaining, using the structures too *and* not enough *with adjectives, adverbs and nouns.*

1 Presentation

- Students look at the sentences and match them with the pictures. Answers:
  Tourist scene: not warm enough; not enough for the children to do.
  Lecture: went on far too long; spoke too fast; room not big enough.
  Party: not enough food; too many people smoking; music too loud.

- Show how *too* and *not enough* are used with adjectives and nouns:

ADJECTIVE or ADVERB	too	long noisy	not	good fast	enough
NOUN	too	much wine many		not enough	people food

  Point out that
  – *enough* comes after adjectives and adverbs, but before nouns
  – we say 'not enough people', *not* 'not enough of people'.

- Ask students to suggest other possible complaints, e.g.
  – He spoke too quietly; there weren't enough seats.
  – There weren't enough glasses; it was too hot.
  – The restaurants were too expensive; the sea was too cold to swim in.

2 Speaking/writing activity

- Pairwork. Students think of suitable continuations for each remark.

- Go through the answers together. Some possible continuations:
  a The teacher spoke too fast; there weren't enough books.
  b The service was too slow; there weren't enough waiters.
  c You eat too much butter; you don't get enough exercise.
  d The workers aren't paid enough; the coffee breaks aren't long enough.

➤ Focus on Form: Exercise 3
➤ Workbook: Exercise B

Presentation option
Establish that
– adjectives are used with nouns or after the verb 'to be' (She's a *good* swimmer, She's *good* at swimming).
– adverbs are used with verbs (She swims *well*).
– *better* is the comparative of both *good* and *well* (She's a *better* swimmer; she swims *better*).

Presentation option
Introduce superlative forms of adjectives and adverbs:
She's *the fastest* swimmer.
She swims *the fastest*.
She's *the most fluent* speaker.
She speaks *the most fluently*.

Optional lead-in
Point out that we can talk about skills in three ways:
– I'm (not) *a good* swimmer.
– I'm (not) *good at* swimming.
– I (don't) swim *well*.

➤ Focus on Form: Exercises 4, 5
➤ Workbook: Exercise C

Language note
The captions include examples of more extended structures with *too* and *not enough*:

too …
not … enough | (for us) to + inf.

If you like, point these forms out and give more examples, e.g.
The river was too wide (for us) to cross.
The wall was too high (for them) to climb over.

Note that with certain structures the object pronoun is dropped:
The water was too cold to swim in (not ~~too cold to swim in it~~).

These structures are practised in Focus on Form Ex. 5 and in the Self-study Workbook, Ex. C.

Alternative
Students work in groups. Give each group a different remark. Together they write down a continuation, and pass their paper to the next group to add another idea. Continue until each remark has five or six continuations, then ask each group to read them out.

2 Who does it best?

Adjectives & adverbs

Amanda

I'm a faster swimmer than Brian, but he's better at singing than I am. His English isn't as fluent as mine, and you should see his handwriting – I write much more neatly!

Brian

Poor Claire – she can hardly sing at all, and she doesn't swim very fast either – not as fast as I do, anyway! But she speaks English more fluently than I do.

Claire

I wish I could sing as beautifully as Amanda – unfortunately I've got a very bad singing voice. But I speak English better than she does, and I certainly write more neatly!

	swimming	singing	English	writing
Amanda				
Brian				
Claire				

1 Which of these three people
- is the fastest swimmer?
- is the best at singing?
- speaks English the most fluently?
- has the neatest handwriting?

2 Work in threes.
Talk about the same activities. Find out who does each of them best.

3 Not good enough

too & enough

He spoke too fast.

There wasn't enough food.

The music was much too loud.

There wasn't enough for the children to do.

It was quite interesting, but it went on far too long.

It wasn't warm enough to sit on the beach.

Too many people were smoking.

The room wasn't big enough.

1 Look at the complaints in the bubbles. Which pictures do you think they go with?

What else do you think was wrong?

2 Continue these remarks with a complaint using *too* or *enough*.
a My first English lesson was a disaster …
b I'll never go to that restaurant again …
c If you carry on like this, you're going to have a heart attack …
d Working conditions at the factory are terrible …

4 Awards

Musician of the Year

Best Place to Live

Politician of the Year

Funniest TV Show

Best Night Spot

Best Restaurant

1 Who or what would you nominate for these awards?
Think of one or two candidates for each.

2 Work in groups. Choose one of the awards, and together decide which candidate should win it.

Tell the rest of the class which candidate you chose, and why.

Grammar Checklist

Comparative adjectives & adverbs

Adjectives: bigger, easier; **more** interesting, **more** careful.
Adverbs: faster, louder; **more** easily, **more** carefully.
Irregular: good → **better**; well → **better**.

Comparative structures

... -er than
more ... than

| Your room is | tidier / more attractive | than mine. |

| She drives | faster / more slowly | than I do. |

as ... as ...
He's **as** tall **as** his father.
I'm nearly **as** old **as** you.
My room isn't **as** tidy **as** yours.
I don't drive **as** fast **as** she does.

Big & small differences

Your room is **far/much** tidier than mine.
My room isn't **nearly** as tidy as yours.

She drives **slightly/a bit** faster than I do.
I don't drive **quite** as fast as she does.

too & not enough

too + *adjective or adverb*
too much/many + *noun*

You work **too** hard.
It's **too** cold to swim.
There are **too many** people here.

not + *adjective or adverb* + **enough**
not enough + *noun*

The table isn't big **enough**.
He couldn't walk fast **enough**.
There isn't **enough** food to eat.

See also Reference section, page 136.

4 Awards

This is a free discussion activity in which students give awards to the best people, places, etc., in different categories. The activity focuses on superlatives (best, funniest, etc.), but also gives an opportunity to make comparisons between people and places in discussing potential candidates.

1 Preparation

- Working alone or in pairs, students consider each category in turn and write down the names of one or two candidates.

2 Discussion

- Students form larger groups (five or six). Taking each category in turn, they read out the names of their candidates, and give reasons why they think they deserve the award. Together, they try to agree on one best candidate for each award.
- As a round-up, ask each group to report back on the candidates they chose and why.

Optional lead-in

To give the idea of the activity, tell the class who you would nominate for one or two of the awards. Explain why, and ask students whether they agree with you.

Optional extension

As a final stage, write a 'short list' of candidates on the board. Students then vote for any of the candidates apart from the one their group chose, and an overall winner is chosen for each award.

Focus on Form

1 *Big and small differences*

> Comparative adjective structures using *slightly / a bit* and *much/far*

- Look at the example. Then divide students into pairs for the activity.
- Go through the answers together. Answers:
  - France uses much more nuclear power than Spain.
  - Elvis Presley lived slightly longer than Mozart.
  - Sugar is a bit more fattening than flour.
  - The French drink far more alcohol than the British.
  - Los Angeles is much bigger than San Francisco.
  - Mount Kilimanjaro is much higher than Mount Fuji.

2 *Not as ... as ...*

> Comparison structures with *not as* + adj. + *as*

- Students write true sentences based on the facts in Exercise 1, using *not quite as ... as* (for small differences) and *not nearly as ... as* (for large differences). Answers:
  - a Spain doesn't use nearly as much nuclear power as France.
  - b Mozart didn't live quite as long as Elvis Presley.
  - c Flour isn't quite as fattening as sugar.
  - d San Francisco isn't nearly as big as Los Angeles.
  - e The British don't drink nearly as much alcohol as the French.
  - f Mount Fuji isn't nearly as high as Mount Kilimanjaro.

3 *Adverbs*

> Adverbs and comparative adverbs

- Students complete the table. Then go through the answers together. Answers:

quickly – more quickly	early – earlier
fast – faster	clearly – more clearly
slowly – more slowly	well – better
hard – harder	

- Students say their sentences round the class, or write them down.

4 *Finding fault: too & enough*

> *too* and *not enough* with adjectives and nouns

- Either ask students to suggest sentences round the class, or let them discuss the items in pairs and then go through the answers together. Possible answers:
  - a It's too cold, it's not strong enough, it's got too much sugar.
  - b It's too slow, there aren't enough buses, the buses are too crowded.
  - c There aren't enough seats, the drinks are too expensive, the service is too slow.
  - d It uses too much petrol, it doesn't go fast enough, it doesn't have enough room for luggage.
  - e They make too much noise, they go to bed too late.

5 *Too/enough to ...*

> Structures with *too/not enough* + *to* + infinitive

- Students do the exercise in pairs. Then go through the answers together. Answers:

  I don't play well enough to get in the team.
  The water's too cold to swim in.
  She speaks too fast (for me) to understand.
  She's too busy to talk to you just now.
  I haven't got enough money to go on holiday this year.
  That road's too dangerous for children to play in.
  My mother's too old to go out on her own.

  Emphasise that we say *too cold to swim in*, *too dangerous to play in*, *too fast to understand*: the final object pronoun is omitted.

6 *Pronunciation*

▢ Ask students to try saying the sentences themselves, then play the recording as a model. Focus on these points:
  - a Reduced vowels in *safer than* /'seɪfə ðən/, *bigger than* /'bɪgə ðən/.
  - b Reduced vowels in *as well as* /əz 'wel əz/.
  - c Pronunciation of *enough*: /ə'nʌf/ or /ɪ'nʌf/.
  - d Contrast between *too* /tuː/ and *to* /tə/ in *too high to* /tuː 'haɪ tə/.

Self-study Workbook

Exercise A: Small and big differences
Comparison of adjectives. Sentence rewriting.

Exercise B: Comparison of adjectives and adverbs
Students fill gaps in sentences from a table of adjectives and adverbs.

Exercise C: Too and enough
Students write explanations of four events, using *too* and *enough*.

Exercise D: I'd rather ...
Students choose from a list of items, and write a paragraph saying which they prefer and why.

Translation
Key sentences for translation.

Listening: Living in Britain
Three people say what they find strange about Britain. Students listen and answer comprehension questions.

Pronunciation: Linking words: consonant + consonant
'Links' between words ending and beginning with consonants. Students read sentences and predict where the links will be.

Reading: Left-handedness
Students read a number of short texts about left-handedness and answer comprehension questions.

Focus on Form

1 Big and small differences

...	slightly a bit	Adj. + -er	than ...
	much far	more + Adj.	

Student A: Can you guess the answers to the questions below? Do you think there's a big difference or a small one? Use the structures in the table.

Student B: Look at the facts on page 118. Tell A if he/she is right or wrong.

Example: *Which is bigger, the Atlantic or the Pacific?*

The Pacific is much bigger than the Atlantic.

a Which country uses more nuclear power, France or Spain?
b Who lived longer, Elvis Presley or Mozart?
c Which is more fattening, flour or sugar?
d Which is bigger, Los Angeles or San Francisco?
e Who drink more alcohol, the British or the French?
f Which is higher, Mount Fuji or Mount Kilimanjaro?

2 Not as ... as ...

Write sentences with *not as ... as ...* based on the facts in Exercise 1.

Example:

The Atlantic isn't (nearly) as big as the Pacific.

3 Adverbs

Look at these adjectives. Write the adverb forms in the table.

	Adverb	*Comparative adverb*
quick	quickly	
fast	fast	
slow		
hard		
early		
clear		
good		

Use three comparative adverb forms in sentences of your own.

4 Finding fault: too & enough

What might be wrong with the things below? Complain about them using *too* and *not enough*.

Example: *a plate of hamburgers and chips*

The chips aren't hot enough.
The hamburgers are too greasy.
There aren't enough chips.
There's too much ketchup.

a a cup of coffee
b the local bus service
c a bar
d your car
e your neighbours

5 Too/enough to ...

Student A: Start a sentence using *too* or *not enough*.

Student B: Complete the sentence using *to* + infinitive.

Example:

A The wall isn't high enough ...
B ... to keep burglars out.

A	B
The wall isn't very high.	She doesn't go out on her own.
I don't play very well.	I can't go on holiday this year.
The water's cold.	It won't keep burglars out.
She speaks fast.	Children shouldn't play in it.
She's rather busy.	I can't understand her.
I haven't got much money.	Don't swim in it.
That road's dangerous.	She can't talk to you just now.
My mother's very old.	I won't get in the team.

6 Pronunciation

How do you say the words and phrases below?

a Japan's much safer than the USA.
   France is a bit bigger than Britain.

b She doesn't play as well as I do.

c It's not fast enough.
   There aren't enough people.

d The wall's too high to jump over.

Now listen and check your answers.

1 In print

1 Look at the picture. What are the people reading?

2 Work in groups. Answer the questionnaire.
How much have you got in common?

Questionnaire

1 Which of your national newspapers do you think is
– the best?
– the worst?

2 Which of these is true?
a I buy a newspaper every day
b I buy one sometimes.
c I read someone else's.

3 Which part of the newspaper do you turn to first?
Which parts do you *never* read?

4 Do you buy
– a weekly magazine?
– a monthly magazine?
What do you like about them?

5 You're in a dentist's waiting room, and these are the only magazines on the table. Which of them would you read?

ON OTHER PAGES

Home news	2–5
International news	6–10
Financial news	11–12
Leading articles	13
Letters	14
Arts & Entertainment	15–16
Obituaries	17
Classified advertisements	17
Horoscope	18
Cartoons	18
TV and Radio	19–20
Sport	21–24
Weather	24
Crossword	24

Now imagine that your group is going on a long train journey. You can only afford *one* newspaper and *one* magazine. Can you agree on what to buy?

This unit is concerned with two language areas:
– vocabulary associated with newspapers and magazines
– language for talking about TV programmes.
The Reading and Listening activity is about the variety of channels available on cable radio in Japan.

1 In print

This exercise introduces language used for talking about newspapers and magazines. The picture and the newspaper 'Contents' list are used to focus on key vocabulary, and this is drawn on in discussing answers to the questionnaire.

➤ Workbook: Exercise A

1 Presentation

● Discuss what the people in the picture are reading: a serious or 'quality' newspaper, a magazine (probably a woman's magazine), a children's comic, a popular ('tabloid') newspaper.

● Look at the Contents list of the newspaper, and check that students understand what all the items mean. Focus especially on:
– Home news = news about your own country
– International or foreign news = news about other countries
– Financial news = news about money and business
– Leading articles = articles written by the editor, giving the newspaper's own opinion
– Arts & Entertainment = what's on at the theatre, cinema, etc., and reviews
– Obituaries = articles about famous people who have died
– Classified advertisements: also called 'small ads'
– Cartoons = picture stories.

Point out that *news* is a singular noun in English, so we say 'The sports news *is* interesting' (not '~~are interesting~~').

Presentation option
To focus on this vocabulary, suggest things students may want to read about, and ask them what page they would turn to, e.g. You want to find out what's happening in Somalia; you want to know what will happen to you next week; a famous actor died yesterday, and you want to read about him.

2 Speaking activity

● Pairwork. Students read the questionnaire and discuss their answers with their partner.

● Go through the questionnaire with the whole class, getting answers to each question from several different students.

Vocabulary option
This is a good opportunity to present adjectives for describing newspapers and magazines:
– *national* and *local* newspaper
– *daily* and *weekly* newspaper; *monthly* magazine.

🔲 Tapescript for Exercise 2: *Changing channels*

And our next guest has come all the way from the United States to be with us tonight. Ladies and gentlemen, Michael Douglas!

It is not yet clear exactly how the accident happened, but police believe that the lorry driver swerved to avoid a child. The driver is ...

(Sound of cars and guns)

It's amazing to think that I am standing at the very spot where, two and a half thousand years ago, the Athenian and Persian armies met at the battle of Marathon. Since then, of course, ...

And as they come into the last lap, it's still the Kenyan way out in front, and if he can keep this up he could be on his way to a new world record. And ...

Aw, you wouldn't want to shoot a friendly little rabbit now, would you? ...

– Samantha – your question for £200. What is a *didgeridoo*?
– A kind of bird?
– Come in. Oh. It's you. What do you want?
– I just ... wanted to say I was sorry about yesterday.
– A bit late for that isn't it?

Hello? Anyone here? Hello?

2 Changing channels

This exercise introduces the vocabulary of types of TV programme and people who appear on them. The last part of the exercise leads into a discussion of types of TV programme, and what students like and don't like watching.

1 Listening & presentation

- Look at the words in the box and check that students understand them. A good way to do this would be by referring to actual TV programmes (e.g. Do you watch the news? What soap operas have you seen on TV?).

- 🔲 Play the tape, pausing briefly after each 'channel change', to allow students time to write down the type of programme. Then check the answers:

  chat show; news; crime series; documentary; sports; cartoon; game show; soap; comedy

- 🔲 Play the tape again, pausing after each channel change. This time, ask students what they imagine on the screen (e.g. Chat show: there are three guests sitting on a comfortable sofa, and the host is asking them questions).

2 Discussion

- Pairwork. Students discuss which of the programmes they would choose to watch.
- As a round-up, ask students what programmes they chose and why, and say which ones you would watch yourself.

➤ Workbook: Exercise B

> *Language note*
> A *soap opera* is a serial that runs over many episodes and follows the lives of a particular group of people (e.g. *Neighbours, Dallas*). It is often called simply a *soap*.

> 🔲 The tapescript is on page T64.

> *Vocabulary option*
> Elicit vocabulary of people who appear on TV and write these on the board: *presenter, newsreader, interviewer, host, guests, actor, comedian, (sports) commentator.*

> *Optional extension*
> This could develop into a more general discussion of TV programmes and what students enjoy watching.

3 On the line

This is a discussion activity about how much freedom the media should have. The headlines are intended to touch on: intrusion by the media into people's private lives; the value of the media in uncovering the truth; censorship of sex and violence.

1 Reading & discussion

- Look at the headlines, and ask students to expand them to explain what the story behind them might have been, and also to comment on it. Help them to do this by asking questions (e.g. What do you think the teenager saw on TV? What did he do? Do you think TV was to blame?). Possible answers:

  – The press keep taking pictures and writing articles about the private lives of members of the Royal Family, and the Royal Family is complaining about it.
  – The star of a soap committed suicide. There were stories in the popular press about his private life, and his girlfriend thinks that's why he killed himself.
  – A teenager saw some violent films on TV, and then went out and started killing people, probably using the same methods as those he saw on TV.
  – A TV play contained a love scene. They decided to cut this scene out.
  – Someone has made a TV documentary about the secret service. The government has banned it because it reveals things they don't want people to know.
  – A newspaper is investigating toxic waste dumps. The government probably claims they don't exist, and the newspaper has proved that they do.

2 Discussion

- Ask students to think about the two opinions in the boxes and decide which they agree with more. To help them decide, remind them of some of the good and bad points about the media which are shown in the headlines, e.g.
  – they often publish details of people's private lives
  – they sometimes find out important secrets that people should know about
  – people may copy what they see on TV, especially scenes of sex or violence.

  When they have decided, they mark a cross on the line to show their opinion.

- Students turn to their partner and compare where they have put their crosses. They explain to their partner why they put their cross in that position.

- As a round-up, find out where most people in the class put their crosses, and who put their cross most towards the left and most towards the right. Finally, tell the class where you would put your cross, and why.

➤ Workbook: Exercise C

> *Language note: headline language*
> Exercise C in the Self-study Workbook deals with the 'grammar' of newspaper headlines.
> You might want to use this workbook exercise (either in class or as homework) before doing this activity.

> *Note*
> The photo shows press photographers trying to get a shot of Princess Diana on a Caribbean beach.

2 Changing channels

1 📼 You will hear someone changing TV channels.
Match what you hear with the programmes in the box.

cartoon
chat show
comedy show
crime series
documentary
game show
news broadcast
soap
sports programme

Now listen again, and imagine what the person can see
on the screen.

2 Which of the programmes would you carry on watching?
Does your partner agree with your choice?

3 On the line

Leave Us Alone, Say Royal Family

SOAP STAR'S SUICIDE:
'I BLAME THE PRESS'
SAYS GIRLFRIEND

TEENAGER KILLS 5
AFTER WATCHING
VIOLENT TV FILMS

LOVE SCENE CUT
FROM TV PLAY

EXCLUSIVE!
SECRET
TOXIC
WASTE
DUMPS:
THEY *DO*
EXIST
*We reveal the truth
behind the lies*

SECRET SERVICE DOCUMENTARY BANNED
Not in the national interest, says Minister

1 Look at these newspaper headlines.
What do you think the stories are behind the headlines?

2 How free do you think the media should be? Mark your position on the line.
What do you think the media should/shouldn't be allowed to do?

| The Press and TV should be allowed to do whatever they like. | | There should be very strict controls on the Press and TV. |

Find someone whose position on the line is different from yours. Compare your opinions.

4 Easy listening

What do trains, frogs, Abba, counting sheep, motorbikes and a mother's heartbeat all have in common?

HOW about tuning your radio to an all-day Swiss yodelling channel or settling down to an evening of uninterrupted Buddhist chanting?

From the 440 radio channels available on Osaka Yusen Broadcasting, Japan's largest cable-radio network, subscribers can tune into a channel featuring 24 hours of croaking frogs, or one that consists of the sound of trains pulling in and out of stations.

As well as the sounds of cicadas or percolating coffee, Osaka Yusen offers nearly 100 channels of announcer-free jazz, rock, classical music, Second World War military marches, and folk music from all over the world. Sheena Easton, Abba and Lionel Richie each have entire channels to themselves, although the repetition rate must be almost as high as that of an in-flight music channel. One student says that he most often listens to the channel that plays the sound of a revving motorcycle engine.

For those in search of more intellectual background sounds for their dinner parties, there is always the abacus-lesson channel or a range of talks on spiritual development. But anyone tired of all the above should adjust their sets to 'drowsing channels' and tune into the sheep-counting station, for example, which features a mature male voice slowly counting from one to a thousand. Then he starts again. In the background, there is the faint sound of a train moving slowly along a railway track.

For busy executives wishing to calm down after an awful day at work, there is a channel of slow synthesiser music, and another carrying only the sound of a mother's heartbeat. According to the company: 'Babies listen to this noise before they are born. It's a natural relaxant.'

4 Easy listening

This combined reading and listening activity is about a private cable radio network in Japan which has 440 different channels. The reading text is adapted from a newspaper article which describes some of the channels that are available. The listening is an interview with two foreigners who live in Japan, who explain what channels they listen to on cable radio.

READING

- Ask students to read the text quickly, just to understand enough to find an answer to Question 1. Answer:

  You can hear them all on Osaka's cable radio network.

- Ask students to read the text more closely and find answers to Question 2. Answers:

  a False. All the channels are available 24 hours a day.
  b False. The music is 'announcer-free', i.e. with no introduction or announcements.
  c True. To drowse means to be half asleep.
  d False. It also helps executives to relax.
  e False. There are 440.

- Look at Question 3, which focuses on particular vocabulary, and get students to answer either by imitating the sounds or with an explanation. Possible answers:

  – traditional Swiss singing
  – religious singing
  – the noise frogs make
  – the sound of coffee being made (a bubbling sound)
  – the sound of someone accelerating an engine while it is not moving

- Pairwork. Students look at the list of programmes and find answers to Question 4. Possible answers:

  C2: to relax; as background to a dinner party; while showing holiday photos.
  C17: to help them wake up in the morning.
  H29: to help their children get to sleep.
  J32: when phoning home or to the office, to make the other person think they are in a café.

- In pairs or groups, students look at the lists and choose three channels they would enjoy. As a round-up, ask a few students which channels they chose, and why.

LISTENING

- ▭ Play the recording, pausing after each part so that students can complete the table. Answers:

  1 Seashore and seagulls (C1); South-east Asian pop music; World Service news. To wake up in the morning.
  2 Karaoke (C25). For fun. / To learn Japanese songs.
  3 Alibi channel (telephone booth, J31). To pretend he was on his way to work.
  4 Music from India and Mexico. As background music for dinner parties.

- ▭ Look at the words in Question 2, and ask students which speaker used them and how. Then play the recording to check. Answers:

  In the morning I use it as an *alarm clock*.
  You sing along to *background music*.
  You become a *pop star* for a few minutes.
  It sounds as though you're in a *phone box*.
  I told the secretary that I'd been to a *meeting*.
  It creates a nice *atmosphere* for dinner.

Optional lead-in
Look at the words in Question 2 before you play the tape, and ask students what they would expect the speakers to say about them.

Note
The listeners mention several channels which are not included in the list on page 67, so students should give the names of the channels they hear, and not try to find them in the list.

▭ The tapescript is on page T67.

📼 Tapescript for Exercise 4: *Easy listening*

1 Sometimes in the mornings I use it as an alarm clock. It's got three different timers and the first alarm that goes off usually starts off with the seashore and seagulls and I listen to that for about 15 minutes. And the next one comes on which is, wakes me up a bit more is more like south-east Asian pop music. And then I get the World Service news at 8 o'clock in the morning to finally wake me up.

2 Also there are these *karaoke* channels, about maybe four or five of them I think. And *karaoke* is the thing where you sing along to background music and you have a microphone and you can become a pop star for a few minutes and sing along to the music so I use this a lot now. I've learnt a few of the Japanese songs now. I can sing maybe five or six of them.

3 About the alibi channels, I did actually use one once. I'd been out quite late one night and overslept and was late for work. So I just got hold of the radio, flipped onto the alibi channel, which is the sound of, sounds as though you're in a phone box in the street with passing cars and sort of horns going. And I turned it up fairly loud, put my telephone next to it and explained to the secretary at work that I was on my way to the office and I'd been to a meeting which started at 8.30 in the morning.

4 Also there are various kinds of music, you can get Indian music and Mexican music for example. So when I'm at home cooking and cooking a Mexican meal and I get my friends to come over and we put the Mexican channel on so it creates a nice atmosphere for dinner.

Self-study Workbook

Exercise A: Which page?
Students match extracts from newspapers with a table of contents.

Exercise B: TV programmes
Students write about two TV programmes, and say what they like / don't like about them.

Exercise C: Understanding the headlines
The use of Present simple, past participle and infinitive forms in newspaper headlines.
Students expand headlines into complete sentences.

New words
Space to record new words with notes and examples.

Translation
Key sentences for translation.

Listening: Media habits
Two people say what newspapers and magazines they read and what radio and TV programmes they like. Students listen and complete a table. They then read remarks and match them to the speakers.

Phrasal verbs: Double meanings
Transitive phrasal verbs that have more than one meaning (e.g. *look someone up*, *look something up*). Students match verbs with their meanings, then use them to complete sentences.

Writing skills: Similarities
Use of *both*, *and*, *so*, *neither*, *nor*, *all* to classify and show similarities. Students write sentences comparing two or three items, then write short paragraphs based on prompts.

READING

1 What is the answer to the question above the text on page 66?

2 Which of these sentences about the text are true, and which are false?

   a You can only listen to the radio channels at certain times of the day.
   b On the music channels, the music is introduced by disc jockeys.
   c 'Drowsing channels' are intended to help you get to sleep.
   d The heartbeat channel is for babies only.
   e There are nearly 100 channels available altogether.

3 What are these sounds like?
   – *yodelling*
   – Buddhist *chanting*
   – *croaking* frogs
   – *percolating* coffee
   – a *revving* motorcycle engine

4 Look at the list on the right. Why do you think people would want to tune in to these channels?

   C2   C17   H29   J32

5 Choose three channels from the list that you think you would enjoy.

LISTENING

[cassette icon] You will hear two foreigners who live in Japan talking about cable radio channels they listen to. The recording is in four short parts.

1 What channels do they mention? What do they use them for? Complete the table.

	Channels	*What do they use them for?*
Part 1		
Part 2		
Part 3		
Part 4		

2 Which of these words were used in each part? How did each speaker use them?

alarm clock	background music	phone box
atmosphere	meeting	pop star

Now listen again and check your answers.

Tropical

C1	Sea, Waves, Seashore
C2	Sea, Waves, Seashore + Music

Japanese Sounds

C3	Waterwheel, Waterfall
C4	Waterwheel, Waterfall + Music

Seasonal Music

C5	New Year's Tunes
C6	Music for the The Dolls' Festival and The Boys' Festival
C7	Hawaiian, Christmas

Background Music

C17	Morning Music with Birdcalls
C18	Midnight Music
C19	Social Dance Music
C20	Sound of Steam Locomotives

Karaoke

C23	Duets
C24	Popular
C25	Lessons in Karaoke

Music for Places of Business

G28	Office (Slow)
G29	Office (Up-tempo)
G30	Bank (Slow)
G31	Bank (Moderate)
G32	Bank (Up-tempo)

For Children

H23	Japanese and Foreign Legends
H24	Songs from TV Cartoons
H26	Nursery Rhymes and Songs
H27	Music for Babies
H28	Bedtime Stories
H29	Lullabies
H30	Mother's Heartbeat

Spiritual Music

H31	Self-realization
H32	Cultivating Innate Ability
H33	Concentration (Enhancing Creativity)
H34	Spiritual Stability (Enhancing Patience)
H35	Easing Stress

Drowsing

H36	Drowsing
H37	Philosophical Talks
H38	Counting Sheep

Sounds of Nature

J21	Rural Scenery (Cows, Insects …)
J22	Rain, Wind, Thunder
J23	Port Town (Ships, Sea …)
J24	Summer Scenery (Cicadas, Frogs …)
J25	Rooster Calls and Bells Ringing

Ceremonial Music

J26	Birthday Song
J27	Japanese Wedding
J29	Hymns

For Alibis

J30	Pachinko & Mah-jong
J31	Telephone Booth
J32	Bar, Coffee Shop

Fun Corner

J33	Jokes & Music
J34	Scary Music
J35	Movie Information
J37	Mental Exercise
J38	Travel Information

Recent events

1 In the news

Present perfect • Past simple

1 These pictures all accompany news stories. What do you think has happened in each case?

   ▭ Now listen to the news stories. For each story answer the questions.
   – What events are reported using the Present perfect tense?
   – What other details are given?

2 Think of something that's been in the news this week. Summarise the story in two or three sentences.

This unit deals with language for talking about recent events, actions and activities. It focuses on two main areas of tense usage:
– Present perfect simple (active and passive) for talking about recent events
– Present perfect continuous for talking about recent activities.

1 In the news

This activity is about news items that might be heard on the radio. It focuses on the use of the Present perfect tense for announcing a piece of news, and shows how we use the Past simple for giving background and further details. Students try to predict the news items from the pictures, then they listen to the recording. Finally they talk about real current news stories.

➤ Focus on Form: Exercises 1, 2
➤ Workbook: Exercise A

1 Presentation & listening

- Remind students of the form of the Present perfect. Point out that as well as being used to describe changes and recent events in general, it is also commonly used to announce news.

- Look at the pictures and ask students to imagine what has happened, e.g.
  - A bomb has damaged a building; a house has been destroyed by fire.
  - Someone has just sailed round the world; a yacht has sunk; police have discovered 20 kilos of heroin on a yacht.
  - A tiger has escaped from a zoo; a child has been injured by a tiger; a zoo has just bought a tiger.

- Use one of the examples to focus on the active and passive forms of the Present perfect, e.g.

> **ACTIVE:** *A bomb has damaged a building.*
> **PASSIVE:** *A building has been damaged (by a bomb).*

- 🔊 Play the recording, asking students to listen out for events reported with the Present perfect. Answers:

Story 1: The body of Clive Robbins has been found.
Story 2: Two people have been killed in an explosion.
A number of bombs and other weapons have been found.
Story 3: Kent Wildlife Park have recovered their van and their tigers.

- Then ask the class to supply other details of the story (e.g. Mr Robbins was reported missing two days ago. The body was found shortly after 6, etc.).

- Point out that
  - we use the Present perfect to announce a piece of news (just to say *that* it has happened, not when or how it happened).
  - if we want to give further details (such as when, where, how, who was involved, etc.), we use the Past simple.

2 Speaking activity

- Ask around the class for current news stories that students know about (these can include local, national and international events), and get them to give whatever details they can. If necessary, prompt students to think of items (e.g. What's happened in China?) and give help with vocabulary. If you like, build up a set of news items on the board.

> *Presentation option*
> If you like, look back at examples in 7.2 and 7.3, or at the Unit 7 Reference section (page 133).

> *Language note*
> Notice that it is not necessary to use the Present perfect only as a beginning. Story 2 switches back to the Present perfect for a second piece of news (*bombs and other weapons have been found*), and in Story 3, the news announcement is kept until the end.

> *Writing option*
> Divide students into groups. Each group takes one news story and writes a brief summary similar to those on the tape.
> As an extension, you could get students to record their news items onto a cassette, as a 'news broadcast'.

🔊 Tapescript for Exercise 1: *In the news*

The news at 6 o'clock.
The body of American TV presenter Clive Robbins has been found off the coast of Florida. Mr Robbins was reported missing two days ago when he failed to appear for breakfast on his yacht while on holiday in the Florida Keys. The body was found shortly after 6 o'clock this morning by a rescue helicopter, and was flown immediately to Miami for a post-mortem examination.

Two people have been killed in an explosion which badly damaged a house in South-east London early this afternoon. First reports say that the explosion was caused by a bomb, and a number of bombs and other weapons have been found in the house. Police believe that a group of terrorists were using the house as a weapons store, and that the bomb went off accidentally.

And finally, thieves got a nasty surprise when they stole a van from a motorway service station yesterday afternoon. When they finally opened the van, which belongs to the Kent Wildlife Park, they found two tigers inside, which were on their way to the Wildlife Park from London Zoo. The thieves, obviously animal lovers, immediately phoned the Wildlife Park, who have now recovered their van – and the tigers – unharmed.

2 Tell me more

This activity shows how the Present perfect combines with other tenses in giving personal news; this is very common in letter writing. During the writing activity, students develop short paragraphs in response to other students' requests for more details.

➤ Workbook: Exercise B

1 Writing & reading activity

- Look at the piece of news. Ask students to suggest other questions, and write them on the board. Some possible questions:

  Was it born in hospital? Have you thought of a name?
  Is it your first child? Was it an easy birth? How much does it weigh?
  Have your parents seen it yet?

- Give time for students to read the letter on page 121, and then establish which of the class's questions were answered. Write brief answers against the questions on the board.

Note
The aim of this activity is to develop the idea that we usually write for an *audience*, i.e. we include information we think our reader will want to know.

2 Writing activity

- Students write a sentence on a piece of paper. Their sentences could either use the Present perfect or Past simple, and they can either be real or invented pieces of news.
- Students pass their paper to their partner, who writes questions asking for further details.
- Students exchange papers again, and expand their sentences into paragraphs, adding details in response to the questions. They then give their paragraphs back for their partner to read.
- As a round-up, ask a few students to read out the paragraphs they received.

Alternative: speaking activity
In groups, students take it in turns to read out their sentence, then answer other students' questions.
Paragraphs can then be written for homework.

3 What have you been doing?

This exercise introduces the Present perfect continuous, used for talking about recent activities. The three texts show examples of this tense, contrasted with the Present perfect simple. In the second part of the exercise, students ask each other about recent activities.

➤ Focus on Form: Exercises 3, 4
➤ Workbook: Exercise C

1 Presentation

- Students read the texts. Establish what the three people's jobs are, and focus on the words that tell you the answer. Answers:

  – Manager of a shop: customers, accounts, ordering stock, delivery van
  – Actor: learning lines, play (the role of)
  – Travelling salesperson: driving, visiting clients, samples, expenses claim

- Use the examples to present the Present perfect continuous:

I've He's They've	been	writing letters. learning English. visiting clients.

Point out that
  – we use the Present perfect continuous to talk about *general activities* in the recent past (how you've been spending your time).
  – we use the Present perfect simple to talk about individual *actions*.

Presentation option
Give more examples to show this difference, e.g.
I've *been ironing*.
I've *ironed* six shirts.
I've *been writing* letters.
I've *written* a long letter to my cousin.

2 Speaking activity

- As a lead-in, get students to ask you the questions, and give answers about yourself. Show how you can answer in a variety of ways: by saying what you've *been doing*, by saying what particular things you *have* or *haven't done*, or by saying when you *did* something.
- Pairwork. Students ask each other the questions.
- As a round-up, ask a few students what they found out about their partner.

2 Tell me more

1 Look at this piece of news. What other details might you want
  to know? Write some questions.

We've just had a baby

Is it a girl or a boy?

hospital?

name?

...?

When was it born?

first?

...?

Now look at the letter on page 121.
Did the writer answer your questions?

2 *a* On a piece of paper, write a sentence giving a piece of news about yourself or
  someone you know. Exchange sentences with your partner.

  b Look at your partner's sentence, and write some questions asking for more
  details. Then give the paper back.

  c Expand your sentence into a paragraph, adding the details your partner asked for.

3 What have you been doing?

Present perfect continuous & simple

> Well, this month I've been serving customers as one of the staff is ill. I've also been doing the accounts, writing letters, ordering new stock. And I've bought a new delivery van.

> Basically, I've been learning my lines. I suppose I've learnt about half of them now. I play an American, so I've also been taking lessons in American English.

> I've been doing all the usual things – driving around, visiting clients, giving out free samples. One thing I haven't done yet is fill in this month's expenses claim. I must do that.

1 *a* Read these texts. What do you think the people's jobs are?

  b What is the difference between the Present perfect simple (*I've done*)
  and the Present perfect continuous (*I've been doing*)?

2 Work in pairs. Find out whether your partner
  has been doing any of these things recently.

  – going out a lot
  – working hard
  – going to bed late

  – spending a lot of money
  – watching TV a lot
  – travelling a lot

  Example:
  A Have you been going out a lot recently?
  B Yes, I have. I've been out four times this week.
    No, I haven't. I've been painting my flat.
    No. I only went out once last week.

---

4 Eavesdropping

1 🔲 You will overhear a couple having an argument. Which of these sentences do you think are true?

> *a* The woman hasn't been sleeping well.
> *b* The man has found a job.
> *c* The woman hasn't been working very hard.
> *d* The man has been sitting around doing nothing.
> *e* They haven't been getting on well for some time.

2 🔲 You will overhear bits of three more conversations. What are the conversations about? Imagine what the people have (or haven't) been doing.

Grammar Checklist

Present perfect active & passive

Active: **have/has** + *past participle*
A prisoner **has** escaped.
They **haven't found** him yet.
Have you **heard** the news?

Passive: **have/has** + **been** + *past participle*
A new planet **has been** discovered.
He **hasn't been** arrested yet.
Have you **been** invited to the party?

Present perfect & Past simple tenses

Present perfect – *for announcing news of recent events (without saying when).*
Past simple – *for giving details.*

Five prisoners **have** escap**ed** from Bedford Prison. They **broke** out late last night and **drove** away in a green van.

– I've **bought** a new coat.
– Really? How much **did** it **cost**?

Present perfect continuous & simple tenses

Present perfect continuous – *for talking about recent activities (how you have been spending your time).*

have/has + **been** + **-ing**
I've **been** going out a lot recently.
She's **been** preparing for her exams.
They **haven't been** speaking to each other.

Present perfect simple – *for talking about single complete events.*

I've **been** tidying my room. *(An activity)*
I've **tidied** my room. (= I've finished it.)

I've **been** going to the cinema a lot recently.
I've **seen** three films this week.

See also Reference section, page 137.

4 Eavesdropping

This is a freer activity involving the Present perfect continuous and simple. Students listen to short snatches of 'overheard' conversations, and interpret the situation and what people have and haven't been doing.

➤ Focus on Form: Exercises 3, 4
➤ Workbook: Exercise C

1 Listening & presentation

● Tell students they will hear a couple having an argument. Write these words and phrases on the board, and check that students know what they mean:

> **to blame someone**   **to imply (that)**
> **it's not my fault**   **twiddling my thumbs**

Optional lead-in
Explain the meaning of the title.
Eavesdropping = to listen secretly to people who are having a private conversation.

● ▭ Quickly read through the list of sentences. Then play the recording and ask students which sentences are true. Answers:

a True
b False
c False – she's got a busy day in front of her.
d False – he's been looking for a job.
e True

2 Listening & speaking activity

● ▭ Play the conversations on the tape. After each one, pause and establish who or what the people are talking about. Then ask students to imagine what the people have (or haven't) been doing. Possible answers:

1 Talking about a student/teenager/schoolgirl. She's been staying out late / going to parties; she hasn't been working/preparing for her exam.
2 A woman talking about her guests (friends or relatives). They've been staying at her home. She's been looking after them / cooking meals / doing a lot of housework. They haven't been helping.
3 Talking about a friend/neighbour/colleague who's got divorced and who has changed a lot. He's probably been going out a lot / meeting people / having a good time.

▭ Tapescript for Exercise 4: *Eavesdropping*

Part 1

A I don't think you can blame me just because you've been sleeping badly. It's hardly my fault, is it?
B I didn't blame you, I didn't, I never blamed you, I just said I'm, I think I'll go to bed early because I've not, you know, didn't sleep very well.
A Yeah OK but you seem to imply that just because I'm not working that somehow I'm just you know sitting around doing nothing.
B I just said I was going to bed early because I was very tired. I slept very badly last night, I'm tired, I've got a busy, you know, busy day ahead of me.
A Oh oh and I haven't. (Well) Because I'm just going to be sitting around watching television and twiddling my thumbs.
B I didn't say that, did I? Look I'm sorry you haven't got enough to do. I'm sorry that you're bored.
A I've got plenty to do, thank you very much. I've been out looking for five different jobs.

Part 2

1 A We've just got to do something. I mean she came home again after midnight last night.
  B I know, she hasn't looked at a book for weeks. She's never going to pass her exams at this rate.
2 A I bet you'll be glad to see them go, won't you?
  B Yeah, it's exhausting, I mean it's nice to see them because they live so far away, but, well it is hard work.
3 A He's so different. He used to be so shy and quiet.
  B I know, it really is incredible. I think he's changed since his divorce, don't you?

Focus on Form

1 *Present perfect or past?*

> Present perfect and past simple

- Give time for students to fill the gaps, working alone or in pairs.
- Go through the answers together. Answers:

  a have decided; told
  b has found; went; offered; have found
  c have made; have been (gone); have shown; have seen

2 *Present perfect active & passive*

> Present perfect active and passive; present tenses

- Go through the example with the class.
- Pairwork. Students look only at their own news stories. Student A asks Student B what has happened. Students can choose to use either active or passive forms.
- Look at the news stories with the class and establish what has happened. Possible answers:

  The power station has been closed.
  The schoolchildren have been rescued.
  Clara Fairbanks has bought the Mona Lisa.
  The Government has sent the refugees back.
  Oliver James has been arrested.
  Miss Botham has been released.
  They've cancelled the rock concert.

3 *Present perfect continuous*

> Present perfect continuous, positive & negative

- Either look at the pictures with the whole class and elicit a range of responses, or let students look at them in pairs and then go through them together. Possible answers:

  B He's been lifting something heavy / hasn't been looking after his back.
  C She's been walking through a snowstorm / skiing.
  D She's been eating chocolate / painting a picture.
  E She's been mending her bicycle / working in a garage.

- Pairwork. Students ask each other the questions, and make up suitable answers, as in the example.

4 *Recent activities & actions*

> Present perfect continuous and simple

- Look at the example. Then go through the exercise, asking students what the people have been doing. Possible answers:

  a He's been looking after the children.
  b She's been cooking/preparing a meal.
  c He's been organising a (children's) party.
  d They've been sightseeing/staying in London.
  e She's been paying bills.

- Go through the exercise again. This time students add something that the person has or hasn't done. Possible answers:

  a He hasn't read them a story.
  b She hasn't cooked the rice yet.
  c He's blown up some balloons.
  d They've travelled on a London bus.
  e She hasn't paid her car insurance yet.

5 *Pronunciation*

[▭▭] Ask students to try saying the sentences themselves, then play the recording as a model. Focus on these points:

a Pronunciation of short forms with the Present perfect tense: *'ve* /v/, *we've* /wiːv/, *you've* /juːv/, *they've* /ðeɪv/. Contrast between *we've had* /wiv hæd/ and *we had* /wi hæd/.
b Reduced vowels in *has been* /həz bin/ and *have been* /həv bin/.
c Full *have* in Yes/no questions: /hæv/. Reduced *have* in Wh- questions: /(h)əv/.

Self-study Workbook

Exercise A: Personal news
Present perfect and Past simple. Students write paragraphs from prompts, then write a real piece of news about themselves.

Exercise B: Asking questions
Students ask questions about a news item, based on prompts, and using a range of tenses.

Exercise C: What have they been doing?
Present perfect continuous and simple. Students read descriptions of various things people have done, and write sentences saying what they have been doing.

Translation
Key sentences for translation.

Listening: What has happened?
Three conversations concerned with personal news. Students listen, and answer comprehension questions.

Pronunciation: Changing stress
Using stress to give prominence to new information. Students listen to two-line conversations and predict which words will be stressed.

Reading: Personal letters
Three letters giving personal news. Students read the letters and answer comprehension questions.

Focus on Form

1 Present perfect or past?

Fill the gaps with the correct form of the verbs in the box. Choose between the Present perfect simple and the Past simple.

be	go	see
decide	make	show
find	offer	tell

a Actress Lana Bernstein and her fourth husband .... to separate after only two months of marriage. They .... reporters yesterday that they both needed more time to follow their own careers.

b Great news! Nina .... a job at last. She .... for an interview last week, and they .... her the job straight away. It's only four days a week, but the pay's good. And we .... someone to look after the children, too.

c I've been having a great time since I came to Barcelona. I .... lots of new friends, and I .... out almost every night. Some friends of mine .... me round the town too, so I .... most of the sights already.

2 Present perfect active & passive

Example:

Last week's news   *This week's news*

> Police are searching for three prisoners who escaped last night from Brixton prison. They

> The three prisoners were back in Brixton prison today after being caught driving a stolen

A What's happened to those prisoners who escaped last week?
B They've been caught.

Student A: Look at last week's news on page 119, and ask B what's happened.

Student B: Look at today's news on page 120, and answer A's questions.

3 Present perfect continuous

Look at the pictures. What do you think the people have (or haven't) been doing?

Example: *Picture A*

He's been watching the late movie.
He hasn't been sleeping well.
He's been working very hard.

4 Recent activities & actions

1 What have these people been doing?
2 Add one more thing that each person has done (or hasn't done yet).

Example: *I've planted some vegetables and I've cut the grass.*

1 She's been working in the garden.
2 She hasn't watered the flowers yet.

a We've done some jigsaw puzzles and painted some pictures, but we haven't been to the playground yet.
b I've washed the vegetables and put the meat in the oven.
c I've bought some paper hats, but I haven't ordered the cake yet.
d We haven't seen Buckingham Palace yet, but we have been to all the big museums.
e I've paid the electricity bill and the rent.

5 Pronunciation

How do you say the words and phrases below?

a 've we've you've they've
We've had a baby.
We had a baby yesterday.

b The money has been found.
The thieves have been arrested.

c Have you been working?
What have you been doing?
I've been watching TV.

[cassette icon] **Now listen and check your answers.**

16 Teaching and learning

1 In the classroom

Morden Park Secondary Sc

Class: .... Name: ....

	Monday	Tuesday	We
9.00	ENGLISH		
9.45	GEOGRAPHY		
10.30	B	R	E	A	K
10.45	COMPUTER		
11.30	STUDIES		
12.15	L	U	N	C	H
1.30			
2.15			

1 *a* Look at the timetable. What other subjects would you expect to find on it?

   b 🔲 You will hear four people talking about subjects they were taught at school.

     What subject are they talking about? How do you know?

2 Work in groups. Choose a subject that you all studied (or are studying) at school. Think about these questions:

  – Did you enjoy it?
  – What was the teacher like?
  – What did you have to do?
  – What *didn't* you do?
  – Did you learn anything useful?

This unit covers three areas of language related to education and learning:
– school subjects and teaching methods
– learning skills
– education systems.
The Reading and Listening activity is about techniques for improving your memory.

1 In the classroom

This exercise introduces the names of school subjects, and also vocabulary used in talking about them (e.g. dates, do experiments, poetry). Students listen to people describing how they were taught at school, and this leads into a discussion of the way school subjects are taught.

1 Presentation & listening

- Look at the timetable, and use it to introduce the words *timetable* and *subject*. Use it as a basis for eliciting other school subjects, e.g.

  science, chemistry, physics, biology, mathematics (maths), history, economics, languages (French, German, Spanish), art, music, religious studies

- Play the recording, pausing after each section to establish what subjects the speakers are talking about. Focus on the key words they use which tell us what subject they are referring to. Answers:

  1 (History of) Art (paintings, monuments).
  2 History (dates, battles, kings, queens).
  3 Music (singing, play, instrument).
  4 English (grammar, speak).
  5 Geography (map, world, country).
  6 Science (experiments).
  7 Literature (stories, poems, poetry).

2 Speaking activity

- Groupwork. Students choose one subject that they all studied (or are studying) at school, and discuss how they felt it was taught. If you like, you could ask them to make notes of the points they agree on.
- Ask one student from each group to report back their conclusions to the rest of the class.

➤ Workbook: Exercises A, B

Language note
Mathematics and *economics* have a plural ending, but are used as singular nouns, e.g. 'Economics *is* a difficult subject'.
Mathematics is often shortened to
– *maths* (British English)
– *math* (US English).

Optional lead-in
To guide the discussion, write a few prompts on the board for students to consider, e.g.

facts or opinions?
boring? interesting?
how useful?

Tapescript for Exercise 1: *In the classroom*

1 We sat in the dark and we watched these slides of different paintings and monuments and it was quite enjoyable.
2 We learnt a lot of dates and we learnt a lot about battles and kings and queens but we never learnt anything about ordinary people who had lived ordinary lives.
3 We did a lot of singing but if you wanted to learn to play an instrument you had to pass a special test.
4 I think my teachers mostly focused on grammar, but we also had the chance to speak in, during the class.
5 I remember we had a map of the world and we used to spin it around and wherever we put our finger on we used to study the country wherever our finger had landed.
6 We had the chance to do a lot of our own experiments which was very good because it gave you the opportunity to see how things worked.
7 We had a very good teacher and we used to write a lot of stories and a lot of poems and I really enjoyed writing poetry. That was great.

2 How to …

This exercise focuses on language used in talking about skills, especially the structures know how to + inf. *and* be good at + -ing. *Students establish which of the activities in the box they can and can't do. They then choose an activity and find out more about it from other students.*

➤ Workbook: Exercise B

1 Presentation & discussion

● To present the key structures, write the sentence 'I can ski' on the board, and then get students to help you build up the following tables on the board:

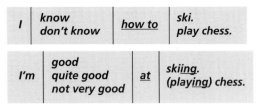

| I | know / don't know | how to | ski. / play chess. |

| I'm | good / quite good / not very good | at | skiing. / (playing) chess. |

Language note
We can often express this idea with the structure *a good* + noun:
I'm quite a good skier.
He's not a very good chess player.

Point out that
– we say 'know *how* to' (not 'know to')
– we say 'good *at*' (not 'good in')
– 'good at' is followed by a *noun* or an *-ing* form.

● Students fill in the table for themselves, adding an item of their own.
● They turn to the person next to them, and compare what they have written.

2 Speaking activity

● Ask students to tell you what skills they added, and write a list on the board.
● Students choose a skill that they'd like to know more about (either from the box or the list on the board), and think of a few questions to ask about it.
● Students move freely round the class looking for someone who can answer their questions.
● As a round-up, ask some students what they managed to find out.

Alternatives
1 Pairwork
Students look at their partner's table, and choose a skill that their partner is better at than they are. They take it in turns to ask their questions.
2 Panel discussion
Choose three or four students who have an interesting or unusual skill to talk about, and ask them to sit at the front of the class. Other students ask the 'panel' questions.

3 Going through the system

This is a freer activity, which introduces vocabulary associated with education systems: schools, university, exams, etc. Students listen to someone talking about the American education system, and use this as a basis for comparison with education in their own country.

➤ Workbook: Exercise C

1 Listening & presentation

● Before playing the recording, read through the questions, and explain any unknown words (e.g. *primary school, secondary school, compulsory, school leaving age, degree*).

● ▭ Play the recording, pausing if necessary. Students make brief notes of the answers. Answers:

a six	e 17 or 18
b 13 (= 'Junior High School' in the USA)	f Diploma
c No – there are compulsory subjects and 'electives'	g (not answered)
d No – they can choose different courses	h (not answered)

Note
The speaker uses a number of American education words. If students are interested, show them the American-British equivalents in the Reference section (page 137).

▭ The tapescript is on page T75.

2 Speaking activity

● To introduce the activity, explain the point of the role-play: to focus on the main differences between education in America and the students' own country.
● Divide the class into pairs. The 'American' finds out about the education system in the other student's country.
● As a round-up, ask some of the 'Americans' what they found out.

Alternative: mixed nationality classes
Instead of doing a role-play, students sit with someone from a different country. They go through the questions, comparing the education system in their two countries. As a round-up, ask one or two pairs what differences they discovered.

2 How to …

1 Do you know how to do any of the things in the box? Complete the table. Add one other thing you know how to do.

windsurf	touch-type
bake bread	ride a horse
ski	shear a sheep
juggle	dance a waltz
read music	draw a bicycle

I don't know how to …	
I know how to … (but I'm not very good)	
I'm quite good at …	
I'm very good at …	

2 Choose one skill you would like to know more about. What would you like to know?

Now find someone who knows more about it than you, and find out as much as you can.

Did you find out what you wanted to know?

3 Going through the system

You will hear someone answering questions about the American education system.

1 Look at the questions in the box. Which questions does he answer?

> a At what age do children start primary school?
> b What about secondary school?
> c Are all subjects compulsory?
> d Do all students follow the same course?
> e What's the school leaving age?
> f What are the most important school exams?
> g How many subjects do they take?
> h How long does it take to get a university degree?

2 *Student A:* Imagine you're an American. Ask about the education system in B's country.

Student B: Answer A's questions.

4 Improve your memory

How many days?

In some cultures, people have no problem remembering which months have 31 days and which have 30. In Iran, for example, the first six months have 31 days, the next five have 30, and the last has 28 or 29. And in Thailand, you can tell from the names of the months: those with 31 days end in *-om* (e.g. January is *Magarakom*), those with 30 days end in *-on* (e.g. September is *Kanyayon*) and February ends in *-an: Kumpapan*.

Most countries, however, use some kind of mnemonic, or memory aid. In Britain, a rhyme is used:

30 days have September
April, June and November.
All the rest have 31
Excepting February alone
Which has but 28 days clear
And 29 in each leap year.

What about your country?

Jan   Feb   Mar   Apr   May   Jun   Jul   Aug   Sep   Oct   Nov   Dec

READING

1 Look at the text called *How many days?*

How do you remember which months have 31 days and which have 30?

2 Look at the text on the opposite page, and read about *one* of the two memory techniques.

Then use the technique you have learned to test yourself.

LISTENING

You will hear someone describing a technique for learning new vocabulary in a foreign language.

1 How does the technique use
   – the learner's mother tongue?
   – a visual image?

2 Look at the four pictures. For each one, note down
   – the foreign word
   – its meaning in English
   – the 'help words' the speaker uses.

3 Choose one of the words from the two lists on the opposite page. How could you use this technique to help you learn it?

4 Improve your memory

This combined reading and listening activity is about techniques for memorising words. Students read an introductory text about mnemonics for remembering the number of days in each month. They then read texts describing two ways of using images to help remember words. Finally they hear about a technique for remembering words in a foreign language.

READING

Part 1

- Give time for students to read the text *How many days?*, and establish what a mnemonic is (= a word, rhyme, etc., that helps you to remember things).
- Discuss with students how they remember the number of days in each month.

Part 2

- Divide the class into pairs. Assign a different text to each pair, alternating round the class. Give time for them to read their text and to use the technique to test each other using the two lists of ten words.
- When students have finished, ask them what they thought of the technique and whether they felt it worked.

LISTENING

- As a lead-in to the listening, write a completely unfamiliar word (in English or another language) on the board, and ask students to suggest good ways of remembering it.
- [cassette icon] Play the tape, pausing after each example, so that students can note down answers to Questions 1 and 2. Then discuss the answers together. Answers:

  1 You think of a similar word in your mother tongue. You imagine a picture that links the similar words and the real meaning.

2 *Picture 1*	*Picture 2*	*Picture 3*	*Picture 4*
skylos	arigato	uchitelj	ogonj
dog	thank you	teacher	fire
ski – loss	alligator	'You cheat!'	gone (out)

- Divide the class into pairs or groups. Each group chooses one of the words on page 75, and discusses how to use the technique on the recording to learn it.
- As a round-up, ask each group to report their ideas to the rest of the class.
- Finally, discuss with the class whether they think the technique is a useful one.

Note
One common method is to use the knuckles of one hand. The four knuckles represent long months, and the depressions between them represent the shorter months.

The months are then: January (knuckle 1 – long), February (depression 1 – short) ... June (depression 3 – short), July (knuckle 4 – long), August (start again at knuckle 1 – long) ... December (knuckle 3 – long).

Alternative
If you are short of time, use just one of the texts.

Optional extension
Students form new pairs so that students in each pair have now read a different text from their partner. They explain their technique to their partner, and try it out.

[cassette icon] Tapescript for Exercise 4: *Improve your memory*

A OK I gather you've got an interesting way of learning words in a foreign language.

B Yes it's actually a very easy way of learning foreign words. What you do is to, you think of a word in your own language, in my case English, which sounds something like the word you're trying to learn and then you just imagine a picture in your mind which links the two ideas – the idea of the foreign word and the idea of the English word.

A Can you give me an example?

B Yeah, an easy example is the Greek word *skylos* which means 'dog'. And this immediately reminds me of the English words *ski* and *loss*, so I just imagine a picture of a skier on a mountain, one of his skis has come off and he's lost it and there's a dog carrying it back to him in his mouth. An example from a different language might be the Japanese word for 'thank you' which is *arigato*. Now that sounds to me a little bit like *alligator*, so I could imagine a rather unpleasant picture of somebody whose leg has just been eaten by an alligator and the alligator's smiling and saying 'Thank you very much.'

A OK I'm going to try you out with some words in Russian (Goodness. Russian, yeah) You don't know Russian, do you?

B No no no.

A OK. Well here's the Russian word for 'teacher', which is *uchitelj*.

B Could you say it again?

A *Uchitelj*.

B *U-chit-elj*. Oh that's easy. The middle of this word is the English word *cheat*, which is something we often associate with teachers and students. So I can imagine a student sitting in an examination and he's cheating, he's copying from the student sitting next to him. And the teacher is standing over him saying 'You cheat!'

A OK, here's another word. It's the Russian word for 'fire' which is *ogonj*. *Ogonj*.

B *Ogonj*. Mm. Oh yes, again, let's take the middle of the word, *gone*. We think of a fire perhaps that's gone out. So I just imagine a picture of a fire in a fireplace and it's gone out. Easy.

A OK. Thank you. I'll try it as a technique.

A At what age do children start school in the States?

B Generally six. That's when I started.

A And that goes up to what age?

B That goes up to grade six, so that would be what? Twelve years old? And then you go to seventh grade in Junior High School, in fact you go for three years to a Junior High School, 7th, 8th and 9th grades.

A And then you go to real High School?

B And then comes the real thing, three years of High School. That's the 10th, the 11th and 12th grades.

A And that takes you up to what age? 16 or …?

B Seventeen, 18. It's quite common to finish High School with your Diploma at age 17.

A And how many subjects do you take for your Diploma?

B Well that depends on what type of Diploma you're doing. There are really two types – there's an academic Diploma, which would prepare you for College, and there's a non-academic Diploma, which is more vocationally orientated. Both types of Diploma have their compulsory subjects, you know, like in the academic Diploma you have to do English. But then in both cases again the student has some choice, so in addition there are what's called 'electives'.

A 'Electives' means you can choose the subject …?

B Exactly, exactly. So in the United States you could do a credit in driving, for example, and learn to drive at High School. Or typing is another skill that you can learn in High School, and that will count towards your Diploma.

Self-study Workbook

Exercise A: School subjects
Students read sentences about different school subjects, and complete an acrostic puzzle.

Exercise B: School report
Students write about three subjects that they are/were good at, and not so good at.

Exercise C: What's the system?
Students answer questions to build up a paragraph about the education system in their country.

New words
Space to record new words with notes and examples.

Translation
Key sentences for translation.

Listening: Three school subjects
Four people remember what it was like learning biology, history and general science at school.
Students listen for the main point each speaker makes.

Phrasal verbs: Prepositional verbs (1)
Common prepositional verbs (e.g. *look after*, *come across*). Students match verbs with their meanings, then put them appropriately in sentences.

Writing skills: Letter writing
Common expressions and formulae used in personal and business letters. Students match different parts of letters written in a variety of styles, then write a short letter in response to an advertisement.

REMEMBERING THINGS IN THE RIGHT ORDER

Suppose you want to remember a sequence of ten unrelated items in a particular order. Here are two techniques that you can use.

Technique 1: Pegwords

First, you have to learn a set of pegwords, one for each of the numbers one to ten. Since each of these rhymes with its number, this is a fairly easy task. Try it for yourself:

One = *bun*	Five = *hive*	Eight = *gate*
Two = *shoe*	Six = *sticks*	Nine = *wine*
Three = *tree*	Seven = *heaven*	Ten = *hen*
Four = *door*		

Having mastered this, you are ready to go; suppose the ten words you are trying to remember are: *battleship, octopus, chair, sheep, castle, rug, grass, beach, milkmaid, binoculars.*

Take the first pegword, which is *bun* (rhyming with *one*), and imagine a picture of a bun interacting in some way with a battleship: you might for example imagine a battleship sailing into an enormous floating bun. Now take the second pegword, *shoe*, and imagine it interacting with *octopus*, perhaps a large shoe with an octopus sitting in it. Pegword nine is *wine*, and the ninth item is *milkmaid*, so you might imagine a milkmaid milking a cow and getting wine rather than

milk. And so on. Having created these pictures, you should be able to come up with an accurate list of the ten words in the right order.

Technique 2: Places

First of all, think of ten locations in your home, choosing them so that the sequence of moving from one to the other is an obvious one – for example, front door to entrance hall, to kitchen, to bedroom, and so on.

Check that you can imagine moving through your ten locations in the same order without difficulty.

Now think of ten items and imagine them in those locations. If the first item is *grass*, you might imagine opening your front door and wiping your feet on a doormat made of grass. If the second is a *cabbage*, you might imagine your hall blocked by an enormous cabbage. If item number three is *sheep*, you could imagine someone in the kitchen trying to put a whole sheep into the oven. And so on.

The locations need not, of course, be in your own home. They could be a typical trip along your high street or around your place of work or school.

Test yourself

Now try to create similarly memorable images for the ten items in either of these lists.

Then cover up the page, and see if you can write down the ten items in order.

If you haven't yet had time to learn the ten pegwords or locations by heart, write them down and use them to help you.

1	shirt	5	camera	8	handkerchief
2	eagle	6	mushroom	9	sausage
3	paper clip	7	crocodile	10	king
4	rose				

1	horse	5	watch	8	typewriter
2	bullet	6	window	9	jacket
3	table	7	ostrich	10	cloud
4	cigar				

Adapted from *Your Memory, A User's Guide* by Alan Baddeley.

1 Flashbacks

Past perfect tense

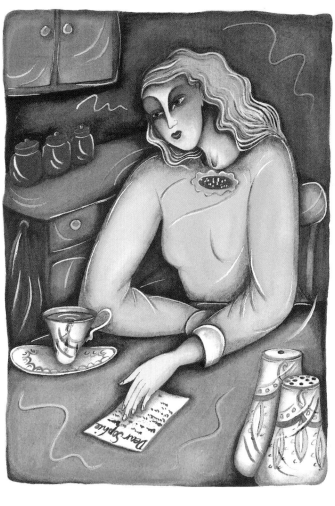

Sophie wandered aimlessly from room to room. The flat,

1

felt empty, too big for one person.

2

she wondered.

3

There was a heavy silence everywhere. She couldn't even put any music on.

4

She made herself a cup of coffee, and sat at the kitchen table, staring at the note with its familiar handwriting.

5   **6**

c/o Ewa Gradowska, ul. Smolna 30 m 21, 00–837 Warsaw, she read. No telephone number. She wondered who Ewa Gradowska was.

7   **8**

Not that it mattered, really. There would be no emergency, she was sure of that.

☐ 'Just in case there's an emergency,' he'd told her.	☐ which had once seemed so small,
☐ Or had they only just met?	☐ He'd taken the cassette player. She'd agreed to that.

☐ Had he known her for a long time? Years perhaps?	☐ Why had she let him leave so easily?
☐ He'd left his address in case she needed to get in touch.	☐ Why hadn't she asked him to wait and think again?

1 Fit the missing parts back into the story. What do they all have in common?

2 Now fill the gaps in the text below with suitable flashbacks.

At the top of the hill he stopped the car and looked down at the village where .... He saw the grey houses, the church, the park, the old schoolhouse where .... It was all exactly as he remembered it: the smoke drifting up from the paper factory; the old garage which had only one petrol pump; the hotel, with its bright yellow walls. And there, in the distance, was the farm. With a grin, he remembered the day, 20 years before, when ....

He drove down to the hotel and went into the bar to get some lunch. He sat at the table by the window, where .... Where was she now, he wondered. Was she still living here? Or ....?

This unit is concerned with narration in the past. It focuses particularly on two areas:
– use of the Past perfect for talking about previous events
– sequence of tenses in reported speech and thought.

1 Flashbacks

This exercise focuses on the use of the Past perfect tense for 'flashbacks', i.e. going back from a point in the past to describe previous events. It shows how this is used to give background information in a past tense narrative.

➤ Focus on Form: Exercises 1, 2
➤ Workbook: Exercise A

1 Presentation

● Look at the picture, and quickly read through the extracts, dealing with any unknown vocabulary (e.g. *wandered aimlessly, staring, emergency, get in touch*). Ask students what kind of book they think the extracts come from. (Answer: a romantic novel.)

● Pairwork. Students decide how the missing parts fit into the story: each number represents one gap.

● Discuss the answer with the whole class. Answer:

1 which had once seemed so small,
2 (or 3) Why had she let him leave so easily?
3 (or 2) Why hadn't she asked him to wait and think again?
4 He'd taken the cassette player. She'd agreed to that.
5 He'd left his address in case she needed to get in touch.
6 'Just in case there's an emergency,' he'd told her.
7 Had he known her for a long time? Years perhaps?
8 Or had they only just met?

● Establish that
– all the missing parts of the story use the Past perfect tense:

had(n't) + past participle

– The main events in the story are set at a particular time *in the past*, and follow a sequence (She wandered … the flat felt empty … she wondered … she couldn't … she made a cup of coffee). The Past perfect tense is used for *going back* to events that had happened *earlier* (what the flat had been like before, what he had said to her, how he had left, etc.).

Presentation option
With single nationality classes, it may help to give the equivalent tense in the students' own language (if one exists), e.g.

l'aveva detto
lo había dicho
il l'avait dit
er hatte es gesagt

2 Writing/speaking activity

● Read the text, and establish that it is about someone returning to the village where he grew up, and that each gap represents a flashback using the Past perfect tense.

● Pairwork. Students imagine suitable flashbacks and write them down.

● Go through the text together, asking students to suggest suitable sentences to fill the gaps. Possible answers:

… he had lived as a child / he had grown up / he had spent so many years
… he had gone to school / he had learned his first words in French
… the farmer had caught him stealing apples / he had learned to milk a cow
… he had first met Ann / he had sat with Ann on their first evening together
… had she moved away? / had she left? / had she gone away?

2 Changes in the past

This exercise shows the relationship between past states (e.g. The lights were on) and previous events that led up to them (e.g. He had turned/left the lights on). This is the same relationship as that between the Present perfect and Present tenses (see Unit 7.2).

➤ Focus on Form: Exercise 2
➤ Workbook: Exercise B

1 Presentation

● After establishing the situation (you let some friends stay in your flat while you were away), use the first example to present two possible ways of talking about a situation in the past:

– by saying what things *were like*, using the Past:

– by saying what *had* or *hadn't happened* earlier, using the Past perfect:

All the lights <u>were</u> on.

They | <u>had left</u> the lights on.
<u>hadn't switched</u> the lights off.

● Go through the other items, asking students to give sentences saying what had or hadn't happened. Possible answers:
  – They'd left the front door open / hadn't closed the front door.
  – They'd gone out / left / gone away.
  – They'd dropped cigarettes on the carpet / hadn't used ashtrays.
  – They'd left dirty dishes everywhere / hadn't washed the dishes.
  – They'd eaten all the food / hadn't bought any food.
  – They'd let the plants die / hadn't watered the plants.

2 Speaking activity

● Pairwork. Students choose one of the remarks and think of suitable continuations, using either Past or Past perfect tenses.
● Go through the answers together. Possible answers:
  a They'd laid the table; they were wearing their best clothes; they'd tidied the room; they seemed a bit nervous.
  b She'd changed a lot; she'd cut her hair short; she was wearing glasses.
  c Inflation had doubled; they'd increased taxes; there was no food in the shops.

> *Presentation option*
> To make this relationship clear, it may help to give similar examples set in the present, using Present and Present perfect tenses:
> NOW: The lights *are* on.
> They*'ve left* the lights on.
> THEN: The lights *were* on.
> They*'d left* the lights on.

> *Presentation option*
> Show how we can also use the Past perfect *passive* to talk about what had happened:
> The front door *had been left* open; cigarettes *had been dropped* on the carpets; the dishes *hadn't been washed*; all the food *had been eaten*; the plants *hadn't been watered*.

3 Reporting

This exercise is concerned with reporting speech and thought in the past. It focuses on the sequence of tenses and introduces the reporting verbs said, told, realised and discovered. In the second part of the exercise, students use these verbs to talk about things they remember happening to themselves.

➤ Focus on Form: Exercise 3
➤ Workbook: Exercises C, D

1 Presentation

● Look at the pictures and the captions, and establish what the speakers actually said or thought. Expected answers:

We're police officers.
I'll meet you at the airport.
Someone's following me.

I fought in the Vietnam War.
The train has already left.
I'm not going to resign.

● Use these examples to present the tense changes involved in reporting speech or thought in the past:

ACTUAL WORDS/THOUGHTS		REPORTED IN THE PAST
does	→	*did*
is doing	→	*was doing*
will do	→	*would do*
did	→	*had done*
has done	→	

2 Writing/speaking activity

● Give time for students to recall an event from their recent past, and write a sentence using *said*, *told*, *realised* or *discovered*.
● Pairwork. Using their sentence as a basis, students tell their partner what happened to them.
● As a round-up, ask students to read out their sentences.

> *Language note*
> The captions include the two commonest verbs of reported speech, *say* and *tell*.
> *Say* is intransitive:
> He *said* (that) he was tired.
> *Tell* is followed by an indirect object:
> He *told me* (that) he was tired.

> *Practice option*
> Give sentences in direct speech and ask students to report them, e.g.
> 'I'm English.'
> → He told me he was English.

> *Alternative: small classes*
> Students read out their sentences in turn. Then the rest of the class choose two or three stories that they want to hear.

2 Changes in the past

Past and Past perfect tenses

1 Read the description below, and say what the guests had (or hadn't) done.

As soon as I got home, I realised that it had
been a mistake to let them use my flat.

– All the lights were on.
– The front door was open.
– There was no-one in the flat.
– There were cigarette burns in the carpet.
– There were piles of dirty dishes
  everywhere.
– There was no food in the fridge.
– The plants were all dead.

2 Choose one of these remarks. Imagine what
things were like and what had happened.

   a Clearly they were expecting some very important guests for dinner.
   b When I saw her again, I didn't recognise her at first.
   c After only one year in power, the government was already very unpopular.

3 Reporting

Reported speech and thought

1 What did these people actually say (or think)? Fill the bubbles.

They said they were police officers.

She said she would meet me
at the airport.

After a time, she realised that
someone was following her.

He told me he'd fought in
the Vietnam War.

When I got to the station, I discovered
that the train had already left.

The Prime Minister told reporters that
he was not going to resign.

2 *a* Think of a time recently when one of these things happened to you:

   – you realised that something was wrong
   – someone told you a surprising piece of news
   – you met somebody interesting.

   Write a sentence about it using *said, told, discovered* **or** *realised*.

   b Tell your partner what happened. Include your sentence in what you say.

4 The dead rabbit

You will hear a story called *The dead rabbit*. The story is in five parts. Listen to each part of the story and answer the questions.

Part 1
– What was the dog like?
– What had it done on previous occasions?

Part 2
– What did the dog bring home?
– What had it done?
– What do you think the man did next?

Part 3
– What hadn't the dog done?
– What do you think the man did next?

Part 4
– What did the man do?
– What happened the next morning?
– What do you think the neighbour said?

Part 5
– Why was the neighbour upset?
– What had the dog done?

Grammar Checklist

Past perfect tense

Active: **had(n't)** + *past participle – for going back from the past to events that happened earlier.*

The house was empty – everyone **had left.**
She **hadn't** changed – she looked just the same.
He showed me photos of the places he**'d** visited.

Passive: **had(n't) been** + *past participle*

They pulled down the buildings that **had been** destroyed in the fire.

Past & Past perfect tenses

There **was** some food on the table.
They**'d left** some food on the table.
Some food **had been left** on the table.

The door **wasn't** locked.
They **hadn't** locked the door.
The door **hadn't been** locked.

Reported speech & thought

Change the verb one tense further back:

Present	→	Past
will	→	would
Past | Present perfect	→	Past perfect

He told me he **was** a tourist.
  (His actual words: '**I'm** a tourist.')

She said she **would** teach me Japanese.
  (She said '**I'll** teach you Japanese.')

I suddenly discovered that **I'd lost** my wallet.
  (I thought '**I've lost** my wallet.')

See also Reference section, page 138.

4 The dead rabbit

In this activity, students listen to a story in sections and predict what they are going to hear next. The aim of this is partly to develop active listening skills, and partly to focus on those parts of the story that involve flashbacks.

Listening & discussion

- Look at the title and the pictures and ask students what they expect the story to be about. (Possible answer: a dog killed a rabbit, or perhaps found a dead rabbit; or someone killed a rabbit, and the dog found the person who did it.)

- 🔊 Play the recording, pausing after each section to discuss the questions. With the prediction questions, try to get a wide range of possible ideas.

  Answers (no answers given to the prediction questions):

  Part 1
  – It was always getting into trouble.
  – It had wrecked (= destroyed) the house and dug up the garden.
  Part 2
  – A dead rabbit.
  – It had killed it.
  Part 3
  – It hadn't damaged the rabbit.
  Part 4
  – He cleaned the rabbit, and put it back in the neighbours' rabbit hutch.
  – The neighbour came round, looking upset.
  Part 5
  – Because she couldn't understand what had happened.
  – It had dug up the rabbit – it was already dead.

> *Vocabulary option*
> In passing, use the picture of the rabbit to teach the word *hutch*, which is used in the story.

> *'Urban myths'*
> This story is an example of an *urban myth*, that is, a story people hear and pass on, usually saying that it happened to 'a friend of a friend': exactly *who* it happened to is never made clear.
>
> There are two more examples of urban myths in Unit 3 of the Self-study Workbook, page 21.
>
> *Optional extension*
> Ask students if they know any other 'urban myths'.

🔊 Tapescript for Exercise 4: *The dead rabbit*

Part 1
Well, this friend of mine had a dog, which he'd bought for his daughter's tenth birthday. This dog was always getting into trouble, and it had already completely wrecked their house and dug up their garden.

Part 2
Anyway, one Friday this dog turned up with a dead rabbit in its mouth, which it brought into the house and dropped on the floor. And my friend's daughter immediately recognised this rabbit as the one that belonged to the little boy next door, and the little boy kept this rabbit in a hutch in his garden, so the dog must have got into their garden and killed it.

Part 3
So my friend had a look at the rabbit, which was all muddy and dirty, but it didn't seem to have any tooth marks on it and it wasn't damaged in any way. So he had an idea.

Part 4
What he did was he cleaned the rabbit up and he dried it with a hairdryer, and made it look really nice, and then later on that night when the neighbours had gone to sleep, he slipped over the garden fence and put the dead rabbit back in its hutch. The next morning there was a ring at the doorbell, and it was the little boy's mother, and she was looking really upset. And my friend said 'What's the matter?'

Part 5
And she said 'It's terrible. It's little Timmy's rabbit. I just can't understand it. The rabbit died two days ago, and so we took it out of its hutch and buried it in the garden, and this morning he went back out into the garden to clean out the rabbit hutch so we could sell it – and there was the rabbit back in the hutch.'

Focus on Form

1 *Which tense?*

> Past simple, Past continuous and Past perfect in narration.

- Students read the text and put the verbs into their correct form. They could either do this together in pairs, or they could do the exercise individually and then sit in pairs to compare their answers. Answers:

  had been; hadn't rung; was

  put; picked; had lost; had pulled; had just divorced; started

  was still doing ; opened; came; was; was wearing; was smoking; looked; hadn't slept; had seen; was; was holding; was

  asked

  said

2 *Explanations: the Past perfect*

> Past perfect tense to refer to previous events

- If necessary, go through the sentences in the box and ask students to change them into the Past perfect.
- Pairwork. One student reads out the sentences, and the other chooses an explanation from the box. Answers:

  b ... because he'd left his wallet at home.
  c ... because he'd passed his exam.
  d ... because he hadn't had any breakfast.
  e ... because he'd studied history at university.
  f ... because he hadn't reserved a table.
  g ... because he hadn't done his homework.
  h ... because he'd lost their address.

3 *Reported speech*

> Reported speech structures involving tense changes

- Look at the example, and if necessary remind students of the tense changes involved in reported speech (see the table in the Reference section, page 138).

- Give each student a letter, A or B, alternately round the class. Students read the remarks either on page 119 or on page 120. Working separately, they think how they would talk about them using reported speech.
- Students form pairs, one A and one B. Without looking at the book, they report the conversation they had at the party, using reported speech.
- As a round-up, look at the remarks together and establish how they could be reported. Possible answers:

  A He told me his name was George and that he came from Texas. He said he owned an oil company. He said he owned three houses in the USA and one in the South of France. He told me he was staying with the Foreign Minister and that he was going to have dinner with the Prime Minister the next day. He told me that he really liked it here because there was so much to buy in the shops. He said he'd never been here before but he'd certainly come again.

  B She told me her name was Ramona and said that she collected antiques and she was planning to open an antique shop here. She said she often went to New York on business and always flew first class. She told me she knew lots of famous people in America and she'd known the Rockefeller family for years. She said it was lovely talking to me and she said she'd give me a ring next week and we could have lunch together.

4 *Pronunciation*

▭ Ask students to try saying the sentences themselves, then play the recording as a model. Focus on these points:

a Reduced vowel in *had* /(h)əd/.
  Full vowel in *hadn't* /hædn̩t/.
b Pronunciation of *There was* /ðeə wəz/ and *There were* /ðeə wə/.
c Pronunciation of *said* /sed/, *told me* /ˈtəʊld‿mi/, *realised* /ˈriəlaɪzd/.

Self-study Workbook

Exercise A: What had happened?
The Past perfect tense for flashbacks.
Students add sentences to a narrative, explaining what had happened.

Exercise B: Past states and previous actions
Two equivalent columns of sentences, saying what things were like and what had happened.
Students write in the missing sentences.

Exercise C: Reported speech
Reported speech with tense changes.
Students match remarks to speakers, and report them.

Exercise D: I realised ...
Students look at pictures and write two paragraphs about people who suddenly realised something.

Translation
Key sentences for translation.

Listening: Locked in!
Someone tells the story of how he was locked in an office building. Students answer comprehension questions and fill gaps in a summary.

Pronunciation: Linking words with /w/ or /j/
'Links' between words ending and beginning in vowel sounds. Students hear examples, then look at sentences and predict where the links will be.

Reading: Strange – but true?
Eight extraordinary news stories – six true, and two untrue. Students match remarks to the stories, then guess which two are untrue.

Focus on Form

1 Which tense?

Put the verbs in brackets into the correct form. Use the Past simple (*did*), the Past continuous (*was doing*) or the Past perfect (*had done*).

The clock said 11.30. I (be) in the office for two hours, and the phone (not ring) once. Maybe I (be) in the wrong business.

I (put) my feet up on the desk, and (pick) up the morning paper. The New York Hurricanes (lose) again. The police (pull) two more bodies out of the river. Myra Halliday (just divorce) her sixth husband. Nothing new there. I (start) doing the crossword.

I (still do) the crossword when the door (open) and a man (come) in. He (be) tall, fairly good-looking, and in his mid-forties. He (wear) a white suit and a loud tie, and he (smoke) an expensive cigar. He (look) as if he (not sleep) for a week. I (see) him before. His picture (be) on the front page of the newspaper that I (hold) in my hand. He (be) Myra Halliday's latest ex-husband.

"Your boss in, honey?" he (ask).

"Where I come from, mister," I (say), "people knock before they open doors. And that's a No Smoking sign on the wall."

2 Explanations: the Past perfect

Student A: Read out the sentences below.

Student B: Give a suitable explanation from the box, using the Past perfect tense.

Example: *He had to go by bus ...*

... because his car had broken down.

a He had to go by bus ...
b He couldn't pay for the meal ...
c His parents bought him a new bike ...
d He was hungry ...
e He knew a lot about the French Revolution ...
f He couldn't get into the restaurant ...
g He had to stay in after school ...
h He couldn't get in touch with them ...

> He didn't reserve a table.
> He passed his exam.
> He lost their address.
> His car broke down.
> He didn't have any breakfast.
> He didn't do his homework.
> He studied history at university.
> He left his wallet at home.

3 Reported speech

Work in pairs. Last weekend you were both invited to a rather smart party. You each spent some time talking to two different people.

Turn to page 119 (*Student A*) or page 120 (*Student B*) to find out what they said to you. Then try and remember what they said, and tell your partner, using reported speech.

Example: '*I'm a film actor. I've just come back from making a film in Hollywood.*'

He told me that he was a film actor, and that he'd just come back from making a film in Hollywood.

4 Pronunciation

How do you say the words and phrases below?

a The guests had arrived.
    Everyone had enjoyed themselves.
    The guests hadn't arrived.
    She hadn't been abroad.

b There was someone in the room.
    There were people everywhere.

c They said they were reporters.
    He told me we'd met before.
    She realised that she'd forgotten his name.

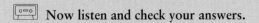 Now listen and check your answers.

Breaking the law

1 Crime ...

A Customs officials found 5 kilos of heroin hidden inside the tyres of the car.

B The two gunmen left the shop with more than £10,000 worth of watches and jewellery.

C When he opened the door, she shot him three times in the chest. According to the pathologist's report he died instantly.

D She said she would publish the photos unless he gave her £5,000.

E A ransom of $1,500,000 dollars was demanded for the child's release.

F Shortly after take-off, they produced guns and forced the pilot to fly to Cyprus, where the plane was given permission to land, and surrounded by armed troops.

G When the school was reopened after the weekend, staff found that three classrooms had been completely wrecked: furniture and windows were broken, and graffiti had been sprayed on the walls.

H He broke into the flat at 3.00 in the morning and took £3,000 from a cupboard.

1 Look at the extracts from newspapers and match them with the crimes in the box.

blackmail	murder
burglary	robbery
hijacking	smuggling
kidnapping	vandalism

What do you call the *people* who commit these crimes?

2 *a* Choose a crime and think of a real incident that you know of.

b Work in groups. Decide which of your stories is the most interesting.

c Tell the story you have chosen to the rest of the class.

This unit is concerned with crime, punishment and the law, and deals with three main vocabulary areas:
– crimes and criminals
– punishments for crimes and other offences
– vocabulary connected with the judicial system (e.g. *trial, judge, guilty*).

The Reading and Listening activity is a series of short crime mysteries that students have to solve.

1 Crime …

This exercise introduces three sets of words for talking about crime: crimes (e.g. robbery), criminals (e.g. robber) and verbs (e.g. to rob). In the second part, students use this vocabulary to talk about real crimes they have heard or read about.

➤ Workbook: Exercise A

1 Reading & presentation

• Give time for students to read the texts and match them with the words in the box.

• Go through the answers. Read through each text, dealing with any unknown vocabulary (e.g. *customs official, heroin, ransom, armed troops, wrecked, graffiti*). If necessary, establish the meaning of each 'crime' word by giving simple glosses and examples (e.g. A burglar steals things from houses). Answers:

A smuggling D blackmail G vandalism
B robbery E kidnapping H burglary
C murder F hijacking

• As you match the texts and crimes, build up a table showing the verb and the word for the person who commits each crime:

VERB	CRIME	PERSON
blackmail	blackmail	blackmailer
burgle (steal)	burglary	burglar
hijack	hijacking	hijacker
kidnap	kidnapping	kidnapper
murder	murder	murderer
rob	robbery	robber
smuggle	smuggling	smuggler
vandalise	vandalism	vandal

2 Speaking activity

• Give time for students to think of a real crime story that they know: it could be something that happened to themselves or to someone they know, or something they have read or heard about. During this stage, students could write brief notes or work in pairs.

• Students sit in large groups (five or six). In turn, they tell their crime story, and then choose the one they think is the most interesting.

• Each group tells their 'best' story to the rest of the class.

Language note
A *burglar* breaks into people's houses and steals things.
A *robber* steals from banks, shops or people, usually with violence.
Thief is a general word for someone who steals (the crime is *theft*).
You steal money and things, but you rob people or places:
– He *stole* £1,000 from the bank.
– He *robbed* the bank.

Optional lead-in
Tell the class about a real incident involving a crime – either something that happened to you or something you've read about.

Alternative: homework project
Let students collect crime stories from outside the class (e.g. from parents, friends, host families), and then use them as material for the next lesson.

2 ... and punishment

This activity is a guided discussion on crime and punishment, and focuses on common expressions for describing punishments (e.g. pay a fine, be sent to prison*).*

1 Presentation

- Look at the offences in the box and check that students know what they mean (*shoplifting* = stealing from a shop by putting things in your bag or in your pocket).
- Look at the list of punishments. To focus on their meaning, ask students questions, e.g. *When do people have to pay a fine? What crimes are people sent to prison for? Are people ever sentenced to death in your country?*
- Working alone, students decide what punishment they would give for each crime, and make brief notes.

2 Discussion

- Students sit in groups to discuss what punishments they would give.
- As a round-up, take each offence in turn and see if different groups agree on a suitable pubishment.

3 Guilty or not guilty?

This is a reading and discussion activity, in which students consider a real court case involving someone who used a swordstick to defend himself against an attacker in an underground train. It introduces a range of vocabulary connected with the judicial system, law courts and trials.

1 Reading & presentation

- As a preparation for reading the text, write key words connected with the law on the board, and see if students can tell you what they mean:

arrest	prosecution	guilty
court	defence	not guilty
trial	judge	
	jury	

- Give time for students to read the text. Then check comprehension by asking questions round the class, e.g. *Where was Mr Cook? Where was he going? What was he carrying? What did the man do? What did Mr Cook do? Was the man injured? Why did Mr Cook use the swordstick? What happened to Mr Cook?* As you do this, present any difficult words (e.g. *strangle, stab*).
- Establish what he was charged with. Answer:

  Possessing an offensive weapon (= having a weapon which could be used to attack someone – his swordstick).

2 Discussion & listening

- Groupwork. Students think of arguments for the prosecution and the defence. Some possible arguments:

  Prosecution: He was carrying a dangerous weapon in public, so he was breaking the law. He didn't need to stab the man – he could have called for help. He could have injured the man seriously, or even killed him.

  Defence: He used the swordstick in self-defence. He had to use it – the man was trying to kill him. He was a respectable citizen, not a criminal.

  They then decide what they think happened at the end of the trial.

- Ask each group what conclusions they came to, and why.
- ▭ Play the recording, and establish what actually happened. Answer:

  The jury found him guilty. He had to pay a fine of £200. He was also given a suspended prison sentence (= he wasn't actually sent to prison, but he would have to serve his sentence if he committed another crime). He also had to pay the costs of the trial, and his swordstick was taken away.

Option
Ask students to put the crimes in order of seriousness.

Language note
Sentence is a noun or a verb. In court, the judge *passes a sentence* (= announces the punishment). He/She may *sentence* the criminal *to imprisonment* or *death*.

➤ Workbook: Exercise B

▭ Tapescript for Exercise 3: *Guilty or not guilty?*

And now the swordstick trial. Mr Edward Cook has been found guilty of carrying an offensive weapon. He was given a 28-day suspended prison sentence, and fined £200. He was also ordered to pay £2,500 towards the costs of the trial, and to hand over his swordstick to the police. Afterwards, Mr Cook said he was shocked at the verdict, and repeated that he had only used the swordstick in self-defence. 'I had to use it,' he told reporters, 'or I'd be a dead man today.'

Alternative
Ask different groups to make a case *either* for the prosecution *or* the defence.

Each group reports its arguments briefly to the rest of the class.

The whole class then votes *guilty* or *not guilty*. If the verdict is *guilty*, they decide on an appropriate punishment.

2 … and punishment

1 What punishments would you give for the offences in the box?

Do you think the person should

– pay a fine?
– be sent to prison?
– be sentenced to death?
– be punished in some other way?
– not be punished at all?

> shoplifting
> dropping litter
> spying for a foreign power
> drunken driving
> smoking marijuana
> shooting a police officer
> not paying income tax

2 In groups, compare your answers.

3 Guilty or not guilty?

1 Read the news story. What was Mr Cook charged with?

2 *a* What arguments do you think were used in court

– by the prosecution?
– by the defence?

b Which of these things do you think happened at the end of the trial?

– Mr Cook was found not guilty.
– He was found guilty and had to pay a fine.
– He was found guilty and was sent to prison.

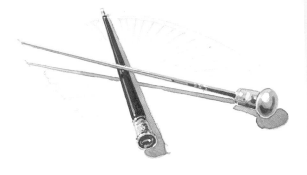 Now listen to a news broadcast about the trial. What happened?

Passenger 'stabbed attacker on Tube with a swordstick'

A COMMUTER carrying a swordstick stabbed a man in the stomach after he tried to strangle him on a London Underground train, a court was told yesterday.

Mr Edward Cook drew his swordstick as he was held by the neck and his head was repeatedly struck against a door, it was said in Wood Green Crown Court.

The court heard that Mr Cook, aged 56, was returning home on the Victoria Line when two young men attacked him.

"One of them pushed him against the door of the carriage, holding him by the neck and banging him against the door. At that stage he took out his sword and used it on the person attacking him," Mr Michael Lawson, for the prosecution, told the jury.

The attacker, who smelled strongly of alcohol, was taken to hospital and treated for the wound. Mr Cook was arrested and charged with possessing an offensive weapon. He told police he carried the swordstick for self-defence while walking in Epping Forest. Mr Lawson said there was no lasting injury to the attacker.

After the incident Mr Cook was interviewed by police and explained why he used the swordstick.

Mr Cook yesterday

He said: "I did it as a last means of self-defence. It was a desperate act as my life was in danger."

The walking stick, which unscrewed to reveal a three-foot long blade and cost Mr Cook £400, was shown to the jury.

The case continues today.

4 Detective Shadow

LISTENING

You will hear two people playing a game in which one person reads out a murder mystery and the other person tries to solve it.

There are three characters:

– Uncle Cecil (the murder victim)
– Harry Fox (his nephew)
– Detective Shadow.

1   Listen to the first part of the recording and answer the questions.

   – What did Shadow see when he arrived?
   – What happened, according to Harry Fox?
   – What happened after Shadow arrived?

2   How does Shadow know that Harry Fox is lying?

    Now listen to the solution.
Were you right?

READING

Here are four more crimes solved by Detective Shadow.
What are the solutions?

1

Shadow opened the door to Dr Adam Apple's office and looked around him. Dr Apple's head lay on his desk surrounded by a pool of blood. On the floor to his right lay a small handgun. There were powder burns on his right temple, indicating that he had been shot at close range. On his desk was a suicide note, and his right hand held the pen that had written it. Shadow recorded the time as 3.30 pm, and ascertained that death had occurred within the past hour. As Shadow was gathering clues, Dr Apple's wife burst into the office and screamed, "Good lord, my husband's been shot!" She ran toward him, saw the note and cried, "Why would he want to kill himself?"

"This was no suicide" said Shadow. "This was clearly a case of murder." How does he know?

4 Detective Shadow

This combined reading and listening activity consists of five short crime mysteries: students listen to the first one and read the other four. In each one, Shadow, the detective, solves the mystery, and students have to say how he knows what the solution is.

LISTENING

- As a lead-in, look at the picture and establish the basic situation: a man's lying on the floor dead (Uncle Cecil), he's probably been murdered, the window's broken, it's night, Detective Shadow has arrived at the scene.

- 🔊 Play the first part of the recording, and use Question 1 to help focus on the main points of the story. Discuss the answers together, making sure that everyone understands the situation. Answers:
  - He saw Cecil lying dead.
  - He says that they were watching TV when someone broke the window, Cecil was shot, there was a crash of thunder and the power went off.
  - The lights came on.

- Give students time to think about Question 2. They can work alone, or in pairs or groups.

- Ask around the class for solutions to the mystery.

- 🔊 Play the second part of the recording, and establish the solution. Answer:

  According to Harry, they were watching TV when the murder took place and the power went off. So the TV should have come back on when the power came back. It didn't – so Harry is lying.

READING

- Students work in pairs or groups. They read through the other mysteries and try to solve them. Give each group a dictionary so that they can look up any unfamiliar words.

- As a round-up, look at each mystery in turn with the whole class, and see if students can tell you the solution. Solutions:

  1 If he shot himself in the right temple, he must have had the gun in his right hand. But his right hand was holding the pen. So the murderer must have put the pen in his right hand after shooting him.

  2 The plant's leaves were facing away from the window. But plants always turn their leaves towards the light, so someone must have moved the plant recently. As Sid Crook had the only key, he must have been in the room and probably took some of the jewels.

  3 Shadow doesn't say 'Sam is dead', but just 'Your brother-in-law is dead'. So how does Grey know which brother-in-law it is? From what he says, he obviously has several.

  4 If Cool's story was true, his fingerprints should have been on the phone on Queen's desk. But when the police examined the phone, they found that Cool's fingerprints weren't there – Cool had forgotten to take his gloves off before he telephoned the police.

Vocabulary option

Before you play the recording, write key words and phrases on the board, e.g.

> **crack of thunder**
> **torch**
> **smashed**
> **the power went off**
> **reading lights**
> **watching TV**

Establish what they mean, and ask students to guess how they will fit together in the story.

🔊 The tapescript is on page T83.

Alternative

Give each group a different mystery to read. They read it and discuss the solution. Then students form new groups and tell other students the mystery they read.

Grammar presentation option

In reporting conclusions about the mysteries, it is natural to use the structure *must have* + past participle, e.g.
– He *must have been* in the room.
– He *must have killed* him.

This is a good opportunity to present this structure.

📼 Tapescript for Exercise 4: *Detective Shadow*

Part 1

A *(Reading)* There was a loud crack of thunder and the power went off. Shadow started to look for a candle when he heard a knock at his door. It was Harry Fox, who lived nearby with his uncle. 'Come quickly!' cried Harry Fox. 'My Uncle Cecil has been shot!' Shadow grabbed a torch and ran to his neighbour's house. When they arrived, Shadow shone the light on Cecil's face, and he knew immediately that he was dead. Harry explained that he and his uncle had been watching TV, when suddenly the window had smashed in and Cecil had fallen forward dead. 'At that moment there was a crash of thunder and the power went out,' Harry said. 'That's when I ran and got you.' Just then the power returned and the two reading lights in the room came on. Shadow and Harry sat in total silence for two minutes, unable to believe the terrible scene before them. Shadow finally turned to Harry and said, 'Your story is obviously completely untrue.' Why does Shadow think Harry's lying?

B So right. So Shadow was in his house (Mm) and Harry Fox and his uncle were nearby, they're neighbours (Mm-hm) …

Part 2

B … Erm, they sat in silence. So the television didn't come on then when the power came on.

A No.

B Ah, right. So in other words Harry had been lying. And that's how Shadow knew, because Harry had said they were watching the television. If they were watching the television, it would have come on again. So, is that right?

A Absolutely right, yes (Good). If Harry Fox and his Uncle Cecil were watching TV, as Harry claimed, the TV should have come back on when the power returned. They sat in silence for a couple of minutes, so it was obvious that the TV had not been on.

B Been on. Ah, OK, yeah.

A Well done.

Self-study Workbook

Exercise A: Criminals and their crimes
Students unscramble nine people's 'names' to find out what kind of criminals they are. They then write short imaginary descriptions of their crimes.

Exercise B: Crime story
An account of a trial with gaps.
Students fill the gaps with words from a box.

New words
Space to record new words with notes and examples.

Translation
Key sentences for translation.

Listening: A case of fraud
The story of an imaginative con trick. Students fill gaps in a text and match what they hear with a written summary.

Phrasal verbs: Prepositional verbs (2)
More prepositional verbs with idiomatic meanings (e.g. *get over*, *do without*). Students match verbs to their context, then use them to replace phrases in sentences.

Writing skills: Defining and non-defining relative clauses
Use of defining and non-defining relative clauses, and differences between them. Students identify the two types in sentences, then rewrite a paragraph using both defining and non-defining relative clauses.

2

"I have the only key to the room containing the jewellery of my late aunt Maggy," said Sid Crook. "Since her death a week ago, neither I nor anybody else has entered this room. I was quite pleased to hear all her jewellery was to be sold and the proceeds to go to charity," continued Crook.

Shadow removed a huge plant whose broad leaves were turned towards the wall, partially covering the safe. While Crook was opening the combination lock, Shadow crossed the room to sit on the ledge of the large bay window. Crook opened the safe, and removed the bag of jewels. "I'm sure these jewels will fetch a fortune for charity," said a smiling Sid Crook. "I'll bet these jewels are either fake or there are a few missing," replied Shadow. What made Shadow suspicious?

3

"Mr Grey?" inquired Shadow, "I'm afraid I have some bad news for you. Your brother-in-law is dead and I have reason to believe he was murdered."

"Oh no!" replied Grey. "I just saw Sam a couple of days ago. To tell you the truth though, I'm not surprised. Sam did have a big mouth and quite a few enemies. As a matter of fact both of my sisters' husbands and Sam had a big fight over a business deal that went wrong. Then there was a friend of my brother's who lent Sam a lot of money and never got it back. Another person is my wife's brother who just got out of jail. He accused Sam of framing him. He swore he would get even." As Grey talked on about Sam's enemies, Shadow got out the handcuffs and arrested him on suspicion of murder. Why?

4

Jim Cool waited until Ed Fry left the office of author Harry Queen. Cool slipped on a pair of gloves, took a handgun from his desk, and crossed the hall to Queen's office. As Queen looked up to see who was there, Cool took aim and shot. Cool dropped the gun on the floor, picked up the telephone on Queen's desk and called the police. He then went back across the hall to his own office and hid the gloves. Shadow arrived moments later and Cool told his story. "I was working at my desk when I heard a shot. I ran to the hall and saw a man fitting the description of Ed Fry running from Queen's office. I went to Queen's office and found him lying on the floor dead. I immediately picked up the phone on Queen's desk and called the police."

Several hours later Shadow arrested Cool for murder. Why was he so easily caught?

All five cases are adapted from *MindTrap* ©, under license to Spears Games ®.

Review: Units 13–18

Find out

1 A Which person in your family are you closest to in age? Tell B who it is.
   B Find out how different A is from the person he/she has chosen. Ask about

   – appearance   – personality
   – interests   – abilities.

2 Find out from other students what kinds of TV programmes they enjoy and don't enjoy watching.

   Who do you have most in common with?

3 In groups, talk about what you've been doing recently. Find out

   – who's been enjoying themselves the most
   – who's been the busiest.

Role-play

MILLIONAIRE FOUND MURDERED AT COUNTRY RESIDENCE

A You're the housekeeper. You discovered the body this morning. What did you find? How had the victim been murdered?
B You're the dead man's secretary. You spent yesterday working with him. Who else was there? Did anything unusual happen?
C You're the police officer investigating the case. What have you found out so far? Do you suspect anyone?
D You're a journalist. Think of questions to ask A, B and C.
   Then interview A, B and C. Report what they said to the rest of the class.

Conversational English

1 Giving advice

1 I think you should ask for your money back.
2 Why don't you turn it on its side?
3 Have you tried cleaning the plugs?
4 You'd better see a doctor straight away.
5 I think you ought to wear your boots.
6 If I were you, I'd apologise.

1 Look at the pictures above. What problems do the people have?
   Which bubble should go with which picture?

2 What advice would you give the person below?

My husband's father came to live with us after his wife died while he looked for somewhere else to live. This was six months ago, and he's still here. I feel sorry for him, but he's quite difficult, and he does nothing to help around the flat. I want him to go, but my husband seems to like having him around.

   Now think of a problem of your own and ask different people for some advice. What was the best (and worst) advice you received?

Find out

1 Revision of language from Unit 13

- Preparation. Tell the class about a member of your family, and make comparisons between that person and yourself. Get the class to ask you questions.
- Establish some of the comparison structures that students might use, e.g. She's a bit taller than I am; I stay up later (than he does); He finds it much easier to make friends.
- Pairwork. Students take it in turns to ask each other questions. Then ask students to tell you what they found out from their partner.

2 Revision of language from Unit 14

- Preparation. Tell the class what TV programmes you like watching, and see if anyone in the class has the same tastes as you.
- Students sit in large groups (five or six).They take it in turns to say what kind of programmes they most enjoy, and find out who they have most in common with.
- Round-up. Ask each group to tell you whether there are any programmes they all like or dislike.

3 Revision of language from Unit 15

- Preparation. Get students to ask you questions to find out how busy you've been and whether you've been enjoying yourself (e.g. Have you been working in the evenings? Have you been to any parties?).
- Pairwork. Students ask each other questions.
- Round-up. Ask a few students what they found out.

Role-play

Revision of language from Units 17 & 18

- Preparation. Take Roles A, B and C in turn and discuss some of the things that the person might talk about, e.g.
  - A Where was the body? What did it look like? Was there anything beside the body? Any weapons?
  - B Did anyone visit him? Did he seem worried about anything? Did he say anything unusual to you?
  - C Where have you looked? Who have you talked to? What clues have you found? Any weapons? Any footprints? Any windows open? Do you suspect anyone?
- Give students roles: A, B, C or D. Give a minute or two for students to prepare what they will say. If you like, pairs of students could share the same role, so that they can prepare together.
- Students sit in groups, so that each group contains students with all four roles. The journalist interviews the others in turn.
- Round-up. Ask each journalist to tell you briefly what he/she found out.

1 Giving advice

This exercise practises ways of giving advice to people who have a problem.

1 Presentation

- Look at the pictures and establish what the problems are and which caption should go with each situation:
  1 It's snowing and he wants to go out.
     I think you ought to wear your boots.
  2 His/her car has broken down / won't start.
     Have you tried cleaning the plugs?
  3 He feels ill.
     You'd better see a doctor straight away.
  4 He's just bought a TV, and it doesn't work.
     I think you should ask for your money back.
  5 They've had an argument / are not talking to each other.
     If I were you, I'd apologise.
  6 They can't get the cupboard through the door.
     Why don't you turn it on its side?
- From the examples, build up a table of advice structures on the board:

You should ...	If I were you, I'd ...
You ought to ...	Have you tried ...?
You'd better ...	Why don't you ...?

2 Practice

- Give time for students to read the problem. Either ask students to suggest possible advice round the class, or give time for them to write sentences first and then read them out. Possible advice:

I think you should ask him to help.
Why don't you try sitting down together and discussing the problem?
If I were you, I'd find somewhere nearby for him to live.

- Give time for students to think of a problem of their own (this could be a real problem or an invented one). Students either sit in groups and tell their problem to the others, or move freely round the class, telling their own problem and also giving other students advice.

⸤▭⸥ Tapescript for *Exercise 2 Making choices, page T85*

1 A What about this one? Is that the kind of thing you have in mind?
   B Um, no, I'd prefer something a little darker.
   A Mm. Well, there's this one.
   B Yes, that's better. I'll have that one.
2 A Come on. Are you ready?
   B Um, actually, I don't think I'll come, if you don't mind. I'd rather finish reading this book.
3 A I'll have the chicken, please.
   B One chicken ... And for you sir?
   A I'd like the lamb, please.
4 A Well we could drive. Or would you rather go by train?
   B Well actually, I'd prefer to fly, if we can afford it.

Talking points

This activity revises language from all six units:

– *Two towns in your country. How are they different?*   Unit 13
– *Radio stations*   Unit 14
– *Today's news*   Unit 15
– *'I'd like to be good at …'*   Unit 16
– *What's wrong with the education system*   Unit 16
– *'Do you know the joke about …?'*   Unit 17
– *'When I was a child, I believed …'*   Unit 17
– *Smuggling*   Unit 18

The activity can be played as a game round the class. One student chooses a topic and says a sentence or two about it. Another student then continues, adding another sentence, and so on.

As a preparation, you could let students choose two or three of the topics and look back at the appropriate unit to recall things they might say. If they like, they could also make brief notes.

Words

1 Revision of language from Unit 16

● Students note down their best and worst subjects.

● Ask students to read out what they wrote, and ask why they were good or bad at these subjects.

2 Revision of language from Units 14, 16 & 18

● Students write down as many words as they can think of.

● Build up lists of expressions on the board, e.g.

Newspaper: business news, crossword, weather forecast
Education: college, university, nursery school
Criminals: blackmailer, smuggler, hijacker

3 Revision of language from Units 14, 16 & 18

● Ask the questions to the whole class, and use them to focus on key vocabulary from the units, e.g.

You'd find a headline at the top of a *newspaper article*.
In a chat show, the *host* invites well-known people to appear as *guests*, and asks them questions.
Things you might learn by heart: *vocabulary* (languages), *tables* (maths), *formulae* (maths/science), *dates* (history).
You might have to *pay a fine*, or *be sent to prison*.
There are usually 12 people on the jury: they sit in the *court*, listen to the *trial*, and decide if the accused person is *guilty* or *not guilty*.

2 Making choices

This exercise practises structures used for choosing and expressing preference.

1 Listening & presentation

● ▣ Play the recording. Establish what's going on, and how the speakers use the structures in the box:

1 Someone's buying something in a shop (e.g. a hat).
   I'd prefer something a little darker. I'll have that one.
2 Someone is about to go out, expecting the other person to come, but she decides not to.
   I don't think I'll come. I'd rather get on with this book.
3 Two people in a restaurant, ordering a meal.
   I'll have the chicken. I'd like the lamb.
4 Two people discussing how to travel somewhere.
   Would you rather go by train? I'd prefer to fly.

● Use the examples to focus on the structures, and make these points:
   – We use *I'll* when we decide to do something; often we add *I think* or *I don't think*:
     I think I'll go for a walk.
     I don't think I'll eat anything.
   – *I'd like* is a less direct way to say 'I want'. The question is *Would you like …?*:
     Would you like some coffee?
     Would you like to come with us?
   – *I'd rather* and *I'd prefer* mean the same. *I'd prefer* is

followed by *to*; *I'd rather* is followed by the infinitive without *to*:
I'd rather go by plane.
I'd prefer to go by plane.

2 Practice

● Look at each situation in turn, and elicit suitable expressions. Possible answers:

A: How would you like to travel? Would you prefer to go first class? Where would you like to stay?
B: I'd like to fly Air France. I'd rather get a morning flight. I'd like a double room, at the back of the hotel.

A: Would you like to come and see the Matisse exhibition? I'll get the tickets. I'll meet you at lunchtime.
B: I'd rather not go today. I think I'll stay at home and watch TV. I'd prefer to go tomorrow.

A & B: I think I'll have the pâté. What starter would you like? I don't think I'll have salmon – I'd rather have chicken. What would you like to drink? I'd like Cola.

● Pairwork. Students choose one of the situations and improvise a conversation.

▣ The tapescript is on page T84.

Self-study Workbook

There is a review test of Units 13–18 on pages 86–7. The test is in six parts:
Sentence rewriting, Verb forms, Vocabulary, Fill the gaps, Writing paragraphs and Dictation.

Talking points

Choose one of these topics. Take it in turns to say a sentence or two about it.

Two towns in your country. How are they different?

Radio stations

Today's news

'I'd like to be good at …'

What's wrong with the education system

'Do you know the joke about …?'

'When I was a child, I believed …'

Smuggling

Words

1 **What are/were**
   - your best three subjects at school?
   - your worst three subjects at school?

2 **Add words to these lists.**
   - foreign news, advertisements …
   - primary school, secondary school …
   - burglar, murderer …

3 **Answer these questions.**
   - Where would you find a *headline*?
   - What happens in a *chat show*?
   - Have you ever learnt anything *by heart*?
   - What's the penalty in your country for *shoplifting*?
   - What does a *jury* do?

2 Making choices

1 You will hear four short conversations in which people make choices.

   a What is going on in each conversation?

   b How do the speakers use the expressions in the box?

> I'll …
> I'd like …
> I'd rather …
> I'd prefer …

2 Look at these situations.
  How do you think the people might use the expressions in the box?

Situation 1

Student A: Your boss B is going abroad on a business trip. You have to arrange travel and hotel accommodation. Find out what he/she wants to do.

Student B: Decide how and when you want to travel and what kind of hotel and hotel room you'd like.

Situation 2

Student A: You want to go to an exhibition which is only open today and tomorrow. You'd like A to come with you.

Student B: There's a good film on TV, and you're feeling tired. You're not busy tomorrow.

Now choose one of the situations and act out a conversation.

Situation 3

A & B: You're in a restaurant. Look at the menu and decide what to order.

STARTERS

Tomato soup   Melon
Pâté with toast and butter   Deep-fried mushrooms

MAIN COURSES

Salmon in cream sauce with seasonal vegetables
Cheeseburger with French fries and mayonnaise
Mushroom omelette with mixed salad
Chicken and prawn with black bean sauce & noodles
Lamb curry (medium hot) with boiled rice and salad

SWEETS

Fresh fruit salad
American apple pie with ice-cream
Death-by-chocolate gateau, served with cream

DRINKS

Mineral water   Cola   Red wine   Coffee
Fruit juice   Beer   White wine   Tea

Up to now

1 Favourite things

1 Read these extracts from a magazine article.

a Which objects is the woman describing?

b How long has she had each one?
Complete these sentences.
   – She's had it for …
   – She's had it since …

Favourite things

Novelist Jo Hamilton, 26, takes us on a guided tour of her favourite possessions

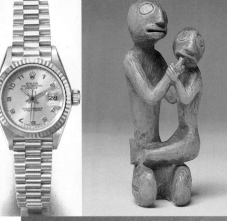

66 I bought this ▨▨▨ while I was travelling in Southern Morocco about eight years ago. It's very precious to me because I had very little money at the time and I spent a whole day bargaining to get it at a good price. I used to have it on the floor, but it started to get a bit worn, so now it hangs on the wall of my living room. 99

66 This was always my favourite ▨▨▨ when I was a child – I was given it for my third birthday, and for years I used to take it everywhere with me. These days I keep it in my bedroom, and even after all this time it's very comforting to know it's there keeping an eye on me while I'm asleep. 99

66 This ▨▨▨ used to be my grandmother's – my grandfather gave it to her when they got engaged. She gave it to me when I got married five years ago, and asked me to pass it on to my own grandchildren, which is just what I intend to do. It's not worth very much, but I think it's beautiful, and I only wear it on very special occasions. 99

2 *Student A:* Write a sentence describing one of your favourite possessions. Don't say how long you've had it or where you got it. Give your sentence to B.

Student B: Imagine how long A has had the thing, and why it is important to him/her. Make some notes.

Now tell A what you thought. How far were you from the truth?

This unit is concerned with duration up to the present (how long things have been going on for or how long it is since something happened). The unit focuses on
– Present perfect continuous and simple with *for* and *since*
– Questions with *How long …?* and *How long ago …?*
– Negative duration structures.

1 Favourite things

This exercise is about possessions and how long people have had them. It focuses on the structure have had *with* for *and* since, *including examples where* since *is followed by a clause (e.g.* since I got married*). The reading texts in the first part lead to a presentation of the main structures; in the second part students talk about their own favourite possessions.*

➤ Focus on Form: Exercises 1, 2
➤ Workbook: Exercise A

1 Reading & presentation

● Look at the pictures and establish what the objects are:

teddy bear, watch, wooden carving (statue), carpet, photo album, brooch, rocking horse

Then students read the texts and decide which pictures they refer to. Answers:

carpet, teddy bear, brooch

● Establish how long the woman has had each object, getting students to make sentences with *for* or *since*. Answers:

Carpet: She's had it for eight years; she's had it since (1986); she's had it since she was in Morocco.

Teddy bear: She's had it for 23 years; she's had it since (1971); she's had it since she was three.

Brooch: She's had it for five years; she's had it since (1989); she's had it since she got married.

● Present structures with *for* and *since* on the board:

She's had it	for	three years. a long time.		She's had it	since	1960. Christmas. she was six.

Point out that
– we use *for* with periods of time, and *since* with points of time (the 'starting point')
– *since* can be followed by a noun or a complete clause. Compare:
She *bought* it *when* she first came here.
She's *had* it *since* she first came here.

Language note
The Present perfect simple is used here instead of the Present perfect continuous because *have* (in the sense of 'possess') is a stative verb and has no continuous form.
See Reference section, page 139.

Practice option
Check that students understand this difference by giving time expressions and asking them to add either *for* or *since*, e.g.
6 months – *for 6 months*
January – *since January.*

2 Speaking & writing activity

● To show how the activity works, write a sentence about one of your possessions on the board, e.g.

I've got a very large English dictionary with a leather cover.

(Alternatively, bring the object into class and show it to the students.) Ask students to imagine how long you have had it, where and how you got it, and why it is special to you; try to get a range of different ideas. Finally, tell them how long you have really had it, etc.

● Students write a sentence about one of their own favourite possessions.

● They exchange sentences with another student. Working alone, they imagine a 'story' for the other's object and make notes.

● When students are ready, they say what they imagined and then find out the true story of the object.

● As a round-up, ask a few students how close their guesses were to the truth.

Alternative
Ask students to bring photos of favourite possessions into class (or the objects themselves if they're small enough) and show them.

Writing option
With a good class, students could write a complete imaginary description, using those in the book as a model.

Homework option
Students write a true paragraph describing one or more of their favourite possessions.

2 Then and now

This exercise focuses on the relationship between events in the past (e.g. met, started playing*) and activities or states over a period up to now (e.g.* have known, has been playing*). It also shows the difference between 'activity' and 'state' verbs. Students complete a table, then write sentences about themselves.*

➤ Focus on Form: Exercise 3
➤ Workbook: Exercise B

1 *Presentation*

● Look at the verbs in the left-hand column of the table. Point out that
  – they are all in the Past simple tense, and are about a single past event
  – the sentences answer the question *When …?* or *How long ago …?*

  Then look at the verbs in the right-hand column. Point out that
  – they are about the period between a past event and now, and use the
    Present perfect continuous or simple tenses
  – the sentences answer the question *How long …?*

● Let students write the missing sentences, and then go through the answers:

  b I joined / became a member of Greenpeace six months ago.
  c Estonia became independent in 1990.
  d They've known each other / been together since 1954.
  e They've been staying with us for three days.
  f He started working / got a job here when he left school.
  g I've had this bank account since I went to college.
  h Mozart has been dead for more than 200 years.
  i He started playing professional football 10 years ago.

● Use the answers to establish the two types of verb in the right-hand column:
  – 'activity' verbs (*play, stay, work*): in the Present perfect continuous
  – 'state' verbs (*be, know, have*): in the Present perfect simple.

2 *Writing & speaking activity*

● Students write sentences about themselves, using verbs from the box.
● Taking each verb in turn, ask students to read out their sentences.

> **Game option**
> Ask students to write some sentences that are true and some that are untrue. They read out their sentences, and other students guess which ones are true.

3 It's a long time since …

This exercise introduces three structures used for saying how long it is since you last did something. Students listen and complete a table. They then talk about activities they themselves haven't done for a long time.

➤ Focus on Form: Exercise 4
➤ Workbook: Exercise C

1 *Listening & presentation*

● 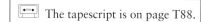 Play the recording, pausing after each speaker. Students listen and complete the table. Answers:

  1 dancing; in September / several months ago; she left France
  2 football; seven or eight years ago; he came to England / it was too cold
  3 ice skating; two years ago; it's too expensive / she doesn't have enough time

● 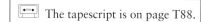 Play the recording again. This time focus on the three key structures:

  1 I haven't been dancing since September.
  2 The last time I played football was when I used to live in South Africa.
  3 It's two years since I last went ice-skating.

● Show how they can be used to give the same meaning:

> **I *haven't* been dancing *for* two years.**
> ***The last time* I *went* dancing *was* two years *ago.***
> **It's two years *since* I *last went* dancing.**

> ▭ The tapescript is on page T88.

2 *Speaking activity*

● Ask students to think of an activity they used to do, and to write a sentence about it, using one of the structures on the board.
● Students sit in groups. Using their sentence as a basis, they each tell the others about the activity and answer other students' questions.
● As a round-up, ask each group about one of the activities they talked about.

> *Optional lead-in*
> Tell students about an activity you haven't done for some time, and get them to ask you more about it.

T 87

2 Then and now

Present perfect simple & continuous • Past simple

1 Write the missing sentences in the table.

How long ago ...?	*How long ...?*
a She started playing the trumpet two years ago.	She's been playing the trumpet for two years.
b	I've been a member of Greenpeace for six months.
c	Estonia has been independent since 1990.
d They met in 1954.	....
e They came to stay with us three days ago.	....
f	He's been working here since he left school.
g I opened this bank account when I went to college.	....
h Mozart died more than 200 years ago.	....
i	He's been playing professional football for 10 years.

2 Write three true sentences about yourself. Choose verbs from the box.

> start live be
> play join meet

3 It's a long time since ...

Negative duration structures

1 🔲 **You will hear three people talking about things they haven't done for a long time.**

a Listen and complete the table.

	Activity	*When did they last do it?*	*Why did they stop?*
1			
2			
3			

b The speakers use three different structures to say when they last did things. What are they?

2 Work in groups.

Think of something you used to enjoy doing that you haven't done for a long time.
Tell the others about it, and answer any questions they may have.

4 Guess how long …

1 'We're just celebrating our diamond wedding anniversary.'

How long have they been married?

2 *a* How long is it since the Big Bang?
  b How old is the Earth?

  c How long have dinosaurs been extinct?
  d How long ago did *homo sapiens* appear?

3 What's wrong with these statements?

  a 'My grandfather's had the same biro since 1935.'
  b 'Shakespeare drank tea constantly while he was writing his plays.'

c 'I've just bought a new Citröen 2CV.'

4 How long have these countries been independent?

  a The United States of America.
  b India.
  c Latvia.

5 How long ago …
  a … was the Great Pyramid built?

  b … did the Beatles have their first No.1 hit?

  c … did Mao Tse-tung die?

1 Work in groups. Do you know the answers to these questions? If you don't know an answer, make a guess.

Now listen to the answers. The group with the nearest answer scores one point. Who won?

2 Now make up two more questions, and see if other groups can answer them.

Grammar Checklist

Present perfect continuous tense

have/has been + -ing – *for talking about activities that started in the past and are still going on.*

He**'s been** trying to phone her for three hours. (*not* ~~he's trying~~)
They**'ve been** going out together since June.

Stative verbs

be, have (= *possess*), **know**
No continuous form – use Present perfect simple.

I**'ve had** these jeans for five years.
She**'s been** away for nearly a month.

for & since

I've known them **for** years.
I've known them **since** 1975.
I've known them **since** we first moved here.

How long …? & How long ago …?

How long + *Present perfect continuous or simple*

– **How long** has she been working here?
– For three months.

– **How long** have you been in this flat?
– Since June.

How long ago (*or* **When**) + *Past tense*

– **How long ago** did she start working here?
– Three months ago.

– **When** did you move into this flat?
– In June.

Negative duration structures

I **haven't ridden** a bike since I was a child.
It's ages **since** I (**last**) rode a bike.
The last time I rode a bike was in 1982.

See also Reference section, page 139.

4 Guess how long ...

This activity is a quiz, in which students make guesses and see how close they were to the correct answers. They then make up quiz questions of their own. This is a free activity, which draws on the duration structures introduced in the unit.

1 Speaking activity

- Divide the class into groups. Together, they look at the questions and guess the answers. One student in the group should act as 'secretary' and write down their guesses.

- Go through the questions with the class, getting guesses from each group and then giving the answers. Give one point each time to the group with the closest guess (keep a running score on the board). Answers:

  1 60 years.
  2 *a* 10–20 thousand million years.
    b 4,600 million years.
    c 65 million years.
    d About 100,000 years ago.
  3 *a* Biros were invented in 1938.
    b Shakespeare died in 1615. Tea was first brought to Britain around 1650.
    c There are no new 2CVs. Production stopped in 1991.
  4 *a* Since 1783.
    b Since 1947.
    c Since 1990.
  5 *a* About 4,600 years ago (2,586–2566 BC).
    b (X) years ago (in 1962). The record was *Please please me*.
    c (X) years ago (in 1976).

2 Writing & speaking activity

- Working together in groups, students think of two similar questions of their own. The questions should be about how long ago something happened, how long something has been in existence, etc.

- In turn, each group reads out their questions, and other students try to answer them.

> *Homework option*
> Students find out facts outside the class, and bring other questions to ask in the next lesson.

🖭 Tapescript for Exercise 3: *It's a long time since ...*

When I was in France I used to go dancing every, every week, and I haven't been dancing since September, which is several months now. And I really miss it because I would go there every Monday, I remember. So I'm just quite looking forward to doing it again when I go back to France.

The last time I played football was when I used to live in South Africa, because it was quite warm and we used to play all year round, it was never cold or anything like that, so that was quite fun. That was about seven years ago that I really, really enjoyed playing football all the time. Then when I moved to England it was a lot colder, and we had to play football in the cold, in shorts, and it was freezing, so I didn't really enjoy it then and I gave it up quite soon after that.

It's two years since I last went ice-skating, and I used to really enjoy ice-skating because you could go with a big group of friends, and you could go for a long time, about three hours. But I haven't been for a very long time now because it's got more expensive and because I don't seem to have very much time.

Focus on Form

1 *For & since*

> Contrast between time expressions with *since* and *for*

- Check that students know what kind of time expressions follow *since*, and what kind follow *for*.
- Take each item in turn, and get one or two answers from different students round the class.
- Pairwork. Students make true sentences about themselves.

2 *Since when?*

> *since* followed by a clause in the past tense

- As a lead-in, make up one or two sentences yourself and see if students can guess the continuation, e.g.
  He's been walking to work …
  … *ever since he crashed his car.*
  He's been eating hamburgers …
  … *ever since he visited the USA.*
- Working alone, students think of a few sentences, and write them down.
- Students read out their sentences and other students guess the continuations. This could be done in pairs, or with the whole class.

3 *How long …? & How long ago …?*

> *How long* + Present perfect; *How long ago* + Past simple

- Look at the questions in the bubbles, and establish what questions could be asked with *How long …?* and *How long ago …?*, e.g.
  (different country): How long have you known each other? How long has he/she been living here?
  (pet): How long have you had it? How long ago did you get/buy it?
  (bike, etc.): How long have you had it? How long have you been riding/driving it? How long ago did you get/buy it?

(keep fit): How long ago did you start (jogging)?
(board games): How long have you been playing (chess)? How long ago did you learn to play / start playing?
(relatives): How long have they been living abroad? How long ago did they go abroad?

- Pairwork. Students ask each other questions.
- Round-up. Ask a few students what they found out.

4 *Negative duration*

> 'Negative duration' structures

- Use the Grammar checklist (opposite page) to remind students of the three 'negative duration' structures.
- Either do the exercise round the class, or let students work in pairs, and go through the answers afterwards. Possible answers:
  a I haven't been there for years; I last went there when I was ten years old.
  b She hasn't spoken to me for weeks; she last wrote to me over a month ago.
  c I haven't used it since I was at school; The last time I was in Spain was ten years ago.
  d I haven't been to the cinema for years; It's three years since I last saw a film.
  e It's a month since he last tidied his room; He hasn't got up early for months.

5 *Pronunciation*

⊡ Ask students to try saying the sentences themselves, then play the recording as a model. Focus on these points:

a Reduced vowels in *he's been* /hiz bin/, *they've been* /ðeɪv bin/.
b Reduced vowels in *How long have you* /haʊ ˈlɒŋ (h)əv ju/, *How long has she* /haʊ ˈlɒŋ (h)əz ʃi/, *How long have they* /haʊ ˈlɒŋ (h)əv ðeɪ/.
c Pronunciation of *haven't* /ˈhævn̩t/ and *hasn't* /ˈhæzn̩t/.

Self-study Workbook

Exercise A: Duration
Present perfect simple and continuous + *for* and *since*. Students rewrite sentences, choosing between alternative forms. They then write duration sentences based on newspaper clippings.
Finally, they write their sentences again, using *since* + clause.

Exercise B: How long (ago) …?
Students write questions with *How long …?* and *How long ago …?*

Exercise C: Negative duration
Students write about three things they haven't done for some time, using negative duration structures.

Translation
Key sentences for translation.

Listening: Favourite things
Three people talk about their favourite possessions. Students listen and fill in a table, identify pictures of each possession, and answer comprehension questions.

Pronunciation: Stress and suffixes
Changes in stress when suffixes are added to words. Students hear examples, then look at sentences and predict where the stress will fall on words with and without suffixes.

Reading: Four logic puzzles
Students solve four logic puzzles, all featuring duration.

Focus on Form

1 For & since

Complete these sentences about yourself (1) using *for* (2) using *since*.

Example: *I've had this watch …*
… for six months.
… since October.
… since my last birthday.

a I've been in this room …
b I've been learning English …
c I've had these shoes …
d I've had this coursebook …
e I've been at this school …

2 Since when?

Student A: Choose one of the events in the box and imagine what things have been like since then.
Student B: Can you guess which item A was thinking of? Complete each sentence using an item from the box.

Examples:
A He's been eating in expensive restaurants …
B … ever since he won the lottery.
A He's been depressed …
B … ever since his girlfriend left him.

… (ever) since	he left school.
	he won the lottery.
	he visited the USA.
	his girlfriend left him.
	he lost all his money.
	he crashed his car.
	he came out of hospital.

3 How long …? & How long ago …?

Ask your partner these questions. If the answer is 'Yes', ask a question with *How long …?* or *How long ago …?*

Example:
A Do you do anything to keep fit?
B Yes. I play basketball.
A How long have you been playing?
How long ago did you start playing?

4 Negative duration

Add a sentence to these remarks, saying how long it is since something happened.

Example: *I'm starving …*
I haven't eaten since breakfast.
I haven't eaten for six hours.
It's six hours since I had anything to eat.

a I'd love to visit Berlin again …
b I don't think she likes me any more …
c I'm afraid my Spanish is rather rusty …
d It's no good asking me what's on at the cinema …
e He's the laziest person I know …

5 Pronunciation

How do you say the words and phrases below?

a He's been trying to phone you.
They've been talking for hours.

b How long have you known him?
How long has she been waiting?
How long have they been talking?

c I haven't been there for years.
He hasn't been out since the weekend.

▭ **Now listen and check your answers.**

Do you know anyone who comes from a different country?

Have you got a pet?

Have you got a bike/ motorbike/car/boat?

Do you do anything to keep fit?

Do you play any board games?

Do you have any relatives living abroad?

20 In your lifetime

1 Birth, marriage and death

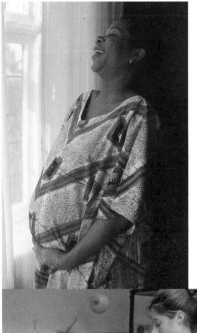

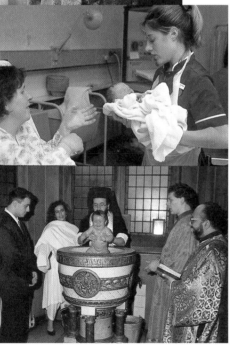

1 What vocabulary do you associate with birth, marriage and death?
Write a list of words for each group of pictures.

2 You will hear five people describing birth, marriage and death customs in different parts of the
world. Here are some of the things they talk about:

silver	money	eating and drinking
a white dress	sweets	dancing
chopsticks	flowers	songs

Which do you expect to be about birth, which about marriage and which about death?

🔲 Now listen to the recording.

Think of birth, marriage and death customs in your own country.
Which do you think a foreigner would find the most unusual?

This unit is about the different stages in people's lives and events connected with them. It focuses on the following vocabulary areas:
– language associated with birth, marriage and death
– vocabulary for talking about different age groups
– language for talking about age and the law.
The Reading and Listening activity is a short story by the Welsh writer, Leslie Thomas.

1 Birth, marriage and death

This exercise is about traditional customs associated with the birth of children, with weddings and with funerals, and it introduces vocabulary used in describing these events. After an initial brainstorming activity, students listen to descriptions of birth, marriage and death customs from different countries. They then discuss similar customs in their own country.

➤ Workbook: Exercise A

1 Presentation & listening

● As a lead-in, look at the three groups of pictures and establish what they show:

birth and baptism/christening; weddings; funerals

● Give time for students to 'brainstorm' vocabulary in pairs or groups, starting with what they can see in the pictures, and then adding any other words they know.

● Ask students what words they thought of, and build up three lists on the board. Important words might be:

Birth: pregnant, expecting a baby, be born, give birth (to), have a baby, midwife, deliver (a baby); baptise, christen.
Marriage: bride, bridegroom, wedding, ring, reception, guests, feast, honeymoon.
Death: funeral, mourn, mourner, cremate, grave, bury, coffin, cemetery, priest.

As you write the words on the board, establish how they are used, e.g. *The bride and bridegroom get married. They invite guests to the wedding.*

> *Optional extension*
> Discuss what countries/cultures the pictures show. The actual answers are:
> *Birth*
> – An African woman
> – English maternity hospital
> – Greek Orthodox baptism
> *Marriage*
> – Traditional Korean wedding
> – Rice throwing at US wedding
> – Romanian wedding party
> *Death*
> – Irish funeral
> – Balinese (Indonesian) cremation pyre
> – Guatemalan (Indian) funeral procession

2 Listening & speaking activity

● Ask students to mark B, M or D against the words in the list. Then discuss together how students expect the words to be used.

● [cassette] Play the recording, pausing after each speaker. Establish what the person is talking about and which of the words they use. Answers:

1 Death: eating and drinking, songs.
2 Marriage: flowers, sweets.
3 Birth: silver (money).
4 Death: chopsticks.
5 Marriage: a white dress, money, dancing.

As you go through, ask a few questions to check comprehension, e.g. Speaker 1: *What country is she talking about? Is the funeral happy or sad? Why is it happy? What do people do?*

● Students sit in groups. They choose a custom that a foreigner would find interesting, and work out what to say about it.

● Tell the class to imagine you are a foreigner who knows nothing about their country. Ask someone from each group to describe the custom they chose.

> [cassette] The tapescript is on page T93.

> *Note*
> The five people are describing:
> 1 A funeral in southern Ireland.
> 2 A Druze wedding in Lebanon.
> 3 Scottish birth customs.
> 4 A Japanese funeral.
> 5 A Hungarian wedding.

> *Alternative: mixed nationality classes*
> Students prepare alone or with a group of other students from their own country.
> They then sit with someone from a different country and tell them about the custom they chose.

2 Age groups

This is a discussion activity about different age groups and the characteristics commonly associated with them. It introduces key vocabulary for talking about people of different ages, and also teaches a range of common 'character' adjectives.

➤ Workbook: Exercises B, C

1 *Presentation*

- Look at the table of age groups, and use it to establish what people are called at each of the ages. Build up a list of words on the board:

> **child**
> **teenager/adolescent**
> **adult/grown-up**
> **middle-aged person**
> **old/elderly person**

Language note
An *adolescent* is someone who is growing up. A *teenager* is someone between 13 and 19.
Elderly is a more polite way to talk about old people.

- Ask the class when they think people move from one age group to the next. This could develop into a general discussion of whether (for example) adolescence or adulthood is a question of actual age or of how you feel or how you behave.

Alternative
Working alone, students write ages at the boundaries between the groups. They then compare what they have written with other students.

2 *Speaking activity*

- Look at the adjectives and check that students understand what they mean. If necessary, give examples of how a shy person might behave, what a rebellious person might do, etc.
- Pairwork. Students decide which adjectives best fit each age group, and think of other adjectives that would go with each group.
- Discuss the answers together. There are of course no 'right' answers, and students might decide that some adjectives could apply to several age groups. Other possible adjectives:
childhood: *loving, innocent, carefree*
adolescence: *active, fashionable*
young adulthood: *self-confident, responsible*
middle age: *conservative, mature*
old age: *peaceful, confused*

3 Legal age

This is a freer discussion activity, which naturally involves expressions for talking about age (e.g. at [the age of] 16, minimum/maximum age), as well as verbs expressing obligation (can, can't, have to, aren't allowed to). Students read the text, which describes the legal age for certain activities in Britain, and then discuss what they think the legal age should be for these activities.

➤ Workbook: Exercise B

Discussion

- Write the expressions *legal age*, *minimum age* and *maximum age* on the board, and check that students understand what they mean:
legal age = the age when you are allowed to do something
minimum age = the lowest age you can do something
maximum age = you can't do something after that age
- Working alone, students read the text and then complete the table with the ages they think people should be allowed to do things.
- Students form pairs or small groups and compare what they have written.
- As a round-up, go through the activities in the table, and find out what most students think the legal age should be for each.

Discussion option
Ask students if they know what the legal ages are for the same activities in their own country, and discuss whether they think the laws in their country are better or worse than those in Britain.

2 Age groups

Childhood
Adolescence
Young adulthood
Middle age
Old age

1 Look at these age groups. At what age do you think you move from one to another?

2 Look at the adjectives. Do you think they apply to any particular age group?

Think of some other adjectives that could go with each age group.

helpless   ambitious   rebellious

self-conscious   naughty   shy

wise   lonely   independent

3 Legal age

Age and the law: some facts about Britain

School-leaving age
Children have to stay at school until the age of 16. There is no upper age limit.

Alcohol
You have to be 18 to buy alcohol in a shop or a pub, but if you're 16 and you're having a meal in a pub, you can drink beer or wine with it.

Prosecution
In Scotland, you can be prosecuted for a crime at the age of 8. In England and Wales, the age is 10. You can't be sent to prison until you're 21.

Motor vehicles
16-year-olds can ride a motorbike of up to 50 cc. At 17 you can ride any bike or drive a car.

Smoking
You can smoke cigarettes at any age, but you can't go into a shop and buy them until you are 16.

Armed forces
Men can join the army at 16, women at 17. If you're under 18, you need your parents' consent.

Marriage
You can get married at 16 with your parents' consent. Otherwise you have to wait till you're 18.

Paid employment
You can take a part-time job at 13, and a full-time job at 16 (i.e. when you've left school).

Voting
Anyone aged 18 or over can vote in a general election.

Retirement age
Women can retire on full pension at 60. Men have to wait till they're 65.

Entering Parliament
The minimum age for becoming a Member of Parliament is 21. The youngest person to become an MP in the 20th century was Bernadette Devlin, who was elected a week before her 22nd birthday.

Read the text about British law.

What do *you* think should be the legal age for these activities? Fill in the table.

Compare your answers with your partner's.

Leaving school		Joining the army	
Drinking alcohol		Getting married	
Being prosecuted		Getting a job	
Riding a motorbike		Voting	
Driving a car		Retirement	
Smoking		Entering Parliament	

4 A Good Boy, Griffith

READING

Read each section of the story in turn and answer the questions.

Section 1
What can you tell about
– Griffith?
– Blodwen?
– Morgan?

Section 2
What else do you now know about the three characters?

Section 3

| Griffith gave a ring to Gwen … | → | … He wants to give the ring to Gwen again. |

What happened in between?

Section 4
What is Griffith's problem?

DISCUSSION

What do you think will happen next? Imagine an ending to the story.

LISTENING

☐ You will hear the last two sections of the story.

Section 5
Does Griffith bring the money?
Does Blodwen give him the ring?
What does Blodwen promise?

Section 6
'Blodwen felt her heart capsize.' Why?
What does Morgan think happened?
What actually happened?

4 A Good Boy, Griffith

This combined Reading and Listening activity is a short story by Leslie Thomas, a modern Welsh writer, about people in a coal-mining village in South Wales. Students read the first part of the story and then guess how it will end. They then listen to a recording of the last part of the story.

READING

- To set the scene for the story, look at the pictures, and ask students what they can tell about the characters: there are two men and one woman, she lives in a cottage, there are coal mines nearby.

- Give time for students to read Section 1 of the story, and then establish basic facts about the three characters:
  - Griffith knows Blodwen, but she's not his wife. He's glad she isn't. He's going to visit her.
  - Blodwen lives in a cottage. She's married to Morgan. She's a very tidy person.
  - Morgan is Blodwen's husband. He works in a garage.

- Give students time to read Section 2, then establish what else we know about the characters:

  Blodwen used to be Griffith's girlfriend/fiancée. She married Morgan instead of Griffith.

- Students read Section 3. Then establish what happened between the events in the boxes. Answer:

  Gwen broke off the engagement and gave Griffith the ring back.
  He got engaged to Blodwen and gave her the ring.
  He broke off the engagement to Blodwen, but she kept the ring.
  Blodwen married Morgan.
  Gwen came back to Griffith.

- Students read Section 4. Then establish what Griffith's problem is:

  Gwen wants the same ring back. She doesn't know he gave it to Blodwen. But Blodwen will only give it back if he gives her £50, and he can't afford it.

DISCUSSION

- Ask students to suggest possible endings for the story. If you like, write a few single sentence 'plots' on the board, e.g. *He shoots Blodwen and steals the ring.*

LISTENING

- ▭ Play the recording of Section 5, and discuss the answers to the questions. Answers:
  - Yes.
  - Yes.
  - Not to tell anyone.
- ▭ Play the recording of Section 6, and discuss the answers to the questions. Answers:
  - Because she thinks Morgan knows what happened.
  - He thinks Griffith borrowed money from him and paid it back to Blodwen.
  - Griffith used Morgan's money to buy the ring back from Blodwen.

Blackboard option
Write the three characters' names on the blackboard, and write brief notes about them as you read the story.
When Gwen is introduced as a character (in Section 3), add her name to the list.

Groupwork option
Students sit in groups and together work out an ending to the story.
Then each group reports back what they decided.

Optional questions
Check more detailed comprehension by asking further questions, e.g.
When did he go back?
Was Blodwen waiting for him?
How do we know?
Why do you think she was 'jumpy'?

Optional questions
Again, check more detailed comprehension by asking questions, e.g.
Where has Morgan come from?
How does Blodwen feel?
How do we know?
How does Morgan feel?

▭ The tapescript is on page T93.

Section 5

The next afternoon he went up the hill to the red brick cottage again. He saw the lace curtains move suddenly as he approached, and the door opened before he had even time to reach the knocker.

'Come back?' she asked. 'If you've not got the money you might as well turn around and go.'

'Steady, steady, girl,' said Griffith, 'don't get so jumpy. I've got the money. Have you got the ring?'

He took the roll of white notes from his waistcoat pocket. 'Come on in then,' she said.

With a quick turn she walked from the room and he heard her going up the stairs. Then she came slowly down.

'There's your ring,' she said, half throwing it on the table. 'Keep it. I'd rather have the money.'

Griffith took the ring. 'One more thing,' he said. 'Nobody must know.'

'All right,' she said quietly. 'Morgan didn't even know I had the thing. I told him I'd given it back to you.'

Section 6

When Morgan came home he washed the grease from his hands under the tap then sat down to his meal. Blodwen poured the tea unsteadily.

'What's up, Blod?' he said. 'You don't look so good, girl.'

'I'm all right,' she said.

'Was Griffith here today?' he said casually, cutting a thick slice from the loaf.

She went pale but he did not look up. 'Yes,' she admitted.

He laughed. 'Good boy, Griff, you know. Sort of steady chap. Can't see why you didn't marry him. Always trust him.'

'Does it matter now?'

'No,' he replied good-humouredly. 'The thing is, did he bring the fifty quid?'

Blodwen felt her heart capsize. 'Yes,' she said shakily. 'Yes, he did ...'

Her husband nodded. 'Good boy, Griff. Came in and asked me to lend it to him so he could get a real special ring for his girl Gwen. Nice girl. Said he'd get it from his savings when his dad came home from the pit and bring it up here. A good boy, Griff; yes a good boy ...'

---

1   After the burial it's very traditional to celebrate the death. And we celebrate that by eating and drinking and in some cases singing traditional Irish songs. Because we consider it to be a happy occasion, especially if the person is old, and they've, they're going to heaven and they're going to be rewarded in the afterlife.

2   The bride is dressed up and she sits in a chair surrounded by flowers and children, and everybody troops past to have a look at her. And then you just sit down, and you're given lots of sweets and drinks, soft drinks. And then the groom and his entourage arrive, and he takes her hand and leads her away.

3   In Scotland, there's a tradition related to birth, where you must present the baby with a piece of silver, a silver coin. And you have to take this coin and actually place it in the baby's hand and make the baby hold it. The idea behind this is that the baby will be rich in later life.

4   After the death of the person, this person's corpse will be taken to the furnace, where the corpse is cremated. And afterwards from the furnace bones are taken out. And all the family members get together to pick up the bones with chopsticks. Each relative takes one bone and put them in a small jar, and we bury it.

5   The bride is dressed in white and the bridegroom is dressed in a black suit and white shirt. At midnight she goes away and takes off her white dress and puts on a red dress. She comes back to dance with the guests, and the guests pay for dancing with her, so she dances with everybody and when she's ready and when the bridegroom thinks that's enough, then he takes her by the hand and they run away and they take all the money with them.

Self-study Workbook

Exercise A: □□□□ □□□□□□ □□ □□□□□
Students write missing words in a text into a grid. If the answers are correct, key letters spell out the title of the exercise.

Exercise B: The time of your life
Students write about the best and worst things about being a particular age.

Exercise C: What are they like?
Adjectives describing people.
Students match adjectives with descriptions of people.

New words
Space to record new words with notes and examples.

Translation
Key sentences for translation.

Listening: Birth and marriage
An unusual birth and an unusual wedding.
Students read a list of expressions and predict which story they will appear in. Then they listen, and answer comprehension questions.

Phrasal verbs: Three-word verbs (1)
Common three-word verbs (e.g. *get on with*, *run out of*). Students use them to fill gaps in sentences.

Writing skills: Joining ideas: showing what's coming next
Use of *in fact*, *(not) surprisingly*, *(un)fortunately*, *on the contrary* and *on the other hand* to show the writer's attitude and signal what is to follow. Students use the key items to link sentences together and to add new sentences.

A GOOD BOY, GRIFFITH

by Leslie Thomas

1 GRIFFITH came over the hill behind the pit and turned the bend in the lane to the red brick cottage. It was too early for Morgan to be home from the garage yet, he knew that. Blodwen would be alone. Walking up to the gate he noticed how the windows shone clean in the late afternoon sun. Just like her, of course; always neat and decent. Never a speck of dust, never a thing out of place. She might have been his wife, but it was a good job she wasn't. He would never have been able to keep things the way she wanted them.

2 She came to the door almost immediately.

Griffith shyly reached for his cap. 'Hello Blod,' he said. 'Hope you don't mind me ...'

'What d'you want, Griffith?' she asked suspiciously. 'It's not decent for you to be calling on me, you know. Not now I'm wed; an' people knowing how we were an' all. What d'you want?'

'Well, let me come in and I'll tell you, girl. Don't keep me out here.'

For a moment she was undecided. Then she opened the door wider and he went into the living room. 'Just as I thought,' he mused. 'Not a plate out of place. Poor old Morgan. A good man, too.'

He looked at her, wondering if this could be the same girl he had asked to marry him on the night of the Institute dance. He realised now what a narrow escape he had had.

3 'Blod,' he said determinedly. 'I've come about the ring.'

A look of slow, smug triumph settled across her face. 'I thought you might,' she said. 'What about it? If you think you're getting it back, think again.'

He paled a little. 'Look, Blod,' he pleaded, 'it's important right now. Anyway, Morgan's given you a tidy little ring. Much better that one is.'

'Who do you want it for this time?' she said craftily. 'Seems that ring's been around a bit already.'

He told her that Gwen had come back.

'You know Gwen,' he said encouragingly.

She laughed, a mean little laugh with no laughter in it. 'Oh, Griffith. You're going round in circles. She was the one before me.'

And the only one, thought Griffith. You caught me on the rebound. Now she has come back from Cardiff, and she is going to stay, and she says it was all her fault, and she wants to start again.

4 'But why do you want the ring, Griff? Jenkins in the High Street has plenty in the window.'

Griffith lost his temper. He went red about the roots of his black hair, and he banged his fist down so that the table shook and it scared her. 'Listen, Blod,' he said. 'I want that ring. I'll pay you. She doesn't know I gave it to you. She wants the same one.'

'Then it's fifty pounds, Griffith,' she said abruptly.

He gasped: 'Fifty! Don't be daft, Blod. It's not worth ten.'

'Fifty,' she repeated firmly.

'But I haven't got that much and I couldn't get it. Talk sense, girl.'

'There's some lovely dresses in Cardiff, Griff. Saw them in the paper. Morgan's taking me down in the car on Tuesday ...'

He went out and slammed the door after him.

* * *

The next afternoon he went up the hill to the red

Finding out

1 Information questions

1 Look at the answers in the bubbles.
  What do you think the questions were?

2 Write down three 'answers' about yourself, and show them to
  your partner. Can he/she guess what the questions are?

This unit is concerned with asking and reporting questions, and covers the following areas:
– Wh- questions
– Indirect questions
– Reported questions
– Question tags.

1 Information questions

This exercise introduces a range of Wh- question types, focusing especially on questions with How and What. Students look at short answers and imagine what the questions might be. Then they think of questions and answers about themselves.

➤ Focus on Form: Exercises 1, 2
➤ Workbook: Exercise A

1 Presentation

● Pairwork. Students look at the remarks in bubbles, and imagine a possible question for each.

● Go through the answers together. Some possible answers:

About an hour by train: How long does it take (you) to get there?
Forty-two: How old is he now? What's six times seven? How many CDs have you got now?
It's my sister's: Whose car is that outside your house? Who does that big dog belong to?
A Porsche: What make of car do you drive? What kind of car would you most like to have?
Aquarius: What birth sign / star sign are you?
I fell off a wall: What happened to your arm? What did you do to your arm?
Nearly four kilos: How much does she weigh? How much weight have you lost? How many potatoes did you buy?
Vanilla, strawberry and chocolate: What flavour ice-cream have you got?
France: What country do you come from? Where did you go for your holiday?
Blue: What's your favourite colour? What colour T-shirt do you want?

● Use these questions to present any Wh- question types that are unfamiliar, focusing on these two groups:

WHAT + NOUN			HOW ...?	
What	flavour (ice-cream) colour (dress) size (shoes) kind of type of (car) make of (car)	**...?**	**How long How much/many How far How often**	**...?**

Point out that most 'What + noun' phrases are followed by a second noun without *of*: we say 'What colour dress ...?', not '~~What colour of dress~~ ...?'. *What kind, What type* and *What make* are followed by *of*.

2 Writing & speaking activity

● To show how the activity works, think of a few questions and answers about yourself. Write the answers on the board, and ask the class to guess the questions.

● Working alone, students think of questions and answers about themselves, and write down only the answers.

● Pairwork. Students show each other their 'answers', and see if their partner can guess the questions.

> *Practice option*
>
> Do basic practice of *What* and *How* questions by giving Yes/No questions as prompts, e.g.
>
> Is your dress blue?
> → What colour is your dress?
>
> Is it ten kilometres to the centre?
> → How far is it to the centre?

2 I'm not sure …

This exercise focuses on the difference between direct and indirect questions, and presents indirect question structures that do not involve a tense change.

➤ Focus on Form: Exercise 3
➤ Workbook: Exercise B

1 Presentation & speaking activity

- Look at the two sets of sentences and establish that
  – the sentences in Column A are *direct questions*
  – the sentences in Column B are *indirect questions*: the 'question' follows a phrase (e.g. *I wonder, I don't know*). They have normal word order: we say 'I wonder where she is', *not* 'I wonder where is she'
  – if we make Yes/No questions into indirect questions, we use *if* or *whether*.
- Show the basic structures on the board:

What <u>is</u> <u>he</u> doing?	→	*I wonder what* <u>he's</u> *doing.*
<u>Are</u> <u>they</u> here?	→	*I wonder* | *if / whether* | <u>they're</u> *here.*

- Pairwork. Students go through the sentences in *b*, making indirect questions.
- Go through the answers together. Answers:

I wonder if they'll come to the party.
I'm not sure how long he's been asleep.
I don't know when the concert begins.

I'm not sure if I've read that book.
Do you know what 'car' is in Spanish?
I can't remember what I was looking for.

2 Writing & speaking activity

- Give time for students to write a few sentences containing indirect questions.
- Ask students to read out some of their sentences round the class.

➤ Focus on Form: Exercise 4
➤ Workbook: Exercise C

3 Getting to know you

This exercise introduces reported questions – indirect questions set in the past, which follow the tense changes of reported speech. Students report short scenes they hear on tape, then improvise their own scenes and report them.

1 Presentation & listening

- Read the three texts and establish what the actual questions were:
  – Which class are you in?
  – Do you know anyone here?
  – How long have you been waiting?

Point out that
– after *asked*, we use an *indirect* question (with normal sentence word order).
– because *asked* is in the past, the verb moves *back* one tense:

ACTUAL QUESTION		REPORTED QUESTION
Which class <u>are</u> you in?		which class I <u>was</u> in.
Do you <u>know</u> anyone?	He / She asked me	if I <u>knew</u> anyone.
How long <u>have</u> you <u>been</u> <u>waiting</u>?		how long I'<u>d been</u> waiting.

- 🔊 Play the recording, pausing after each scene and asking students to report the other questions. Answers:
  1 She asked him if he was enjoying it; whether he'd ever been to Japan.
  2 She asked him if he knew anyone; if he was from the States.
  3 She asked her whether she was going into town; if she was going shopping.

🔊 The tapescript is on page T96.

2 Speaking activity

- Preparation. Either ask students to suggest suitable questions round the class, or give time for students to write down a few questions they might ask.
- Pairwork. Students choose one of the situations and improvise a conversation.
- Ask a few pairs to report their conversations. At this stage, make sure students use reported speech and reported questions where appropriate.

Language note
This exercise deals with indirect questions involving no tense change. Reported questions (involving a tense change) are presented in Exercise 3.

Language note
Examples beginning 'Can you tell me …' and 'Do you know …' are indirect questions embedded in normal direct questions, so they have a question mark at the end.
Compare:
– I don't know where she is.
– Do you know where she is?

Option: suggest topics
Suggest topic areas, e.g. things in the news, other people in the class, addresses and telephone numbers, early childhood, English vocabulary, how to get to places, authors and books.

2 I'm not sure …

Indirect question forms

A	B
Who is she going out with?	I wonder who she's going out with.
How much money do I owe you?	I can't remember how much money I owe you.
How long is the Amazon?	I've no idea how long the Amazon is.
Have you met before?	I'm not sure whether you've met before.
When did they arrive?	Can you tell me when they arrived?
Has the train left yet?	Do you know if the train's left yet?

1 *a* **What's the difference between the sentences in Column A and those in Column B?**

   b **Combine these sentences to make indirect questions.**

   – Will they come to the party? I wonder.
   – How long has he been asleep? I'm not sure.
   – When does the concert begin? I don't know.
   – Have I read that book? I'm not sure.
   – What's 'car' in Spanish? Do you know?
   – What was I looking for? I can't remember.

2 **Write some true sentences beginning:**

   I wonder …   I'm not sure …

   I don't know …   I can't remember …

3 Getting to know you

Reported question forms

I was in the students' room
waiting for my class to begin when
the girl in the next seat asked me
which class I was in …

I was sitting in a corner when a
guy came up and asked me if I
knew anyone at the party. I said
I didn't …

I was waiting for my bus yesterday
when a woman came and stood
next to me and asked me how long
I'd been waiting …

1 *a* **Read the texts. What do you think were the actual questions?**

   b 🔲 **Now listen to the scenes, and report the other questions.**

2 **In pairs, choose one of the situations above, and improvise a short conversation.**

   Student A: **You want to get to know B. Think of one or two questions you might ask
   to get a conversation going.**

   Student B: **Respond in any way you want.**

   Now report your conversation to the class.

4 Tags

It's a bit cold today, …

Auckland isn't the capital of New Zealand, …

… can they?

… don't they?

They speak Arabic in Iran, …

They didn't stay very long, …

… is it?

… have you?

You haven't seen my glasses, …

That film was awful, …

… isn't it?

… did they?

Penguins can't fly, …

… wasn't it?

1 **Add the missing question tags to these remarks.**

   ▣ **Now listen to the same remarks. In which ones**
   – does the speaker really want to find out something?
   – is the speaker just expressing an opinion or belief?

2 **What question tags might you use in these situations?**
   – You've just seen someone you think you recognise.
   – You're driving to the airport to go on holiday.
   – Your dinner guests have just left.
   – You've just seen a Charlie Chaplin film.

   Choose one of the situations and improvise a short conversation.

Grammar Checklist

Wh- questions

What kind of coffee do you like?
What make is your cooker?
What happened to your coat?
How long did it take to get there?
How much does the suitcase weigh?
Whose coat is this? (*not* ~~Who's~~)

Indirect questions

Wh- *word + normal word order*
I don't know **what** his name **is**.
   (*not* … ~~what is his name~~)
I wonder **where** they **went**.
Can you tell me **when** he's **coming** back?

if/whether + *normal word order*
I can't remember **if I posted** the letter.
   (*not* … ~~did I post~~ …)
Do you know **whether** Mr Smith **lives** here?

Reported questions

Wh- *word or* **if/whether** + *normal word order.*
Verb tense changes as in reported speech. (See Unit 17.)
'Do you know many people?' he asked.
→ He asked me **if I knew** many people.
'Where are you going?' she asked.
→ She asked him **where** he **was going**.

Question tags

They **live** here, **don't** they?
You **phoned** him, **didn't** you?
He's very talkative, **isn't** he?
You **can** drive, **can't** you?

She **doesn't** like fish, **does** she?
They **haven't** forgotten, **have** they?

See also Reference section, page 140.

---

4 Tags

This exercise presents question tags, used for checking or for getting agreement from the person we're talking to. The first part of the presentation is intended to establish whether students are familiar with the form of question tags; the second part focuses on the two main <u>uses</u> of question tags.

➤ Focus on Form: Exercise 5
➤ Workbook: Exercise D

1 Presentation & listening

- To present question tags, write *It's a bit cold today* on the board. Show how we can make this a question by adding a *tag*:

  It's a bit cold today, <u>isn't it</u>?

- Point out that in English, question tags *vary* according to the verb in the main part of the sentence. Ask students to match the tags to the remarks. Answers:

  It's a bit cold … isn't it?   They didn't stay … did they?
  They speak … don't they?   That film was … wasn't it?
  You haven't seen … have you? Penguins can't … can they?
  Auckland isn't … is it?

- Use these examples to establish that
  – auxiliary verbs (*is, was, have, will*, etc.) are repeated in the tag
  – main verbs (Present & Past simple) are replaced by *do/does* or *did* in the tag
  – if the sentence is positive, the tag is negative, and vice versa.

- Point out that we use question tags in two ways:
  – to check something we're not sure of, e.g. *It's three o'clock, isn't it?* In this case we use *rising intonation*.
  – just to express an opinion, and get agreement, e.g. *It's a nice day, isn't it?* In this case we use *falling intonation*.

- 🔲 Play the recording, and let students hear this difference. After each remark, establish whether it was a real question or just an opinion. Answers:

  1 Opinion   3 Question   5 Opinion   7 Question
  2 Question   4 Question   6 Opinion

2 Speaking activity

- Look at the situations, and elicit some question tags students might use, e.g.

  – That's Michael, isn't it? He's the new English teacher, isn't he?
  – You've packed the sunglasses, haven't you? The plane leaves at 10, doesn't it?
  – They didn't say much, did they? They're interesting people, aren't they?
  – That was a good film, wasn't it? Charlie Chaplin's really funny, isn't he?

- Pairwork. Students improvise short conversations based on each situation. Encourage them to include one or two question tags each time.

Presentation option

Build up a table of the main forms on the board:

it is	…	isn't it?
he was	…	wasn't he?
she goes	…	doesn't she?
they went	…	didn't they?
he can	…	can't he?
they will	…	won't they?
he's seen	…	hasn't he?

Practice option

Give sentences using different tenses. Students add the tag.

Language note

There are also 'positive question tags', in which both the sentence and the tag are positive. These are used especially in making deductions (e.g. *Ah, so you're a doctor, are you?*). These are not dealt with in this exercise.

Optional lead-in

Improvise a conversation yourself with a good student, to show how the conversation might develop.

🔲 Tapescript for Exercise 4: *Tags*

1 It's a bit cold today, isn't it?
2 They speak Arabic in Iran, don't they?
3 You haven't seen my glasses, have you?
4 Auckland isn't the capital of New Zealand, is it?

5 They didn't stay very long, did they?
6 That film was awful, wasn't it?
7 Penguins can't fly, can they?

🔲 Tapescript for Exercise 3: *Getting to know you*

1 A Hi. Which class are you in?
   B I'm studying Japanese.
   A Oh, I'm in the same class. (Ah) Yeah, I've just joined, this is my first time. Are you enjoying it?
   B Yes, I am. It's fine.
   A Have you ever been to Japan?
   B I've been once, yes.
2 A Hi. I'm Ian. Do you know anyone here?
   B Only a few people. Oh, I'm Alison. (Hi) Do you know anyone here?
   A Er just Bob, who I, I think it's his party actually, he met

me when he came in.
   B Yes. Are you from the States?
   A No, I'm from Canada, but you know, it's sort of the same accent, but I'm Canadian, actually.
3 A Excuse me, how long have you been waiting?
   B Um, about half an hour now. These buses are always late.
   A Are you going to town?
   B Yes, yes I am.
   A Are you going shopping?
   B Er no, I'm meeting a friend there.

Focus on Form

1 *Questions with How ...?*

> Questions with *How* and with *How* + adverb

- Students fill the gaps, working alone or in pairs.
- Go through the answers together. Answers:

a How many	e How	i How much
b How	f How long	j How
c How far	g How often	
d How much	h How long	

- Students write their own questions, which they can try out on other people in the class.

2 *Questions with What ...?*

> Questions beginning with *What* + category noun

- Students make up sentences, either orally or in writing.
- Ask students what sentences they thought of for each of the words in the right-hand box. Some sample answers:
  - What flavour soup shall I buy?
  - What kind of flowers did she give you?
  - What size T-shirt does he want?
  - What sort of music do they play?

3 *Quiz: indirect questions*

> Indirect questions beginning *Do you know ...?*

- Go through the questions and ask students to change them into indirect questions with *Do you know ...?*
- Pairwork. Students ask each other the questions.
- Go through the questions (and the answers) together. Questions (answers in brackets):

  Do you know...
  - a ... when St Valentine's Day is? (February 14th)
  - b ... if/whether spiders are insects? (No – they're arachnids)
  - c ... how many days there are in a fortnight? (14)
  - d ... why you can't swim in the Sea of Tranquillity? (It's on the Moon, and has no water in it)
  - e ... what nationality Christopher Columbus was? (Italian)
  - f ... when he discovered America? (1492)
  - g ... if/whether Denmark is a monarchy? (Yes)

  - h ... what a *didgeridoo* is? (A traditional Australian musical instrument)
  - i ... where Batman lives? (Gotham City)

4 *Reported questions*

> Reported questions involving tense changes

- Either do the exercise round the class or let students do it in pairs and then go through the answers together. Expected answers:
  - a They asked me if I'd ever done that sort of work before; when I would be able to start (the job); whether I could speak Spanish.
  - b The doctor asked me where it hurt; if I'd been taking anything for the pain; when the trouble had started.
  - c The customs officer asked me if I was on a business trip; how long I was planning to stay; if I could speak Spanish.

5 *Checking: question tags*

> Question tags for checking what you're not sure about

- Go through a few of the items, asking students to add both positive and negative tags, e.g.

  You were born in this country, weren't you?
  You weren't born in this country, were you?

- Pairwork. Students ask each other the questions, choosing a positive or negative form according to what they expect the answer to be. The other student should reply truthfully.
- Ask if anyone guessed right in all seven questions.

6 *Pronunciation*

⊞ Ask students to try saying the sentences themselves, then play the recording as a model. Focus on these points:

- a Assimilation of /t/ sound in *What ...?* questions: *What kind of* /wɒk‿ˈkaɪnd əv/; *What flavour* /wɒ[ʔ]‿ˈfleɪvə/; *What colour* /wɒk‿ˈkʌlə/.
- b Pronunciation of *I wonder* /aɪ ˈwʌndə/, *I'm not sure* /aɪm nɒt ˈʃɔː/.
- c Pronunciation of consonant cluster in *He asked me* /hiː‿ˈaːs(k)t miː/.
- d Rising and falling intonation in question tags.

Self-study Workbook

Exercise A: Questions
Students write questions with *What ...?* and *How ...?*

Exercise B: They don't know ...
Indirect questions beginning *They don't know ...*

Exercise C: Reported questions
Reported questions with tense changes.
Students match questions to speakers, and report them.

Exercise D: Question tags
Students rewrite remarks using question tags.

Translation
Key sentences for translation.

Listening: Phone conversation
Students hear one speaker, and guess what the other person says. Then they hear the whole conversation.

Pronunciation: Changing tones
Falling tones to give new information, rising tones to repeat what has been said before.

Reading: A bit of luck
A short story followed by comprehension questions.

Focus on Form

1 Questions with How ...?

How	How long	How much
How far	How many	How often

Fill the gaps with expressions from the box.

a .... children have you got?
b .... did you get here? On foot?
c .... is it from Rome to Pisa?
d .... did it cost?
e .... expensive was it?
f .... does it take you to get to work?
g .... does the ferry go? Once or twice a day?
h .... have you known them?
i .... sugar do you take?
j .... high is Mount Everest?

Now write three questions of your own.

2 Questions with What ...?

Make questions with *What ...?* plus an item from each box.

kind of	flavour
sort of	colour
type of	size
make of	

soup	music
flowers	crisps
curtains	car
shoes	T-shirt

Examples:

What sort of shoes should I wear?
What size curtains do we need?
What colour T-shirt did you get?

3 Quiz: indirect questions

Ask your partner questions beginning *Do you know ...?*

Examples:

When is St Valentine's Day?
Do you know when St Valentine's Day is?

Are spiders insects?
Do you know if spiders are insects?

a When is St Valentine's Day?
b Are spiders insects?
c How many days are there in a fortnight?
d Why can't you swim in the Sea of Tranquillity?
e What nationality was Christopher Columbus?
f When did he discover America?
g Is Denmark a monarchy?
h What is a *didgeridoo*?
i Where does Batman live?

4 Reported questions

Are you on a business trip?

Have you ever done this sort of work before?

Where does it hurt?

Have you been taking anything for the pain?

How long are you planning to stay?

When will you be able to start?

When did the trouble start?

Can you speak Spanish?

Report the questions you think were asked

a at a job interview
b at the doctor's
c going through customs.

Example:

The doctor asked me where it hurt ...

5 Checking: question tags

Decide whether you think these statements are true of your partner. Check by asking question tags.

Example: *You like spicy food.*

You like spicy food, don't you?   *or*
You don't like spicy food, do you?

a You like spicy food.
b You were born in this country.
c You can say 'Thank you' in Arabic.
d You've had measles.
e You believe in ghosts.
f You're left-handed.
g You know how to ski.

6 Pronunciation

How do you say the words and phrases below?

a What kind of biscuits do you want?
   What flavour ice-cream is that?
   What colour is his shirt?

b I wonder what they're doing.
   I'm not sure if we've met.

c He asked me if I spoke Japanese.

d You're not going, are you?
   (*I really want to know.*)

   You're not going, are you?
   (*I'm just checking.*)

Now listen and check your answers.

22 Speaking personally

1 Feelings

1 How might you feel in these situations? Choose the best words from the box.

a You're sitting chatting to friends after a good meal.
b Somebody has slashed the tyres on your car.
c You're introducing someone to a friend and you get his name wrong.
d It's your sixth birthday tomorrow.
e Your best friend is much more popular than you are.
f You're about to make a speech in public for the first time.
g You're alone in a house at night and you hear a window being opened downstairs.
h You've lost your wedding ring.
i Your neighbour keeps coming round and asking to borrow things.
j All the news in the papers seems to be about wars and disasters.
k You've heard a rumour that the factory where you work is going to close down.

angry
annoyed
depressed
embarrassed
excited
frightened
jealous
nervous
relaxed
upset
worried

2 What makes you angry? depressed? jealous? ...?
Choose three feelings and write down a situation for each.

Find out if other students would feel the same.

22

This unit deals with three language areas concerned with feelings and reactions:
– saying how you feel in particular situations
– talking about situations in the past which involved feelings
– giving positive and negative reactions.
The Reading and Listening activity is about smiling and laughter, and how they can be used to cure illness.

1 Feelings

This exercise hinges on the fact that people do not always react to the same situations with the same feelings. In the first part, students match a list of adjectives describing feelings with 'typical' situations, and then go on to write and talk about situations in which they themselves have various feelings.

➤ Workbook: Exercise A

1 Presentation

● As a lead-in, look at the pictures and ask students to say how they imagine the people are feeling and what has happened to them. They could talk about this using basic words for feelings (e.g. *happy*, *sad*), but it is also a chance to present some of the adjectives that will be needed for the exercise.

Note: The pictures are intentionally ambiguous. So the woman in the bottom left picture might be worried (e.g. her children haven't come home from school) or upset (e.g. she's just heard she hasn't been given a job she wanted).

● To introduce the activity, focus on the word *angry*. Ask students what makes them angry and what they do if they feel angry. Then look at the situations in the exercise and ask them which one goes with *angry* (Answer: *b*).

● Pairwork. Students match the other situations with the adjectives in the box.

● Go through the answers. If necessary, give further explanations or examples to make sure students understand what the adjectives mean (e.g. If you're *embarrassed*, you go red and your face feels hot). Expected answers:

a relaxed	d excited	g frightened	j depressed
b angry	e jealous	h upset	k worried
c embarrassed	f nervous	i annoyed	

> *Language note*
> Note that some of these adjectives are used differently in English from many other languages:
> *nervous* = slightly afraid of something that's going to happen (you have 'butterflies in your stomach')
> *annoyed* = a bit angry
> *excited* = happy about something that's going to happen (you might feel like jumping up and down).

2 Writing/speaking activity

● Working alone, students choose five of the adjectives, and write a situation for each one (this could be in the form of a sentence or just a phrase, e.g. *angry – people smoking in restaurants*).

● To introduce the next stage, present the basic verbs needed to describe feelings:

> | I | feel | angry when ... |
> |---|---|---|
> | | get | |
> | ... makes me (feel) angry. | | |

● Pairwork. Students tell each other what they have written and find out if their partner would react in the same way.

● As a round-up, ask a few pairs of students how similar/different their reactions would be.

> *Optional lead-in*
> Choose a few adjectives yourself and tell the class what situations make you feel these things.

> *Language note*
> You can't say 'get relaxed'.

> *Alternative: class survey*
> Students move freely round the class, and find out how many students would react in the same way as themselves. They then report their findings to the class.

> *Homework option*
> Students write complete sentences giving situations for each feeling adjective, including those they didn't choose for the class activity.

2 Reactions

In this exercise, students practise reporting conversations in which people expressed feelings. This involves using particular verbs that describe people's reactions (e.g. refuse, cheer ... up*) as well as adjectives describing feelings.*

➤ Workbook: Exercise B

1 Presentation & listening

- Check that students understand the expressions in the bubbles (do this by asking e.g. *When would you calm me down? What would you say to me?*).
- [cassette] Play the recording, pausing after each scene to elicit a brief description of what happened, using a pair of the expressions. Possible answers:

  1 He *gave her* a birthday present and she *was absolutely delighted.*
  2 She *got angry* and he *tried to calm her down.*
  3 She *tried to persuade him* to go for a walk, but he *refused.*
  4 He *complained* about the noise, and the neighbour *apologised.*
  5 He *was very upset*, and she *tried to cheer him up.*

- [cassette] Play the recording again. This time, establish a more detailed 'storyline' for each scene, e.g.

  2 She was angry because a close friend had ignored her in the street. Her boyfriend tried to calm her down and convince her that it was just a mistake.

> **Language note**
> We *calm someone down* if they are angry or excited. We *cheer someone up* if they are sad, depressed or upset.

> [cassette] The tapescript is on page T101.

2 Writing/speaking activity

- Pairwork. Students choose any pair of expressions (e.g. *gave her ... was very angry; was very upset ... apologised*) and make up a short scene like those on the recording. They could either write the scene as a dialogue, or make notes for an improvisation.
- In turn, pairs act out their scene in front of the class. The other students guess what pair of expressions they chose.

> **Homework option**
> If pairs improvised scenes, they could write them as dialogues for homework, and then write a 'reported' version of what happened.

3 Reviews

This exercise introduces adjectives that are commonly used in giving positive and negative reactions to films, books, performances, sports events, etc.

➤ Workbook: Exercise C

1 Presentation

- Begin by asking students to imagine they saw a film yesterday, and write these structures on the board:

  It was
  I found it ························

  Add different adjectives to the sentences, and ask what they mean, e.g. *It was awful = it was very bad; I found it dull = it wasn't interesting.*

- Establish that the adjectives on the left are 'normal', and those on the right are 'extreme'. To show the difference, write these examples on the board:

  It was _very_ interesting.
  It was _absolutely_ fascinating.

  Fascinating already means 'very interesting', so we can't say 'very fascinating'. Instead we use *absolutely* if we want to emphasise how fascinating it was.

- Give a few examples to show how the other 'extreme' adjectives are used, e.g. *I think X is an absolutely brilliant singer; That film was absolutely terrible.*

> **Language note**
> *Dull* and *boring* both mean 'not interesting'.
> *Fascinating* = 'very interesting'.
> *Brilliant, terrific* and *wonderful* all mean 'very good'.
> *Awful, dreadful* and *terrible* all mean 'very bad'.

> **Language note**
> *Really* can be used with both 'normal' and 'extreme' adjectives:
> It was *really* interesting.
> It was *really* fascinating.

> **Language note**
> The normal/extreme distinction also applies to a large number of other adjectives, e.g. *hot – boiling; cold – freezing; tired – exhausted; big – enormous; clever – brilliant; hungry – starving.*

2 Reading & writing activity

- Read through the reviews and establish what they're about:
  – a sports event (e.g. a football match)   – a novel   – a film

- Agree on a few 'topics' to review. These could be recent films, TV shows, sporting events, books – anything that most students are familiar with.

- Students choose one of the topics and write a two-sentence review.

- As a round-up, students read out their reviews and compare their reactions with other students. This may lead to a general class discussion.

> **Alternative**
> Students read out their reviews, and other students guess which topic their review is about.

2 Reactions

1 🔲 You will hear five short scenes. For each one, find two expressions that describe what happened.

Now listen again, and say what happened in more detail.

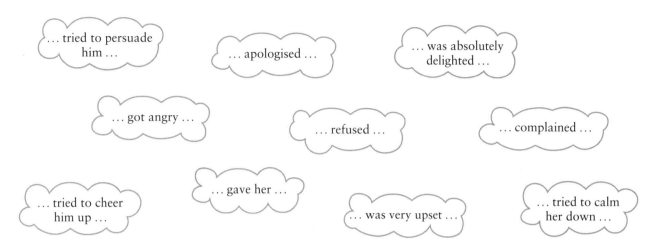

... tried to persuade him ...

... apologised ...

... was absolutely delighted ...

... got angry ...

... refused ...

... complained ...

... tried to cheer him up ...

... gave her ...

... was very upset ...

... tried to calm her down ...

2 Work in pairs. Choose any two of the expressions and prepare a short scene of your own.

3 Reviews

1 Look at the words in the box.

 a Which of them are positive and which are negative?

 b Which adjectives would fit in these sentences?
 – It was very ....
 – It was absolutely ....

amusing	awful
boring	brilliant
disappointing	dreadful
dull	fascinating
enjoyable	terrible
entertaining	terrific
exciting	wonderful
interesting	

2 a Look at these extracts from reviews. What do you think they're about?

It was a terrific match. Hodges is one of the most exciting players I've seen for ages.

The plot was entertaining enough, but I wish the author hadn't included all those long, boring descriptions of southern England.

This was a complete waste of an evening. The script was awful, the acting was wooden, and the camerawork was dreadful.

 b Choose something that several of you have seen or read recently, and write a short review.

 Now find out if other people agreed with you.

4 What's in a smile

READING

1 **Before you read:**

  a Which of these smiles do you think are real? Which are false? How can you tell?

  b Look at these faces. Which smile do you find the most attractive, and which the least attractive? Why?

  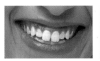

2 **Read the magazine article and find the answers to these questions.**

  a Do people smile in every culture in the world?
  b How many facial muscles do you use to smile?
  c What happens to your blood pressure when you smile?
  d What's the difference between a false smile and a real smile?
  e How did Norman Cousins cure himself?
  f Where can you find 'laughter rooms' and what are they for?
  g Why did Aristotle Onassis wear dark glasses?
  h What does a professional laugher do?

3 **Note down any points in the article that you disagree with or find hard to accept. Compare notes with your partner.**

LAUGHTER CLINIC

Robert Holden, whose handbook *Laughter, The Best Medicine?* will be published early next year, runs the only NHS Laughter Clinic in Britain. Holden believes that laughter and smiling can not only heal the mind but the body as well.

LISTENING

1 Read the text about the Laughter Clinic.
  What kind of activities do you imagine take place there?

2 🖭 You will hear someone describing a typical session at the Clinic.
  Make a list of all the activities she mentions.

  Now compare your list with your partner's. Did you have the same answers?

4 What's in a smile

This combined reading and listening activity is about smiling and laughter, and how it can be used as a form of therapy. The reading text is a magazine article which describes the difference between real and false smiles, and tells the story of a man who cured himself from a serious illness by laughing. The listening is an interview with someone who went on a course of 'laughter therapy'.

READING

- As a lead-in, ask students to look at Questions 1a and 1b in pairs. Then find out what they thought, and whether they all agree.
- Students read the text and find answers to Question 2.
- Go through the answers together, and ask students to say which part of the text gives the information. Answers:

    a Yes.
    b One.
    c It goes down.
    d In a false smile, the eyes don't change. False smiles start too early or too late, and they go on too long.
    e He stopped taking drugs, moved into a hotel room, watched comedy films and laughed a lot.
    f American hospitals – to cheer people up.
    g So that people couldn't see from his eyes whether he was interested or not during business negotiations.
    h Laughs non-stop for money, to make you laugh too.

- Give time for students to make brief notes of points in the text they don't agree with or can't accept. Then discuss these together.

> *Note*
> The aim of these questions is to help students scan for specific information. It isn't necessary for students to understand every word of the text.

> *Note*
> This could lead to a more general discussion of the value of smiling and laughter, and of whether it is possible to cure disease 'psychologically'.

LISTENING

- Look at the picture and the text beneath it, and ask students to suggest some of the activities they imagine taking place at a Laughter Clinic. If you like, write ideas on the board in note form, e.g.

listening to jokes	*remembering something funny*
watching comedy films	*tickling each other*

- 🔲 Play the recording, pausing from time to time. Students listen and list the activities she mentions.
- Pairwork. Students compare their list with the person next to them, and together make a 'collective' list of activities.
- Go through the answers together, and build up a list of activities on the board. Answers:

    – breathing exercises ('breathing in happiness')
    – smile
    – remember the last time we felt happy
    – lecture: how we forget to laugh
    – remember things that made us laugh (and the last thing that made us laugh)
    – listen to laughter on tape
    – homework: laugh in front of a mirror

> 🔲 The tapescript is on page T101.

A So you've just been on a smile therapy course. What was it like?

B It was really good. I enjoyed it.

A What did you have to do on the course?

B We started off by doing breathing exercises so we could feel about breathing in happiness and of course we had to smile, we had to smile a lot, and the idea is that if you smile you feel better, it puts you in a good mood, so we tried that. We had to try to remember the last time we felt happy and think about that feeling. Then we were given a lecture and that helped to explain how we forget to laugh. When we grow up we forget to laugh. As children you play and you laugh and you smile and you have fun and as you get older life is much more serious. And they're trying to help us to go back to that feeling of childhood and the fun that we had.

A So did you do any activities on the course?

B Yes, they got us into groups, and we had to think back to things that had made us laugh. That was really interesting because it's surprising how there's some people who just can't remember what last made them laugh.

A What about you? Could you remember?

B Oh yes I could remember because I watch funny things on the telly.

A And what else happened on the course?

B Well, the last bit was really the best. That's when they put on a tape of somebody laughing and they were just laughing really out of control and it was really good because we all started to laugh and one by one everybody was laughing because laughing is infectious and that was really good fun.

A What about homework? Do you do anything at home in between the sessions?

B Oh yes, we have this homework to do. We have to practise to laugh. It sounds a bit strange at first, you have to stand in front of the mirror and laugh, sort of like laugh at yourself, which the first time feels embarrassing but it does work and it makes you feel better. Yes. It's good.

A So in general do you think the course has helped to make you feel better about yourself?

B Yeah I do and it is good fun, and it's nice to be with a group, and I can think of some bad-tempered people who I would recommend should go on it.

---

1 A Happy birthday, Annie.
   B Oh thank you! Can I open it now?
   A Of course.
   B Oh it's lovely. Thank you very much.

2 A What's the matter?
   B My girlfriend Mary just walked right by me in the street and didn't even say hello.
   A Maybe she didn't see you.
   B She saw me all right. She's just, I don't know, mad at me or something.
   A I'm sure she isn't darling – don't get too worried about it. She probably just didn't see you.

3 A Do you want to go for a walk?
   B No I've got far too much work to do.
   A Oh please, it's a lovely day.
   B I know, but let's go later, eh?

4 A Would you mind keeping the noise down, please? I'm trying to get to sleep, I've got to get up early in the morning, this has been going on for two hours.
   B Yeah well I'm sorry. It's just, a friend of mine's just got married, you see. We're having a party.
   A Ah well I hope he's very happy. The thing is I've got to get up early. When are you going to stop?

5 A Is anything the matter?
   B It's Caroline. She's left me.
   A Oh no. I don't believe it. What happened?
   B Oh nothing really happened. She just said she was moving out and she didn't want to see me any more. I think she's met someone else.
   A Oh that's terrible. Look, tell you what, I'll make us some coffee, and then we'll get in the car and go for a drive.

Self-study Workbook

Exercise A: Three ways of talking about feelings
Students complete a table of feelings adjectives and verbs, then choose words from the table to fill gaps in sentences.

Exercise B: A time when ...
Students choose feelings-related topics from a box, and write about two things that happened to them.

Exercise C: Good and bad
'Normal' and 'extreme' adjectives describing reactions. Students answer questions by selecting from a list.

New words
Space to record new words with notes and examples.

Translation
Key sentences for translation.

Listening: James Bond films
Three people give their opinions of James Bond films. Students mark their own opinions in a table, then listen and complete the table for each speaker.

Phrasal verbs: Three-word verbs (2)
More three-word verbs (e.g. *put up with, get down to*). Students look up their meanings in a dictionary, then use them to fill gaps in sentences.

Writing skills: Sequence: unexpected events
Use of *after, while, before* for showing normal sequence, and *had just done ... when, was just doing ... when, was just about to ... when* for signalling unexpected events. Students fill gaps in sentences, then reorganise a story using sequence expressions.

What's in a smile

Eyes are important in other ways, too. When you feel good, your pupils get larger; when you feel bad, they become small. Ancient Chinese traders always looked their customers straight in the eye. If the pupils became big, the person was interested, and they could ask for more money.

DARK GLASSES

One reason why shipping tycoon Aristotle Onassis always wore dark glasses may have been so that his eyes would not give him away during delicate business negotiations.

Smiling is ...

universal. In his travels, Charles Darwin discovered that smiling was the only facial expression which was recognised instantly all over the world.

easy to see. It is possible to recognise a smile on someone's face at a distance of 45 metres. You'd have to be much closer to decide whether the person was showing surprise, anger or fear.

simple. You only use one facial muscle to smile. This is the zygomatic major muscle, which reaches down from the cheekbone to the corners of the lips. To look sad or angry, you need to use at least two muscles.

good for you. Studies in the USA have shown that when you smile your heart rate slows down, your blood pressure goes down and the body begins to relax. This happens whether you are feeling happy or not. In fact, if you're feeling unhappy, the simple act of smiling is the first step to feeling better.

attractive. According to American dentists Melvin and Elaine Denholtz, an attractive smile should show most of the upper teeth, at least two thirds of the length, and just the tips of the lower teeth.

Real smiles and false smiles

When you smile a real smile, two things happen to your face: your lips move up towards your cheeks, and your cheeks themselves go up and gather in the skin around the eyes. And a real smile will usually only last for up to four seconds.

False smiles are seen on the faces of politicians who have just lost an election, people who are pretending they're pleased to see you, and door-to-door salesmen. False smiles usually appear slightly too early or too late, and they tend to go on for too long.

But if you really want to know if a smile is real or false, look at the eyes. In a false smile these don't change – however much the person has practised smiling.

Laughter: the best medicine

In 1964 an American journalist called Norman Cousins developed a serious problem with his back. It turned out that he had an illness called ankylosing spondylitis, which was extremely painful and, according to doctors, incurable. He was admitted to hospital, unable to move, and prescribed a course of strong pain-killing drugs. Cousins knew that negative emotions could make you ill, and began to wonder whether positive emotions – and particularly laughter – might make you better.

He stopped taking the drugs, and moved out of the hospital into a hotel room, which was not only a more cheerful place to be but was also much cheaper. There he hired a lot of Marx Brothers and *Candid Camera* films, and started to watch them. He found that every time he laughed, the laughter acted as an anaesthetic and gave him relief from pain. And the effect lasted some time: 10 minutes' laughter could give him around two hours free from pain.

More important, he found that he was slowly getting better, and eventually recovered completely from the illness.

For many years, the medical profession refused to take Cousins' claims seriously, but now things are changing and some American hospitals have set up 'laughter rooms', where patients can watch videos, listen to cassettes and read joke books, instead of sitting around feeling depressed.

LAUGHING FOR MONEY

A Frenchwoman, Julie Hette, works as a professional laugher. For a fee, she will come and laugh non-stop for you. Her record is 90 minutes. She guarantees that you will soon be laughing with her – even though you might not know what you're laughing about.

23 The unreal past

1 Dilemmas

would have done

On 13 October 1972 a plane carrying 45 passengers and crew bound for Santiago, Chile, crashed in a remote part of the High Andes. After waiting several days, the 27 survivors of the crash realised that they had no chance of being rescued. They were stranded high in the mountains above the snow line, and although they could shelter from the worst of the cold inside the plane, they had nothing to eat except snacks and chocolates that the plane had been carrying. These soon ran out, and they were faced with starvation. Then one of the survivors suggested that there was just one chance of survival: they could eat the flesh of the passengers that had died in the crash ...

1 *a* Read the story about the crash in the Andes. What was the dilemma facing the survivors?

   Imagine you were one of the survivors. What would you have done?

  b 🎞 You will hear three people saying what they would have done in the situation.

   Which speaker's opinion is closest to your own?

2 Work in groups. Look at one of these other dilemmas. What would you have done?

When the nine-year-old daughter of Ernest and Regina Twigg died in 1988, the post-mortem examination showed that she was not in fact their daughter. They made enquiries, and discovered that someone had made a mistake at the hospital where Mrs Twigg had had her baby girl: their daughter had been given to another couple, and the Twiggs had been given the other couple's baby. Their daughter, they learnt, was living with her 'family' in another part of the USA, 1,500 kilometres away ...

In August 1991, Dr Nigel Cox was treating a 70-year-old woman who was extremely ill with rheumatoid arthritis, and in constant pain. There was no chance that she would ever leave her bed again. The only way Dr Cox could relieve her pain was by giving her large doses of heroin. After a time, however, heroin was not enough to stop the pain, and the woman begged Dr Cox to give her a drug that would kill her ...

This unit introduces language for talking about situations in the past that are unreal. This includes:
– *would have* + past participle
– Past conditionals with *If* + Past perfect
– *I wish* + Past perfect and *should(n't) have* + past participle for expressing regret.

23

1 Dilemmas

This exercise shows how we imagine things in the past using the structure would(n't) have + *past participle. Students look at true stories in which people faced dilemmas, and consider what they would have done themselves.*

➤ Focus on Form: Exercise 1
➤ Workbook: Exercise A

1 Presentation & listening

● Give time for students to read the text. Then establish what the passengers' dilemma was: whether to eat the flesh of the dead passengers or starve to death themselves.

● Write these two sentences on the board:

> **A I would have eaten the flesh of the dead passengers.**
>
> **B I wouldn't have eaten the flesh of the dead passengers.**

Ask students to decide whether they agree with sentence A or sentence B. Then find out how many 'A's and 'B's there are in the class.

● 🔲 Play the recording. Pause after each speaker and ask whether the speaker is an 'A' or a 'B', and what his/her reasons are. Answers:

1 B She's a vegetarian.
2 A He wouldn't have minded other people eating him.
3 A It isn't morally wrong if you need to survive.
4 B It is morally wrong.

● Find out how many students agreed with each speaker. This may develop into a more general discussion of the issue.

● Before going on to the other dilemmas, look again at the sentences on the board. Point out that
– the structure is formed *would(n't) have* + past participle.
– we use it to *imagine* something in the past that wasn't real (we weren't really in the plane crash – we're just imagining it).

2 Discussion

● Divide the class into groups, and ask each group to choose one of the other dilemmas. Together, they discuss what they would or wouldn't have done.

● Ask each group to say what they would have done and why. Find out if others in the class agree with them, and give your own opinion.

● As a round-up, tell the class what actually happened to the people involved:

> Mrs Twigg contacted her daughter, who went to stay with the Twiggs several times. The girl found these visits increasingly difficult, and wanted to break the contact with her real family. When she was 14 she went to court to try and get a 'divorce' from her real parents, and won her case. A year or so later, she changed her mind and went back to live with her real parents.

> Dr Cox injected his patient with a drug that killed her. He was later tried for attempted murder, and was found guilty. However, he was only given a *suspended* 12-month sentence. The British Medical Association said that what he had done was wrong, but they allowed him to keep practising as a doctor.

Optional lead-in
Look at the picture and ask students if they know the story (they might have seen the film *Alive* or read the book). If they do, ask them to say what happened in their own words.

🔲 The tapescript is on page T104.

Blackboard option
Draw a grid on the board, and fill it as you elicit answers from the class:

	A or B?	Reasons
1		
2		
3		
4		

Vocabulary option
Read through the texts with the whole class, explaining any difficult words, e.g. *post-mortem examination, in constant pain, relieve, doses.*

2 If ...

This exercise shows how the structure would have + *past participle is used in complete Past conditional sentences with* If + *Past perfect. Students interpret remarks and then write* If ... *sentences themselves.*

➤ Focus on Form: Exercise 2
➤ Workbook: Exercise B

1 Presentation

- Look at the remarks and establish the three situations:
  - He lost a tennis match because he hurt his wrist.
  - She was busy and didn't have time to write to a friend.
  - He bought e.g. a second-hand car, then found that it was in bad condition.

- Use the first example to present Past conditional structures:

> **The facts: He <u>hurt</u> his wrist. He <u>didn't win</u>.**
> **He says: If I <u>hadn't hurt</u> my wrist, I <u>would have won</u>.**
> **IF + HAD(N'T) DONE   WOULD(N'T) HAVE DONE**

Point out that
- we use this structure to imagine something *unreal* in the past (in fact he *did* hurt his wrist, so he *didn't* win).
- the verb moves *back*, so to talk about the past we use the *Past perfect tense*.

> **Practice option**
> Give other situations and ask students to make Past conditional sentences, e.g.
> I didn't have the car. I didn't offer her a lift.
> → If I'd had the car, I would have offered her a lift.

2 Writing/speaking activity

- Ask students to suggest *If ...* sentences for the first item. Possible answers:

  If you'd told me you were ill, I would have come to see you.
  If I'd known you were ill, I wouldn't have cooked all this food.

- In pairs, students look at the other remarks and write *If ...* sentences.
- Ask students to read out their sentences. Possible answers:
  - If I'd known it was your birthday, I would have sent you a card.
  - If the weather hadn't been so bad, I would have gone sailing.
  - If they'd opened my suitcase, they would have found the gun.
  - If I'd had some money with me, I would have got a taxi.

3 A better place

This activity shows how we can 'mix' second and third conditional structures, depending on whether we are referring to the present or the past. Students consider what would make the world, their country, etc., a better place.

➤ Focus on Form: Exercise 3
➤ Workbook: Exercise C

1 Presentation & listening

- Go through the sentences and ask students whether they agree with them.
- To focus on the tenses used, write on the board:

> **The world <u>would be</u> a better place**

Point out that this is a 'second' conditional structure (like those in Unit 9), used to imagine the world *now*. Then add the first two examples:

> **The world <u>would be</u> a better place   <u>if</u> women <u>were</u> in control.**
> **   <u>if</u> Karl Marx <u>had died</u> young.**

The first continuation is about *now*, and uses *if* + *Past* tense.
The second continuation is about the *past*, and uses *if* + *Past perfect* tense.

- Ask students to make up other continuations, either about now or the past.

> **Practice option**
> Take each of the opinions in turn, and ask students to add to them, e.g.
> If scientists hadn't split the atom, Hiroshima wouldn't have been destroyed.
> If women were in control, there wouldn't be so many wars.

2 Writing & speaking activity

- Working alone, students write continuations for the three sentences, e.g.

  This country would be a better place if they reduced taxes.
  This country would be a better place if they hadn't built so many motorways.

- Pairwork. Students read out their sentences, and see if their partner agrees.
- As a round-up, ask a few students to read out their sentences.

2 If ...

1 Look at the remarks above. What are the speakers talking about?
What happened (or didn't happen)?

2 Write *If* ... sentences based on the remarks below.

Why didn't you tell me you were ill?

Sorry. I didn't know it was your birthday.

It's a pity the weather was so bad.

It's a good thing they didn't open my suitcase.

I didn't have any money with me.

3 A better place

2nd & 3rd conditionals

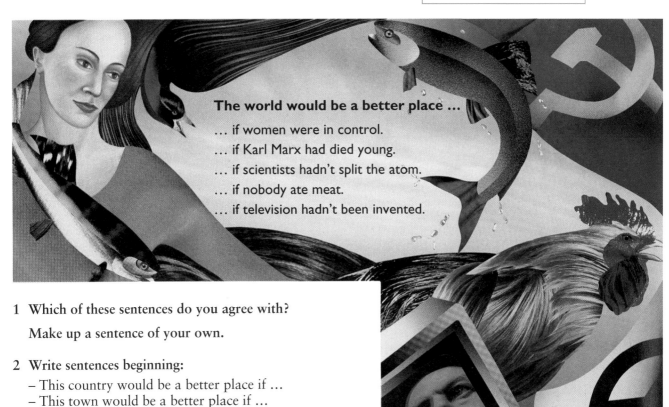

The world would be a better place ...

... if women were in control.
... if Karl Marx had died young.
... if scientists hadn't split the atom.
... if nobody ate meat.
... if television hadn't been invented.

1 Which of these sentences do you agree with?

Make up a sentence of your own.

2 Write sentences beginning:
– This country would be a better place if ...
– This town would be a better place if ...
– This school would be a better place if ...

Show your sentences to your partner. Does he/she agree?

4 I wish I hadn't …

> I wish + Past perfect • should(n't) have

⟨⟨⟨ ARE YOU THE PERSON YOU'D LIKE TO BE? ⟩⟩⟩

Analysing your regrets is the first step to finding out

From time to time, we all find ourselves regretting things we've done and things we haven't done. But there's no point in getting depressed about it. In fact, looking at our regrets can be a very useful way of finding out more about ourselves.

Try this test.

FIRST fill in the table. Put a tick against each regret, to show whether you feel it often, sometimes or never.

THEN add two more regrets that you often (or sometimes) feel.

NOW look at the results. What do they tell you about yourself?

Here are ten common regrets. How often do you say them to yourself? Add two more of your own.	often	some-times	never
1 I shouldn't have lost my temper.			
2 I should have said what I really thought.			
3 I wish I'd kept my mouth shut.			
4 I wish I hadn't spent so much money.			
5 I shouldn't have left it to the last minute.			
6 I wish I'd been a bit friendlier.			
7 I should have offered to help.			
8 I wish I'd remembered …			
9 I shouldn't have let it upset me.			
10 I should have refused.			
11			
12			

1 Look at the sentences in the table.
   How do we use *I wish* and *I should* to express regret?

2 Read the article and follow the instructions.
   What do your answers tell you about yourself?

Grammar Checklist

would have done

would have + *past participle – to refer to the unreal past.*

I **would have** phoned you, but I was too busy. (= actually I didn't phone you)
I **wouldn't have** enjoyed living in the 16th century.

3rd conditional structures

If + *Past perfect* … **would have** + *past participle*

I **would have** phoned you if I **hadn't been** so busy.
If he'd **taken** a map, he **wouldn't have got** lost.
If I'd **known** they were at home, I **would have** visited them.
If she **hadn't left** the window open, the cat **wouldn't have got** in.

'Mixed' conditionals

These mix 2nd and 3rd conditionals. One part of the sentence is about the past, the other is about the present.

If he **hadn't stolen** the money, he **wouldn't be** in prison. (= he stole the money, so now he's in prison)
Inflation **would be** higher (now) if the Democrats **had won** the election (last year).

(For 2nd conditionals, see Unit 9.)

Structures for expressing regret

I wish + *Past perfect*

I wish I'd apologised.
I wish I **hadn't lost** my temper.

I should(n't) have + *Past participle*

I should have apologised.
I shouldn't have lost my temper.

See also Reference section, page 141.

4 I wish I hadn't ...

This exercise uses a magazine-style questionnaire to introduce the structures I wish + Past perfect and I should(n't) have + past participle, used for expressing regret. Students complete the table and then discuss what this reveals about their personalities.

➤ Focus on Form: Exercise 4
➤ Workbook: Exercise D

1 Reading & presentation

- Read through the text, and show how we use the word *regret* as a verb or a noun:

I *regret* many things.
being rude to him.   I have many *regrets*.

- Use the first regret in the table to present the key structures on the board:

> **I wish I hadn't**
> **I shouldn't have** <u>lost my temper.</u>

Point out that
– after *I wish* we use the Past perfect tense to refer to the past
– instead of *I wish*, we can use *I should have (done)*.

- To check comprehension of the structures, point to the first regret and ask 'What did the person do wrong?' Answer:

She *lost* her temper (and now she wishes she *hadn't*).

Get students to explain the other regrets in the same way, e.g.

She *didn't say* what she really thought.
She *didn't keep* her mouth shut.
She *spent* a lot of money.

2 Writing & speaking activity

- Working alone, students complete the table and then add two more regrets of their own.

- Students turn to the person next to them and compare their answers. They discuss what they think their answers tell them about the kind of person they are.

- Ask the class whether they think the test reveals anything about their personality, and if so, what.

Optional lead-in
Ask the class the question 'Are you the person you'd like to be', and ask students to raise their hands for 'Yes', 'No' and 'Not sure'.

Presentation option
Remind students of the two other *I wish* structures (for talking about the present and the future) introduced in Unit 9:
I wish + Past tense.
I wish + would/could.

🔲 Tapescript for Exercise 1: *Dilemmas*

1 Well this is very difficult, but I'm vegetarian, and I don't think I could have eaten the flesh of another person. I don't think I could have lived with myself afterwards if I'd survived. So no, I wouldn't have eaten the flesh of another human being.

2 I think I would have eaten the flesh of the other passengers. If I looked at it from a point of view that I was one of the dead passengers, I wouldn't have minded my body helping other people live. So I think I would have reluctantly done it.

3 I think I probably would have ended up eating the flesh of my fellow passengers if I needed to to survive. I find the idea physically revolting when I think about it, but I don't find it morally revolting. I don't see any moral reason for not doing that if it's necessary to survive, so I probably would have done.

4 I would not have eaten the flesh of my fellow passengers, quite simply because I believe it's morally wrong to do so. So if it was a choice between starving to death and eating the body of another person, I would have chosen starvation.

Focus on Form

1 *Would(n't) have done*

> *would(n't) have* + past participle

- Read the introduction together, and give time for students to read through the text.
- Ask students to give reasons why Moriarty didn't commit the crime, using *would(n't) have* ... . Other possible answers:

  He wouldn't have dropped the sword; he would have taken it away with him.

  He wouldn't have left his fingerprints on the sword; he would have wiped them off.

  He wouldn't have left his ring by the body.

  He would have killed the victim properly, or he would have cleaned up the blood.

  He wouldn't have written his name on the note.

  He would have entered the building without being seen.

  He would have worn a disguise.

2 *Past conditionals*

> *If* + *had(n't)* ... *would(n't) have* + past participle

- Read the example. Then read the second sentence from Box A and ask students to find a continuation. Ask them what the complete answer should be, and write it on the board:

  If they'd known you were coming, they wouldn't have eaten all the food.

- Pairwork. Students change the other items from Box A and find continuations from Box B.
- Go through the answers. Answers:
  - If they'd had life-jackets, they wouldn't have drowned.
  - If they hadn't lit a fire, they wouldn't have been rescued.
  - If they'd been insured, they would have got their money back.
  - If they'd checked the plane, they would have found the bomb.
  - If the dog hadn't barked, they wouldn't have woken up.

3 *Mixed conditionals*

> Mixed 2nd and 3rd conditional structures

- Look at the example and establish that
  - the first part of the sentence is about the present (she wouldn't be so lonely now)
  - the first continuation is also about the present (she doesn't know many people) and uses the *Past tense*
  - the second continuation is about a past event (she moved away from home) and uses the *Past perfect*.
- Go through the exercise, asking students to put the verbs in the correct tense. Answers:
  - a ... if they *hadn't bought*; ... if they both *had*
  - b ... if she*'d passed*; ... if she*'d worked* (... if she *worked*)
  - c ... if he *lived*; ... if his wife *hadn't left*; ... if he *hadn't spent*

4 *Regrets*

> *I wish* + Past perfect; *I should(n't) have* + past participle

- Go through the example with the class.
- In pairs, students make sentences for the other situations.
- Go through the answers together. Some possible answers:
  - a I wish I hadn't left school so early. I should have gone to university. I wish I had better qualifications.
  - b I shouldn't have picked the briefcase up. I wish I hadn't opened it. I wish I'd never seen it.
  - c I wish I'd married him/her. I shouldn't have hesitated. I wish he/she hadn't got married.

5 *Pronunciation*

[cassette icon] Ask students to try saying the sentences themselves, then play the recording as a model. Focus on these points:

a Reduced vowels in *would have* /wʊd (h)əv/ and *wouldn't have* /wʊdn̩t (h)əv/.

b Stress and rhythm of Past conditional structures: If he **had**n't left **fin**gerprints they **would**n't have **caught** him.

c Reduced vowels in *should have* /ʃʊd (h)əv/ and *shouldn't have* /ʃʊdn̩t (h)əv/.

Self-study Workbook

Exercise A: What would you have done?
Students read about what people did in different situations, and say what they themselves would have done.

Exercise B: Third conditionals
Students complete conditional sentences.

Exercise C: It's all your fault
Mixed 2nd and 3rd conditionals.
Students write sentences from prompts.

Exercise D: It's all my own fault
I wish + *had(n't)*; *I should(n't) have*.
Students write wishes for the situations in Exercise C.

Translation
Key sentences for translation.

Listening: A better place
Five views about what would make the world a better place. Students listen for each speaker's main point.

Pronunciation: Common suffixes
Common suffixes and their pronunciation. Students make predictions, then check their answers on the tape.

Reading: If things had been different ...
A person writes about his regrets.
Students read the texts, and answer true/false questions.

Focus on Form

1 Would(n't) have done

For many years, Detective Shadow has been pursuing Sid Moriarty, a master of disguise and the cleverest criminal in North America ...

Read the story. How many reasons can *you* find?

Example:

Moriarty wouldn't have used his own sword. He would have used another weapon.

2 Past conditionals

Student A: Read out the items from Box A. Use *If + had(n't)*.

Student B: Complete each sentence with a suitable item from Box B. Use *would(n't) have*.

Example:

A If they'd promised to lower taxes ...
B ... they would have won the election.

```
A   They didn't promise to lower taxes.
    They didn't know you were coming.
    They didn't have life-jackets.
    They lit a fire.
    They weren't insured.
    They didn't check the plane properly.
    The dog barked.
```

```
B   They were rescued.
    They drowned.
    They woke up.
    They didn't find the bomb.
    They ate all the food.
    They didn't win the election.
    They didn't get their money back.
```

3 Mixed conditionals

Put the verbs in brackets into the right form. Use the Past or Past perfect tense.

Example: *She wouldn't be so lonely ...*

... if she *knew* more people.
... if she *hadn't moved* away from home.

a They'd be much better off ...
    ... if they (not buy) such a big house.
    ... if they both (have) jobs.
b She'd still be at university ...
    ... if she (pass) her exams.
    ... if she (work) harder.
c He'd be much happier ...
    ... if he (live) in a warmer climate.
    ... if his wife (not leave) him.
    ... if he (not spend) all his savings.

Now make some continuations of your own.

'We've got him this time, sir!' the Sergeant told Shadow excitedly. 'It was Moriarty all right!'

'Tell me about it, Sergeant,' said Shadow.

'Well, sir, for a start, the victim was killed with a 17th century Italian sword, of a kind that Moriarty is known to have in his collection.'

'How do you know?' asked Shadow.

'We found it, sir. He dropped it in the hallway. And it's got his fingerprints on the handle. Not only that, a ring with *SM* engraved on it was found by the body.'

'Mm,' said Shadow. 'Anything else?'

'Plenty! It seems the victim didn't die immediately: he had time to write *MORIA* in his own blood before he died. And we found a note in his pocket: it said *Tonight you die*, and it was signed *Sid M.*'

'Is that all?' asked Shadow, smiling.

'Not quite,' said the Sergeant. 'There's a neighbour, a Mr Sam Crook, who says he saw someone answering Moriarty's description enter the building just before midnight.'

'Right,' replied Shadow. 'You'd better arrest Sam Crook.'

'Sam Crook, sir? But ...'

'Sergeant,' said Shadow patiently, 'I can think of at least seven reasons why Sid Moriarty didn't commit this crime.'

4 Regrets

Make sentences with *I wish* or *I should(n't)* for these situations.

Example: *You were behind a lorry on a narrow road; you tried to overtake it; you didn't see a car coming the other way, and you crashed.*

I shouldn't have overtaken the lorry.
I wish I'd seen the car coming the other way.
I should have been more careful.
I wish I hadn't crashed.

a You left school at 16; you didn't go to university; now you haven't got enough qualifications to get a good job.
b You found a briefcase lying on the pavement; you picked it up and opened it; it exploded, and now you're in hospital.
c You met someone you liked; he/she wanted to marry you but you weren't sure; he/she married someone else and now you're alone.

5 Pronunciation

How do you say the words and phrases below?

a I would have waited.
    You wouldn't have liked the film.
    If I'd known you were busy, I would have waited.

b If he hadn't left fingerprints, they wouldn't have caught him.

c I should have apologised.
    I shouldn't have bought it.

 Now listen and check your answers.

1 Global issues

1 Every week, a staggering 10,000 square kilometres of tropical rainforest are cut down. An area the size of France disappears every 12 months.

2 The nations of the world, rich and poor alike, continue to regard the sea as a convenient place to dump millions of tons of chemicals, sewage and industrial waste.

3 There are now more than 800 nuclear power stations throughout the world. Although this is supposed to be a 'clean' form of energy, there are in fact very high risks associated with it.

4 Smoke from factories and coal-fired power stations not only pollutes the air, but also causes chemical changes in the atmosphere which result in acid rain.

5 In 1985 it was noticed that there was a hole in the ozone layer over the Antarctic. Scientists now believe that the loss of ozone may be as much as 30%, and still rising.

6 Over the last 10 years, the Sahara has advanced southwards by an average of 20 kilometres per year, and 250,000 square kilometres of land has turned into desert.

7 A major report on global warming has warned that average world temperatures will rise by several degrees in the next century, due to the build-up of carbon dioxide and other 'greenhouse gases' in the Earth's atmosphere.

1 Look at the texts, and give a title to each one.
   Which picture best illustrates each text? What's the connection?

2 Together, choose one of the issues. Then work in pairs.

   Pair A: You think Pair B should be more worried about this issue. What will you say to them?

   Pair B: You think Pair A are worrying about nothing. What will you say to them?

   Now get together. Can you persuade the others to change their minds?

This unit is concerned with language used to talk about environmental issues. It deals with three main areas:
– global issues concerning the environment
– individual and government action to help the environment
– endangered species of wildlife.
The Reading and Listening activity is about asteroids and the threat they pose to life on Earth.

1 Global issues

This exercise is about general environmental issues that affect the whole world, and which are often referred to in everyday conversation. The pictures and texts are used to introduce a range of key vocabulary, which is then used in discussing the problems in a role-play activity.

➤ Workbook: Exercise A

1 *Presentation & discussion*

- Give time for students to read the texts and think of a suitable title for each; the purpose of this is simply to focus on the seven issues.
- Discuss possible titles together, and build up key concepts on the board (given in italics below). Possible answers:
  1 Destruction of the *tropical rain forest*
  2 *Pollution of the sea*
  3 The dangers of *nuclear power*
  4 *Air pollution; acid rain*
  5 The *ozone layer*
  6 The growth of deserts; *desertification*
  7 *Global warming*; the *greenhouse effect*

- Ask students to match the pictures with the texts, and discuss how they are connected. This should lead to a discussion of what the problems are and how they are caused. Possible answers:
  1 C: if the rainforest is cut down, many species of animals and plants will become extinct. (Some of these may be very valuable for medicine.)
  2 F: pollution of the sea kills wildlife.
  3 D: in 1986, the nuclear power station at Chernobyl caught fire, and radioactivity leaked into the atmosphere.
  4 E: acid rain causes damage to trees, and also kills fish and other wildlife.
  5 G: as the ozone layer gets thinner, there is more risk of skin cancer from sunbathing.
  6 A: as the deserts spread, thousands of people are losing their homes and are forced to move.
  7 B: global warming is leading to changes in climate throughout the world, including an increase in storms, hurricanes and floods.

Optional questions
If necessary, lead students to see the connections by prompting with questions, e.g.
Where do you think frogs like this one live? Why has this man covered himself?

2 *Speaking activity*

- Ask the class to choose one of the issues to discuss. Then divide the class into pairs and give pairs a letter, A or B, alternately round the class. 'Pair A' students should be concerned about the issue, 'Pair B' should be unconcerned.
- To prepare for the role-play, each pair prepares arguments they will use to persuade the other pair. If they like, they could make brief notes.
- 'A' and 'B' pairs get together to make groups of four. They discuss the issue, trying to persuade each other.
- As a round-up, ask each group what happened in their discussion.

Alternative
Divide the class into groups of four to choose an issue. They then divide into two pairs, A and B, to prepare their argument.

Homework option
Students choose one of the issues and design a poster alerting people to the problem and (possibly) suggesting solutions.
This could be done as a group project outside the class.

2 Going green

This exercise is concerned with steps that can be taken, by individuals and by governments, to help the environment. It introduces a range of common verbs used for talking about saving, wasting and using products.

➤ Workbook: Exercise B

1 Presentation

● Look at the suggestions for individual action, and establish what the point of each one is. Use students' answers to present these key verbs:

save	*re-use*
waste	*recycle*
use	*destroy*

Possible answers:

1 It saves petrol / doesn't contribute to global warming.
2 It saves electricity and water (showers use less water than baths).
3 It wastes plastic bags to only use them once.
4 The glass can be re-used/recycled.
5 It helps to stop people destroying the rainforest.

● Look at the suggestions for govenment action, and discuss in each case whether the government should take action rather than expecting action from individuals. Encourage students to consider the plus and minus points of each suggestion (e.g. doubling the price of petrol would encourage people to use cars less often, but would be bad for people who really need to use their car).

2 Writing/speaking activity

● Pairwork. Students write another pair of suggestions. Both should concern the same problem, but one is aimed at individuals, the other at governments.

● Students form groups and read out their suggestions. They discuss which of the two suggestions they think is more practical.

● As a round-up, ask groups to read out their best suggestions.

Alternative
Students move freely round the class, reading out their pair of suggestions to other students. They ask the other students to comment on the suggestions.

---

3 Endangered species

This is a freer activity, in which students discuss and read about the dangers facing four endangered species of animals. It introduces a range of vocabulary used in talking about wildlife (e.g. species, habitat, extinct, hunt).

1 Writing & reading activity

● Groupwork. Give each group a different animal to talk about. Together, they make notes of everything they know about it, including things they are not sure of, e.g. *Elephant:*
Very big
Two kinds – African and Indian
People hunt them for ivory
They eat leaves (?)
It's illegal to kill them (?)

● Each group turns to the back of the book and reads about the animal they discussed (pandas, p.118; tigers, p.119; rhinos, p.120; elephants, p.121).

2 Speaking activity

● Ask each group in turn to tell the class about their animal, and why it needs special protection.

● Ask students to imagine that they each have $500 to spend on endangered species. Give time for them to decide which animal(s) to spend their money on, and to write out 'cheques' (e.g. Elephant $300; Tiger $100; Rhinoceros $100) on pieces of paper.

● Ask four students to go round the class and collect the cheques.

● Find out how much money was donated to each species.

Whole class option
Choose one of the animals, and elicit information from the whole class, building up notes on the board. Then divide the class into groups to talk about the other three animals.

Language note
The texts contain a range of vocabulary that is commonly used in talking about wildlife, e.g.

species, common, rare, extinct, habitat, protected, hunt.

You could focus on these words during the group presentations.

Note
Groups could also consider other species at this point, e.g. whales, dolphins, turtles, or endangered species in their own country.

---

2 Going green

FIVE THINGS YOU CAN DO TO HELP THE ENVIRONMENT

❶ If it isn't very far, walk or cycle – leave the car at home.

❷ Have a shower instead of a bath.

❸ When you go shopping, don't ask for a bag – take one with you.

❹ Don't throw away old bottles – take them to a bottle bank.

❺ Don't buy furniture made from tropical hardwoods.

FIVE THINGS GOVERNMENTS COULD DO TO HELP THE ENVIRONMENT

❶ Double the price of petrol.

❷ Introduce water meters.

❸ Put a tax on plastic bags.

❹ Put a deposit on bottles to encourage people to return them.

❺ Ban the import of tropical hardwoods.

1 Which suggestions do you think are better – those for individuals or those for governments?

2 Add another pair of suggestions, one for individuals and one for governments. Ask other students which suggestion they think is better.

3 Endangered species

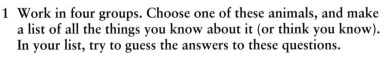

1 Work in four groups. Choose one of these animals, and make a list of all the things you know about it (or think you know). In your list, try to guess the answers to these questions.

– Where does it live?
– Why is it in danger?
– Roughly how many are there in the world?
– Is the number increasing or decreasing?

Turn to the back of the book and read about the animal. Were your guesses correct?

2 Tell other groups what you know about your animal.

Now hold a collection. Each student has $500 to spend on the animal(s) of their choice.

Which group collected the most money?

Death of the Dinosaurs

65 MILLION YEARS AGO, dinosaurs suddenly became extinct, together with a large number of other species. But why did it happen?

Many scientists believe that the cause was a large asteroid crashing into the Earth. According to this theory, the asteroid threw huge amounts of dust and water vapour into the atmosphere, blocking out the light of the sun, the vegetation died off, and the dinosaurs starved to death.

Evidence for the theory came in 1992 when scientists in Mexico uncovered an underground crater 175 kilometres wide, which turned out to be exactly 65 million years old. The crater was probably caused by an asteroid 10 km in diameter hitting the Earth at thousands of miles an hour, with the force of 70 million one-megaton bombs.

According to David Raup of the University of Chicago, this was just one of many such cases. He says that asteroids have caused more than half of species extinctions since life on Earth began 600 million years ago. If he's right, it seems likely that *Homo sapiens* will end its days in the same way.

READING

Find answers to these questions in the texts.

1 Look at the pictures at the top of page 109. Which shows
   - an asteroid?
   - a comet?

2 How did dinosaurs become extinct? What evidence is there?

3 Which asteroid has caused the most damage during the 20th century?

4 What damage would the following cause?
   - an asteroid 30 metres wide
   - an asteroid 1 kilometre wide
   - Swift-Tuttle's comet

5 What are the chances of
   - a 1 km wide asteroid hitting Earth during your lifetime?
   - a 5 km wide asteroid hitting Earth next year?
   - Swift-Tuttle's comet hitting Earth on August 14, 2116?

6 How is NASA planning to use
   - telescopes?
   - nuclear bombs?

DISCUSSION

1 Do you think that the human race will go the same way as the dinosaurs?

2 Do you think NASA's plans are
   - sensible?
   - pointless?
   - dangerous?

LISTENING

1 Imagine that you read the following headline in your daily newspaper:

10 KM ASTEROID HEADING FOR EARTH
**Due to arrive in 6 months' time
The chances of impact are 70%**

What would you do?

2 🔲 You will hear five people saying what they would do in the same situation.

If you had to spend the next six months with one of the speakers, which one would you choose?

4 The Doomsday Asteroid

This combined reading and listening activity is about the risks of an asteroid hitting the Earth and destroying the human race. The reading consists of a series of short texts adapted from newspapers and magazines which describe asteroid encounters in the past and the future. In the listening, five people say how they would spend the rest of their lives if they believed an asteroid was about to hit the Earth.

READING

- Give time for students to work through the questions and find answers from the texts. They could do this working with a partner, or they could work alone and then compare answers with their partner afterwards.

- Discuss the answers together and ask students to tell you where they found the relevant information. Answers:

  1 *Asteroid* = the round object.
    Comet = the one with the tail.
  2 A large asteroid crashed into the Earth, and dust blocked out the sun. The evidence: an asteroid crater in Mexico. (*Death of the Dinosaurs* text)
  3 The one in Tunguska in 1908. (*Some Recent Encounters* text)
  4 *30 metres wide*: it would probably explode in the atmosphere and cause no damage.
    1 km wide: it would kill people, destroy cities, block out the sun for years.
    Swift-Tuttle's comet: it would probably destroy the human race (it's five–ten km wide). (Statistics table and *End of the World* text)
  5 – about 1 in 4,000. (*NASA to the Rescue* text)
    – 1 in a million. (Statistics table)
    – 1 in 400. (*End of the World* text)
  6 *Telescopes*: to spot approaching asteroids.
    Nuclear bombs: to move an approaching asteroid out of the way. (*NASA to the Rescue* text)

DISCUSSION

- Use the two questions to find out what students think of the ideas expressed in the texts. If they disagree with them, ask them to say why and give their own opinion.

LISTENING

- Look at the newspaper headline and ask students to imagine the situation. Ask students what they would do, getting a range of different ideas. If you like, write the ideas in note form on the board.
- ▭ Play the recording, pausing after each speaker to establish what he/she would do.
- Ask students to decide which speaker they'd choose to spend the next six months with, and why. If you like, you could take a class vote on each of the speakers.

Vocabulary option

As you go through the answers, deal with key vocabulary, e.g. *fragment, chunk, dust, explode, explosion, equivalent to, encounter, block (out), the human race, impact, collision, risk.*

Groupwork option

Students discuss what they would do in groups. Then ask each group to tell you one or two of their 'best' ideas.

Optional questions

Help students by asking 'prompt' questions, e.g. *She'd 'live it up'. What does that mean? What does she say about money? What's an overdraft? What about food?*

▭ Tapescript for Exercise 4: *The Doomsday Asteroid*

1 Well if I only had one month left to live I'd certainly live it up. I'd spend every penny I have, I'd run up an enormous overdraft at the bank, buy everything I've ever wanted, eat anything I've ever wanted to eat, I don't care how bad it is for me – I'd just have a wild time.

2 I think I would go to Spain and get a really nice house on the beach, and have a month on the beach with my children, playing by the seaside, just having fun.

3 I'd buy a wonderful pair of walking boots and an enormous rucksack, and set off with my partner to walk around the entire coast of the British Isles and just stick to the coast, and just keep going, until the end.

4 Well it isn't absolutely certain that the world would end in six months, so I think I'd probably just carry on as normal really. But I think I'd try and do all those things that I've always wanted to do that I've never done. Like I'd learn to fly, and I'd try parachute-jumping, and I think I'd like to go scuba-diving. And that's what I'd do. I'd live normally, but I'd make sure that I really filled up my time with enjoyable things.

5 I suppose in such a situation, most people would just want to travel around. So I would open a travel agency and organise trips to the most exotic places, just like palm beaches, and exotic islands, visiting relations, and so on and so forth. And I would just earn a fantastic amount of money. There is a 30% chance that the asteroid wouldn't hit the Earth, so I'd become just fantastically rich. And when everybody goes to work after the panic has gone I would just retire and enjoy myself.

Tapescript for *In the street* (*Conversational English, page T111*)

1 A Excuse me. Do you know if there's a Post Office near here?
  B Yes. There's one just round the corner.
2 A Excuse me. I wonder if you could tell me what the time is.
  B Yes. It's nearly half past three.
3 A Excuse me. Do you know if there's anywhere around here I can change some money?
  B Well there's a bank in the next street.
4 A Excuse me. Can you tell me when the bus leaves?
  B I think it goes in about ten minutes.
5 A Excuse me. Could you tell me the way to North Street?
  B Yes. Carry on up here and it's the second on the left.

Self-study Workbook

Exercise A: Environment quiz
An acrostic puzzle. The answers are key vocabulary items related to the environment.

Exercise B: Agree or disagree?
Students agree or disagree with three opinions on the environment, and give their reasons.

Exercise C: How green are you?
Students write about how green they are in their everyday life, using pictures as prompts.

New words
Space to record new words with notes and examples.

Translation
Key sentences for translation.

Listening: How green are you?
Three people answer the question 'How green do you think you are in your everyday life?' Students assess each speaker, and answer comprehension questions.

Phrasal verbs: Review
A review of all the previous phrasal verbs exercises. Students match phrasal verbs to contexts, and complete sentences using phrasal verbs.

Writing skills: Organising ideas
Using linking expressions (*The main reason …, The problem with …, One advantage of …*, etc.) to show the connection between ideas in a paragaph. Students use the key expressions to join sentences together and develop them into a paragraph.

ASTEROIDS AND COMETS

Asteroids are lumps of rock flying around in space. They are fragments of planets that have broken up.

Comets are chunks of ice surrounded by dust. The dust is visible as a long tail trailing behind the comet.

Some recent encounters with asteroids

1908
A 60-metre asteroid exploded in the air about 8 kilometres above the Tunguska region of Siberia, destroying hundreds of square kilometres of forest. The explosion was equivalent to 20 hydrogen bombs.

1978
A huge explosion equivalent to 100,000 tons of TNT was detected in the South Pacific. This was first thought to be a secret nuclear test, but most experts now think it was an asteroid strike.

1991
An asteroid 10 metres in diameter passed between the Earth and the Moon, scoring a near miss.

1992
An asteroid called Toutatis, measuring 3 km across, passed within 3 million km of Earth. Toutatis is a regular visitor, and in 2004 it is expected to come even closer, within 1.5 million km of Earth.

Size	How often?	Damage
10 m–100 m	every 300 years	Most explode on hitting the Earth's atmosphere, and cause no damage. Some of the larger ones, however, get through, including two this century. If either of these had arrived over a major city, millions of people would have been killed.
1 km	every 300,000 years	An asteroid this size could affect whole countries, with tens of millions of deaths in a densely populated region. The impact would throw up enough debris into the atmosphere to block out the light of the sun for several years.
5 km	every million years	This would be big enough to cause mass extinction. Agriculture and civilisation would certainly be destroyed, and the human race might not survive.

The bigger they are, the harder they fall: some vital statistics about asteroids

NASA to the rescue

As we can't predict when a really big asteroid will arrive, is there really any point in worrying about it? NASA thinks there is. It estimates that there are between 1,000 and 4,000 asteroids at least 1 kilometre in diameter which regularly cross Earth's orbit. If such an asteroid hits the Earth once every 300,000 years, this gives the average person roughly a one in 4,000 chance of being around when it happens. A small risk, maybe, but much bigger than the risk of dying in an air crash, which is one in 20,000.

NASA aims to set up six new telescopes and spend the next 25 years working out which large asteroids are likely to arrive within the next century or two.

The idea is that once they've identified an asteroid heading straight for us, they can move it out of the way by hitting it with powerful nuclear bombs. One expert recently proposed inventing a new nuclear bomb, 10,000 times as powerful as anything we have at the moment. He did not explain how.

August 14, 2116 – the End of the World?

Dateline 26 October 1992

WHILE SOME BELIEVE man-made pollution or a nuclear war may bring civilisation to a close, the end of the world is more likely to come in the shape of a huge chunk of ice and dust called Swift-Tuttle's comet, an Australian Conference was told yesterday.

New research indicates that its probable date of impact with Earth is August 14, 2116, said David Steel of the Anglo-Australian Observatory. It is not known if the collision will come in the morning or afternoon.

The size of Swift-Tuttle, which is travelling at 200,000 kph, is calculated at between five and 10 kilometres wide. The chance of collision is calculated at one in 400. Scientists

Adapted from *New Scientist, The Times.*

Review: Units 19–24

Find out

1 Find out what hobbies other students have got, and how long they've been doing them.

2 Find out about a time recently when your partner felt one of the following:

– angry   – embarrassed   – nervous
– frightened   – worried   – jealous

3 Work in groups. Find out how 'green' other students are. How do they try to help the environment? What do they do that's bad for the environment? Who's the 'greenest' person in the group?

4 In groups, choose a TV programme that you all watched recently. What did you think of it?

Role-play

1 Choose one of these situations, and improvise a conversation:

– A is interviewing B for a job.
– A is a police officer who has just stopped B for driving too fast.
– A is going through customs. B is a customs officer.

Now report your conversation.

2 Imagine that you're a famous person (dead or alive). What is your main regret? See if other students can guess who you are.

3 A You're in favour of nuclear power.
B You're against nuclear power.
C You're a TV interviewer. Interview A and B for a TV documentary.

Conversational English

1 Making offers

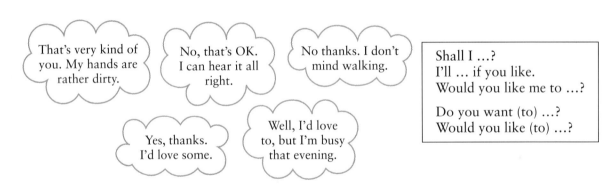

That's very kind of you. My hands are rather dirty.

No, that's OK. I can hear it all right.

No thanks. I don't mind walking.

Yes, thanks. I'd love some.

Well, I'd love to, but I'm busy that evening.

Shall I …?
I'll … if you like.
Would you like me to …?

Do you want (to) …?
Would you like (to) …?

1 Here are some replies to offers. What offer do you think the other person made? Use expressions from the box.

🔲 Now listen to the conversations.

2 Work in pairs.

Student A

B has got a lot of problems, and you want to help. Decide what you could do to help B with each problem.

Now get together with B. Keep making offers until you offer what B wants.

You've been thrown out of your flat.

You've hardly got any money.

If you find somewhere to live, you don't know how you can move all your things.

You haven't had a good meal for days.

The whole thing has made you ill and exhausted.

Student B

You've got a lot of problems, but A is going to help you. For each problem, decide exactly *how* you'd like A to help you.

Now get together with A. Keep refusing A's offers until he/she offers what you want.

Find out

1 Revision of language from Unit 19
- Lead-in. Tell the class about a hobby of your own and get the class to ask you a few questions.
- Pairwork. Students ask each other questions in turn.
- Round-up. Ask a few students what they found out.

2 Revision of language from Unit 22
- Lead-in. Ask students to tell you typical situations when they might feel angry, frightened, etc.
- Pairwork. Students work through the list of adjectives, taking it in turns to ask each other questions.
- Round-up. Ask a few students what they found out.

3 Revision of language from Unit 24
- Preparation. Build up a list of headings on the board (e.g. car, rubbish, aerosols, electricity, water).
- Students sit in large groups (5–6). They take it in turns to say what they do, and find out who is 'greenest'.
- Round-up. Find out what the 'greenest' (and the least 'green') students in each group do and don't do.

4 Revision of language from Unit 22
- Preparation. Remind students of the adjectives from 22.3, and also the structure *I found it (exciting)*.
- Groupwork. Students choose a TV programme that they've all seen and discuss what they thought of it.
- Round-up. Ask each group to comment briefly on the programme they chose.

Role-play

1 Revision of language from Unit 21
- Preparation. Establish some of the questions students could ask, e.g. Situation 2: *Why are you in such a hurry? Have you got a driving licence? Is that your own car?*
- Pairwork. Students improvise the conversation.
- Remind students of 'reported questions' structures (see Unit 21 Reference section). Then ask one student from each pair to report their conversation.

2 Revision of language from Unit 23
- Preparation. Choose a famous person, and get students to suggest some of the regrets they might have.
- Pairwork. Students think of a famous person and write a few regrets.
- In turn, pairs read out their regrets and other students guess which person they chose.

3 Revision of language from Unit 24
- Preparation. If necessary, establish basic arguments for and against nuclear power (e.g. clean, doesn't cause acid rain; expensive; accidents – danger of radiation).
- Divide the class into groups of As, Bs and Cs, and give them time to prepare their arguments or questions.
- Students form new groups, so that each group contains one A, one B and one C. They improvise the interview.
- Round-up. Groups report briefly on what happened in their interview.

Making offers

This exercise practises structures used for offering to do things yourself and to let other people do things.

1 Listening & presentation
- Present two simple situations to show how the expressions in the box are used, e.g.
  You haven't got a coat; I'm offering to lend you one:
  – Shall I lend you a coat?
  – I'll lend you my coat if you like.
  – Would you like me to lend you my coat?
  I'm going away; I'm offering to let you stay in my flat:
  – Do you want to stay in my flat?
  – Would you like to stay in my flat?
- Look at the replies, and ask students to suggest what the person is talking about and what offer the other person has just made. Try to get a range of suggestions, using expressions from the box, e.g. (first bubble) *Shall I open the door for you? Would you like me to carry the sandwiches? Do you want to use the bathroom?*
- 🔲 Play the recording. Students listen and say what the actual offers made by the speakers were.

2 Practice
- Look at the problems in the box, and explain that these are B's problems and A will offer to help him/her. Look together at the first one and discuss what A might do to help, e.g. invite B to stay with him/her, help B find another flat, lend B a tent and a sleeping bag.

- Give each student a letter, A or B, alternately round the class. Working alone, Student As note down what they will do to help with each problem, and Student Bs note down what they would like A to do.
- If necessary, demonstrate part of the pairwork stage by choosing a Student B and taking the part of Student A yourself.
- Students form pairs, one A and B. Student B states a problem, and Student A offers help. Student B keeps refusing until Student A offers what he/she wants.
- As a round-up, ask a few pairs if A offered what B wanted.

🔲 Tapescript for *Making offers*

1 A Would you like me to open the door for you?
   B That's very kind of you. My hands are rather dirty.
2 A Shall I turn the volume up a bit?
   B No, that's OK. I can hear it all right.
3 A I'll give you a lift to the station if you like.
   B No thanks. I don't mind walking.
4 A Do you want some cream on it?
   B Yes, thanks. I'd love some.
5 A Would you like to come to a concert on Friday?
   B Well I'd love to, but I'm busy that evening.

Talking points

This activity revises language from all six units:

– *It's ages since ...*	*Unit 19*
– *Getting old*	*Unit 20*
– *Young people and the law*	*Unit 20*
– *Things I can never remember*	*Unit 21*
– *Showing your feelings*	*Unit 22*
– *I'd be happier if ...*	*Unit 23*
– *Regrets*	*Unit 23*
– *Are human beings an endangered species?*	*Unit 24*

The activity can be played as a game round the class. One student chooses a topic and says a sentence or two about it. Another student then continues, adding another sentence, and so on.

As a preparation, you could let students choose two or three of the topics and look back at the appropriate unit to recall things they might say. If they like, they could also make brief notes.

Words

1 Revision of language from Unit 21

- Students complete the sentences.
- Go through the answers:
  - What flavour (kind of) ice-cream ...?
  - What size shoes ...?
  - What make of (kind of) car ...?

2 Revision of language from Unit 22

- Pairwork. Students discuss each situation.
- Go through the answers, focusing on language for describing feelings and reactions. Possible answers:
  - A's very angry; B is trying to calm him/her down.
  - A's upset; B is trying to cheer him/her up.
  - A is trying to persuade B to do something; B is refusing.

3 Revision of language from Units 20 & 24

- Establish what each of the categories is: marriage, death, dangers to the environment.
- In pairs, or working alone, students continue the lists.
- Build up lists of words on the board, e.g.
  - bride, guests, reception, get married, priest, honeymoon
  - death, grave, corpse, bury, cremate, priest, mourner
  - acid rain, (destruction of the) ozone layer, (air/sea) pollution, nuclear radiation, (destruction of) rainforests

2 In the street

This exercise practises polite ways of asking for information, using indirect question structures. These are particularly useful when asking strangers questions, e.g. stopping people in the street.

1 Listening & presentation

- To remind students of indirect questions, look again at the examples in Unit 21.2. Show how we can make questions less direct (and therefore more polite) by beginning *Can/Could you tell me ...?* or *Do you know ...?*, and even more indirect by beginning *I wonder if you could tell me ...*

DIRECT:	**Where's the bus stop?**	
INDIRECT:	**Do you know / Can/Could you tell me**	**where the bus stop is?**
VERY INDIRECT:	**I wonder if you could tell me where the bus stop is.**	

- Look at the conversation, and ask students to complete the questions. Possible answers:
  1. ... where there's a baker's near here?; ... where I can find a post box?
  2. ... what the time is?; ... what time it is?
  3. ... where I can change some money?; ... if there's a cash machine near here?

4. ... when the train to X leaves?; when the bus leaves?
5. ... where Queen Street is?; the way to Station Road?

- 🔲 Play the recording, and establish what the actual questions were.
- Ask students to change the questions in *b* into a more indirect form. Possible answers:
  - Could you tell me where the station is?
  - Do you know what time the bank opens?
  - Do you know if there's a bookshop near here?
  - I wonder if you could tell me where I can buy a newspaper.

2 Practice

- Students think of a question to ask, and write it down.
- Students move freely round the class, as if they were walking in a street. They 'stop' other students (by saying 'Excuse me') and ask them their questions.

> 🔲 The tapescript is on page T109.

Self-study Workbook

There is a review test of Units 19–24 on pages 112–3. The test is in six parts:
Sentence rewriting, Asking questions, Vocabulary, Fill the gaps, Writing paragraphs and Dictation.

Talking points

Choose one of these topics. Take it in turns to say a sentence or two about it.

It's ages since …

Getting old

Young people and the law

Things I can never remember

Showing your feelings

I'd be happier if …

Regrets

Are human beings an endangered species?

Words

1 Complete these questions:
   – What .... ice-cream do you want?
   – What .... shoes do you take?
   – What .... car do you drive?

2 Look at these remarks. What's happening?
   – 'There's no need to get so angry.'
   – 'Don't cry. It'll all turn out all right.'
   – 'No. I've already told you. I won't do it.'

3 Continue these lists:
   – wedding, bridegroom …
   – funeral, coffin …
   – global warming, desertification …

2 In the street

1 Excuse me. Do you know …?

2 Excuse me. I wonder if you could tell me …?

Yes. There's one just round the corner.

Yes. It's nearly half past three.

3 Excuse me. Do you know …?

5 Excuse me. Could you tell me …?

Well there's a bank in the next street.

Yes. Carry on up here and it's the second on the left.

Excuse me. Can you tell me …?

I think it goes in about ten minutes.

4

1 *a* Complete the questions in these conversations.

   🔲 Now listen to the recording.

 b Make these questions more polite.
   – Where's the station?
   – What time does the bank open?
   – Is there a bookshop near here?
   – Where can I buy a newspaper?

2 Think of a polite question to ask someone in the street outside your school.
  See how many people know the answer.

Additional material

1·Focus on Form·2 *Student A*

Text 1 **Ask B questions to find the missing words.**

The Tuareg live in .... People call them
................., because they .... Both men and
women ...., as a protection against sand and
duststorms. Traditionally, the Tuareg breed ....,
and take .... across the Sahara. Nowadays, many
Tuareg live in ...., where they work as
....

Text 2 **Use this text to answer B's questions.**

The Dinka live in the southern
part of the Sudan. The men of the
tribe look after cattle, and they
regard them as extremely
important. When a boy grows up,
his father gives him a special bull,
and he looks after it for the rest of
its life. He plays with it and sings
songs to it, and when it dies he
mourns for it like a friend.
Although the Dinka get milk from
their cattle, they don't normally
eat them. If they want meat, they
usually hunt hippopotamus in the
River Nile.

3·Focus on Form·2 *Student A*

**Use these facts to ask your partner questions.
The answers are the words in *italics*.**

1 *Margaret Thatcher* became Prime Minister
of Great Britain in 1979.
2 The Second World War began *in 1939*.
3 Archimedes was *having a bath* when he
shouted 'Eureka'.
4 *Paul McCartney* wrote the song 'Yesterday'.
5 In the film 'From Russia with Love', *Sean
Connery* played James Bond.

5·1 Overseas experience

Interplex

Qualifications
Applicants must be between 18 and 26 years old. They should
have a basic knowlege of English, and be physically fit. A driving
licence and experience in hotel work is an advantage but is not
essential.

Travel
Interplex International will pay 50% of the cost of return air or
train fare. This will be paid to employees on completion of their
contract.

Contracts and pay
Contracts will be for a minimum of 6 weeks. Employees will be
paid at standard local rates, and local tax and insurance will be
deducted.

Work permits will be arranged by Interplex International. Please
enclose *two* passport photos with your application form.

Conditions of work
Employees will do a variety of jobs, including cleaning,
bedmaking, acting as porters and waiters, helping in the kitchens,
and driving between the hotel and airports/stations.

The working day is from 6.00 am till 9.00 pm. This will include
two hours for meals, plus a two-hour free period which may be
from 10.00–12.00 or 2.30–4.30.

Employees will have one free day per week. This can be any day
except Saturday and Sunday.

Employees are expected to look smart at all times, and will be
provided with a uniform, which they must wear during working
hours. The hotel will be responsible for cleaning the uniforms.

Accommodation and food
Accommodation will be provided in the hotel or an annexe, in
rooms shared between four employees.

Meals will be provided free of charge by the hotel.

Hotel facilities
Outside working hours, employees may use the hotel's facilities,
including the swimming pool, sauna and tennis courts. They will
be charged for these at 40% of normal·rates.

6 You've had an astonishing two years. Not only did you get married, but your father-in-law died, leaving you a large house and an even larger sum of money. You invested it, and you now have £200,000 more than two years ago.

Your parents wrote to you recently, saying there's still a job open to you in the Civil Service if you want it. Or you could stay where you are, and carry on having beach barbecues.

Stay in Brazil	➤ **22**	(p.116)
Join the Civil Service	➤ **16**	(p.115)

7 You arrive in Los Angeles and manage to find a place to live, but there aren't many jobs around. After doing casual work for a time, you manage to get a job as a taxi driver – not a quick way to make a million dollars, but the money's not bad. At the end of two years, you've increased your total wealth by £10,000 – LA's an expensive place to live.

You could either stay in LA and drive your taxi, or go back home – there's still a job open for you in the Civil Service.

Stay in Los Angeles	➤ **25**	(p.116)
Join the Civil Service	➤ **16**	(p.115)

8 The country has been suffering from serious economic problems for more than a year now, and recently a lot of companies have gone bankrupt – including yours. You're unemployed, and there aren't any jobs in advertising – not even for someone as good as you. Still, you did well enough last year, and you now have £20,000 more than you had two years ago.

A friend told you about an interesting job you can get – working as a crew member on a yacht in the Caribbean, taking wealthy Americans to Caribbean islands. Otherwise, there's always the Civil Service ...

Go to the Caribbean	➤ **4**	(p.23)
Join the Civil Service	➤ **16**	(p.115)

9 For the last two years, you've been running your own business as a financial consultant. Unfortunately, running a business is more expensive than you imagined, and not enough people want your financial advice. At the end of two years, you have £5,000 less than you had when you resigned.

One day, your former boss rings you and asks you if you'd like your old job back. You accept the offer.

Rejoin the Civil Service	➤ **5**	(p.23)

10 You had a good time at design college – it was very interesting and you made a lot of friends. Unfortunately, you also spent quite a lot of money: you now only have half of what you had two years ago.

You could now get a well-paid job in an established advertising agency. Alternatively, you could go to Brazil for a couple of years – a friend of yours is working there and says she could probably find you a job. You've heard the beaches are unbelievable ...

Go into advertising	➤ **19**	(p.115)
Go to Brazil	➤ **14**	(p.114)

11 You've joined the Civil Service, and you're finding the work quite interesting, although you aren't being promoted as fast as you hoped. Still, you're earning enough to buy your own flat and a car. In the last two years, you've become £20,000 better off.

You met a friend the other day who works in an advertising agency, and makes nearly twice as much money as you. It might be a good time to change jobs ...

Stay in the Civil Service	➤ **16**	(p.115)
Go into advertising	➤ **19**	(p.115)

7·2 **Changes** *Student A*

1·Focus on Form·2 *Student B*

Text 1 **Use this text to answer A's questions.**

The Tuareg live in the Sahara region of North Africa. People call them the 'Blue People', because they wear blue robes. Both men and women cover their faces with veils, as a protection against sand and duststorms. Traditionally, the Tuareg breed camels and take camel caravans across the Sahara. Nowadays, many Tuareg live in towns and cities, where they work as servants and nightwatchmen.

Text 2 **Ask A questions to find the missing words.**

The Dinka live in .... The men of the tribe look after ...., and they regard them as extremely important. When a boy grows up, his father gives him ...., and he looks after it for the rest of its life. He .... it and .... it, and when it dies he .... like a friend. Although the Dinka get .... from their cattle, they don't normally eat them. If they want meat, they usually hunt .... in the River Nile.

3·Focus on Form·2 *Student B*

Use these facts to ask your partner questions. The answers are the words in *italics*.

1 *Bill Clinton* beat George Bush in the 1992 American Presidential Election.
2 Isaac Newton was *sitting under an apple tree* when he discovered gravity.
3 *Napoleon* invaded Russia in 1812.
4 In Shakespeare's play, Othello killed *his wife Desdemona*.
5 Björn Borg won the men's tennis championship at Wimbledon *five times*.

4·4 Can you make a million? *Cards 12–15*

12 You're doing quite well at university, although economics isn't very interesting. If you carry on, you'll probably get a good degree. Or you could drop out and go on a two-year course at design college.

You're not spending much money – at the end of the two years you have £1,000 less than you had before.

Continue at university	➤ **2**	(p.23)
Go to design college	➤ **10**	(p.113)

13 So much for your career in the Civil Service! The government made huge cuts this year, and you were made redundant. Fortunately, you got a large redundancy payment – you now have £100,000 more than two years ago.

Now you have to look for a job – times are hard and you're not as young as you were. You could get a job with a firm of accountants. Or you could join a friend who's starting up a business designing children's toys. It's not a very good time for small businesses, but you never know ...

Join a firm of accountants	➤ **24**	(p.116)
Go into the toy business	➤ **3**	(p.23)

14 You've had a wonderful time in Brazil – beach barbecues, lots of parties, swimming ... Your friend helped you find a part-time job with a computer company – not very well paid, but it leaves you time to travel around and see Brazil. You've spent quite a lot of money on food and air fares, but you've still managed to save a bit. You have £5,000 more than two years ago.

Recently, you met someone you like a lot – you could settle down here. Alternatively, some friends of yours are travelling overland to the USA and have invited you to go with them.

Stay in Brazil	➤ **6**	(p.113)
Go to the USA	➤ **20**	(p.115)

15 The last two years have been bad for small businesses, including yours – you made a loss again in both years, and now have £25,000 less money than two years ago.

Designing toys is still hard work, and you and your friend are not working together quite as well as you were before. This might be the moment to give up and get that job with a firm of accountants. On the other hand, you've invested four years of your life in this business now ...

Stay in the toy business	➤ **21**	(p.115)
Join a firm of accountants	➤ **24**	(p.116)

4·4 Can you make a million? *Cards 16–21*

16 You're working in the Civil Service, and you're now £25,000 better off than you were two years ago. You're still in a fairly junior post, and your salary hasn't risen as much as you hoped. Never mind – it's a good steady job and you bought a new car this year.

On the other hand, several of your friends are self-employed, and this might be a good time to start your own business – as a financial adviser, for example …

Stay in the Civil Service	➤	**5**	(p.23)
Start your own business	➤	**9**	(p.113)

17 You've been round the world. You've seen temples in Bali, lions in Africa, penguins in the Antarctic, the Himalayas, the Grand Canyon … and you've spent and spent and spent.

After two years of luxurious travel, you now have only 25% of your money left, and it's time to go back home. The trouble is, you aren't so young any more, and there are two possibilities open to you. You could get a job with a firm of accountants. Or you could join a friend who's starting her own business designing children's toys …

Join a firm of accountants	➤	**24**	(p.116)
Go into the toy business	➤	**3**	(p.23)

18 In the last two years, you've increased your savings by £5,000. You've got a good steady job, but it isn't exactly exciting. If you carry on working here, you'll probably be a manager by the time you're 45 – but you certainly won't be a millionaire!

You'd do better to go back to university or design college and get some qualifications.

Go to university	➤	**12**	(p.114)
Go to design college	➤	**10**	(p.113)

19 This is the job for you. You've got a natural talent for it, and you really like the people you work for. Your company's designing a new series of soft drinks advertisements, so there's plenty of money coming in – at the end of the two years you have £45,000 more than you had before.

You're doing well, and there's no reason to change jobs at the moment – although your friend in Brazil wrote recently, inviting you to go there, and this could be your last chance …

Stay in advertising	➤	**8**	(p.113)
Go to Brazil	➤	**14**	(p.114)

20 Everything was fine until you got to a remote part of Central America, where you were kidnapped by bandits and held prisoner for two years. Eventually, you managed to buy your freedom, but it was expensive, and you're now down to your last £2,000.

One of your group has friends in Los Angeles – if you can get there you should be able to find a job. You've also heard that you can get jobs on yachts in the Caribbean, working as crew members for rich Americans – might be worth a try.

Go to the Caribbean	➤	**4**	(p.23)
Go to Los Angeles	➤	**7**	(p.113)

21 You're a genius! You designed a family of toy dinosaurs from outer space (called *Galactosaurs*) that became an instant success. They've sold all over the world, they appear on T-shirts, cups, bags, socks … There are even plans to make a series of cartoon films about them.

In the last two years, you have made a staggering £600,000.

You don't need to go anywhere from here: by now, you're either 36 years old or a millionaire – or both!

7·2 Changes *Student B*

7·1 Ancient civilisations

4·4 Can you make a million? *Cards 22–25*

22 Bad news! The Brazilian economy has collapsed and inflation is running at 30% a month. You can't find a job anywhere. Worse still, your partner has left you for someone else, and taken half the money. You now only have a third of what you had two years ago.

You've heard from a friend who's working on a yacht in the Caribbean as a member of the crew. He says he could get you a job too, and that the pay is quite good.

Or maybe it's time to go back home to the Civil Service …

Go to the Caribbean	➤ **4**	(p.23)
Join the Civil Service	➤ **16**	(p.115)

23 You should have left the ship when you had the chance. On your last trip to Miami you were all arrested for smuggling gold and jewels (lucky for you it wasn't drugs or arms!). You were sentenced to six years in prison, and fined £10,000. Fortunately you've invested your money, which makes up for the fine.

Add *four* years to your life (you only served four years because of good behaviour): you have the same amount of money as before.

Someone you met in prison says he can help you get a job in Los Angeles. Or you could go back home and try the Civil Service (you'd better not tell them you've been in prison!).

Go to Los Angeles	➤ **7**	(p.113)
Join the Civil Service	➤ **16**	(p.115)

24 You're working for *Jarvis, Jarvis & Jarvis, Accountants, Ltd*. It's not the most interesting job in the world, but it's a safe, established firm, and the pay's reasonable.

Your friend in the toy business has found another partner, and there aren't any other good jobs around. It looks as if you'll be working here for at least another four years.

For each two-year period you work here, add 10% to your savings.

25 A year ago, you were driving your cab when you saw a couple fighting in the street. The woman shouted 'He's going to kill me!' and jumped into your cab. She turned out to be a Hollywood movie star – she gave you a large tip and asked for your address. Last month she died, leaving you £500,000 in her will, 'To the taxi driver who saved my life'. Add that to your savings, plus £10,000 from driving your taxi.

A friend back home is starting up a business designing children's toys and has invited you to join her – it might be a good way to invest all that money. Or you could celebrate by going on a trip round the world …

Go into the toy business	➤ **3**	(p.23)
Go round the world	➤ **17**	(p.115)

A NEW ICE AGE?

MOST OF THE TALK these days is about global warming. But in fact the opposite could happen: it would only take the tiniest change in the Earth's orbit round the Sun to bring another Ice Age. A change of as little as 5°C would have a dramatic effect on life on Earth.

CLIMATE SHIFT

The main effect would be to shift climate about 1,500 kilometres towards the Equator, so that Spain, say, would have a climate much the same as England's is now, and Buenos Aires could look forward to the kind of weather now found around Cape Horn.

FOOD

The same would be true of crops: wheat would grow in Spain, but no longer in Britain; it would be impossible to grow rice in most of China; and grapes would be much happier growing in Africa than in France.

CATASTROPHE

In the colder regions of the world, the results would be devastating. Large parts of Northern Europe, Canada, Chile and Argentina would be covered in snow and quickly become uninhabitable. Huge numbers of people would be forced to migrate to warmer climates, bringing with them economic catastrophe, and probably war.

A sign of things to come?

TURNING THE DESERT GREEN

On the brighter side, a number of inhospitable places would become more pleasant to live in. Cave paintings in the Sahara Desert show that it was once full of people and animals. A drop in temperature – together with increased rainfall – might begin to turn the desert green again.

A cave painting in the Sahara, 1300 BC

12.2 Emergency

Snake bite

Movement helps the poison to spread, so try not to walk about: if possible, send someone else to get a doctor. Meanwhile, tie something (e.g. a handkerchief) fairly tightly above the bite, to stop the poison spreading. If you have a sharp knife, make a cut and suck out as much of the poison as you can.

Cut wrist

If possible get someone to call a doctor right away. Meanwhile, try to stop the bleeding: close the wound and apply pressure with your other hand (or get someone else to), until bleeding begins to stop. This may be some minutes. Any bandages should be applied tightly: if blood soaks through the bandage, don't remove it – just add another bandage on top.

Hotel fire

Wet towels or sheets and use them to block the gap under the door. Then open the window, try to attract the attention of people outside, and wait for help to arrive. If you can't open the window, and the room becomes smoky, go down to floor level: it's easier to breathe near the floor, because smoke rises upwards.

Boiling water

Reduce the heat as quickly as possible by putting the arm in cold water or under a cold tap for at least 10 minutes. Remove anything tight such as jewellery, and cover the burn with a clean smooth cloth to avoid infection. Then take the person to hospital.

Heart attack

If the patient is conscious, place her in a half-sitting position, with her head and shoulders supported with pillows or cushions, and with another cushion placed under her knees. Then call a doctor or an ambulance. Loosen clothing around the neck, chest and waist. Do *not* give the patient anything to eat or drink, and do *not* allow her to move unnecessarily.

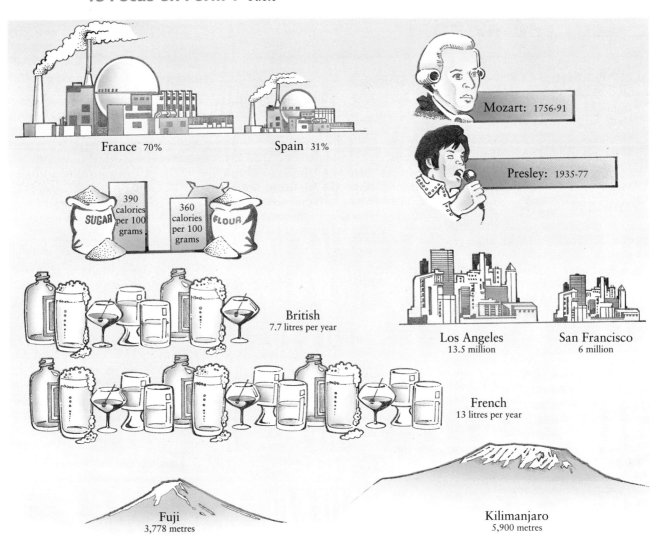

France 70% Spain 31%

Mozart: 1756-91

Presley: 1935-77

390 calories per 100 grams SUGAR

360 calories per 100 grams FLOUR

British
7.7 litres per year

Los Angeles
13.5 million

San Francisco
6 million

French
13 litres per year

Fuji
3,778 metres

Kilimanjaro
5,900 metres

24·3 Endangered species: *pandas*

- Pandas are one of the rarest animals in the world. They live only in a small area in the mountains of South-western China.
- There are only 500–1,000 pandas surviving in the wild, and the number is decreasing all the time. There are about 100 more in zoos and research stations.
- Although they are protected, pandas are still poached for their skins. Because they are so rare, their skins are very valuable.
- Pandas live in mountain forests, and can only eat bamboo. As their habitat is getting smaller and smaller, pandas are in danger of dying from lack of suitable food.
- Zoos are making efforts to breed pandas in captivity, but this is very difficult. Also, baby pandas weigh only 100 grams at birth, so they need to be looked after very carefully. Since 1963 about 50 baby pandas have been born in captivity, and around half of them are still alive today.

15·Focus on Form·2 *Student A*

This is last week's news. Find out from B what has happened since then.

There were worries last night about the safety of the Claxton nuclear power station, after reports of leaks

The search is continuing in the French Alps for a party of schoolchildren who failed to return from a

There are rumours that the Louvre is planning to sell the priceless Mona Lisa, the most

A group of 200 refugees crossed the border last night without passports or visas and

Police were questioning billionaire Oliver James last night about the disappearance of millions of dollars

The Government has denied that Miss Botham is a spy, and has demanded that she should be released immediately and

Only 3,000 tickets have so far been sold for the 'Rock Show of the Century' due to take place

17·Focus on Form·3 *Student A*

My name's George.

I come from Texas.

I own an oil company.

I own three houses in the USA and one in the South of France.

I'm staying with the Foreign Minister.

I'm going to have dinner with the Prime Minister tomorrow.

I really like it here because there's so much to buy in the shops.

I've never been here before, but I'll certainly come again.

24·3 Endangered species: *tigers*

- There are six species of tiger still in existence. They are found in Siberia, India and South-east Asia.
- 50 years ago, tigers were common throughout much of Asia, living in many different habitats from tropical forest to semi-desert.
- Because people thought they were dangerous, they were hunted and trapped, and tiger skins were considered very valuable.
- By 1970, there were fewer than 5,000 tigers left, and many of their habitats had been destroyed.
- In 1972, Operation Tiger was launched: tigers were protected by law and reserves were created to protect the species.
- Gradually, numbers began to increase, and there are now some 8,000 tigers living in the wild.

17·Focus on Form·3 *Student B*

My name's Ramona.

I collect antiques.

I'm planning to open an antique shop here.

I often go to New York on business, and I always fly first class.

I know lots of famous people in America.

I've known the Rockefeller family for years.

It's lovely talking to you.

I'll give you a ring next week and we can have lunch together.

15·Focus on Form·2 *Student B*

This is today's news. Answer A's questions using the Present perfect tense, active or passive.

The power station will stay closed until engineers have

The schoolchildren were taken to Moutiers by helicopter after being found by rescue workers

The new owner of the Mona Lisa, billionaire Clara Fairbanks, who paid a record $900 million for

There were angry protests yesterday against the Government's decision to send back 200 refugees who had

Billionaire Oliver James was arrested last night on charges of fraud and theft. He will appear in court

Sarah Botham flew back home yesterday to be reunited with her family after her release from

Angry fans protested yesterday after the organisers cancelled the 'Rock Show of the Century', which

24·3 Endangered species: *rhinos*

- Most rhinos live in Africa. There are two African species: the black rhino, which lives in East Africa and the white rhino, which is found in Southern Africa. There are also a few rhinos in Asia, mainly in India.
- Over the last 20 years, numbers of rhinos have dropped rapidly: there are now fewer than 10,000 in the whole world, and the number is still falling.
- The main threat to rhinos is from poachers, who hunt them for their 'horns', which are in fact made of stiff hair. The horns are sold in the Middle East, where they are used to make dagger handles, and also in the Far East, where they are used in medicines and aphrodisiacs.
- Trading in rhino horn is illegal, but it is still continuing. Unless more is done to protect them, they will almost certainly become extinct.

23 Morrison Drive
Redbridge
Monday 16th

Dear Lucy and Fred,

Just to let you know that the baby's arrived! It's a girl, and we've called her Frances, after Theresa's mother. She's a lovely baby, with blue eyes and black hair.

We went into hospital at 9 o'clock last night, when the labour started, and the baby was born just after 2 o'clock this morning — not bad! Theresa was wonderful. I was there the whole time, and the birth wasn't too difficult this time, thank goodness, although she's a big baby — nearly 4 kilos!

Theresa is fine, and sends her love. They're coming out of hospital on Friday, so do come and see us next week some time.

Henry's seen his little sister, and seems quite excited by the whole thing. I expect he'll change his mind before long!

See you soon.

Love,
David

24·3 Endangered species: *elephants*

- Elephants are found in Africa and in Asia (mainly India). African elephants are slightly larger and have much bigger ears.
- Elephants in Africa are in serious danger: nearly a million have been killed in the last 10 years, and only about 600,000 are left.
- In Asia, there are only about 50,000 elephants left in the wild. However, Asian elephants are used for transporting timber, so many are now born in captivity.
- Elephants are killed by poachers for their tusks, which they sell as ivory. Elephant ivory is made into ornaments, piano keys, chopsticks and other objects.
- In 1989, governments of 79 countries agreed to ban all trade in ivory, and this ban came into effect in 1990. Unfortunately, as long as people buy ivory, poaching will continue and elephants will be in danger.

Tapescripts

1·4 At the moment …

1 I'm a journalist. I work for the *Daily Mirror*. I report on foreign news, so I spend quite a lot of time abroad. At the moment I'm covering the American elections.

2 I work as a secretary for a firm of accountants, so I answer the phone, type letters, things like that. At the moment I'm typing out our annual report, which I have to finish by Friday.

3 I'm a research student. I spend a lot of time in libraries and on the phone to people, trying to get information. I study the history of medicine, and at the moment I'm doing some research on the First World War, finding out what kind of medicines they used in the army.

4 I work on a farm, a potato farm. I drive a tractor and I help with all the jobs around the farm. There's not much going on at the moment, being winter. We're cutting down some of the trees and mending fences, mostly.

5 I work for the United Nations as an engineer. I'm involved in development projects in Africa. Just at the moment there's a big project we're doing – we're building a dam in Ethiopia.

2·1 Easy to live with?

1 Well, she helps a lot with cleaning the flat, but she's not very tidy. She always leaves books and magazines lying around, and she never puts things away when she's finished using them.

2 He's only been in a couple of weeks, but he's a good cook, and he's very tidy. He never makes a mess when he's cooking, and he always washes up afterwards.

3 Oh no, I like Jane – she's really great. Oh, apart from one thing – she spends hours in the bathroom. I can never get in to have a shower. And another thing – she uses up all the hot water.

4 Well, his room's always in rather a mess – he never tidies up, never puts his clothes away. Oh he's OK otherwise – he's quite quiet, doesn't make too much noise.

5 The worst thing about her is she leaves all the lights on. She never switches the light off when she goes out of the room, so I have to go round switching them off after her. And she leaves all the doors open.

2·3 A place to relax

A OK, I'd like you to imagine an ideal room, a place to relax.

B I see windows, big windows that look out on the sea. A small room with wooden walls, wooden furniture, wooden floors, a thick rug, a thick woollen rug on the floor, and a dog – I love dogs. On the floor also a table, a small table with papers, magazines, books on it. Music coming from a CD player.

A What about you? What are you doing?

B Reading. Listening to the music and reading at the same time. I'm reading a novel. And the room is warm – I'm alone.

2·4 Snow house

Now we'll cut a small hole for a chimney, and meanwhile John is packing snow over the outside just to make it all nice and strong and close up any gaps so the wind doesn't get through.

Now we're building the blocks round and round in a spiral. They're very firm, very firm, and there's no chance of them falling in.

Now we're cutting blocks from the floor of the igloo, so it will be below ground level, and we're building the walls from the inside.

So that's it, and it's very strong, you see – well, take a chance here, here we go. Yes, I can climb on the top of it, no problem, no problem. And it's very strong. So, it took just over an hour to build, and that's not bad for a place to live.

So now we've just got one block to put on the top. So I'm going to push it up through here and then let it fall into position – there, ah there, good. And now we're going to make the entrance tunnel.

Now I've marked out a circle for the igloo, and I'm cutting blocks from the entrance tunnel first. So this, this will go down below ground level.

Well, we've found some nice firm deep snow here, and it looks like a really good place to build an igloo. So we'll get started. So first of all we're going to mark out a shape for the tunnel and for the igloo itself.

3·3 The first time …

1 How did I learn to swim? It was when I was 11. It was just after we'd moved from Berlin to the south of Germany to a small village and I was the last one in the class of 28 who could not swim, but as I was very good in sports otherwise I decided that I will be able to swim in no time. So I didn't want

to be taught, I just stepped on the diving board and jumped in and somehow struggled with the water and managed to move back to the side of the river bank and got out, and that was it.

2 I learnt to swim when I was about five or six during the summer holidays, and I remember my father putting me in the swimming pool in the shallow end and at the other end of the pool he put I think it was a chocolate bar on a plate, and he said 'If you can swim to the other end all on your own you can have the chocolate bar', and I did.

3 It was while I was at infants school, which would make me five or six, I suppose. My brother and I used to be taken for lessons on a Tuesday evening. My brother learnt to swim a lot sooner than I did, and so I used to watch him jumping into the deep end, while I was sort of guided up and down the shallow end on the end of a pole. I used to look forward to the hot chocolate that we used to buy in the foyer afterwards.

4·2 Exchanges

1 A Do you think you could lend me £20?
  B Um, well I'm not sure.
  A I can pay you back on Friday.
  B Well OK, here you are. (Thanks)

2 A I'd like to pay my bill, please.
  B Right, yes, it's all made out. There you are.
  A Thanks. Do you take credit cards?
  B No, I'm afraid we don't. You can pay by cheque or by cash if you've got it.

3 A I bought a shirt here the other day and it's got a little tear here (Oh yes, yes) on the back of the collar, so I'd like a refund please.
  B Right. Did you bring your receipt with you?
  A No, I haven't got one.
  B Well I'm afraid without the receipt we can't really give you a refund.

4 A Excuse me, I'm sorry to bother you. Can you give me change for a £10 note? I need to make a phone call and I haven't got any change.
  B Sorry, I can only give you change if you buy something.
  A Oh really? OK well, can I just buy some chewing gum, please?

5 A I'd like to cash some traveller's cheques, please.
  B Certainly. Can I see your passport? (Yes) Right. Thank you. OK, you'll need to sign them just here please.

4·4 Can you make a million?

A So Gareth, you're going to tell us how to make a million.

B Well, to go back to the beginning, um I went to study graphic design after leaving school. And I was there for two years, and when I left college I decided to go off and see a bit of the world.

A Where did you go?

B Well a friend of mine got a job in Brazil, so I decided to go and have a look at Brazil. And I had a wonderful time. The social life was terrific, and I made a lot of wonderful friends. Some of these friends then decided to drive up to the USA. It seemed like a very good opportunity to see some more of the world, so I joined them. But we had a bit of a mishap in Central America. We were kidnapped by bandits, believe it or not, (Good Lord) and it was two years before I got away from them.

A What an extraordinary experience ...

B ... And eventually that was the way that we escaped from them, by paying our way out.

A So what happened then?

B Well, having got away from there I went to the States, as I planned to do two years before, to Los Angeles, without any money of course, and for four years I drove a cab in LA.

A Did you meet any of the stars? ...

B ... But when she died only a year later, she left me half a million pounds in her will.

A That is extraordinary. What a stroke of luck. So what did you do?

B Well, fortunately a friend wrote to me to say that she was starting up her own toy-making business. So I came home and I worked helping her design, and of course business was very slow to start with. But then I had a great stroke of luck. I found a design that was very popular – I designed the Galactosaurs (Of course) which are a family of toy dinosaurs, and they proved to be a great hit all over the world. And that was the beginning of my great good fortune, and I've just become a millionaire.

A And congratulations.

5·3 Punishments

1 The worst punishment I can remember was when I was at primary school, and I'd stayed in the school building at lunch time, because I felt it was too cold to go out. And for that they made me go down to the class below, and do all their lessons for a whole week. And I wasn't even allowed to see my own friends during the break times.

2 I remember I was about seven and I got punished because I held my prayer book too low in morning prayers. They made me stand up in front of the class and recite a prayer in front of everybody, and I was terribly embarrassed.

3 When I was about eight years old and I was at school, I remember we were having a Latin lesson, and the teacher asked me something, and I was extremely rude back to him. And to punish me, he made me write out 'I must not be cheeky' something like 500 times in Latin one Saturday afternoon.

6·3 Festival

The Dragon Boat Festival commemorates the death of a national hero, Chow Yen, who threw himself into the river and drowned himself in protest against a corrupt Government, and that happened about oh over 2,000 years ago in China. But the people saw the incident and they felt very sorry for him, and they collected a fleet of boats and beat the drums, made a lot of noise and raced the boat in the river trying to scare away the creatures in the river which were about to eat Chow Yen's body. And other people made up dumplings of rice, meat, beans, and they threw these dumplings into the river to feed the fish and other creatures in the river. That's how it started originally.

And nowadays people still make dumplings but they do not throw the dumplings into the river any more. They eat the dumplings, which is really very delicious. And they still hold boat races, anywhere in China, in Hong Kong and any parts of the world where there is a sizeable Chinese community, they still hold dragon boat races. The dragon boats are quite narrow and long and they have the head of a dragon in the front and the tail of a dragon at the back and they have about 22 people on each boat. They have a drum, a big drum at the end of the boat as well, so while the people are racing one person will be beating the drum and the people have to row together to the rhythm of the drum.

6·4 Culture shock

I was travelling in the Sudan by train and the journey I had to make was going to last about 48 hours and about an hour into the journey someone in my compartment, I think there were another seven people in the compartment, someone spread a large cloth on the floor and people began to bring out food. No-one had a knife, so people were breaking up the food and placing it on the cloth ...

... I realised this was the thing to do so all I had was three or four tomatoes. So I broke up my tomatoes and put them on the cloth and then we all started to eat the food. And there was bread and beans and lamb and many different things and people were eating and I noticed that no-one was eating my tomatoes. So I encouraged them to eat and everyone smiled very politely but wouldn't actually take any. And slowly the food disappeared and disappeared and my tomatoes were left. So at the end of the meal there was nothing left except my tomatoes. And I felt slightly uneasy about this, I didn't know why ...

... I thought probably it was because I was a foreigner and perhaps the Sudanese people didn't want to take a foreigner's food from them. So in fact I ate the tomatoes myself. It was only some time later that I realised that in fact the reason that people hadn't eaten my tomatoes was because I had broken up the tomatoes with both hands.

On the phone

1 A Hello. 305 8442.
   B Hello. Is that Carol?
   A Speaking.
   B Hi. This is Bill.

2 A Hello. Fletcher's Bookshop.
   B Hello. Could I speak to Mr Taylor, please?
   A Certainly. Can I have your name, please?
   B My name's Linda Holden.
   A Hold on. I'll put you through.

3 A Hello. Fletcher's Bookshop.
   B Hello. Could I speak to Mr Taylor, please?
   A I'm afraid he's not in at the moment.
   B Oh, OK. Can I leave a message?

7·4 For and against

1 Well I have to get up very early in the mornings, so I have to go to bed very early the night before. So it's great for me because I can, when there's good programmes on, I can record them late at night and watch them later on.

2 The problem is they just taste so awful. In the old days food used to really taste of something, but this stuff just tastes of nothing.

3 In the old days, say 50 years ago, nobody knew what was going on in the world. But nowadays you can actually see what's happening anywhere in the world, almost as it's happening.

4 I type with two fingers, and when I used to type letters I'd always make a mistake and then have to type the whole letter all over again – drove me crazy. But now I can just correct it on the screen as I go along, and when I'm happy with it I'm finished. It's perfect, brilliant.

5 At school I learnt how to add up in my head, and children just can't do that any more. My son can't add up at all.

8·2 What's the system?

1 To use a public telephone, first you lift the receiver and then you put in the coins. You can use as many coins as you like, because at the end of the call the coins which haven't been used are returned. And then after putting in the coins, you dial the number. Alternatively you can use a phone card, with which you can talk until the number of units on the telephone card has been used up.

2 To use libraries in England, you join the library. They'll give you a ticket, that means that you can keep books that you take out for up to two weeks. If you bring the books back late you have to pay a fine. There's also a reference section which you can use, but you can't take those books out, you can just use the books in the library.

3 To send a parcel abroad, you take the parcel to the post office, and have it weighed. And they give you stamps, which you stick on the parcel, and they also give you a customs form which you have to fill in, and then you stick that on the parcel as well. Now if you want to send something valuable, then it's normal to send that by registered post, which is rather more expensive than normal post.

8·4 Jobs we love to hate

1 I hate it when you ring up a big company, for example, and you're trying to get through to someone, and all you get is the ▓▓▓▓▓▓ who tells you to hold the line. And then they just leave you there – they don't tell you what they're doing, sometimes they play a horrible little tune that repeats itself over and over again, and you just – you don't know what's happening at all. And it's particularly annoying if it's a long-distance call, because it's costing a lot of money.

2 I don't like ▓▓▓▓▓▓ because I think that a lot of the time they take advantage of your vote. And they tell you that they're going to do one thing, but they're not, they don't have any intention of doing it. They're liars, basically. And I think that you put your trust in them by giving them your vote, and nine out of ten times they let you down.

3 I hate ▓▓▓▓▓▓, you know the people who ring you up and try and sell you something over the phone. And they always start off with a really stupid question like 'Would you like to make more money?' or 'Do you care about the environment?' And they always seem to ring up at the worst possible moment, like when you've just sat down to have tea or something. And they sound so cheerful, they really annoy me.

4 Oh, ▓▓▓▓▓▓ that try and sell you things that you don't want. You go into a shop, you want to buy a dress, you try it on, it doesn't look good, you come back out of the changing room and say 'No, thank you'. The ▓▓▓▓▓▓ says 'Oh well why don't you try another size?' You say 'No, I'm fine about it, I don't want it.' 'Oh well why don't you try another colour?' 'No, I don't want another colour.' They won't let you get out of the shop – it drives me mad.

9·1 What would you do?

A Your teenage daughter has started using the telephone to chat to her friends in the evening and quite often she talks for more than an hour, and it means that you can't use the phone yourself. Now you've told her to stop phoning her friends but now her friends phone her instead. Now what would you do about that? Rebecca?

B Oh it's a difficult one. I think I'd try to reason with her and say – I mean I wouldn't say 'You must not ring your friends and your friends must not ring you' because I think that's unfair. What I would say is 'If your friends ring you, can you just keep the conversation a bit short so that other people can use the phone?', which seems quite reasonable to me.

A Nick, what do you think?

C I think what I'd do is stop my daughter from answering the phone and monitor the calls as they came in. And she would only be allowed to take one call in the evening from a friend, and any other calls that came in from her friends, we'd say 'No I'm sorry, she's already talked to Angela or Julia or whatever and so she can't talk to anyone else' and take control of it that way.

A Aisha, do you agree with that?

D Not really. I think you should always try and remember what it felt like at that age and actually how important it felt to try and talk to your friends. What I'd do I think is really encourage her to visit her friends and to have her friends round more so they could actually talk in person rather than on the telephone.

9·4 Wishes

– I wish I could take more time off work. I work at home, and I find it very difficult to stop at the end of the day.

– I wish I had time to do more exercise. I used to do a lot of aerobics, but now that I'm studying I find that I have very little time to attend the classes.

– I wish I could play the guitar. I used to try to teach myself, but I wasn't very good, so I gave up.

– I really wish it was warmer in the North of England, that's where I study, and I pay a lot of money for the rent and electricity to heat up the house. It would make me a lot happier to study in a warmer country.

– I wish I didn't have such an old car. I'd like to have one with central door locking and power steering and an open sun roof.

– I wish I lived in a smaller house. The house that I live in at the moment is very big. There are six of us living there, and it gets very noisy sometimes. In a smaller house I'd feel more comfortable and I'd have the quiet that I need to study.

– I wish my children would leave home. They're over 20, but they're still living with us, and they use the telephone all the time, and they invite all their friends around, and they're very nice kids but I just wish they'd go.

10·1 I don't know what it's called but …

1 I need a pair of those things you use for pulling nails out. They look like scissors but they're not sharp.

2 Have you got one of those spoons that I can use because I'm frying eggs in the frying pan and I need something to turn them over. You know those big spoons made of metal I can use.

3 Please, I'm writing my composition and I've made a mistake. Do you have this white stuff that you use for correcting mistakes? You know, it's got a little brush and you paint it over the wrong word.

4 Have you got one of those things to eat Chinese food? You know those long sticks, and they're usually made of wood or plastic.

5 I'd just like to find out how much fatter I've become. Have you got this thing I can stand on and find out how much I weigh?

10·4 Great ideas?

1 It looks rather dangerous because if you were at the top of a hill, could you hold yourself so that you just didn't go down the hill really, really fast? I don't know. And then it says here that it floats on the water. Well that's fine, but if you were in a fast moving river and you were trying to get across, surely the water would take you with it and you'd just go on and on and never be seen again.

2 This is called a natural flying machine, but it doesn't seem very natural to me. How do you get the man inside, in the middle bit of this machine? And where do you find ten eagles? How do you actually put them inside their jackets? And just because we know that eagles can carry heavy weights, I mean we don't know how long they can carry heavy weights for. So they

may be able to lift a man for ten seconds or something, but they may not be able to keep going. But it's a nice idea.

3 My main fear is that it looks really claustrophobic once you're in there, especially with the lid down. It says you can have enough supply of food, a month's supply of food and drinking water in there – I'm a bit worried about the smell, for instance, of the food going off. Also, there's no mention of how you go to the toilet in it. Also, I should imagine you'd get quite seasick in it, especially with the lid on.

11·3 In five years' time

A So when are you planning to leave for Australia?

B I'll be going in a few months' time. I'm supposed to be staying there at least five years, but I don't know, I'll have to wait and see if I like it.

A And do you have a job to go to?

B Oh yes, I'm a nurse. I'm going mainly for the job that I've found there. I've found quite a good job in a university hospital, and I get a free apartment and I'll be earning twice as much as I do now, so it's not bad.

A That's good. And are you going by yourself?

B No, no I'm going with my boyfriend, who will by then be my husband. We're getting married before we go.

A And is he going to be working out there?

B Well hopefully he'll find a teaching job out there.

A And will you stay in one place in Australia?

B Oh I hope not. We really want to travel as much as possible. There's so much to see, I mean the whole of the Far East and the Pacific Islands, yeah.

A So you won't be starting a family straight away?

B Er, not just yet.

12·1 Narrow escapes

1 Well I had these friends round to dinner and, I don't know, for some reason I had this candle and I put it on the plastic lid of the record player, and forgot all about it. We went into another room to have some coffee, and I went into the kitchen to get some more coffee for a top-up, and as I went out I noticed this dreadful smell of burning. And I realised that the lid of the record player was on fire, and I looked in, there was this thick black smoke everywhere. So, well I didn't really know what to do – so I thought 'Don't throw water, get a wet towel', and I threw that over the record player lid, and went to call the fire brigade. And luckily everything was OK.

2 Well my mother tells me that when I was small, just around about a year, I very nearly drowned. I was playing by the pond in the garden, and apparently I slipped and fell in, and somehow I stood up just enough so my mouth was sticking out above the water. And I didn't cry out – I was apparently just too busy trying to breathe. And eventually my mother, who was wondering where I'd got to, came out, found me standing in the pond with my head just above the water, and she pulled me out before anything bad happened.

3 Oh, it was awful. I'd left some money on the table, and I turned round just for a second to do the dinner, and the baby put it in his mouth. It got stuck in his throat, and he couldn't breathe properly – he was choking. Well I had no idea what to do, so I called an ambulance … But what happened was Jacky, my next-door neighbour was there, and she just turned the baby upside down, slapped him on the back, and the coin came out.

12·4 You're on your own

A Forward on the controls. That's fine. Let the aeroplane fly itself.

B I wish it would.

A Read the air speed.

B The air speed is about 105.

A I am on your right-hand side. Just relax …

A … We are going to do a left-hand circuit. Try to keep that height. Keep the turn going all the way round again.

B I understand but how do you stop it?

A Maintain the height, little more power. That's good. Keep turning to the left. Roll the aircraft in a gentle bank to the left. That's fine. Gently bank to the left, if necessary a little bit of power …

A … I'm going to attempt to get you down.

B Going down, are we?

A We are shortly, yes. Bank gently to the right. We are aiming for the wide tarmac strip to the right of the white and red lights. Can you see it?

B Affirmative.

A Pull back very gently on the control column. Close the throttle, just hold it there. Hold it. Hold it. Hold it. Hold the control column back. Relax. OK …

A … Press the top of the rudder pedals. You will find the brakes. Press both rudder pedals together … you will find the brakes.

B The engine still hasn't stopped.

A Can you see some keys in the ignition?

B Affirmative.

A Turn the keys to 'off' and take them out. The engine should then stop.

B The key's out.

A Has the engine stopped?

B Just stopping now.

A Unstrap yourself and the emergency services will see to you.

B Thank God.

A You're welcome. All in a day's work.

Making suggestions

– Shall we drive down to the coast?

– We could always just have some bread and cheese.

– Let's have an early night.

– I suppose we could just talk to each other.

– What about going for a picnic?

– Let's go and get a Coke.

– We could always play cards.

– Why don't we try that new restaurant?

– Why don't you go and sit in the shade?

– How about getting a take-away pizza?

13·1 National differences

1 In France most of the people want to have a very long time for lunch. In Britain it doesn't seem to be important because people take a cup of tea and a very quick sandwich and it's OK.

2 Another very surprising thing for the foreigner is the way the people obey the law – you seem to have much more discipline than in France, and you respect the police much more than we do. For instance, people park their car everywhere, and they know it is forbidden but they do it – in Britain people don't do that.

3 In England it's easier to feel alone, people don't bother you, don't look after you or worry about you so much, so it's easy to get sort of, to get lost or to hide away here. When you're in the United States people want to know who you are, they tend to speak to you, to find out who you are, what you're doing.

4 Yes, one thing I should mention is that the United States is I think a much more exciting place to be than England, but there is a drawback and that is, you do have this sense of danger in the United States, especially in big cities, that you don't get so much in England or Britain as a whole. You feel safe in England.

5 Japanese houses are really small and people live close to each other, and there aren't so many parks, there aren't so many places where you can play when you are little, and it's very difficult for people to relax.

6 Japan is quite safe, and you can leave your handbag behind when you leave the room without being really careful about it. But in Britain you really have to keep eye on your handbag when you leave the room, and you have to take it with you when you leave.

14·2 Changing channels

And our next guest has come all the way from the United States to be with us tonight. Ladies and gentlemen, Michael Douglas!

It is not yet clear exactly how the accident happened, but police believe that the lorry driver swerved to avoid a child. The driver is …

(Sound of cars and guns)

It's amazing to think that I am standing at the very spot where, two and a half thousand years ago, the Athenian and Persian armies met at the battle of Marathon. Since then, of course, …

And as they come into the last lap, it's still the Kenyan way out in front, and if he can keep this up he could be on his way to a new world record. And …

Aw, you wouldn't want to shoot a friendly little rabbit now, would you? …

– Samantha – your question for £200. What is a *didgeridoo*?
– A kind of bird?
– Come in. Oh. It's you. What do you want?
– I just … wanted to say I was sorry about yesterday.
– A bit late for that, isn't it?

Hello? Anyone here? Hello?

14·4 Easy listening

1 Sometimes in the mornings I use it as an alarm clock. It's got three different timers and the first alarm that goes off usually starts off with the seashore and seagulls and I listen to that for about 15 minutes. And the next one comes on which is, wakes me up a bit more is more like south-east Asian pop music. And then I get the World Service news at 8 o'clock in the morning to finally wake me up.

2 Also there are these *karaoke* channels, about maybe four or five of them I think. And *karaoke* is the thing where you sing along to background music and you have a microphone and you can become a pop star for a few minutes and sing along to the music so I use this a lot now. I've learnt a few of the Japanese songs now. I can sing maybe five or six of them.

3 About the alibi channels, I did actually use one once. I'd been out quite late one night and overslept and was late for work. So I just got hold of the radio, flipped onto the alibi channel, which is the sound of, sounds as though you're in a phone box in the street with passing cars and sort of horns going. And I turned it up fairly loud, put my telephone next to it and explained to the secretary at work that I was on my way to the office and I'd been to a meeting which started at 8.30 in the morning.

4 Also there are various kinds of music, you can get Indian music and Mexican music for example. So when I'm at home cooking and cooking a Mexican meal and I get my friends to come over and we put the Mexican channel on so it creates a nice atmosphere for dinner.

15·1 In the news

The news at 6 o'clock.

The body of American TV presenter Clive Robbins has been found off the coast of Florida. Mr Robbins was reported missing two days ago when he failed to appear for breakfast on his yacht while on holiday in the Florida Keys. The body was found shortly after 6 o'clock this morning by a rescue helicopter, and was flown immediately to Miami for a post-mortem examination.

Two people have been killed in an explosion which badly damaged a house in South-east London early this afternoon. First reports say that the explosion was caused by a bomb, and a number of bombs and other weapons have been found in the house. Police believe that a group of terrorists were using the house as a weapons store, and that the bomb went off accidentally.

And finally, thieves got a nasty surprise when they stole a van from a motorway service station yesterday afternoon. When they finally opened the van, which belongs to the Kent Wildlife Park, they found two tigers inside, which were on their way to the Wildlife Park from London Zoo. The thieves, obviously animal lovers, immediately phoned the Wildlife Park, who have now recovered their van – and the tigers – unharmed.

15·4 Eavesdropping

Part 1
A I don't think you can blame me just because you've been sleeping badly. It's hardly my fault, is it?
B I didn't blame you, I didn't, I never blamed you, I just said I'm, I think I'll go to bed early because I've not, you know, I didn't sleep very well.
A Yeah OK but you seem to imply that just because I'm not working that somehow I'm just you know sitting around doing nothing.
B I just said I was going to bed early because I was very tired. I slept very badly last night, I'm tired, I've got a busy, you know, busy day ahead of me.
A Oh, oh and I haven't. (Well) Because I'm just going to be sitting around watching television and twiddling my thumbs.
B I didn't say that, did I? Look I'm sorry you haven't got enough to do. I'm sorry that you're bored.

A I've got plenty to do, thank you very much. I've been out looking for five different jobs.

Part 2
1 A We've just got to do something. I mean she came home again after midnight last night.
   B I know, she hasn't looked at a book for weeks. She's never going to pass her exams at this rate.
2 A I bet you'll be glad to see them go, won't you?
   B Yeah, it's exhausting, I mean it's nice to see them because they live so far away, but, well it is hard work.
3 A He's so different. He used to be so shy and quiet.
   B I know, it really is incredible. I think he's changed since his divorce, don't you?

16·1 In the classroom

1 We sat in the dark and we watched these slides of different paintings and monuments and it was quite enjoyable.
2 We learnt a lot of dates and we learnt a lot about battles and kings and queens but we never learnt anything about ordinary people who had lived ordinary lives.
3 We did a lot of singing but if you wanted to learn to play an instrument you had to pass a special test.
4 I think my teachers mostly focused on grammar, but we also had the chance to speak in, during the class.
5 I remember we had a map of the world and we used to spin it around and wherever we put our finger on we used to study the country wherever our finger had landed.
6 We had the chance to do a lot of our own experiments which was very good because it gave you the opportunity to see how things worked.
7 We had a very good teacher and we used to write a lot of stories and a lot of poems and I really enjoyed writing poetry. That was great.

16·3 Going through the system

A At what age do children start school in the States?
B Generally six. That's when I started.
A And that goes up to what age?
B That goes up to grade six, so that would be what? Twelve years old? And then you go to seventh grade in Junior High School, in fact you go for three years to a Junior High School, 7th, 8th and 9th grades.
A And then you go to real High School?
B And then comes the real thing, three years of High School. That's the 10th, the 11th and 12th grades.
A And that takes you up to what age? Sixteen or …?
B Seventeen, eighteen. It's quite

common to finish High School with your Diploma at age seventeen.

A And how many subjects do you take for your Diploma?

B Well that depends on what type of Diploma you're doing. There are really two types – there's an academic Diploma, which would prepare you for College, and there's a non-academic Diploma, which is more vocationally orientated. Both types of Diploma have their compulsory subjects, you know, like in the academic Diploma you have to do English. But then in both cases again the student has some choice, so in addition there are what's called 'electives'.

A 'Electives' means you can choose the subject …?

B Exactly, exactly. So in the United States you could do a credit in driving, for example, and learn to drive at High School. Or typing is another skill that you can learn in High School, and that will count towards your Diploma.

16·4 Improve your memory

A OK I gather you've got an interesting way of learning words in a foreign language.

B Yes it's actually a very easy way of learning foreign words. What you do is to, you think of a word in your own language, in my case English, which sounds something like the word you're trying to learn and then you just imagine a picture in your mind which links the two ideas – the idea of the foreign word and the idea of the English word.

A Can you give me an example?

B Yeah, an easy example is the Greek word *skylos* which means 'dog'. And this immediately reminds me of the English words *ski* and *loss*, so I just imagine a picture of a skier on a mountain, one of his skis has come off and he's lost it and there's a dog carrying it back to him in his mouth. An example from a different language might be the Japanese word for 'thank you' which is *arigato*. Now that sounds to me a little bit like *alligator*, so I could imagine a rather unpleasant picture of somebody whose leg has just been eaten by an alligator and the alligator's smiling and saying 'Thank you very much.'

A OK I'm going to try you out with some words in Russian (Goodness. Russian, yeah) You don't know Russian, do you?

B No no no.

A OK. Well here's the Russian word for 'teacher', which is *uchitelj*.

B Could you say it again?

A *Uchitelj.*

B *U-chit-elj.* Oh that's easy. The middle

of this word is the English word *cheat*, which is something we often associate with teachers and students. So I can imagine a student sitting in an examination and he's cheating, he's copying from the student sitting next to him. And the teacher is standing over him saying 'You cheat!'

A OK, here's another word. It's the Russian word for 'fire' which is *ogonj*. *Ogonj.*

B *Ogonj.* Mm. Oh yes, again, let's take the middle of the word, *gone*. We think of a fire perhaps that's gone out. So I just imagine a picture of a fire in a fireplace and it's gone out. Easy.

A OK. Thank you. I'll try it as a technique.

17·4 The dead rabbit

Well, this friend of mine had a dog, which he'd bought for his daughter's tenth birthday. This dog was always getting into trouble, and it had already completely wrecked their house and dug up their garden.

Anyway, one Friday this dog turned up with a dead rabbit in its mouth, which it brought into the house and dropped on the floor. And my friend's daughter immediately recognised this rabbit as the one that belonged to the little boy next door, and the little boy kept this rabbit in a hutch in his garden, so the dog must have got into their garden and killed it.

So my friend had a look at the rabbit, which was all muddy and dirty, but it didn't seem to have any tooth marks on it and it wasn't damaged in any way. So he had an idea.

What he did was he cleaned the rabbit up and he dried it with a hairdryer, and made it look really nice, and then later on that night when the neighbours had gone to sleep, he slipped over the garden fence and put the dead rabbit back in its hutch. The next morning there was a ring at the doorbell, and it was the little boy's mother, and she was looking really upset. And my friend said 'What's the matter?'

And she said 'It's terrible. It's little Timmy's rabbit. I just can't understand it. The rabbit died two days ago, and so we took it out of its hutch and buried it in the garden, and this morning he went back out into the garden to clean out the rabbit hutch so we could sell it – and there was the rabbit back in the hutch.'

18·3 Guilty or not guilty?

And now the swordstick trial. Mr Edward Cook has been found guilty of carrying an offensive weapon. He was given a 28-day suspended prison sentence, and fined £200. He was also ordered to pay £2,500 towards the costs of the trial, and to hand over his swordstick to the police. Afterwards, Mr

Cook said he was shocked at the verdict, and repeated that he had only used the swordstick in self-defence. 'I had to use it,' he told reporters, 'or I'd be a dead man today.'

18·4 Detective Shadow

A *(Reading)* There was a loud crack of thunder and the power went off. Shadow started to look for a candle when he heard a knock at his door. It was Harry Fox, who lived nearby with his uncle. 'Come quickly!' cried Harry Fox. 'My Uncle Cecil has been shot!' Shadow grabbed a torch and ran to his neighbour's house. When they arrived, Shadow shone the light on Cecil's face, and he knew immediately that he was dead. Harry explained that he and his uncle had been watching TV, when suddenly the window had smashed in and Cecil had fallen forward dead. 'At that moment there was a crash of thunder and the power went out,' Harry said. 'That's when I ran and got you.' Just then the power returned and the two reading lights in the room came on. Shadow and Harry sat in total silence for two minutes, unable to believe the terrible scene before them. Shadow finally turned to Harry and said, 'Your story is obviously completely untrue.' Why does Shadow think Harry's lying?

B So right. So Shadow was in his house (Mm) and Harry Fox and his uncle were nearby, they're neighbours (Mm-hm) …

B … Erm, they sat in silence. So the television didn't come on then when the power came on.

A No.

B Ah, right. So in other words Harry had been lying. And that's how Shadow knew, because Harry had said they were watching the television. If they were watching the television, it would have come on again. So, is that right?

A Absolutely right, yes (Good). If Harry Fox and his Uncle Cecil were watching TV, as Harry claimed, the TV should have come back on when the power returned. They sat in silence for a couple of minutes, so it was obvious that the TV had not been on.

B Been on. Ah, OK, yeah.

A Well done.

Making choices

1 A What about this one? Is that the kind of thing you have in mind?

B Um, no, I'd prefer something a little darker.

A Mm. Well, there's this one.

B Yes, that's better. I'll have that one.

2 A Come on. Are you ready?

B Um, actually, I don't think I'll come, if you don't mind. I'd rather get on with this book.

3 A I'll have the chicken, please.
B One chicken … And for you sir?
A I'd like the lamb, please.

4 A Well we could drive. Or would you rather go by train?
B Well actually, I'd prefer to fly, if we can afford it.

19·3 It's a long time since …

1 When I was in France I used to go dancing every, every week, and I haven't been dancing since September, which is several months now. And I really miss it because I would go there every Monday, I remember. So I'm just quite looking forward to doing it again when I go back to France.

2 The last time I played football was when I used to live in South Africa, because it was quite warm and we used to play all year round, it was never cold or anything like that, so that was quite fun. That was about seven years ago that I really, really enjoyed playing football all the time. Then when I moved to England it was a lot colder, and we had to play football in the cold, in shorts, and it was freezing, so I didn't really enjoy it then and I gave it up quite soon after that.

3 It's two years since I last went ice-skating, and I used to really enjoy ice-skating because you could go with a big group of friends, and you could go for a long time, about three hours. But I haven't been for a very long time now because it's got more expensive and because I don't seem to have very much time.

20·1 Birth, marriage and death

1 After the burial it's very traditional to celebrate the death. And we celebrate that by eating and drinking and in some cases singing traditional Irish songs. Because we consider it to be a happy occasion, especially if the person is old, and they've, they're going to heaven and they're going to be rewarded in the afterlife.

2 The bride is dressed up and she sits in a chair surrounded by flowers and children, and everybody troops past to have a look at her. And then you just sit down, and you're given lots of sweets and drinks, soft drinks. And then the groom and his entourage arrive, and he takes her hand and leads her away.

3 In Scotland, there's a tradition related to birth, where you must present the baby with a piece of silver, a silver coin. And you have to take this coin and actually place it in the baby's hand and make the baby hold it. The idea behind this is that the baby will be rich in later life.

4 After the death of the person, this person's corpse will be taken to the furnace, where the corpse is cremated. And afterwards from the furnace bones are taken out. And all the family members get together to pick up the bones with chopsticks. Each relative takes one bone and put them in a small jar, and we bury it.

5 The bride is dressed in white and the bridegroom is dressed in a black suit and white shirt. At midnight she goes away and takes off her white dress and puts on a red dress. She comes back to dance with the guests, and the guests pay for dancing with her, so she dances with everybody and when she's ready and when the bridegroom thinks that's enough, then he takes her by the hand and they run away and they take all the money with them.

20·4 A Good Boy, Griffith

Section 5

The next afternoon he went up the hill to the red brick cottage again. He saw the lace curtains move suddenly as he approached, and the door opened before he had even time to reach the knocker.

'Come back?' she asked. 'If you've not got the money you might as well turn around and go.'

'Steady, steady, girl,' said Griffith, 'don't get so jumpy. I've got the money. Have you got the ring?'

He took the roll of white notes from his waistcoat pocket. 'Come on in then,' she said.

With a quick turn she walked from the room and he heard her going up the stairs. Then she came slowly down.

'There's your ring,' she said, half throwing it on the table. 'Keep it. I'd rather have the money.'

Griffith took the ring. 'One more thing,' he said. 'Nobody must know.'

'All right,' she said quietly. 'Morgan didn't even know I had the thing. I told him I'd given it back to you.'

Section 6

When Morgan came home he washed the grease from his hands under the tap then sat down to his meal. Blodwen poured the tea unsteadily.

'What's up, Blod?' he said. 'You don't look so good, girl.'

'I'm all right,' she said.

'Was Griffith here today?' he said casually, cutting a thick slice from the loaf.

She went pale but he did not look up. 'Yes,' she admitted.

He laughed. 'Good boy, Griff, you know. Sort of steady chap. Can't see why you didn't marry him. Always trust him.'

'Does it matter now?'

'No,' he replied good-humouredly. 'The thing is, did he bring the fifty quid?'

Blodwen felt her heart capsize. 'Yes,' she said shakily. 'Yes, he did …'

Her husband nodded. 'Good boy, Griff. Came in and asked me to lend it to him so he could get a real special ring for his girl Gwen. Nice girl. Said he'd get it from his savings when his dad came home from the pit and bring it up here. A good boy, Griff; yes a good boy …'

21·3 Getting to know you

1 A Hi. Which class are you in?
B I'm studying Japanese.
A Oh, I'm in the same class. (Ah) Yeah, I've just joined, this is my first time. Are you enjoying it?
B Yes, I am. It's fine.
A Have you ever been to Japan?
B I've been once, yes.

2 A Hi. I'm Ian. Do you know anyone here?
B Only a few people. Oh, I'm Alison. (Hi) Do you know anyone here?
A Er just Bob, who I, I think it's his party actually, he met me when he came in.
B Yes. Are you from the States?
A No, I'm from Canada, but you know, it's sort of the same accent, but I'm Canadian, actually.

3 A Excuse me, how long have you been waiting?
B Um, about half an hour now. These buses are always late.
A Are you going to town?
B Yes, yes I am.
A Are you going shopping?
B Er no, I'm meeting a friend there.

21·4 Tags

1 It's a bit cold today, isn't it?
2 They speak Arabic in Iran, don't they?
3 You haven't seen my glasses, have you?
4 Auckland isn't the capital of New Zealand, is it?
5 They didn't stay very long, did they?
6 That film was awful, wasn't it?
7 Penguins can't fly, can they?

22·2 Reactions

1 A Happy birthday, Annie.
B Oh thank you! Can I open it now?
A Of course.
B Oh it's lovely. Thank you very much.

2 A What's the matter?
B My girlfriend Mary just walked right by me in the street and didn't even say hello.
A Maybe she didn't see you.
B She saw me all right. She's just, I don't know, mad at me or something.
A I'm sure she isn't darling – don't get too worried about it. She probably just didn't see you.

3 A Do you want to go for a walk?
B No I've got far too much work to do.
A Oh please, it's a lovely day.
B I know, but let's go later, eh?

4 A Would you mind keeping the noise down, please? I'm trying to get to sleep, I've got to get up early in the morning, this has been going on for two hours.

B Yeah well I'm sorry. It's just, a friend of mine's just got married, you see. We're having a party.

A Ah well I hope he's very happy. The thing is I've got to get up early. When are you going to stop?

5 A Is anything the matter?

B It's Caroline. She's left me.

A Oh no. I don't believe it. What happened?

B Oh nothing really happened. She just said she was moving out and she didn't want to see me any more. I think she's met someone else.

A Oh that's terrible. Look, tell you what, I'll make us some coffee, and then we'll get in the car and go for a drive.

22·4 What's in a smile

A So you've just been on a smile therapy course. What was it like?

B It was really good. I enjoyed it.

A What did you have to do on the course?

B We started off by doing breathing exercises so we could feel about breathing in happiness and of course we had to smile, we had to smile a lot, and the idea is that if you smile you feel better, it puts you in a good mood, so we tried that. We had to try to remember the last time we felt happy and think about that feeling. Then we were given a lecture and that helped to explain how we forget to laugh. When we grow up we forget to laugh. As children you play and you laugh and you smile and you have fun and as you get older life is much more serious. And they're trying to help us to go back to that feeling of childhood and the fun that we had.

A So did you do any activities on the course?

B Yes, they got us into groups, and we had to think back to things that had made us laugh. That was really interesting because it's surprising how there's some people who just can't remember what last made them laugh.

A What about you? Could you remember?

B Oh yes I could remember because I watch funny things on the telly.

A And what else happened on the course?

B Well, the last bit was really the best. That's when they put on a tape of somebody laughing and they were just laughing really out of control and it was really good because we all started to laugh and one by one everybody was laughing because laughing is infectious and that was really good fun.

A What about homework? Do you do anything at home in between the sessions?

B Oh yes, we have this homework to do. We have to practise to laugh. It sounds a bit strange at first, you have to stand in front of the mirror and laugh, sort of like laugh at yourself, which the first time feels embarrassing but it does work and it makes you feel better. Yes. It's good.

A So in general do you think the course has helped to make you feel better about yourself?

B Yeah I do and it is good fun, and it's nice to be with a group, and I can think of some bad-tempered people who I would recommend should go on it.

23·1 Dilemmas

1 Well this is very difficult, but I'm vegetarian, and I don't think I could have eaten the flesh of another person. I don't think I could have lived with myself afterwards if I'd survived. So no, I wouldn't have eaten the flesh of another human being.

2 I think I would have eaten the flesh of the other passengers. If I looked at it from a point of view that I was one of the dead passengers, I wouldn't have minded my body helping other people live. So I think I would have reluctantly done it.

3 I think I probably would have ended up eating the flesh of my fellow passengers if I needed to to survive. I find the idea physically revolting when I think about it, but I don't find it morally revolting. I don't see any moral reason for not doing that if it's necessary to survive, so I probably would have done.

4 I would not have eaten the flesh of my fellow passengers, quite simply because I believe it's morally wrong to do so. So if it was a choice between starving to death and eating the body of another person, I would have chosen starvation.

24·4 The Doomsday Asteroid

1 Well if I only had one month left to live I'd certainly live it up. I'd spend every penny I have, I'd run up an enormous overdraft at the bank, buy everything I've ever wanted, eat anything I've ever wanted to eat, I don't care how bad it is for me – I'd just have a wild time.

2 I think I would go to Spain and get a really nice house on the beach, and have a month on the beach with my children, playing by the seaside, just having fun.

3 I'd buy a wonderful pair of walking boots and an enormous rucksack, and set off with my partner to walk around the entire coast of the British

Isles and just stick to the coast, and just keep going, until the end.

4 Well it isn't absolutely certain that the world would end in six months, so I think I'd probably just carry on as normal really. But I think I'd try and do all those things that I've always wanted to do that I've never done. Like I'd learn to fly, and I'd try parachute-jumping, and I think I'd like to go scuba-diving. And that's what I'd do. I'd live normally, but I'd make sure that I really filled up my time with enjoyable things.

5 I suppose in such a situation, most people would just want to travel around. So I would open a travel agency and organise trips to the most exotic places, just like palm beaches, and exotic islands, visiting relations, and so on and so forth. And I would just earn a fantastic amount of money. There is a 30% chance that the asteroid wouldn't hit the Earth, so I'd become just fantastically rich. And when everybody goes to work after the panic has gone I would just retire and enjoy myself.

Making offers

1 A Would you like me to open the door for you?

B That's very kind of you. My hands are rather dirty.

2 A Shall I turn the volume up a bit?

B No, that's OK. I can hear it all right.

3 A I'll give you a lift to the station if you like.

B No thanks. I don't mind walking.

4 A Do you want some cream on it?

B Yes, thanks. I'd love some.

5 A Would you like to come to a concert on Friday?

B Well I'd love to, but I'm busy that evening.

In the street

1 A Excuse me. Do you know if there's a Post Office near here?

B Yes. There's one just round the corner.

2 A Excuse me. I wonder if you could tell me what the time is.

B Yes. It's nearly half past three.

3 A Excuse me. Do you know if there's anywhere around here I can change some money?

B Well there's a bank in the next street.

4 A Excuse me. Can you tell me when the bus leaves?

B I think it goes in about ten minutes.

5 A Excuse me. Could you tell me the way to North Street?

B Yes. Carry on up here and it's the second on the left.

Reference section

1 Regular events

Present simple tense

* We use the Present simple:
  - to talk about repeated or habitual actions:
    I often *go* to Berlin.
    He *has* a shower every morning.
  - for talking 'in general':
    I *enjoy* dancing.
    She *studies* music.
* To focus on *what happens* rather than *who does it*, we often use the *passive* form:
  The bridge *is painted* every five years.
  BMWs *are made* in Germany.
  In Britain, most babies *are born* in hospital.
* Active forms:

I	work don't work	at weekends.
She	works doesn't work	

Do you Does she	like horror movies?

* Passive forms:

Wheat is Potatoes are	grown in England.

Is wheat Are potatoes	grown in England?

Frequency expressions

once twice three times ...	a day a week a year ...	(once) every 6	hours days months years

* Often we can choose between two frequency expressions with the same meaning:
  every 6 months = twice a year.

Present continuous tense

* We use the Present continuous tense to talk about:
  - things happening 'now', at the moment of speaking:
    They*'re watching* the news.
    The Earth *is* gradually *warming* up.
  - current activities, things happening 'around now':
    I*'m going* out a lot at the moment.
    Everyone*'s wearing* hats this year.
* Compare the Present simple and continuous in talking about jobs and what they involve:
  I'm a history teacher. I *teach* class 2B. At the moment we*'re doing* a project on the Russian Revolution.

2 Around the house

Behaviour at home

* Some things you are supposed to do (and not to do) in your house or flat:
  - *tidy* things *up* and *put them away* when you've finished using them (don't *leave* them lying around)
  - *wash up* (or *wash the dishes*) after a meal, and *clear* things *away*
  - *keep* your room *clean* and *tidy* (don't *make a mess*)
  - don't *make* too much *noise*
  - *switch/turn* lights *off* when you leave a room (don't *leave* them *on*)
  - don't *use up* too much hot water.

Jobs in the home

* Labour-saving devices (= machines or appliances that save time and work in the home):

Appliance	Activity
vacuum cleaner	cleaning carpets
washing machine	washing clothes
sewing machine	sewing, making clothes
food processor	preparing food
cooker	cooking food
microwave oven	cooking food quickly
electric drill	repairing things, drilling
iron	ironing clothes
dishwasher	washing dishes

* Vacuum cleaners are also called *hoovers*, and we use the expression *to hoover the carpets*.
* *Cooker* is only used for the appliance. A person who cooks is a *cook*.
* *do the + -ing* is used for regular activities. It is only used if no noun follows (we say *do the cleaning* but not *~~do the cleaning the floors~~*). Compare:

do the washing	wash the clothes
do the washing up	wash the dishes
do the cleaning	clean the floor
do the cooking	cook a meal
do the ironing	iron the clothes

Describing rooms

* Features of a living room:
  Rooms may have old or modern *furniture*.
  This may include *armchairs*, a *sofa*, or *bookshelves*.
  People often use *rugs*, *cushions* and *plants* to add colour to a room, and put *ornaments*, *pictures* or *photographs* round the walls.
  The walls may be *painted* or have *wallpaper*.
  The room may have doors or *French windows* (= glass doors) leading onto a *balcony* or a *patio*.

3 Past events

Past simple and continuous tenses

- We use the Past simple to talk about things that happened in the past:
  He *went* abroad in 1980.
  They *arrived* at 1 o'clock.
- Positive and negative forms:

I	saw	the film.
He	didn't see	

- We use the Past continuous to talk about the background to past events (things that were going on at the time):
  The children *were playing* outside.
  I *was having* lunch (when they arrived).
- Positive and negative forms:

I was(n't)	feeling very tired.
We were(n't)	

- The Past simple and continuous are often joined with *when*, *while* or *as*:
  I was having lunch *when* someone rang the doorbell.
  A woman came up to me *while* I was walking home.
  They arrived just *as* I was leaving.

Past time expressions

- *when* can be followed by Past simple or continuous:
  I met her *when* I was on holiday.
  I met her *when* I was living in London.
- *during* is followed by a noun phrase:
  I met her *during* the summer holidays.
- *before* & *after* can be followed by Past simple or -*ing*:

Before I *went*	to college, I worked as a waiter.
Before *going*	

Subject and object questions

- Subject questions ask about the subject of the sentence. They keep normal word order:
  Someone *told* you → Who *told* you?
  Something *happened* → What *happened*?
- Object questions ask about other parts of the sentence. They have question word order:
  You *told* someone → Who *did* you *tell*?
  You *left* it somewhere → Where *did* you *leave* it?
  She *was eating* something → What *was* she *eating*?

Past simple passive

- We often use the Past simple passive to focus on *what happened* rather than what people did:
  He *was killed* in a road accident.
  The baby *was born* last night.
- Forms of the Past simple passive:

The building was(n't)	damaged in the fire.
The buildings were(n't)	

Was the building	damaged in the fire?
Were the buildings	

4 Money

Cost

- It *cost* £20.
  I *paid* £20 *for* it.
  I *bought* it *for* £20.
  I *spent* £200 *on* clothes.
- It's *cheap* = it doesn't cost much.
  It's *expensive* = it costs a lot.
  I can't *afford* (to buy) it. (= It's too expensive for me.)
- You should buy it – it's (*well*) *worth the money*.

Don't buy it – it's	a waste of money.
	not worth the money.

  These jeans are *good value* (*for money*). (= They're not expensive considering how good they are.)
  These jeans are a *bargain*. (= They're cheaper than they should be.)

Using money

At a bank	open/close an account, pay in / draw out money, cash a cheque
At an exchange office	change money, cash traveller's cheques, change francs into dollars
In a shop	buy something, ask the price, pay for it, get a receipt, bring it back, get a refund
In a hotel, restaurant, etc.	pay the bill, pay by cheque / by credit card / in cash

- Useful expressions:
  How much is it? How much does it cost?
  Do you take credit cards?
  Will you accept a cheque?
  Can you give me change for £10?
  Have you got any change?
- *lend* = give money (for a time).
  borrow = take money (for a time).
  Can you *lend* me $50?
  Could I *borrow* $50 (from you)?
  I'll *pay* you *back* next week.

The cost of living

Bills	medical bills, heating (fuel) bills, repair bills, rent
Taxes	income tax, sales tax, car tax, VAT (= European Community tax)
Insurance	property insurance, health insurance, life insurance, car insurance

- Some things that governments do:
  – *introduce* or *abolish* taxes
  – *increase* or *reduce* taxes
  – *spend money on* health, transport, education, defence, housing.

5 Obligation

Obligation and permission

have to need to (must)	don't have to don't need to (needn't)
can are allowed to	can't aren't allowed to (mustn't)

- *don't have to* and *don't need to* mean 'it isn't necessary':
  You *don't have to* bring any food with you (it's provided).
- *can* and *can't* are modal verbs. They are followed by the infinitive without 'to':
  We *can't* go in that room.
- *must*, *mustn't* and *needn't* are mainly used for giving orders or instructions. Compare:
  Parent to teenager: You *must* be home by 11; you *mustn't* stay out later than that.
  Teenager to friend: I *have to* be home by 11; I'm *not allowed to* stay out later than that.

make and let

- They *make* me stay in = I have to stay in.
  They *don't make* me stay in = I don't have to stay in.
  They *let me* go out = I'm allowed to go out.
  They *don't let* me go out = I'm not allowed to go out.
- Like modals, *make* and *let* are followed by infinitive without 'to', but they have the form of normal verbs:
  She *lets* her children *stay* up late.
  They *didn't make* us *wear* a uniform.
- Past tense forms:

I had to stay in. They made me stay in.	I didn't have to stay in. They didn't make me stay in.
I was allowed to go out. They let me go out.	I wasn't allowed to go out. They didn't let me go out.

Freedom from obligation

- Two ways of expressing freedom from obligation: structures with *-ever* and structures with *any-*:

You can do it	wherever *or* anywhere whenever *or* any time however *or* any way	you like.
You can see	whatever *or* anything whoever *or* anyone	

- With adjectives and adverbs, we use *as ... as ...*:

You can sing as	loud often much many songs	as you like.

6 On holiday

Holidays

- We say *go on holiday* and *be on holiday*:
  They're on holiday in Italy.
- The period when children are not at school is called *the holidays* (e.g. the summer holidays) or *the vacation* (e.g. the summer vacation).
- A day when people don't work (e.g. May 1st, New Year's Day) is a *national holiday* or *public holiday*.
- *Festivals* are special occasions (e.g. Christmas, Ramadan, Carnival) which people *celebrate* by taking part in *traditional* activities.

Types of holiday

- A holiday that is organised and paid for in advance is called a *package holiday*:
  They went on a package holiday to Ibiza.
- Some common types of holiday:
  – a seaside holiday (at a seaside resort)
  – a walking holiday
  – a camping holiday (at a camp site)
  – a coach tour (going from place to place by coach)
  – a cruise (going from place to place by ship)
  – an activity holiday (doing a special activity, e.g. painting, climbing, sailing).

Holiday activities

beach	sunbathing, swimming, waterskiing, windsurfing, diving
mountains and lakes	walking, climbing, skiing, camping sailing, canoeing, fishing
towns and cities	sightseeing, visiting churches, cathedrals, mosques, museums, art galleries, castles

- for activities we use *go + -ing*, e.g. go skiing, go camping, go fishing.
- You *go on* a journey, a trip, a tour, a picnic, an excursion (= a short organised trip).
- Cathedrals, castles, etc., are *sights* (= things people go to see). Tourists often *go sightseeing* or *see the sights*.
- Things that come from the place we visit are *local*. So we talk about *local specialities* (in restaurants) and *local produce* (in shops and markets).

Some things to take on holiday

clothes	anorak, T-shirts, swimming costume, shorts, walking boots, trainers, sandals
equipment	tent, sleeping bag, skis, face mask, map, camera, film, binoculars, beach mat
first aid kit	insect repellent, aspirin, suntan cream
luggage	suitcase, bag, rucksack (or backpack)
documents	passport, traveller's cheques, tickets, (international) driver's licence, insurance

7 Past and present

used to

- We use *used to* to talk about:
  - repeated actions in the past:
    I *used to* get up at six every morning.
  - past states:
    I *used to* live in the country.
- *Used to* emphasises that these actions or states are no longer true:
  I *used to* get up at six (but now I get up later).
  I *used to* live in the country (but now I live in town).
- Instead of *used to*, we can use the Past simple tense:
  I *got up* at six when I was at school.
- Forms of *used to*:

I	used to didn't use to	play with dolls.
Did you use to play with dolls?		

Note: We can also say *used not to*, but this sounds more formal.

- *Used to* is only used in the past, and has no present form. Note the difference between:
  - I *used to* ride a bike. (= I rode a bike earlier, but I don't now.)
  - I'*m used to riding* a bike. (= I often do it, I'm accustomed to it.)

Present perfect tense

- We use the Present perfect tense to talk about recent events:
  I'*ve finished* the book.
  They'*ve arrived*.
  (See also Unit 15.)
- We often use this tense to talk about *changes* that have taken place (what is different now from before):
  BEFORE: He used to be single.
  NOW: He's married.
  CHANGE: He'*s got* married.
- Active forms:

I've (= have) He's (= has)	mended the window.
Have you mended the window?	

- Passive forms:

The windows have The window has	been mended.
Have the windows Has the window	been mended?

- Some common verbs of change:
  get: The weather has got worse.
  become: Jazz has become less popular.
  start: I've started wearing glasses.
  stop: I've stopped seeing her.

8 At your service

Services

Place	You can ...
dentist's	have your teeth filled/cleaned
garage	have your car repaired/serviced
electrician's	have your TV mended/repaired
hairdresser's	have your hair cut/washed
optician's	have your eyes tested
dry cleaner's	have your clothes cleaned
photographer's	have your photograph taken

- Instead of *have your hair cut*, we can also say *have a haircut*.
- Shops and places that offer services often add *-'s*, e.g. we can say *baker* or *baker's* (= *baker's shop*), *hairdresser* or *hairdresser's*, *optician* or *optician's*. Nowadays, the apostrophe is often left out.

Having things done

- If other people do things for us, we say that we *have* these things *done*, e.g. We have our windows cleaned once a month. (= Someone cleans them for us.)
- *Have something done* is a form of the passive. Compare:
  Someone *cleans* our windows once a month.
  Our windows *are cleaned* once a month.
  We *have* our windows *cleaned* once a month.
- Like the passive, the structure *have something done* can be used in any tense – past, present or future:
  I *had* my car serviced yesterday.
  I usually *have* my car serviced at Johnson's Garage.
  I think I'*ll have* my car serviced soon.

Systems

- *Using a public library*
  If you want to *borrow* books from a library, you have to *join* or *become a member*. To borrow a book, you show your *ticket* to the *librarian*, and *return* it (or *bring it back*) after a week or two. Most libraries also have a *reference section*, where you can read *reference books* (e.g. dictionaries, encyclopaedias, atlases).
- *Using a public phone*
  To make a *call* from a public *phone box*, you *pick up the receiver* and put in some money. You *dial the number*, and wait till the person answers. If the number is *engaged*, you'll have to try again later.
- *Sending things by post*
  You can *post a letter* in a *post box*, but if you want to send a *parcel*, you have to take it to the *post office*. There they will *weigh* it, and sell you *stamps* to put on it. You can send letters and parcels abroad *by air mail* or *by surface mail*. You can send valuable things *by registered post*.

9 Imagining

Conditional structures

1st conditional

> If + Present tense, … will/won't …

- We use the first conditional to talk about things that we think might happen in the future:
  If I *find* your watch, I'*ll* tell you.
  (You've lost your watch, and I'll look for it – perhaps I'll find it.)
- In first conditionals, we use *if* + Present tense to talk about the future.

2nd conditional

> If + Past tense, … would/wouldn't …

- We use the second conditional to *imagine* things that we don't expect to happen:
  If I *found* a watch in the street, I'*d* take it to the police.
  (No-one has really lost a watch – I'm just imagining the situation.)
- We also use the second conditional to imagine things that can't be true:
  If I *lived* in Hawaii, I'*d* go swimming every morning.
  (I don't live in Hawaii – I'm just imagining it.)
- To form second conditionals, the verbs move 'one tense back' from the first conditional:
  Present   →   Past
  will   →   would
  Note: in second conditionals the Past tense does *not* refer to *past time* – it is used to show that the condition is *unreal*.
- In second conditionals, we can use *were* instead of *was*. This is used in a more formal style, and also in the phrase *If I were you*:
  If he *were* older, I'd take him swimming.
  If I *were* you, I'd see a doctor.
- To talk about imaginary situations, we can also use *would* on its own:
  I don't think I'*d* enjoy having children. They'*d* take up too much of my time, and I *wouldn't* be able to go out and enjoy myself.

I wish

I wish	I *had* more money. I *could* go home. he'*d* stop shouting.

- After *I wish*, we use Past tense or *could/would*.
- We use *I wish* + Past to talk about the present:
  I wish I *had* a car.
  (I don't have a car.)
- We use *I wish* + *could/would* to talk about things we want to do and things we want to happen:
  I wish I *could* go out.
  (I want to go out but I can't.)
  I wish they'*d* pay me more money.
  (I want them to pay me more but they won't.)

10 Describing things

Ways of describing objects

shape	round, square, oval, triangular; flat
dimensions	long, short; wide, narrow; thick, thin
texture	rough, smooth; hard, soft
material	made of wood, metal, plastic, rubber, glass, pottery

- Expressions with adjectives: a glass bottle, a plastic cup, a metal table, a wood*en* spoon.
- *made of* = the actual material:
  The bottle is *made of* glass.
  made from = the original material:
  Glass is *made from* sand.

Use

- *use for*:
  You *use* a corkscrew *for opening* bottles.
  A corkscrew *is used for opening* bottles.
- Noun phrases:

-ing + noun	noun + noun	noun + -er/-or
writing paper frying pan washing powder	table lamp face cream kitchen knife	can opener pencil sharpener word processor

  – writing paper = paper you use for writing
  – table lamp = a lamp you put on the table
  – can opener = something you use for opening cans.
- Some commonly used nouns are written as one word: *penknife, newspaper, notebook, saucepan*.
- General words for describing objects:
  It's a *thing* you use for opening bottles.
  It's a kind of white *liquid* which is used for correcting typing mistakes.
  It's soft, coloured *stuff* that children use for making models.

Features

- My car *has got* electric windows.
  I've got a car *with* electric windows.
- His guitar *has got* 12 strings.
  He's got a *12-string* guitar.

Buying and selling

- To save money, you can buy things *second-hand* (= someone else has owned them before you). To find second-hand things, you can look through the *classified advertisements* (or *small ads*) in newspapers, which tell you what people have *for sale*.
- Some questions you might ask:
  – How much does it cost?
  – How long have you had it?
  – Is it in good condition?
  – Does it work?

11 The future

will, won't and might

- *will*, *won't* and *might* are followed by the infinitive (without *to*):

| He | will (probably)
might
(probably) won't | give up his job.
go and live abroad.
become a novelist. |

might = perhaps he will.
probably comes after *will* but before *won't*.

- *will*, *might* and *won't* can also be followed by the passive infinitive (*be* + past participle):

| He | will (probably)
might
(probably) won't | be invited to the party.
be released from prison.
be promoted. |

expect and hope

| I expect
I don't expect | the President will resign. |

| I hope | the President resigns.
the President doesn't resign. |

- *I hope* is usually followed by the Present simple, but it is also possible to use the future:
  I hope the President *will/won't* resign.
- *I hope* is not used in the negative form (we can't say 'I don't hope …').

Future continuous and Future perfect tenses

- We use the Future continuous tense to say what will be *going on* at a point in the future.

| In 5 years' time I'll | be living in London.
be working for Esso. |

- We use the Future perfect tense to say what will be *completed* at a point in the future:

| By next month he'll | have left university.
have found a job. |

Linking expressions

- *in case* and *so that* are followed by the Present simple tense to express the future.
- *Otherwise* usually begins a new sentence.

| You should take a torch | *because* it might get dark.
in case it gets dark.
so that you can see.
Otherwise you won't be able to see. |

12 Accidents

Accidents and injuries

- If you *have an accident*, you may *injure* yourself. If the *injury* is serious, you may have to go to hospital for *treatment*.
- Common accidents and injuries:
  - Oil splashed out of the pan and he *burnt* his hand.
  - The knife slipped and she *cut* herself.
  - He tripped and *twisted* his ankle.
  - She fell and *broke* her leg.
  - He touched the wire and *got an electric shock*.
  - She was going upstairs when she *had a heart attack*.
  - The roof collapsed and they *were trapped*.
- Expressions connected with fire:
  - The candle fell over and *set fire to* the carpet.
  - The carpet *caught fire*.
  - The carpet was *on fire*.
  - They tried to *put the fire out*.

Accidental death verbs

Verb	Cause
suffocate	you can't breathe
choke	something sticks in your throat
drown	your face is under water
starve	you have nothing to eat
die of thirst	you have nothing to drink

- There are many expressions with the form *die of* + noun: die of exhaustion, die of cold, die of old age.

Acting in an emergency

- In an emergency, you may need to *call for help*, *call an ambulance* or *the fire brigade*, or *give first aid*.
- Other common actions:
  - Keep the person calm/warm/still.
  - Comfort the person, stay with him/her.
  - If he/she has a cut, clean it, put a plaster on it or a bandage round it.

Driving

- To go faster, you *accelerate* (or *speed up*).
  To go slower, you *slow down*.
  To stop, you *brake* (or *put the brake on*).
  If a car is going slowly in front of you, you can *overtake* it.
- To avoid something on the road, you may need to *swerve*.
  If the road is wet or icy, you may *skid*.
  If you aren't careful, you may *crash into* another car, or you may *run* someone *over*.

13 Comparing and evaluating

Comparison of adjectives

- My car isn't nearly as fast = his car is much faster. (a big difference)
  My car isn't quite as fast = his car is slightly faster. (a small difference)

His car is	much far a bit slightly	faster more expensive	than mine.

My car isn't	nearly quite	as	fast expensive	as his.

- We can also make positive sentences with ... *as ... as*:
  I'm (just) *as* clever *as* you.
  She's nearly *as* tall *as* her mother.

Comparison of adverbs

- If the adverb is formed by adding *-ly*, add *more*: quickly – more quickly; easily – more easily.
- If the adverb is the same as the adjective, add *-er*: hard – harder; fast – faster; early – earlier.
- Irregular: well – better.

too and enough

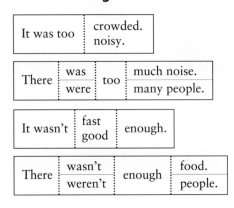

It was too	crowded. noisy.

There	was were	too	much noise. many people.

It wasn't	fast good	enough.

There	wasn't weren't	enough	food. people.

- *too* is followed by an adjective or adverb, or by *much/many* + noun.
- *enough* comes after adjectives and adverbs, but before nouns.

too/enough + infinitive

He was too ill. He couldn't go to work.
→ He was *too* ill to go to work.
The table was too heavy. I couldn't lift it.
→ The table was *too* heavy (for me) *to* lift.
(*not* ... ~~to lift it~~)
The water wasn't warm enough. We couldn't swim in it.
→ The water wasn't warm *enough* (for us) *to* swim in.
(*not* ... ~~to swim in it~~)

14 The media

- *The media* is a general term describing newspapers and magazines ('the Press') and radio and television. It is also called the *mass media*, because it brings information to large numbers of people.

Newspapers and magazines

- You buy newspapers and magazines from a *newsagent* or *news-stand* (or, in some countries, from a *kiosk*).
- Most newspapers appear *daily* or *weekly* (*once a week*). Magazines are usually produced *weekly*, *fortnightly* (*once a fortnight*) or *monthly* (*once a month*).
- Newspapers contain *articles* and *features*, which are written by *journalists*. Usually they also have a *leading article* or *editorial*, which is written by the *editor* and gives the point of view of the newspaper.
- In many countries, the press is *independent*, and newspapers may be *right-wing* or *left-wing*. In some countries, the press is *controlled* by the state and may be *censored*.
- Typical contents of a newspaper:

news	home news, foreign/international news, business/financial news, sports news
regular features	weather forecast, TV & radio programmes, horoscope, cartoons, letters, reviews, obituaries, advertisements, crossword

Radio and TV

- To listen to a radio programme, you *tune in* to the *station* (or *wavelength*) you want. When you watch TV, you choose the *channel* you want.
- Some types of TV programme and the people involved:

Programme	People
news	newsreader
documentary	presenter
sports programme	commentator
chat show	host, guests
soap (opera)	actors
comedy show	comedian

Note: Chat show is British English. In the USA it's called a *talk show*.

15 Recent events

Present perfect simple tense

- We use the Present perfect simple to talk about recent events. It is often used for *announcing news* of something that has happened recently:
  Sarah *has got* engaged.
  There *has been* a plane crash at Heathrow Airport.
- If we want to focus on *what has happened* rather than on *who* has done the action, we often use the passive:
  A thief *has been arrested* (by the police).
  A new motorway *has been built*.
  (For tables of active and passive forms, see Unit 7.)

Present perfect and past simple tenses

- We use the Present perfect when we are not interested in *when* things happened, but only in *the fact* that they have happened. If we mention *when* or *how*, we use the Past tense:
  Sarah *got* engaged at the weekend.
  A plane *crashed* at Heathrow Airport last night as it was coming in to land.
- In a single paragraph, it is common to use the Present perfect for *announcing* a piece of news, followed by the past tenses for *going into details*:
  There *has been* a plane crash at Heathrow Airport. The crash *took place* late last night as the plane *was coming* in to land. Five passengers *were killed* and …

Present perfect continuous tense

- We use the Present perfect continuous to talk about *recent activities*. It answers the question 'How have you been spending your time?':
  I've *been writing* letters.
  I *haven't been working* very hard.
- Like the Present perfect simple, this tense cannot be used with past time expressions, but we can use it with expressions such as *recently, this week, over the last few days*:
  I've been writing a lot of letters *recently*.
  I haven't been working very hard *this week*.
- Forms of the Present perfect continuous:

I've She's	been working hard.
Have you Has she	been working hard?

Present perfect continuous and simple tenses

- Present perfect continuous and simple tenses are often used together. We use the continuous form to talk about *activities*, and the simple form to talk about individual *actions*:
  I've *been getting* ready for my trip. I've *packed* my case, I've *collected* my tickets and I've *changed* some money.
  I've *been writing* an essay. I've *written* it in rough but I *haven't typed* it out yet.

16 Teaching and learning

School subjects

Subject	Typical activities
languages	learning vocabulary; doing exercises; practising; translating
literature	reading novels, poetry, plays; writing essays
maths	making calculations; using tables
science	doing experiments
geography	using maps
history	learning dates; learning about governments, wars, leaders
art	painting, drawing
music	playing musical instruments
sport	playing football; doing athletics

- You *go to* (or *attend*) school.
  You *study* or *do* school subjects (e.g. I never did French at school).
  You *take* or *sit* examinations (exams), and you either *pass* or *fail* them.

Skills

- *good at + -ing* or noun.

I'm	(very) good quite good not very good no good	at	football. French. speaking French. singing.

- We can also say:
  I'm a good singer.
  She isn't a very good dancer.
- I *know how to* dance the tango. (= I can do it.)
  I *don't know how to* read music. (= I can't do it.)
  I *learnt how to* ride a horse when I was a child.

Schools and universities

- British and American equivalents:

GB	USA
nursery school	
primary school	grade school
secondary school	junior high school high school
university	college

- Before you leave school, you take a *school-leaving examination*. This qualifies you to go to *university*, where you study for a *degree*. When you get your degree, you *graduate* from university. Someone who has graduated from university is called a *graduate*. Note the pronunciation difference:
  to *graduate* /ˈgrædjʊeɪt/
  a *graduate* /ˈgrædjʊət/.

17 Narration

Past perfect tense

- We use the Past perfect tense to *go back* from a point in the past to events that had happened *earlier*:
  I came home at 4 o'clock, but I was too late: my brother *had* already *left*.
  The woman opposite me looked very familiar; I was sure I'*d seen* her somewhere before.
- Active and passive forms:

I He	had(n't)	met them before.

The car	had(n't) been	serviced. stolen.

I had, he had, etc., are often shortened to *I'd, he'd*.

- Notice the relationship between *how things were* in the past and *what had happened* earlier:

Past state	Previous event
The light *was* off.	Someone *had switched* the light off.
He *was* abroad.	He'*d gone* abroad.
There *wasn't* any hot water.	All the hot water *had been used* up.

Reported speech and thought

- Often we report what people said or thought in the past using verbs such as *said, told, discovered* and *realised*. When we do this, what the person actually said or thought usually changes *one tense further back*:
  'I'*m* French,' he said.
  → He said he *was* French.
  'I'*ve been* here before,' I thought to myself.
  → I realised that I'*d been* there before.
  'I'*ll* meet you at six,' she told me.
  → She told me she'*d* (= *would*) meet me at six.
- Tense changes in reported speech and thought:

Actual words		Reported
does	→	did
is doing	→	was doing
will do	→	would do
did has done	→	had done

- *say* and *tell*
  say is not followed by an object; *tell* is followed by an indirect object:
  He *said* he was French. (*not* ~~he said me~~)
  He *told me* he was French. (*not* ~~he told he was~~)
- Common reporting verbs:
  SPEECH: say, tell, explain, point out, reply, deny.
  THOUGHT: realise, discover, know, think.
- In certain cases (e.g. when reporting general facts or very recent speech) no tense change is necessary:
  Our teacher told us that penguins *live* in Antarctica.
  He said he'*ll* be there by 10 o'clock tonight.

18 Breaking the law

Crimes and criminals

A *criminal* is someone who *commits* a *crime*.

Crimes		Criminals
Verb	*Noun*	
rob	robbery	robber
(burgle)	burglary	burglar
(steal)	theft	thief
murder	murder	murderer
kidnap	kidnapping	kidnapper
hijack	hijacking	hijacker
blackmail	blackmail	blackmailer
spy (on)	spying	spy
smuggle	smuggling	smuggler
(vandalise)	vandalism	vandal

- You *steal* money or other things from people:
  He *stole* $100 *from* his cousin.
  They broke into our house and *stole* our TV.
  You *rob* people or places:
  They stopped him in a dark street and *robbed* him (of all his money).
  They *robbed* the National Bank.
- A *burglar* breaks into homes or shops and steals money or goods.
  A general word for someone who steals is a *thief*. The crime is *theft*.

Punishments

- If you commit a minor offence (e.g. parking your car in the wrong place), you may have to *pay a fine* (= pay money).
  If you commit a more serious crime, you may *be sent to* (or *go to*) *prison*.
  In some countries, people are *sentenced to death* for serious crimes (e.g. murder).

Trials

- The accused person *goes on trial* or *is tried* or *appears in court*.
- The *judge* is in charge of the trial.
  The *jury* decides if the accused is *guilty*.
  The *prosecution* tries to prove that the accused is guilty.
  The *defence defends* the accused.
  Witnesses give *evidence*.
- At the end of the trial, the jury give their *verdict* (either *guilty* or *not guilty*).
  If the accused is guilty the judge passes *sentence* (= decides on a punishment).

19 Up to now

Present perfect tenses with for and since

- We use the Present perfect continuous to talk about the duration of activities that started in the past and are still going on now:
  I've *been travelling* for 3 days.
  He's *been doing* the same job for 40 years.
- Some verbs are not normally used in the continuous form. With these verbs, we use the Present perfect simple:
  I've *had* this bicycle since I was a child.
  They've *been* here since Saturday.
- *for* is used with periods of time:
  for a year, for two weeks, for ages
  since is used with points of time:
  since 1950, since last week, since my birthday
  since can also be followed by a clause with a Past simple verb:
  I've been writing to her *since we met on holiday.*
  I've loved horses (ever) *since I was a child.*

Origin and duration

- When we talk about activities or states continuing up to now, we can focus on when they *started* (*origin*) or on *how long* they've been going on (*duration*).
  ORIGIN: He *became* a teacher five years ago.
  DURATION: He's *been* a teacher for five years.
  ORIGIN: They *started* building the dam in July.
  DURATION: They've *been building* the dam since July.
  Some common pairs of 'origin' and 'duration' verbs:

become	be
buy/get	have
move to	live (in)
meet / get to know	know
learn (how to)	know (how to)
fall in love	be in love
die	be dead

How long ...? and How long ago ...?

- Questions with *How long ago ...?* ask about *origin*:
  How long ago *did* you *meet* each other?
  – A year ago. / Last Christmas.
- Questions with *How long ...?* ask about *duration*:
  How long *have* you *known* each other?
  – For a year. / Since last Christmas.

Negative duration

- To express negative duration (how long something *hasn't* happened for), use the Present perfect simple:
  I *haven't visited* them for years.
  I *haven't spoken* French since I was at school.
  (*not* ~~I haven't been speaking~~ ...)
- Other structures that express negative duration:
  – *The last time* I visited them *was* years ago.
    The last time I spoke French *was* at school.
  – *It's* years *since* I (*last*) *visited* them.
    It's three years *since* I (*last*) *spoke* French.

20 In your lifetime

Birth, marriage and death

Event		Ceremony
Noun	*Verb*	
birth	be born	
	give birth (to)	
marriage	get married	wedding
	marry	
death	die	funeral

- Before a baby is born, its mother is *pregnant*, or *is expecting a baby*. Then she *gives birth* (or *has the baby*), either in hospital or at home. A *midwife* helps to deliver the baby.
- In Britain and the US, many parents *christen* (= give a name to) or *baptise* their babies in church.
- At a wedding, the two people getting married are the *bride* and *bridegroom*. A wedding can be a *religious* ceremony (e.g. in church) or a *civil* ceremony (at a registry office). After the wedding, friends and relatives are invited to a *reception*. Then the couple go away on a *honeymoon*.
- When someone dies, the body is usually put into a *coffin*. At the funeral, the body may be *cremated* (= burnt) or *buried* in a *cemetery* (or *graveyard*). The *grave* is marked with a *gravestone* or *headstone*. Close relatives of the dead person usually go into *mourning*.

Ages

Person	Stage of life
child	childhood
adolescent/teenager	adolescence
adult/grown-up	adulthood
middle-aged person	middle age
old/elderly person	old age

- an *adolescent* is someone who is *growing up* (between child and adult). A *teenager* is someone between 13 and 19.
- *adult*, *grown-up* and *adolescent* can be used as nouns or adjectives:
  He behaves like a grown-up.
  He behaves in a very grown-up way.
- *Elderly* is a polite way to refer to old people.
- Other ways of talking about age:
  She's *in her* (*early/mid/late*) *twenties.*
  She's a *seven-year-old* (child).

Age and the law

In most countries, there is a *legal age* for certain activities.
- Often this is a *minimum age*:
  You *can't* drive a car *until* you are 17.
  You *have to* be 18 before you *can* vote.
- Or it may be a *maximum* age:
  You *have to* retire *at the age of* 65.

21 Finding out

Information questions

- Questions with *What ...?*

What	*kind of* bread shall I buy?
	type of music does she like?
	make of fridge have they got?
	colour paper did you get?
	size shoes does he wear?
	flavour soup would you like?

- *kind*, *type* and *make* are followed by *of*. Other category words are followed directly by another noun.
- Other questions with *What ...?*:
  What happened to your finger?
  What did you do to your finger?
  What happened to my coat? (= Where is it?)
- Questions with *How ...?*:
  – *How much/many, How long, How far, How often*:
  How much do you weigh?
  How far is it to the beach (from here)?
  – *How + adjective*:
  How expensive are the tickets?

Indirect questions

I wonder	if they're here.
I don't know	where they are.
Do you know	where they are?

- Indirect questions have normal word order. Compare:
  DIRECT: *Does* she *live* here?
  INDIRECT: I wonder if she *lives* here.

Reported questions

- As in reported speech (see Unit 17), the verb in a reported question changes one tense further back:
  '*Are* you French?'
  → He asked if I *was* French.
  '*Have* you *been* here before?'
  → She asked him if he'*d been* there before.
- Like indirect questions, reported questions keep normal word order:
  He asked me *where I lived*. (*not* ~~where did I live~~)

Question tags

- We use question tags:
  – to check things when we're not quite sure:
  You don't eat beef, do you? (rising intonation)
  – to express an opinion or belief:
  It's cold in here, isn't it? (falling intonation)
- To form question tags, repeat the auxiliary verb:
  They'*re* coming tomorrow, *aren't* they?
  You *can* swim, *can't* you?
  With Present and Past simple sentences, use *do(n't)* or *did(n't)*:
  She works for IBM, *doesn't* she?

22 Speaking personally

Feelings

angry	embarrassed	jealous	upset
annoyed	excited	nervous	worried
depressed	frightened	relaxed	

- *annoyed* = slightly angry.
  nervous = slightly afraid of something that's going to happen (e.g. an exam, a visit to the dentist).
  upset = very unhappy about something that's happened (you feel like crying).
- All these adjectives are used with *feel*, *get* and *make*:
  I *feel/get* frightened if I'm alone at night.
  Being alone at night *makes* me frightened.
- Adjectives ending in *-ed* have three equivalent forms:
  It *frightens* me.
  I makes me (feel) *frightened*.
  I find it *frightening*.

Reporting verbs

Notice how we use these verbs to report conversations:
  'Come on, cheer up – don't be sad.'
  – I tried to *cheer* him *up*.
  'OK, don't get angry – calm down.'
  – I tried to *calm* her *down*.
  'I'm very sorry.'
  – I *apologised*.
  'Go on – have a drink.'
  – He tried to *persuade* me to have a drink.
  'No, I don't want one.'
  – I *refused* (to have one).
  'This food's terrible.'
  – She *complained* about the food.

Reactions

'*Normal*' *adjectives:*
- With these adjectives we can use *very* or *quite*:
  The film was *very* disappointing.
  I found the film *quite* amusing.

Positive	Negative
good	bad
interesting	boring
enjoyable	dull
amusing	disappointing
entertaining	
exciting	

'*Extreme*' *adjectives:*
- *Wonderful*, *brilliant* and *terrific* all mean 'very good'. *Awful*, *dreadful* and *terrible* all mean 'very bad'.
- Because these adjectives already have the sense of 'very', we can't use the word *very* with them. Instead we use *absolutely* for emphasis:
  The film was *absolutely* wonderful.
  I found the film *absolutely* terrible.
- We can use *really* with normal or extreme adjectives:

Positive	Negative
wonderful	awful
brilliant	dreadful
terrific	terrible
fascinating	

The film was *really* | interesting.
fascinating.

23 The unreal past

'Unreal' conditionals

2nd conditionals

> If + past tense ... would/wouldn't (do)

- We use the second conditional to imagine unreal things in the *present*:
  If I were rich, I'd give a lot of money to help poor people. (I'm not rich – I'm just imagining it.)
  She'd be happier if she had a more interesting job. (In fact she's *not* very happy and her job *isn't* very interesting.)
  (See also Unit 9.)

3rd conditionals

> If + past perfect tense ... would/wouldn't have (done)

- We use the third conditional to imagine unreal things in the *past*:
  If I'd *known* you were alone, I *would have visited* you. (Unfortunately I *didn't* know, so I *didn't* visit you.)
  I *would have been* upset if they *hadn't invited* me to the party. (In fact they did invite me, so it was all right.)
- Notice that to form unreal conditionals, the verb moves *one tense back*. So to talk about the present, we use the *Past tense*; to talk about the past, we use the *Past perfect tense*.

Mixed conditionals

- We can mix second and third conditionals in one sentence. One part can refer to the present (second conditional) and one part to the past (third conditional):
  If you'd *remembered* to buy some petrol, we'd *be* home by now.
  (You *didn't* remember, so we're *not* home now.)

Expressing regret

- *I wish* + Past perfect tense is used for regretting past actions:
  I wish I'd *gone* to university. (I didn't go, and I regret it.)
  I wish I *hadn't shouted* at him. (I shouted at him, and now I'm sorry.)
  (For the use of *I wish* to make wishes about the present and future, see Unit 9.)
- *should(n't) have* + past participle is used for expressing regret or criticising past actions:
  I *should have* gone to university.
  I *shouldn't have* shouted at him.
  You *should have* told me. (You didn't tell me – that was wrong.)
  They *shouldn't have* stayed up so late. (They stayed up too late – now they're tired.)

24 Life on Earth

Global issues

Issues	Causes and effects
Air pollution	Factories, power stations and cars pollute the air → acid rain → trees are damaged.
Pollution of the sea	Industrial waste and sewage is dumped in the sea → wildlife is killed.
Global warming	Gases from cars and power stations → 'greenhouse effect' → the Earth becomes warmer → the climate changes → sea level rises.
Destruction of the rain forest	Trees are cut down → species become extinct, increases 'greenhouse effect'.
Nuclear power	Nuclear accidents → radioactive material escapes into the atmosphere → causes cancer.
Ozone layer	Chemicals destroy the ozone layer → sun causes skin cancer, damages crops.
Desertification	Overuse of farmland → desert spreads → farmland is lost.

- Notice these verb/noun pairs:

Verb	Noun
destroy	destruction
pollute	pollution
damage	damage (to)
protect	protection

Environmental action: verbs

- To help the environment:
  – *save* electricity; don't *waste* it
  – don't *use* more electricity than you need
  – *recycle* glass and paper; don't *throw* it *away*.
- Governments can *increase* or *decrease* (*raise* or *lower*) the price of certain products.
  They can *tax* (or *put a tax on*) products or *ban* them (= make them illegal).
- These are all things that can be done to *protect* the environment.

Wildlife

- Animals, birds, fish and insects are forms of *wildlife*.
- Many animals that were once *common* have become *endangered species*: they are so *rare* that they could *become extinct*.
- Some animals are *hunted* for their meat or skins; others are in danger because their *habitat* is being destroyed.
- Many rare animals are *protected* by law (= it is illegal to kill them), and live in *wildlife reserves*; some also live *in captivity* (e.g. in zoos).

Verb forms

Verb tenses

Here is a summary of verb tenses taught in this book (numbers refer to units).

	Simple	Continuous
Present	go/goes (1)	am/is/are going (1)
Past	went (3, 7, 19)	was/were going (3)
Present Perfect	have/has gone (7, 15, 19)	have/has been going (15, 19)
Past Perfect	had gone (17, 23)	(had been going)
Future	will go (11)	will be going (11)
Future Perfect	will have gone (11)	(will have been going)
Conditional	would go (9)	(would be going)
Past Conditional	would have gone (23)	(would have been going)

The Passive

The passive is formed with *be* + past participle. It can be in any tense: past, present or future:

Present: Wheat *is grown* all over Europe.
Past: They *were rescued* by helicopter.
Present perfect: The house *has been sold*.
Past perfect: I noticed that the lights *had been left* on.
Future: The road *will be opened* in six months' time.

The passive also has a continuous form, but this is commonly used only in the Present and Past tenses:

Present: My flat *is being redecorated*.
Past: He *was being questioned* by the police.

Infinitives

The infinitive is the basic form of the verb. It is used after *to* and after modal verbs. There are four possible forms: present or past, simple or continuous:

	Simple	Continuous
Present	work	be working
Past	have worked	have been working

Examples:
Be quiet now – I want to *work*.
He's not at the office – he must *be working* at home today.
No wonder you failed the exam – you should *have worked* harder.
She's nearly 70, so she must *have been working* here for at least 50 years.

Common functions

Asking people to do things

– *Would you* pass the salt, please?
– *Could you* give me a lift to the station?
– *Would you mind* tak*ing* your shoes off?

Asking permission

– *Can I* take my shoes off?
– *Do you mind if I* turn the radio on?
– *Is it all right if I* bring a friend?

Making suggestions

– *Let's* go for a swim.
– *Why don't we* buy a CD player?
– *How about* (mak*ing*) a cup of coffee?

Giving advice

– *I think you should* go to bed earlier.
– *You'd better* tell the police immediately.
– *If I were you, I'd* complain about it.

Deciding and choosing

– *I think I'll* buy a newspaper.
– *I'd like* an orange juice, please.
– *I'd rather* stay at home and watch TV.

Making offers

– *Shall I* bring some food?
– *I'll* call a taxi *if you like*.
– *Would you like to* see my holiday photos?

Asking for information

– *Can you tell me* what time the film starts?
– *Do you know* where I can find a dictionary?
– *I wonder if you could tell me* the way to the station.

Irregular verbs

Infinitive	Simple past	Past participle
be	was/were	been
beat	beat	beaten
become	became	become
begin	began	begun
bend	bent	bent
bite	bit	bitten
blow	blew	blown
break	broke	broken
bring	brought	brought
burn	burnt	burnt
build	built	built
buy	bought	bought
can	could	(been able)
catch	caught	caught
choose	chose	chosen
come	came	come
cost	cost	cost
cut	cut	cut
do	did	done
draw	drew	drawn
dream	dreamt	dreamt
drink	drank	drunk
drive	drove	driven
eat	ate	eaten
fall	fell	fallen
feed	fed	fed
feel	felt	felt
fight	fought	fought
find	found	found
fly	flew	flown
forget	forgot	forgotten
forgive	forgave	forgiven
freeze	froze	frozen
get	got	got
give	gave	given
go	went	gone (been)
grow	grew	grown
hang	hung	hung
have	had	had
hear	heard	heard
hide	hid	hidden
hit	hit	hit
hold	held	held
hurt	hurt	hurt
keep	kept	kept
know	knew	known
lay	laid	laid
lead	led	led
learn	learnt	learnt
leave	left	left
lend	lent	lent
let	let	let
lie	lay	lain
lose	lost	lost
make	made	made
mean	meant	meant
meet	met	met
pay	paid	paid
put	put	put
read	read	read
ride	rode	ridden
ring	rang	rung
rise	rose	risen
run	ran	run
say	said	said
see	saw	seen
sell	sold	sold
send	sent	sent
set	set	set
shake	shook	shaken

Infinitive	Simple past	Past participle
shine	shone	shone
shoot	shot	shot
show	showed	shown
shut	shut	shut
sing	sang	sung
sink	sank	sunk
sit	sat	sat
sleep	slept	slept
smell	smelt	smelt
speak	spoke	spoken
spell	spelt	spelt
spend	spent	spent
spread	spread	spread
stand	stood	stood
steal	stole	stolen
sweep	swept	swept
swim	swam	swum
swing	swung	swung
take	took	taken
teach	taught	taught
tear	tore	torn
tell	told	told
think	thought	thought
throw	threw	thrown
understand	understood	understood
wake	woke	woken
wear	wore	worn
win	won	won
write	wrote	written

Phonetic symbols

Vowels

Symbol	Example
/iː/	tree /triː/
/i/	many /'meni/
/ɪ/	sit /sɪt/
/e/	bed /bed/
/æ/	back /bæk/
/ʌ/	sun /sʌn/
/ɑː/	car /kɑː/
/ɒ/	hot /hɒt/
/ɔː/	horse /hɔːs/
/ʊ/	full /fʊl/
/uː/	moon /muːn/
/ɜː/	girl /gɜːl/
/ə/	arrive /ə'raɪv/
	water /'wɔːtə/
/eɪ/	late /leɪt/
/aɪ/	time /taɪm/
/ɔɪ/	boy /bɔɪ/
/əʊ/	home /həʊm/
/aʊ/	out /aʊt/
/ɪə/	hear /hɪə/
/eə/	there /ðeə/
/ʊə/	pure /pjʊə/

Consonants

Symbol	Example
/p/	pull /pʊl/
/b/	bad /bæd/
/t/	take /teɪk/
/d/	dog /dɒg/
/k/	cat /kæt/
/g/	go /gəʊ/
/tʃ/	church /tʃɜːtʃ/
/dʒ/	age /eɪdʒ/
/f/	for /fɔː/
/v/	love /lʌv/
/θ/	thick /θɪk/
/ð/	this /ðɪs/
/s/	sit /sɪt/
/z/	zoo /zuː/
/ʃ/	shop /ʃɒp/
/ʒ/	leisure /'leʒə/
/h/	house /haʊs/
/m/	make /meɪk/
/n/	name /neɪm/
/ŋ/	bring /brɪŋ/
/l/	look /lʊk/
/r/	road /rəʊd/
/j/	young /jʌŋ/
/w/	wear /weə/

Stress

We show stress by a mark (/'/) before the stressed syllable: later /'leɪtə/; arrive /ə'raɪv/; information /ɪnfə'meɪʃn/

Acknowledgements

The authors would like to thank the following for their contributions to *Language in Use* Intermediate:

– for contributing to the listening and reading material: Carlos Aradas-Balbás, Carolyn Becket, Mª Celina Bortolotto, Jake Bundy, Lucy Bundy, Deb Clark, Bryan Cruden, James Dingle, Maria Dingle, Kayoko Enomoto, Jahel Fabris, Amy Fisher, David Fisher, Colette Fitzpatrick, Véronique Foray, Genevieve Higgins, Laura Jerran, Sakae Katoh, Catriona Maclachlan, Jonathan Mullan, Sally Mullan, Mike Mendenhall, Alan Ogilvy, Shane Pope, Helen Sandiford, Ewa Simbieda, Aileen Smith, Carsten Williams, Ingrid Williams, Jan Williams, Larissa Williams, Tony Williams, Gabriela Zaharias; and all the actors whose voices were recorded in studio sessions.

– for the production of the recorded material: Martin Williamson (Prolingua Productions), Peter Taylor (Taylor Riley Productions Ltd.), and Peter and Diana Thompson (Studio AVP).

The authors would also like to thank the following at Cambridge University Press:

– Colin Hayes for his continuing support and help.
– Peter Donovan for organising and steering the project through its various stages.
– Nick Newton and Anne Colwell for organising and overseeing design and production.
– Joanne Currie for her excellent design.
– Catherine Boyce for her work on the Pilot edition.
– Molly Bannister, Sue Featherstone and Val Grove for general administrative help.
– James Dingle, our Editor, for his tireless dedication, constructive ideas and good judgement.

The authors and publishers would like to thank the following institutions and teachers for their help in testing the material and for the invaluable feedback which they provided:

A.C.T., Paris, France; Rowan Ferguson, Executive Language Services, Paris, France; Lanser SA, Paris, France; The British Council, Athens, Greece; John Eaglesham, British School, Milan, Italy; Centro Linguistico di Ateneo, Parma University, Parma, Italy; Ridge International, Osaka, Japan; Tessa Pacey, ILC, Tokyo, Japan; Sunshine College Tokyo, Japan; Janaka Williams, Simul Academy, Kyoto, Japan; Lexis, Granada, Spain; LinguaSec, Madrid, Spain; Joe Hogan, The House, Palafrugell, Spain; English 1, Seville, Spain; Istanbul Technical University, Istanbul, Turkey; Özel Eyüboğlu Lisesi, Istanbul, Turkey; Roger Scott, Bournemouth, UK.

The authors and publishers are grateful to the following copyright owners for permission to reproduce copyright material. Every endeavour has been made to contact copyright owners and apologies are expressed for any omissions.

pp. 30–1: Times Editions Pte Ltd for texts adapted from *Britain, Singapore, Spain* and *Thailand* in the *Culture Shock* series, published by Kuperard (London) Ltd; The Rough Guides for text adapted from *The Rough Guide to West Africa*; p. 38: advertisements and Yellow Pages cover reproduced by kind permission of BT Yellow Pages. 'Yellow Pages' is a registered trademark of British Telecommunications plc in the United Kingdom; pp. 40–1: GE Magazines for text adapted from 'HELP! nobody loves us!' from *Me*, 10 July, 1989; pp. 48–9: John Murray (Publishers) Ltd for pictures and text adapted from *Victorian Inventions* by Leonard de Vries, 1991; p. 50: Simon & Schuster, Inc. for text adapted from *The Great Reckoning*, © James Dale Davidson and Lord William Rees-Mogg, 1993; p. 57: *Daily Record* and *Daily Mail*, © *Daily Mail* / Solo, for adapted text; p. 64: *The Beano*, © D. C. Thomson & Co. Ltd., *Car Magazine, Hello!, Homes and Gardens* and *Reader's Digest* for permission to reproduce covers; p. 66: *The Times* for text adapted from 'Easy Listening' by Joanna Pitman from *The Times* 22 May, 1992, © Times Newspapers Ltd. 1992; pp. 74–5: Multimedia for text adapted from *Your Memory, A User's Guide* by Alan Baddeley, © Multimedia Books Limited, published in the UK by Pelican and USA by Prion; p. 81: *The Times* for text adapted from 'Passenger "stabbed attacker on Tube with swordstick"' from *The Times* 10 September, 1987, © Times Newspapers Ltd. 1992. The names have been changed to protect those involved in the case; pp. 82–3: MindTrap Games Inc. for texts adapted from the board game *MindTrap*, © MindTrap Games Inc.; p. 93: Leslie Thomas for *A Good Boy, Griffith* , © Leslie Thomas; p. 100: *The Observer* for text from 'The medicine' by Thomas Quirke, © *The Observer*; p. 101: Little, Brown and Co. (UK) Ltd. for text adapted from *Smile Therapy* by Liz Hodgkinson; pp. 108–9: *New Scientist* for adapted texts; p. 109: *The Times* for text adapted from 'August 14, 2116 – the End of the World?' by Nick Nuttal from *The Times* 26 October, 1992, © Times Newspapers Ltd. 1992.

The authors and publishers are grateful to the following illustrators and photographic sources:

Illustrators: Julie Anderson: pp. 51 *t*, 58, 71; Peter Byatt: pp. 13 *t*, 15, 17, 56, 66 *br*; Celia Chester: pp. 13 *b*, 92–3; Jerry Collins: pp. 55 *b*, 91 *b*, 118; Joanne Currie: p. 16 *t*; Richard Deverell: pp. 37, 94; Paul Dickinson: pp. 8, 65, 82–3; Lisa Hall: pp. 61 *b*, 66 *t*, 77 *b*; Sue Hillwood-Harris: p. 76; Phil Healey: pp. 74–5, 101; Frank Langford: pp. 16 *b*, 79; Angela Joliffe: pp. 64, 91 *t*; Vicky Lowe: pp. 66 *bl*, 78; Michael Ogden: pp. 11, 14, 88, 109 *t*; Amanda MacPhail: pp. 51 *b*, 55 *t*, 95, 117; Carl Melegari: p. 77 *t*; Nigel Paige: pp. 21, 84, 109 *b*; Bill Piggins: pp. 29, 42, 53, 61 *t*, 103 *t*, 113, 115, 119, 120; Tracy Rich: pp. 72, 103 *b*; Chris Ryley: p. 108; Jane Smith: pp. 23, 62; Sue Shields: p. 25; Kathy Ward: p. 98; Rosemary Woods: p. 43; Annabel Wright: pp. 10, 70, 81.

Photographic sources: Mohamed Ansar / Impact Photos: p. 90 *bl*; Apple Computer UK Ltd.: p. 36 *t*; Aqualisa for the focus spray from the Aqualisa Turbostream Power Shower System: p. 12 *bl*; Art Directors Photo Library: p. 24; Barnabys Picture Library: pp. 90 *br*, 117 *r*; The J. Allan Cash Photolibrary: pp. 90 *bc*, 117 *c*; Casio Electronics Ltd.: p. 36 *mc*; The Associated Press Ltd.: p. 65; Chinese and Japanese Special Fund, courtesy Museum of Fine Arts Boston for *Court Ladies Preparing Newly Woven Silk*: p. 34; Bruce Coleman Ltd.: pp. 107 *b*, 118; Colorific Photo Library: pp. 18, 73 *bl*, 117 *l*; Editions Minerva SA for pictures from *Life of the Aztecs in Ancient Mexico*, published by Productions Liber SA, 1978: p. 116; Mark Edwards / Still Pictures: p. 106 *m*; Greg Evans International: p. 68 *b*; Chris Fairclough Colour Library: p. 28 *bcr*; Mike Feeney / TRIP: p. 30; Sally and Richard Greenhill: pp. 31 *t*, 90 *ml*; Juliet Highet / TRIP: p. 90 *tl*; David Hoffman: p. 68 *tl*; The Hutchison Library: p. 106 *tl*; The Image Bank: p. 73 *br*; The Kobal Collection: p. 50; Peter Lake: pp. 12 *t*, *bc* & *br*, 20, 31 *b*, 39, 40–1, 44, 46, 54, 64, 81, 86 *br* (with thanks to Kate Dickens) & *bl*, 100, 104; Phil Loftus / Retna Pictures Ltd.: p. 66 *m*; Caroline Penn / Impact Photos: p. 90 *tcr*; Pictor International Ltd.: p. 86 *t*; Picturepoint-London: pp. 28 *bcl*, 66 *b*, 90 *mr*, 106 *tr*; Quadrant Picture Library: p. 52; Rex Features Ltd.: pp. 80, 106 *bl*; Helene Rogers / TRIP: pp. 31 *ml*, 86 *mr*; The Rolex Watch Company Ltd.: p. 86 *mcl*; Michael Rutland / Retna Pictures Ltd.: p. 86 *ml*; Sony United Kingdom Ltd.: p. 36 *mr*; South West News Service: p. 57; Tony Stone Images: pp. 9, 15, 28 *tl*, *bl* & *br*, 60, 73 *tl* & *br*, 106 *bc*, 107 *tl* & *tr*, 114, 120, 121; Sygma: p. 102; Syndication International: p. 66 *t*; Topham Picture Source: p. 86 *mcr*; Toshiba (UK) Ltd.: p. 36 *ml*; TROPIX / M. & V. Birley: p. 31 *mr*; TROPIX / M. Jory: p. 106 *tc*; Rob Turner / TRIP: p. 86 *bc*; Viewfinder Colour Photo Library: p. 29; Visionbank and England Scene: p. 68 *tr*; Zefa: pp. 28 *tr* & *m*, 73 *tr*, 90 *tcl* & *tr*, 107 *tc*, 112, 119.

t = top   *m* = middle   *b* = bottom   *r* = right   *c* = centre   *l* = left

Picture research by Sandie Huskinson-Rolfe of PHOTOSEEKERS.

4.4 Can you make a million?

This diagram shows the possible routes that can be followed. The route followed by the millionaire in the interview is shown by red lines.

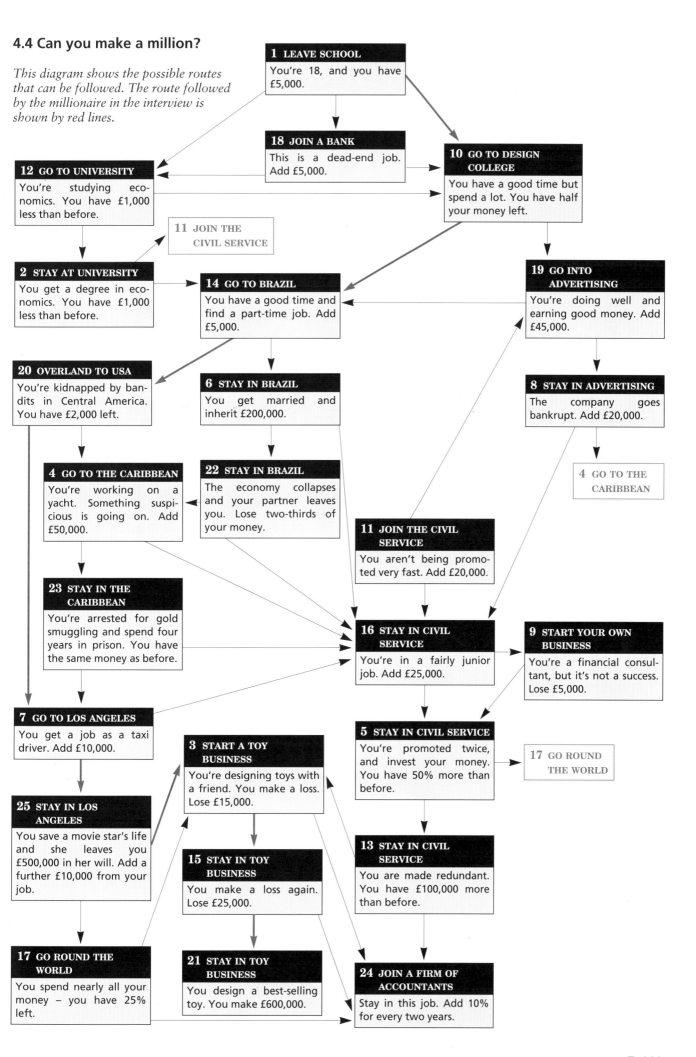